THE COST OF TALENT

How Executives and Professionals Are Paid and How It Affects America

Derek Bok

THE FREE PRESS
A Division of Macmillan, Inc.
New York
Maxwell Macmillan Canada
Toronto
Maxwell Macmillan International
New York Oxford Singapore Sydney

THE FREE PRESS
A Division of Simon & Schuster
1230 Avenue of the Americas
New York, NY 10020

Manufactured in the United States of America

10 9 8 7 6 5 4 3 2 1

Library of Congress Cataloging-In-Publication Data

Bok, Derek Curtis.
The cost of talent : how executives and professionals are
Paid and how it affects America / Derel Bok.
p. cm.
Includes bibliographical references and index.
ISBN: 0-7432-3632-7
1. Executives—Salaries, etc.—United States. 2. Professional
Employees—Salaries, etc.—United States. I. Title.
HD4965.5.U6B65 1993
331.2'816584'00973—dc20 93-27892
CIP

For information regarding special discounts for bulk purchases, please contact Simon & Schuster Special Sales at 1-800-456-6798 or business@simonandschuster.com

CONTENTS

PREFACE

I first conceived the idea of this book in 1988 when I was locked in my annual struggle to find a suitable topic for my commencement address at Harvard University. All over the country, I mused, speakers at similar exercises would be exhorting graduating classes to devote their lives to improving society by helping the poor, defending the environment, fighting for racial justice, and pursuing other worthy ends. The more I thought about this yearly ritual, the more hollow, even hypocritical these speeches seemed. In fact, notwithstanding the commencement rhetoric, society was making it extremely difficult for graduating students to follow the advice of the speakers. Moreover, the problem was steadily growing worse, much worse.

When I graduated from Harvard Law School in 1954, I could have taken a job with a Wall Street firm for $4,200 a year or joined a firm in a smaller city for two or three hundred dollars less. If I had decided instead to serve the government as an attorney, I could have gone to the Justice Department for almost as large a salary as private law firms were offering. Or else, by giving up only a few hundred dollars in starting pay, I could have become a teacher and devoted myself to helping young people.

By 1987, the outlook for graduating law students was radically different from the one that I had encountered. They could teach school for approximately $16,000 per year. They could work for the Justice Department for $25,000. Or they could join a Wall Street firm at a starting salary of $65,000 to $70,000.

Clearly, the financial rewards had shifted dramatically in favor of the private sector. Checking further, I found that much the same process had occurred in other professions, such as medicine and corporate management. Moreover, financial considerations couldn't help but loom larger for today's students than they had during my law school days. In contrast to the situation that I and my classmates faced, most students now were leaving the university with large educational debts that they were required to start repaying immediately. Surely, it must be difficult for many of these young people to accept the message of graduation speakers exhorting them to stop thinking only of themselves and start devoting their lives to noble causes.

I had a chance to reflect further on this problem during the ensuing months as a member of the National Commission on Public Service under the chairmanship of Paul Volcker. In our meetings and at hearings around the country, I learned in more detail about the problems the Civil Service was encountering in attracting and retaining able people to work for the federal government. As our project proceeded, articles and studies were heaped upon us bearing grim titles such as "The Quiet Crisis in the Federal Civil Service" or "Brain Drain from the Federal Government." Meanwhile, starting salaries in law firms, corporations, and medical practice continued to move steadily upward.

Eventually, I finished preparing my speech. When Commencement Day finally arrived, however, and I looked out over the vast, happy throng of students, parents, and alumni, I felt a sudden pang of fear that I had chosen a grossly inappropriate topic. After all, Harvard graduates are especially well represented among the ranks of successful, highly paid executives and professionals. Could I really listen to loyal alumni making the usual announcements of exceptionally generous reunion gifts and then address the donors in the audience about bloated paychecks and burgeoning stock options? For a moment, I hesitated, but my anxiety did not last long. One of the joys of presiding over an ancient Puritan institution is the constant sense of being able to speak frankly to alumni about difficult, contentious topics even when they strike uncomfortably close to home.

Once again, I was not disappointed. After explaining in detail how private-sector salaries had ballooned while earnings in the public sector were eroding, how chief executives of American corporations were earning several times the salary of their more successful Japanese competitors, how students were flocking in ever-growing numbers to Wall Street rather than to schools, churches, and government agencies, I received the longest, warmest ovation I had experienced in fifteen years of giving commencement addresses.

Clearly, I thought, something in my remarks had struck a responsive chord, even among those who had benefited the most from rapidly rising incomes in the private sector.

As a onetime labor law professor, however, I realized that problems of compensation were far from simple and that it might be difficult to find cures that were not worse than the disease they sought to remedy. Accordingly, as I began to think about leaving my post at Harvard, I decided to devote the first year of my new life to exploring the topic more carefully.

By the time I had completed my twentieth year as president and given my last commencement address, I had arranged to spend a month at the Rockefeller Foundation villa at Bellagio, Italy, followed by a year at the Center for Advanced Study in the Behavioral Sciences at Stanford, California. I cannot imagine more favorable settings in which to try to write a serious book after two decades of university administration.

In the course of working on the project, I was fortunate to have the assistance of four exceptional Harvard students: Kathryn Boudett, Susan Haber, Gina Raimondo, and Cecilia Rouse. Without their help, I could never have ferreted out all the data on salary and student trends in the various professions I studied. I have also benefited greatly from many friends and colleagues who were kind enough to read individual chapters and rescue me from egregious errors: Philip Areeda, George Baker III, William Bowen, Christine Cassell, John Dunlop, Richard Freeman, Patricia Graham, Betsy Hicks, Lawrence Katz, Dan Mayers, Mark Moore, David Nathan, Jeffrey O'Connell, Joseph Newhouse, and Daniel Rezneck. John Roberts read several chapters of an early draft and gave me many valuable suggestions, while Henry Rosovsky made his way through the entire manuscript and offered numerous helpful comments.

Special thanks go to two loyal assistants, Susan Kearney and Connie Higgins, who typed and retyped more drafts than I care to remember. I appreciate their patience and hard work more than I can say.

Above all, I am grateful to my most faithful and perceptive critic, Sissela, who read every chapter of the manuscript more than once. As always, she gave unfailing encouragement during periods of gloom while finding countless ways to improve what I had written. No words could describe the debt I owe to her.

INTRODUCTION

In 1987, hard times overtook the three major television networks. While costs continued to spiral upward, revenues failed to keep pace. Something had to be done, and soon. As the networks searched for ways to economize, even the nightly news programs were vulnerable. Heated discussions took place at CBS between the new chief executive, Leonard Tisch, who pressed hard to reduce costs, and Dan Rather, who fought to avoid massive layoffs and to protect the quality of his program. At last, all parties agreed on cuts totaling $36 million per year. Two hundred fifteen people lost their jobs. For a brief time, the problem seemed to be solved.

Ten days later, Mr. Tisch was startled to read an Op Ed piece in the *New York Times* in which Rather publicly condemned the cuts and questioned Mr. Tisch's commitment to quality. "Our new executive officer," Rather declared, "told us when he arrived that he wanted us to be the best. Ironically, he has now made that task seem something between difficult and impossible."[1]

What irked Mr. Tisch even more than the Op Ed piece was another quote from Rather in a front page article the same day alleging that he had offered to cut his own $3.5 million salary to avoid such heavy layoffs.[2] Tisch could not remember any such offer. Summoning the president of CBS News, Howard Stringer, he demanded to know whether Rather had actually proposed lowering his own salary.

"Not exactly," answered Stringer.

"They never approached you on anything?" continued Tisch.

"Yes," answered Stringer, "but Rather's agent, Richard Leibner, and several well-paid members of the news division raised the issue vaguely."[3]

It is still not clear how much of a pay cut Rather was willing to accept or just how serious he was about pressing such a proposal.

Nor would it have been easy to advise him. His predicament exposes many of the problems that trouble us most in thinking about the subject of compensation. Could a television anchorman actually be worth more than $3 million a year? Should he feel morally obliged to take a pay cut rather than allow so many fellow professionals, working for only a small fraction of his salary, to lose their jobs? If he continued to earn such a lordly sum while colleagues were tossed out on the street, would the Evening News team feel betrayed or would they continue loyally to perform to the very best of their ability?

Concern over bloated earnings has steadily grown as the public has learned of one spectacular pay package after another. In the 1970s, athletes and entertainers led the way by repeatedly cracking the million-dollar ceiling. In the 1980s, financiers, CEOs, attorneys, and doctors came to reap similar rewards, or even more. In 1988, the top ten trial lawyers in the country, none of them household names, earned amounts ranging from $6 million to $450 million. By helping to save Chrysler, Lee Iacocca took home $20 million in a single year, to be quickly topped by Michael Eisner's $45 million at Disney and Steven Ross's $78 million at Time-Warner. Leading all competitors for the decade was Michael Milken, recently behind bars, who parlayed junk bonds and corporate takeovers into an astonishing $550 million of income in 1987.

These earnings were merely among the more riveting examples in a rising flood of pay for top professionals and executives in the 1980s. By the end of the decade, the total compensation of CEOs in the largest two hundred companies *averaged* almost $3 million per year. At least as many lawyers were pocketing more than $1 million per year, and similar earnings for doctors were not unknown. With paychecks like these, it is not surprising that the number of millionaires increased more rapidly than in any other decade in history—from fewer than 600,000 to over 1,500,000.[4] Deca-millionaires multiplied more than threefold as did centi-millionaires. Billionaires—still a rare breed—rose from only a handful in 1980 to more than fifty at the end of the decade. More arresting still, the number of people reporting an adjusted gross income of *more than one million dollars per year* rose from 642 in 1970 to 60,677 in 1990.

Some prominent observers look upon this accumulation of wealth as a sign of vigor and prosperity. In their view, the United

States has always been a land of opportunity that attracts people who prefer to take risks in order to make a fortune. Americans don't mind huge incomes; they hope to have one themselves some day. As Jack Kemp put it, "Why should we say to a guy who has invented some microsystem or some new business that there is a limit to his achievement? That is at such odds with the American dream."[5]

In fact, fewer people than one might think appear to share Mr. Kemp's dream. Americans may have greater tolerance for economic inequality than citizens of other advanced countries, but they do not approve of the huge incomes currently being earned in the United States. In the 1970s, Republicans, Democrats, union representatives, farmers, and intellectuals all agreed that top executives were being paid too much.[6] Even CEOs agreed. Most of these groups (not CEOs) would have cut executive compensation by 40 or 50 percent or more. Since then, periodic surveys continue to show substantial majorities of the public favoring higher taxes on all incomes above $100,000 per year.[7]

Popular concern over huge paychecks is not the only reason for paying attention to executive and professional compensation. What individuals earn in different vocations is also important because it influences the way in which talent is distributed in our society. If gardeners were paid more than $250,000 per year while surgeons earned only $25,000, we would quickly find that we had many more gardeners and many fewer surgeons than is currently the case. As our economy becomes more complicated, the demand for able, highly educated people increases constantly, so that the way in which this talent is allocated takes on greater and greater importance. Consequently, the variations in pay that professionals earn in different occupations assume a greater significance as well.

Today, for example, college seniors majoring in mathematics and computer science can often find jobs in industry that pay 50 percent more than the salaries of beginning teachers. Predictably, properly trained math teachers are hard to find; up to one-third of those currently hired are not certified as qualified to teach the subject. In a nation threatened with shortages of scientists and engineers and increasingly in need of numerate workers at all levels, such shortages cannot help but arouse concern. Similarly, high salaries on Wall Street seem to have attracted large fractions of the graduating classes of leading business schools in the 1980s. At a time when our manufacturing corporations are engaged in a battle to hold their own against foreign competition, one can legitimately worry lest too much talent be diverted to investment advising, consulting, and other fields of business less vital to our national interests.

Finally, the terms on which people are compensated may affect how effectively they perform. Few individuals manage to work at a level close to their full potential. The puzzle is to discover how to induce them to achieve more. Many believe that the answer lies in rewarding better performance with higher pay. Most employers seem to agree. All manner of piece rate programs, bonuses, profit-sharing plans, and stock option schemes have been devised to capitalize on this possibility. Such incentives spread rapidly in the 1980s. Merit pay made an appearance in the federal civil service and in many school districts across the country. At the opposite end of the pay spectrum, the ten-, twenty-, and fifty-million-dollar incomes that a few CEOs received in recent years were chiefly the result of stock options designed to motivate them to exert every effort on behalf of their shareholders.

The way in which earnings are structured not only affects how hard people work but where they direct their effort. If police officers receive a bonus for each stolen car they recover, they are likely to spend more of their time looking for missing automobiles. Corporate CEOs may think less about the long-term prospects for their company if they receive a year-end bonus for increasing profits than if they have an option to buy company stock at today's price exercisable only after seven years. Now that we are so worried about the performance of our economy, our schools, and our government, we cannot help but take an interest in whether our executives, teachers, and public officials are paid in ways that motivate them properly.

These concerns point to the three critical questions about what professionals earn in this country. Are some of them paid too much and some too little? Do existing differences in pay help to allocate talent among the various occupations in a manner that corresponds to society's needs and priorities? Is compensation structured to motivate people to work appropriately hard in pursuit of the right goals?

These questions have been the subject of many articles and books over the years. But almost all of the books are concerned with the wages of blue-collar workers. Newspaper accounts and articles in learned journals sometimes take up the earnings of top executives, physicians, or even sports stars. Only rarely, however, do they consider more than a single calling. In this book, I take a different tack and examine the compensation for six important groups of highly educated professionals and managers: doctors, lawyers, corporate executives, university professors, teachers, and high federal civil servants. Although these groups are less numerous than blue-collar workers, they wield extraordinary influence in our society. Together, they affect the nature of health care, the progress of the economy, the effectiveness of public policy, the pursuit of justice, and the quality of education in America.

At a more profound level, the compensation paid to members of these groups has further lessons and larger meanings to convey. The amounts people are paid and the ways in which they respond reflect our deepest values, motivations, and priorities. For better or for worse, we can often learn more about what matters in this country by observing what we are willing to pay for than by studying the messages that come to us from pulpits and campaign hustings, lecture halls and editorial pages. If we truly wish to understand our society, then, and appreciate its problems, its contradictions, its aspirations, and its values, we would do well to pay some heed to the ways in which we reward different kinds of work throughout the land.

PART I

CHAPTER 1

THE ROLE OF COMPENSATION

In central California, migrant laborers stoop under a hot sun for hours on end picking fruits and vegetables for a few dollars a day. In Manhattan skyscrapers, scores of secretaries sit in long rows in large, windowless rooms typing letters at $500 a week. In Detroit factories, workers hurt by overseas competition operate machines for $14 an hour, substantially less than they earned a decade ago. In airplanes far above the earth, rows of business executives and lawyers take papers from their briefcases and start to prepare, at $200 or more per hour, for the negotiations that await them in Dallas, Los Angeles, or some other commercial center.

All of these people are working hard at tasks that are vital to maintaining our society and helping it to prosper. Yet each group earns a very different reward than the others. Why? Is there any convincing rationale to justify these wide variations in pay or are they simply the result of luck, convention, or arbitrary privilege?

JUSTIFYING THE DIFFERENCES

Differences in pay are ubiquitous. They go back to early civilization and extend worldwide to every kind of society and regime. Thinkers centuries ago undoubtedly puzzled over the reasons for these differences. Not until 1776, however, when Adam Smith produced his *Wealth of Nations,* did anyone succeed in offering a detailed, plausible explanation of why earnings varied so much among different kinds of occupations.[1]

Smith is renowned for his analysis of how competitive markets channel the selfish desires of participants toward socially desirable ends. In the course of describing how competition rewarded different factors of production, he sought to explain why the law of supply and demand did not bring about equal wages for everyone.[2] One might have thought, he mused, that anyone offering a wage above the normal level would quickly attract a host of laborers seeking the higher pay. This influx of workers would simultaneously allow the employer to reduce his wages while forcing other firms to raise theirs to keep the workers they needed. In this way, supply and demand would continuously force wage differences back to a common level. Yet one had only to look around to discover that no such equality existed. Why?

Smith gave several reasons to explain the persistent differences:

1. Some jobs are unusually dirty, disagreeable, or arduous to perform and thus require extra compensation to attract enough people to do the work. Coal mining and butchering were prominent examples in the England of Smith's day.

2. Other occupations carry greater risks of layoffs or unemployment. Employers must pay higher wages to compensate for these hazards. Seasonal jobs, such as construction work, are a case in point.

3. Some jobs require individuals to sacrifice income for a while to acquire special knowledge and skills. Such positions must pay above-average rates to induce enough people to incur the necessary training costs. Preparation of this kind is particularly important for the professions. As Smith put it, "Education in the ingenious arts and in the liberal professions is still more tedious and expensive. The pecuniary recompense, therefore, of painters and sculptors, of lawyers and physicians, ought to be much more liberal, and it is so accordingly."[3]

4. Some occupations, such as scientific research, violin playing, or professional athletics, need special intelligence or special skills. Because relatively few people possess these talents, the demand for their services often exceeds the supply, and the price they can charge increases accordingly.

5. Some occupations command higher incomes because the risk of failure is far greater than normal. Here, Smith uses the

example of law. For every successful attorney (he claims), there will be twenty or more who fail to finish their legal studies and build a viable practice. Because the chances of success are so small, much larger rewards are needed to induce enough young people to undertake the long, arduous process of acquiring legal training and trying to establish a successful practice. In principle, Smith argues, "the counsellor of law who, perhaps near forty years of age, begins to make something by his profession, ought to receive the retribution, not only of his own so tedious and expensive education, but that of more than twenty others who are never likely to make anything by it."[4] In fact, he asserts, the premium earned by successful professionals is usually much less than this amount because young people tend to take too little account of long-term risks and to overestimate their own chances of success.

6. Finally, Smith gave one last explanation for high professional earnings. In his words, "we trust our health to the physician, our fortune and sometimes our life and reputation to the lawyer and attorney. Such confidence could not be safely reposed in people of a very mean or low condition. Their reward must be such, therefore, as may give them that rank in society which so important a trust requires."[5]

In the ensuing years, other reasons for differences in pay have come to light. Many workers have managed to obtain premium wages by forming a union or otherwise limiting the supply of their labor. Many others have been forced to accept lower pay because of their nationality, their gender, their religion, or their skin color. Still others have earned less than they might because they were ignorant of higher pay elsewhere or unwilling to leave their homes and neighborhoods to find more lucrative jobs in other communities. These reasons, however, complement Smith's theories; they do not weaken his explanations or contradict his insights.

Differing rates of pay have also appeared in Communist regimes for reasons similar to those put forward by Smith and his followers. Karl Marx may have envisaged a utopia that would operate on the principle "from each according to his abilities, to each according to his needs." In practice, however, the Communist world never behaved this way. Although pay differentials may have narrowed in countries such as Cuba or China, substantial disparities have remained. There is simply no other way to attract enough qualified, motivated workers to the more difficult, hazardous, disagreeable jobs that Communist and capitalist societies alike require.

Although Smith and his followers have done much to explain many of the differences in pay we see around us, they do not offer convincing reasons for the high compensation given to many professionals. For example, the work of lawyers, doctors, and business executives is hardly more arduous or disagreeable than that of ditchdiggers, garbage collectors, or many other low-paid occupations. On the contrary, many studies show that work in the learned professions is widely thought to be more interesting and desirable than in most other occupations. Some investigators have even found that most people consider the nonpecuniary attractions of professional work *several times* more valuable than the greater compensation that practitioners usually command.[6] Hence, the differences in satisfaction of various kinds of work hardly justify paying professionals even more money. On the contrary, the most vexing moral question posed by professional and executive compensation is why so many people fortunate enough to hold the most interesting, prestigious jobs in society should earn many times the pay of those condemned to work that is much more boring and disagreeable.[7]

The answer is surely not that executives and professionals must endure unusual hazards. Police officers, fire fighters, and truck drivers routinely face much greater physical danger than lawyers, doctors, and corporate executives. Even the odds of being fired or laid off are typically worse for blue-collar workers. It is rare for a physician to lose hospital privileges or for a law partner to be dismissed. Chief executives are not forced to leave as often as their workers, and when they are pushed out, most of them get golden parachutes or other kinds of severance pay, often running into millions of dollars, to ease the pain of losing their jobs.

There is likewise not much left of the heavy risk of failure Smith describes in speaking of aspiring lawyers and other professionals. Today, anyone admitted to medical school can count on living at least a comfortable, if not opulent, life. Graduates of law schools and business schools may not always fare quite so well, but even they face little danger of being unemployed or being forced to abandon their profession. Hence, one can scarcely describe these professions as a lottery in which a few winners deserve ample rewards for having survived against great odds.

A more plausible reason why professionals earn more than factory workers is that they must go to the trouble and expense of acquiring a considerable amount of advanced training. Doctors and lawyers must complete years of education beyond college, and companies seem increasingly inclined to look for management trainees with M.B.A. degrees. This extra education costs a tidy sum in tuition and forgone earnings. But even that amount does not begin to offset the premiums earned by the most successful professionals. *Average* earnings for corporate executives, attorneys, and physicians yield higher-than-normal returns on the total investment in special training, and the best-paid professionals earn several times the average.[8]

In addition to longer preparation, Adam Smith pointed to the special skills that highly successful professionals must exhibit in order to reach the top. Certainly, exceptional talents of some sort are required of anyone who becomes the head of a large company, a successful trial lawyer, or a leading heart surgeon. These abilities help to justify the healthy premiums such professionals enjoy over the salaries earned by the typical teacher or government attorney. But even the most generous allowance for special talent cannot explain why a CEO, a neurosurgeon, or a corporate lawyer can earn several times the salary of a university president, a Nobel prize winner, or a United States senator. Some other cause must plainly be at work.

Could the huge earnings of top private-sector professionals have something to do with the grave responsibilities they bear for the lives of patients, the welfare of clients and employees, or the incomes of tens of thousands of stockholders? Like the special talents just discussed, these responsibilities are impressive. Yet they are hardly weightier than those of a superintendent of schools for a major metropolis, or the head of a large government agency, not to mention the president of the United States.* It is also unclear why

* A CEO might reply that high public officials have the special satisfaction of wielding great powers to serve humankind in exciting, visible ways. But such an argument can easily be turned on its head. The awesome challenges and responsibilities of government leaders and the consequences of their actions for the welfare of the citizenry

greater responsibility should warrant more pay. True, it makes a job more difficult and important and hence seems to justify higher compensation. On the other hand, it also makes a position more attractive to many ambitious people and hence makes it less necessary to offer large rewards to attract qualified candidates.

In short, although Adam Smith gave many good reasons to explain why some workers earn more than others, his writings do not convincingly explain why professionals today are paid so much more than other types of workers or why some professionals receive much greater compensation than others. More than a century after *The Wealth of Nations* first appeared, however, several economists in different countries—Knut Wicksell in Sweden, Leon Walras in France, John Bates Clark in the United States, and Alfred Marshall in England—arrived independently at another insight that shed further light on these questions.[9] Their idea has come to be known as the theory of marginal productivity.

The theory itself is mercifully simple, to the point of seeming self-evident. Employers will keep on hiring workers, and paying what it takes to attract them, until the cost of further hiring equals the price to be obtained from selling the extra output that the added employees make possible. In this way, employers will maximize their profits and workers will receive a wage equal to the market value of what they produce. No employees need toil for a lesser sum, because they are always free to leave a penny-pinching employer and find work elsewhere at the market rate. Conversely, no one will be paid more than the market rate or competitors will be able to undercut the price and force wages down to proper levels. Best of all, the wages and jobs that emerge from this process will be exactly the ones needed to attract the mix of skills required to produce the pattern of goods and services that the public most desires.

Even this simplified model helps to show how individuals with rare talents can command very high salaries. Monica Seles earns

---

can just as well be used to justify *larger* salaries than those available in the private sector. Besides, most CEOs do not consider their jobs less challenging or attractive than positions in the public sector. Nor do they claim that they deserve their paychecks because they have to assume heavy responsibilities on behalf of uninspiring ends, such as producing underarm deodorants or pet foods. If salaries were truly supposed to decline in return for the chance to serve a worthy cause, one would expect to find CEOs of firms producing health-preserving drugs and life-support systems earning much less than their luckless counterparts who have to settle for selling Fig Newtons or video games. Yet this is plainly not the case.

over a million dollars per year because no woman has the ability to beat her at tennis more than occasionally, and many people want to watch the best player compete. Michael Jackson takes home still greater sums because even more people want to hear him perform and can satisfy their desires thanks to television, discs, and cassettes. The rewards for such scarce talents dwarf the earnings of those who labor no less hard in factories and fields. But economists view these huge paychecks as legitimate, because the talented few are being paid only in accordance with how the public values their services.

The theory of marginal productivity, together with the insights of Adam Smith, seem to have persuaded the general public, as well as economists, that large differences in compensation are indispensable to progress and prosperity. Even philosophers strongly attracted to the ideal of economic equality acknowledge that marked disparities in pay are needed both to attract people to the occupations for which they are best suited and to induce them to acquire the skills and exert their best efforts at work for the ultimate benefit of the entire society. As Thomas Nagel puts it, "Perhaps there is some alternative method of using straightforward economic incentives in such a way that large economic inequalities do not develop from their operation; but no one has yet dreamed up such a system."[10]

Notwithstanding this consensus, the theory of marginal productivity is not entirely satisfactory in justifying the pay of successful professionals and executives. For one thing, the theory is based upon an earlier economy very different from the one we know today. In the nineteenth century, many industries were packed with small, competing firms employing workers who could see what they produced each week with their own hands. As time went on, however, simple forms of production gave way to much more complex operations and much larger enterprises. It became impossible to measure the output of individual employees, let alone be sure that the wages paid to additional workers equaled the value of the goods they produced. In a world crowded with technical knowledge and surfeited with information of all kinds, one could hardly assume that all producers and consumers were totally informed. Once industries came to be dominated by a few large companies (often bargaining with powerful unions), one could scarcely feel confident that wages would correspond closely with those that

Marshall envisaged in markets served by scores of small, competing enterprises.

These changes not only called the older theories into question; they also undermined belief in a moral basis for the prevailing levels of compensation. One could tolerate vast differences in pay so long as they were considered necessary to produce the mix of talents, effort, and skills required to maximize the welfare of the entire society. But the more these differences came to be seen as affected by monopoly power, political influence, or consumer ignorance, the less one could assume they were exactly what the economy needed to promote everyone's welfare to the fullest.

Technology also weakened our faith in the theory of marginal productivity by pushing its logic to lengths that strained belief. In earlier generations, one could question a system in which business executives earned so much more than poets and philosophers. But there was at least an observable link between reward and talent, entrepreneurial success and social welfare. Today, what is one to make of a world in which modern communication allows Madonna to earn tens of millions of dollars, while a rock group, New Kids on the Block, with claims to enduring musical distinction that are tenuous at best, receives over one hundred million dollars in a single two-year period? Economists will respond that if we do not let the market decide matters of compensation, who will? Yet even if no better alternative comes to mind, thoughtful people will look upon the results, not with comprehension and respect, but with bewildered disbelief.

Efforts to justify compensation have been further weakened by changing perceptions of inequality in American society. From colonial times until World War II, most Americans clung to the view that all persons had an equal opportunity to succeed according to their abilities and efforts. From *Poor Richard's Almanac* to the Horatio Alger books, this message was constantly repeated and eagerly accepted by the public. As late as the 1930s, opinion polls could report that large majorities of the public answered yes to the question, "Do you feel that your child has as good a chance as any other to be President of the United States?"

In such a world, it was natural to look upon individuals with high salaries as fully deserving of their earnings. According to Francis Bowen, a nineteenth-century Harvard professor of practical ethics, "In a free and just commonwealth, property rushes from the idle and the imbecile, to the industrious, brave and persevering."[11] Why shouldn't entrepreneurs reap a handsome reward if their success was simply the result of hard work and good character?

Fifty years of research in the social sciences have shaken the faith of many Americans that economic success is open to all on the same terms. Scholars have documented in ever greater detail the many reasons why all children do not begin school, still less their careers, with an equal capacity to succeed. Native intelligence, prenatal care, family support, nutrition, and a host of other forces combine to produce marked differences in ability and ambition at a very early age. Race, gender, family income, schooling, and community influences of all kinds continue to limit the chances of some while enhancing the prospects of others. In such a world, effort and character undoubtedly count for something, but it is hard to be as confident as before that the high salaries earned by so many doctors, lawyers, and business executives are simply rewards for the "industrious, brave and persevering."

In short, now that our perceptions of the world have changed so drastically, it is more difficult than it seemed a century ago to justify the vast differences in earnings we see all around us. That is the way the market works, apologists assure us. Yet more and more skeptics are unconvinced that the market produces ideal results or that the paychecks many leading professionals receive need be so large to achieve the greatest prosperity and well-being for the society as a whole.

MONEY AND THE CHOICE OF CAREERS

In Adam Smith's day, when most people lived at the edge of poverty, modest differences in wages must have had a potent effect on workers choosing their calling and deciding where to look for a job. For the past one hundred years, however, intellectuals have wondered whether money would gradually lose its power to affect behavior as more and more people grew prosperous enough that they no longer needed to worry about acquiring the necessities of life. Utopians, in particular, looked forward to a society so affluent that few individuals would care enough about what they were paid to be influenced in their choice of career. It was this thought that inspired

Edward Bellamy in *Looking Backward* to conjure up a world in which everyone received equal rewards and worked only to serve the community.[12]

Economists have never taken kindly to these imaginings. Thorstein Veblen, for example, offered a much more cynical assessment of the place of money in society.[13] In contrast to Bellamy, Veblen noted how persistent the motives were for accumulating wealth and how enduring the human weaknesses were that underlay them. As he put it, in his characteristically ornate prose:

> In the nature of the case, the desire for wealth can scarcely be satiated in any individual instance, and evidently a satiation of the average or general desire for wealth is out of the question. However widely, or equally, or 'fairly' it may be distributed, no general increase of the community's wealth can make any approach to satiating this need, the ground of which is the desire of everyone to exceed everyone else in the accumulation of goods. If, as is sometimes assumed, the incentive to accumulation were the want of subsistence or of physical comfort, then the aggregate economic wants of a community might conceivably be satisfied at some point in the advance of industrial efficiency; but since the struggle is substantially a race for reputability or the basis of an invidious comparison, no approach to a definitive attainment is possible.[14]

The debate over the power of money has hardly ended. Some social scientists detect a new strain of postmaterialism in advanced societies, more common among young adults than among their parents and especially prevalent in affluent professional circles. Postmaterialists seem to pursue other aims than financial gain in their search for a meaningful life.[15] They shun luxury and disdain material values. How deep these sentiments go, however, remains a puzzle; answers to questionnaires may not provide a valid index of people's innermost feelings when they are face-to-face with hard choices and dwindling incomes. Already, there are indications that the number of people expressing postmaterialist attitudes may have stopped growing and even begun to fall back under pressure from the economic slowdown that most Western economies have experienced in recent years.

For the foreseeable future, then, pecuniary ambitions seem likely to survive, if only because the uses of money are so numerous. The desire for wealth is neither static nor merely the outgrowth of a yearning for material goods. New appetites are constantly emerging under the stimulus of ingenious entrepreneurs and advertisers. Beyond possessions, money brings security and freedom from a host of petty worries. It often yields power, influence, and at least the illusion of popular esteem. It signals personal achievement and bolsters feelings of self-worth. For some, money is simply the best way of keeping score in an ambiguous world. For a miserly few, it is an end in itself, quite apart from anything it buys in the marketplace.

These multiple attractions have persuaded economists to stick with the premise that money is the primary motive in modern society and that differences in pay remain the principal force regulating the distribution of labor among the various occupations. Not that economists are unaware that there are other reasons for choosing a career. How else to explain the continuing supply of priests and social workers? But these motives, once acknowledged, are quickly brushed aside. "Other things being equal," economists maintain, the supply of labor in any occupation is determined by the income it promises to yield in comparison with prospective earnings in alternative callings.

While economists have continued to spin their theories, investigators in a neighboring discipline have offered a more complicated set of reasons for choosing one occupation over another. In study after study, when psychologists ask college seniors what they look for most in a job, money finishes far down the list. Typical of these findings are the results of a 1989 survey of over nine thousand seniors from a group of thirty selective private colleges and universities.[16] For these students, the most important reasons for choosing a career were those having to do with the interest of the work involved—its intellectual challenge, the opportunities to be creative and exercise initiative. Next came aspects of the job relating to other human beings—the kinds of people that will be your colleagues, the freedom to live by your own ethical values, the chance to be helpful to others. Somewhat lower in importance were matters affecting freedom of choice—the opportunity to keep your options open, to have a flexible schedule, to be relatively free from supervision. Only after all these considerations did seniors value "high income potential." In a list of twenty-one separate factors, income rated fourteenth, surpassing only such items as "social recognition or status," "acceptability to my family," "not much pressure or stress," and "does not require an extended period of training beyond college."

Such findings, repeated many times for many kinds of college students, appeared to cast doubt on the power of money to shape career choices, at least among the highly educated. If these results were correct, economists would have to revise their theories. Employers would be well advised to rethink their approach to recruitment. Law firms, corporations, and government agencies would do better emphasizing challenging work with interesting colleagues instead of talking so much about their starting salaries and earnings potential.

Rather than debate their differences, psychologists and economists continued for years to plough their respective fields in seeming indifference to one another. Psychologists deplored the economists' philistine preoccupation with money. Economists scoffed at the naïveté of supposing that answers to surveys could reveal the true values of students. For them, as Frank Hubbard wrote, "When a fellow says it hain't the money but the principle of the thing, it's the money."[17]

In 1972, however, a Harvard economist, Richard Freeman, sought to reconcile the two bodies of work.[18] Freeman acknowledged that most students were motivated primarily by reasons other than money and that many of them would stick with their chosen career regardless of any conceivable change in the earnings offered. Based on his own student surveys, however, he insisted that income was at least *one* relevant consideration for most and the principal factor for a significant minority (perhaps 15 percent). In particular, he found that many students were torn among several career possibilities and that money could be a decisive factor in making up their minds. From this evidence, Freeman concluded that compensation was significant for enough college seniors that it performed its classic function of altering the flows of students from one profession to another to adjust to the shifting needs of society.

With the aid of these findings, Freeman was able to make predictions about the number of students who would graduate as physicists, engineers, and Ph.D.s of all kinds, predictions that differed significantly from those of other scholars in the field. By and large, his forecasts proved more accurate than the conventional estimates.

Since his findings first appeared in print, similar work by other scholars has lent added support to his thesis.[19]

In the years that followed, circumstances have changed in ways that would appear to make compensation even more powerful in affecting students' career choices. Undergraduates seem to have become much more materialistic. According to a well-known annual survey, the number of freshmen who regard "being very well off financially" as a "very important" goal rose from 40 percent in 1970 to 75 percent in 1990.[20] Thanks to college placement offices, undergraduates also have much better information about prospective earnings in different professions, which they can use in their quest for financial security. In addition, because of the federal government's financial aid programs, student loans have grown tremendously over the past twenty years, and more and more seniors are graduating with substantial debts. To those with large sums to repay, earning good money ought to seem much more important than it did to their parents.

Despite these recent trends, neither mounting debts nor creeping materialism has settled the argument over how students choose their life's work. University officials deeply involved with the career decisions of students continue to act as though financial considerations were of distinctly minor importance. When applications to medical schools dropped sharply in the early 1980s, admissions officers attributed the slump to worries about malpractice suits and mounting regulations and red tape; they pointed to surveys showing that surprising numbers of doctors would no longer recommend that their own children become doctors. When applications to law schools surged unexpectedly in the late 1980s, admissions deans linked the increase to the rise of television shows such as "L.A. Law." When college seniors turned away from Ph.D. programs in the 1970s, professors insisted that it was not lagging salaries but the fear of not being able to find an academic job that prompted their students to look for other careers. Buttressing these opinions, surveys continued to pile up showing that when it came to choosing a vocation, college seniors still placed a high income very low in their list of considerations.

Apart from these discordant voices, economists themselves are not entirely clear about important details of their theory of career choice. Exactly what kinds of comparisons are students supposed to make? Between related occupations such as law and business? Between going to professional school and starting work? And what calculations do students make? Do they look simply at starting salaries or do they look at projected earnings over a lifetime? If it is the latter, as some economists seem to claim, are college seniors really capable of making the kinds of sophisticated projections described in the scholarly journals? Amid these doubts, the role of compensation in determining career choice continues to provoke disagreement.

MOTIVATING EMPLOYEES

Controversy has also been simmering over how effective money is in persuading people to work harder. With relentless consistency, economists have insisted that economic rewards are a powerful tool not only for influencing career choices but also for determining how hard individuals work and what they try to achieve. A whole industry of consultants has grown up to advise employers about bonuses, piece-rate plans, and ever more elaborate schemes to link pay and performance. Corporate executives receive hundreds of thousands, even millions of dollars in bonuses and stock options on the theory that money will motivate them to work more effectively.

This view seems plausible enough at first blush. But dissenting voices have not been hard to find. In that classic of management texts, *The Functions of the Executive,* Chester Barnard observed that "the unaided power of material incentives . . . is exceedingly limited."[21] During the years that followed, many psychologists voiced the same opinion.[22] So did W. Edwards Deming, father of "total quality management" and guru to many of the Japanese industrialists who built great global enterprises.[23]

According to these critics, human beings, especially in the professions, are motivated more by the intrinsic interest of their work and the opinions of their colleagues than by crass material rewards. Most of the psychologists were influenced by the work of Abraham Maslow, who claimed that human beings had a hierarchy of needs and that once their basic material requirements of comfort and well-being were assured, they responded to other concerns such as self-fulfillment and personal growth.[24] A slightly different approach was used by Frederick Hertzberg, who took to asking employees what incidents had pleased them most and provoked them most in their working experience.[25] Repeatedly, he found that inadequate wages were a cause of discontent that could be relieved only temporarily by a raise in pay but that moments of achievement, mastery, and recognition were much more likely to account for employees' lasting satisfaction with their work.

In yet another challenge to the conventional economic wisdom, Mark Lepper and other experimental psychologists began to raise further questions about the effects of monetary rewards. When investigators paid children to perform a challenging and absorbing task, their enthusiasm for the work diminished as soon as the payments stopped.[26] In some way, money seemed to snuff out spontaneous interest. Other psychologists claimed that financial rewards undermined young people's creativity as well.[27] Such findings created suspicion that paying employees for performing well might somehow stunt other qualities important to their life and work.

After decades of debate and experience, then, much controversy remains over the role of compensation in our society. The complexities of our modern economy cast doubt on whether theories of competitive labor markets drawn from a simpler age can justify the earnings of successful professionals. Experts still differ over how important compensation is in influencing college students deciding on their careers. Psychologists and economists disagree over what monetary rewards can do to motivate people to work more effectively.

In recent years, these issues have taken on renewed importance. In the face of widespread poverty and deprivation, and with money to address these problems in such short supply, one cannot read about the soaring incomes of so many executives and professionals without wondering whether these vast earnings could be better used to help meet urgent human needs. With so many successful students flocking to management consulting organizations and corporate law firms, one has to ask whether money has become too dominant in shaping the career choices of talented undergraduates—and whether the nation is being disserved as a result. As the economy sputters and dissatisfaction grows over the performance of our schools, our companies, our universities, and our health care system, one cannot help but take an interest in whether bonuses, merit pay, stock options, and similar devices can induce professionals and executives to work more effectively. To explore these questions adequately, we need to move from theory to experience and observe how the compensation of executives and professionals has changed over the years and what effects these changes have had on the behavior of the recipients.

CHAPTER 2

THE RISE OF THE PROFESSIONS

Most of us think of attorneys and physicians as fortunate in income and social status. On both scores they rank high in every survey and tabulation. Yet such good fortune was not always their lot. In the eighteenth and nineteenth centuries, many a father cursed his son for wanting to become a doctor, and many a community tried to discourage attorneys from entering their midst.

THE EARLY YEARS

Not until the 1890s did physicians begin to earn significantly more than skilled laborers. In earlier times, practitioners were too numerous in cities to allow most of them to make a good living from the patients wealthy enough to pay for their services. In the countryside, where doctors were fewer, their practice was limited by the distance they could travel in a day by horse or carriage. As a result, they seldom had enough patients to keep them fully employed and had to seek other part-time jobs to make ends meet.

Doctors also suffered in the eyes of the public because they lacked an impressive body of scientific knowledge about the causes and cures for disease. Benjamin Rush, the foremost physician of the late eighteenth century, believed that all illnesses were caused by a "morbid excitement induced by capillary tension" and that only one remedy—bloodletting—was effective.[1] Although the first medical school in America opened in Philadelphia as early as 1765, so limited was the doctor's expertise that even in 1850, the course of study at a leading university such as Harvard lasted only four months, and much of what was taught there was wrong. According to the dean, Jacob Bigelow, "The unbiased opinion of most medical men of sound judgment and long experience" is that "the amount of death and disaster in the world would be less if all disease was left to itself."[2] Another Harvard dean, Oliver Wendell Holmes, added with refreshing candor, "If the whole *materia medica*, as now used, could be sunk to the bottom of the sea, it would be all the better for mankind—and all the worse for the fishes."[3]

Lacking a body of specialized knowledge, doctors found it difficult to impose educational requirements for entry to the profession. Whatever headway they made in setting standards prior to the Revolution soon vanished in a nineteenth-century America hostile to any barriers to freedom of opportunity. At least ten states repealed earlier legislation authorizing medical societies to examine candidates and grant licenses to aspiring physicians. Proprietary schools sprung up offering training that was even more dubious in quality than that of the university-based medical schools. Homeopathy, botanic medicine, chiropraxis, and other more exotic forms of healing flourished in a sea of ignorance and superstition.

Beset by all these difficulties, doctors earned remarkably little throughout the nineteenth century. In 1850, the average income of physicians was thought to be no more than $600 per year. As late as 1904, the American Medical Association estimated median annual earnings at only $750 (roughly $12,000 in today's currency).[4]

Lawyers too had a difficult history in the United States. Throughout the seventeenth century, they were the object of active suspicion and dislike. According to Perry Miller, a majority of Americans in the colonies "hated the law as an artificial imposition on their native intelligence" and thought it "a gigantic conspiracy of the learned against their helpless integrity."[5] Although these sentiments are not unknown today, the early settlers were much more willing to act on their prejudices. Several colonies actually tried to eliminate lawyers altogether. A typical statute of the period provided that "all mercenary attorneys [i.e., attorneys who charged for their services] be expelled from that office."[6] By 1705, there were only three lawyers in Philadelphia; forty years later, records reveal no more than eight members of the bar in New York City. One can even find reports of defendants in big cities accusing their opponents of denying them justice by hiring away all the local attorneys.[7]

Eventually, citizens found that they needed skilled representation when they became embroiled in legal disputes. Rather than prohibit lawyers altogether, therefore, legislatures placed strict limits on attorneys' fees and ordered stiff fines for anyone charging above the maximum. Gradually, however, the status of lawyers improved, and they steadily grew in number and influence throughout the eighteenth century. Inspired by the gentlemanly traditions of Great Britain, aristocratic members of the bar favored voluntary honoraria rather than fees, and stoutly opposed suing for nonpayment. To elevate standards, they formed legal societies, argued that all lawyers should have some college education in the liberal arts, and actually persuaded several colonial legislatures to pass laws allowing professional bodies to set qualifications for admission to the bar. By the outbreak of the Revolution, in Roscoe Pound's words, "the legal profession in most of the colonies had become well-established in public estimation, well educated, and well qualified by study of law."[8]

Efforts to improve the profession, however, quickly lost momentum after the Revolution, when many leading lawyers turned out to have Tory sympathies and had to flee the colonies. With much legal work shifting to the unpopular task of collecting debts, the status of lawyers plunged again to a low level. As John Quincy Adams wrote in a letter to his mother, "The popular odium which has been exerted against the practitioners in this Commonwealth prevails to so great a degree that the most innocent and irreproachable life cannot guard a lawyer against the hatred of his fellow citizens."[9]

In the decades that followed, educational requirements for the bar were swept away by the same tides of egalitarianism that overwhelmed medical licensing statutes. The years from 1830 to 1870 proved to be the nadir of the legal profession. Educational standards suffered as apprenticeship continued to be the preferred means to prepare for the profession. Although Harvard had opened a law school as early as 1817, and many other schools sprang up thereafter, fewer than a thousand students were enrolled in the country as late as the Civil War. Only nine jurisdictions still imposed any educational requirements, and most states seemed to believe that any person of good character could teach himself to practice adequately. The chairman of Vermont's committee on admission to the bar caught the spirit of the times in commenting on two young applicants who came before him in 1850:

> Of any branch of the law, they were as ignorant as so many Hottentots . . . I frankly told them that for them to attempt to practice law would be wicked, dangerous, and would subject them to suits for malpractice. They begged, they prayed, they cried. . . . I, with much self-reproach, consented to sign their certificates, on condition that each would buy a copy of Blackstone, Kent's Commentaries, and Chitty's Pleadings, and immediately emigrate to some western town.[10]

With the floodgates open, young men flocked to the profession. By 1880, there were more lawyers for every thousand people than America would see again until 1960. Such fragmentary evidence as remains suggests that lawsuits may have reached a peak, relative to the size of the population, that would not be matched even in the so-called litigation explosion of the 1970s and 1980s.

Other professions and quasi professions suffered from a similar lack of quality and prestige through much of the nineteenth century. Prior to the Civil War, college instructors were not expected to do research or to possess any special knowledge or scholarly training. The institutions in which they taught were more like preparatory schools than universities. At Harvard, Charles Eliot observed in his inaugural address in 1869, "it is very hard to find competent professors for the University. Very few Americans of eminent ability are attracted to this profession. The pay has been too low, and there has been no gradual rise out of drudgery such as may reasonably be expected in other learned callings."[11]

In the public schools, teaching was originally a temporary job for young men preparing for the ministry or some other occupation. In the nineteenth century, however, the nation's children were increasingly taught by young women trained in normal schools that were attached not to colleges but to local secondary schools. Universities prior to the Civil War showed little interest in accepting any responsibility for preparing their students either to teach in schools or to administer them.

As for the federal government, jobs at every level were overrun by the spoils system after Andrew Jackson's presidency. Each national election brought floods of hungry office seekers to Washington and carried away previous beneficiaries on the ebbing tides of defeat. Few of these officials were prepared at college for their public responsibilities, and the nation's universities did not seriously contemplate creating any special training for this purpose.

THE GROWTH OF PROFESSIONALISM

Toward the end of the nineteenth century, the mood of the country gradually turned to favor greater professionalism. Knowledge accumulated, placing a stronger foundation under the professions and, for the first time, allowing serious, specialized courses of training. After 1870, aided by advances in germ theory and scientific physiology, medical education began to undergo a transformation at Johns Hopkins and other leading universities. At about the same time, Christopher Columbus Langdell revolutionized the study of what he was pleased to call the "science of law" by championing the case method. Under the leadership of Daniel Coit Gilman and Charles W. Eliot, Johns Hopkins and Harvard introduced the Ph.D. in the late 1870s, featuring serious attention to research methods along lines already familiar in Germany.

Business education arrived several decades later, even though professional managers had already begun to appear in railroads and telegraph companies as early as the 1850s. At the end of the century, only the University of Pennsylvania offered an undergraduate business major, and graduate schools of management did not emerge until the early 1900s. Training for teachers was almost as slow in coming, with the first teachers' college starting only in 1887 and the first university graduate programs in education opening at Columbia only in 1891. Last of all to appear was special preparation for government service. The Maxwell School of Public Administration at Syracuse University did not open its doors until 1924. By the end of the 1920s, however, the educational foundations had been laid, and all of the aspiring professionals and executives covered in this study could receive some form of advanced training for their calling.

THE PATTERN OF EARNINGS

The growth of specialized knowledge did more than allow the training of specialists. It permitted certain professions to limit entry by persuading legislators to impose licensing requirements administered by professional organizations. Speaking for the United States Supreme Court in 1888 in the case of *Dent* v. *West Virginia,* Justice Stephen Field upheld a state board of health in expelling a graduate of the American Eclectic College of Medicine as incompetent.[12] In

Field's words, "no one has the right to practice medicine without having the necessary qualifications of learning and skill."

After medical societies had gained control over entry to the profession, Abraham Flexner issued his famous report in 1910 condemning much of existing medical education.[13] Flexner offered a powerful rationale for closing down scores of proprietary schools and other institutions of doubtful merit. The message gave impetus to a process of reform that was already well underway. In the name of quality, the number of accredited medical schools dropped by almost half, the period of study grew longer and more demanding, and licensing requirements became more stringent. As the quality of medicine improved, fewer students went to medical school, and the number of doctors for every one hundred thousand Americans fell from 173 in 1900 to 125 in 1930. Through the magic of supply and demand, the incomes of physicians started to rise at a professionally gratifying pace. After so many frustrating decades, a bright new day was dawning for practitioners.

A similar pattern of events took place in the legal profession after the founding of the American Bar Association (ABA) in 1878. Among the Association's aims was to "uphold the honor of the profession" by supporting efforts to improve the preparation required to become a lawyer.[14] Apprenticeship rapidly fell away, and the responsibility for preparing attorneys shifted to the law schools. With ABA encouragement, more and more law faculties insisted on at least two years of college as a prerequisite to admission.

In the 1920s, the ABA turned its attention to legislation to strengthen entry requirements even further. Gradually, more and more states passed laws requiring that candidates have at least a few years of college and a law school degree from an accredited institution (or equivalent law office study). In addition, most states insisted on the successful completion of a detailed bar examination and a finding of good moral character.

Because of these requirements, the number of lawyers began at last to grow less rapidly than the population. No longer could enterprising bloods without training or qualifications learn to practice on their own at their clients' expense. As in the case of doctors, the new restrictions not only improved the quality of the bar; they also had the satisfying effect of lifting lawyers' incomes to more respectable levels.

In contrast to law and medicine, the teaching professions were either unwilling or unable to limit entry successfully. Even toward the end of the nineteenth century, when states began to require that teachers be certified, professional associations such as the National Education Association (NEA) never sought to control the number of students crowding into the teachers' colleges. If teachers had any collective aim, it was not to limit supply but to increase demand by pressing for smaller class sizes.

Had the NEA tried to control entry, it would have quickly encountered the objection that professional training for teachers was unnecessary because education lacked a specialized body of knowledge comparable to that of doctors or lawyers. Then as now, teachers have failed to persuade the world that they are highly skilled practitioners entitled to the emoluments of a learned profession. Instead, their fortunes have depended on the level of prosperity in the economy and, even more, on the rise and fall of the student population. Those fortunes, alas, have fluctuated around a very low base. There is a persistent myth that mature and dedicated teachers abounded in the public school classrooms of the early 1900s. A few such paragons doubtless existed, but they were the exception. As David Tyack has observed, "The concept of a golden age in the past is untenable. Throughout most of our history, teachers have been young and poorly paid."[15]

Like teachers, university professors could not hope to control supply effectively, because they would have a hard time convincing anyone that the new Ph.D. degree was a proper requirement for faculty status in all the tiny colleges and professional schools that sprang up during the nineteenth century. By the early 1890s, however, some graduate training was a prerequisite for appointment in any first-rate university. In addition, rising enrollments and the emergence of Cornell, Stanford, Chicago, and other new institutions led to an active competition for talented scholars and a rapid growth in their salaries. By the mid-1890s, only twenty-five years after Eliot complained about low faculty pay, the average professor's salary was $1,470 (over $23,000 in today's currency), or at least twice that of a doctor and five times the average pay of a teacher. As it happened, however, this affluence was short-lived. Earnings for professors would not rise above the level of the 1890s (in constant dollars) for more than sixty years, . . . but that is to get ahead of the story.

By 1930, the pattern of compensation in the several professions had come to reflect the differences in their market power. In 1900, doctors were paid, on average, only half as much as university professors, less even than federal employees, and about the same as ministers. Once they succeeded in creating stiff requirements for licensure, however, they quickly moved to the top of the professional heap, overtaking even the lawyers, who were not quite as successful in limiting the influx of new members. Professors, who were paid substantially more than doctors at the beginning of the century, lagged far behind by the time of the Great Depression. Bringing up the rear were teachers, who had fared relatively well since the turn of the century but started from such a low base that they still could not equal the pay of skilled workers in 1930.

AVERAGE ANNUAL EARNINGS, 1930[16]

Medicine	$5,600
Law	5,100
College teaching	2,792
School teaching (urban)	1,392
Skilled labor	1,700
Unskilled labor	1,080

Outside the traditional professions, trends were also taking shape in the early twentieth century that would become increasingly marked in later decades. In the federal government, the passage of the Pendleton Act and the gradual expansion of a merit-based civil service helped lift the educational attainments of government officials far above those of the nation as a whole. By the turn of the century, over 20 percent of those who passed the Civil Service Examination had attended college, compared with only 4 percent in the general population. Even so, federal employees watched their compensation steadily erode. By 1916, for the first time in memory, their pay scales were clearly surpassed by those in industry, and significant gaps appeared between the earnings of higher-level officials and their counterparts in the private sector.[17] By 1930, according to a Personnel Classification Board study, "the salaries paid by private concerns to their major executives exceed those paid by the Federal Government to positions of similar responsibility anywhere from 100 to 500 percent."[18]

As the previous sentence implies, very different patterns were beginning to unfold in the boardrooms of American corporations. Business did not enjoy the status of a profession requiring special qualifications. Long after World War I, the MBA was still considered an exotic degree possessed by only a small fraction of executives. The key to raising executive salaries lay not in limiting entry but in gaining control of the corporation. So long as owners remained in charge and hired managers to help run the business, salaries were ample but not extravagant. J. P. Morgan, for example, made it a point never to pay an executive more than twenty times the earnings of the lowliest employee in the organization. As late as 1900, salaries of $5,000–$6,000 (or $80,000–$95,000 in today's currency) were not uncommon for presidents of substantial manufacturing companies, and the average compensation for top managers of large firms prior to World War I was slightly below $10,000—less than the pay of a major university president.[19] Not until owners relinquished power, and managers were accountable only to thousands of shareholders, was the way clear to granting emoluments on the lavish scale we know today.

Once professional managers gained control, however, their salaries rocketed upward. In the booming 1920s, a few chief executives, such as Charles Schwab of U.S. Steel, Eugene Grace of Bethlehem, and George Washington Hill of American Tobacco, received bonuses in good years that lifted their total pay above $1 million (or roughly $8 million in today's currency). By 1929, the median compensation of top executives in one hundred large industrial firms reached $101,000 (or approximately $800,000 in today's currency).[20]

The Great Depression caused professional incomes to decline severely. During World War II and thereafter, however, earnings began to evolve once again in much the same fashion as they had during previous decades.

ANNUAL RATES OF INCREASE IN COMPENSATION (%)[21]

	1930–52	1952–61	1961–70
Doctors	5.13	7.35	6.73
Lawyers	2.54	7.14	5.51
Professors	2.08	5.21	5.58
Teachers	4.12	5.18	5.55
Federal officials (GS 15)	1.20	2.71	5.95
All employees	4.42	4.46	5.23

By continuing to limit entry to the profession, doctors managed to push up their annual earnings at rates well above the cost of living. In the Depression, as physicians' incomes fell, the American Medical Association persuaded medical schools to cut enrollments substantially and hence avoid a glut of doctors. After 1933, their incomes began to rise rapidly again. Attorneys were not so fortunate. It was easier for the public to dispense with their services, and the demand for lawyers has always been sensitive to the growth of the economy. For these reasons, real legal earnings rose little until the late 1940s, when the economy surged, causing incomes to grow more rapidly.

In contrast, teachers and professors continued to be hostages to the ebb and flow of student populations. As a result, their salaries rose at lower-than-average rates until 1950, only to exceed the average in the following two decades when returning GI's and then the baby boom generation lifted enrollments to unprecedented heights.

Federal officials, on the other hand, continued to have a hard time of it. Taxpayers never displayed much enthusiasm for increasing the pay of bureaucrats, and professionals and managers in the civil service were squeezed especially hard. When money was available, Congress tended to favor the lower-level public employees, who were much more numerous and hence more politically influential. Top civil service pay rates were tied to congressional salaries, which lawmakers were reluctant to raise for fear of angering their constituents. From 1930 to 1960, therefore, pay increases for high civil servants consistently lagged the average for all workers. Only when President Kennedy arrived on the scene, determined to attract "the best and the brightest" to the nation's service, did federal managers see a marked improvement in their paychecks.

Corporate executives, finally, had surprising difficulty pushing their earnings much above the high-water mark of 1929. Their total compensation dropped by over one-third in the early years of the Depression before returning to previous levels in the latter years of the decade. In 1936, a study of one hundred large companies revealed that chief executive officers were being paid $93,000, down from $101,000 in 1929.[22] Even so, as the authors point out, "justification of these large amounts has been a constantly recurring problem . . . raised by economists, business men, and ordinary citizens interested chiefly in dividend payments." After World War II, executive pay continued to move erratically, so much so that by the early 1960s, average salaries and bonuses (in real dollars) still did not exceed the levels reached in 1940.[23]

THE DISTRIBUTION OF TALENT

There are no records from the nineteenth century to tell us how the most intellectually gifted members of society made their living. All we possess are fragmentary records of the occupations of men who graduated from a number of the better-known colleges. From this, we can learn something of the changing demands of the several professions for educated personnel.

PERCENTAGE OF COLLEGE GRADUATES PURSUING VARIOUS CAREERS[24]

	Teaching	Business	Medicine	Ministry	Law
1801–1820	5	5	28	20	24
1821–1840	7	5	35	22	19
1840–1860	9	9	28	18	23
1861–1880	12	12	28	10	29
1880–1900	13	13	21	6	23

As late as 1900, managers and professionals together made up barely 10 percent of the entire labor force. Over the next fifty years, however, undergraduate and graduate degrees grew eightfold, and managers and professionals steadily increased their share of the work force. The growth was highly uneven, reflecting the differing power and policies of the several professions. Managers multiplied rapidly, almost doubling their share of all employed persons by 1950. Teachers and professors did the same. But doctors, by limiting entry to the profession, continued to make up only half of 1 percent of the work force. Lawyers actually reduced their share; by midcentury, they accounted for only four-tenths of 1 percent of all male workers.[25]

These trends continued in much the same fashion for at least two decades after World War II. The number of physicians and attorneys continued to grow at a pace only slightly faster than the entire population. In contrast, lifted by a rising tide of new students, teachers and professors multiplied much more quickly, increasing their share of the work force at a rate three times that of doctors and lawyers. Managers likewise grew steadily, as business prospered in the postwar economy. Overall, managers and professionals together accounted for 28 percent of all male workers by 1970—almost three times their share in 1900—while the fraction of both groups holding at least a college degree climbed continuously.[26]

These patterns of growth tell us little about the distribution of intellectual talent among the several callings. Evidence on this score was not available until World War II, when men were required to take aptitude tests in connection with military service and, later, the draft. Aptitude tests, of course, like college grades, are admittedly crude indexes for measuring intellectual talent, let alone the other qualifications needed to do well in one's chosen occupation. Everyone knows that perseverance, judgment, imagination, interpersonal skills, and just plain luck have decisive effects on success in one's career. In assessing talent, however, we are forced to concentrate on grades and test scores, because measures of other important traits are simply unavailable.

Fortunately for our purposes, grades and test scores appear to have some significant effect on success in one's career. For example, David Wise found that the rate of salary increase for managers and professionals in large corporations varied consistently in accordance with the selectivity of the college they had attended, the grade averages they achieved, and their rank in graduate school.[27] Another study concluded that college graduates with A records received salaries averaging 9 percent more than graduates with B records, who in turn received 9 percent more than graduates with C records.[28] In still another survey, Ronald Ferguson found that the scores Texas teachers received on the state qualifying exam accounted for about one-fifth to one-quarter of the differences in the average performance of their students on the statewide assessment of minimum skills.[29] After reviewing many studies of this kind, Robert Klitgaard concluded that "across a rather large spectrum of the population, both test scores and grades tend to have a modest predictive power for many kinds of later life contributions" with correlations running higher for managerial and professional occupations.[30]

There is every reason to believe that intelligence and analytic ability will be even more important in years to come. Whether in medicine, with its ever-greater technological sophistication and its steadily expanding corpus of knowledge, or in business, with its increasing dependence on science and its growing involvement with other countries and cultures, or in teaching, with its newly discovered emphasis on higher-level problem-solving skills, every profession and near profession is becoming more complex and making greater intellectual demands on its practitioners.

There is one final reason for paying attention to grades and test scores, despite their evident shortcomings. Professions that can attract disproportionate numbers of students with exceptional academic records are also likely to interest large numbers of young people with other abilities that will help them get ahead. As a result, unless employers are incapable of choosing intelligently among applicants, professions that are attractive to students with academic talent will presumably be able to enlist aspiring young managers and professionals possessing other important skills as well. For this reason, changes in the employment patterns of academically talented students are likely to signal similar changes in the career choices of young people with other traits that lead to success.

With these qualifications in mind, we can learn something about the distribution of talent around 1950 by observing the following table, which lists the average test scores of students enrolled in various professional programs at that time.

DISTRIBUTION OF SCORES ON ARMY GENERAL CLASSIFICATION TEST[31]

	Test Scores		
Academic Program	**Bottom 25%**	**50th Percentile**	**Top 25%**
Medicine (M.D.)	120	127	135
Law (L.L.B.-J.D.)	115	127	128
Business (M.B.A.)	114	121	128
Education (Masters)	114	122	129
Business (B.A.)	112	119	126
Education (B.A.)	111	118	126

These figures suggest that academic talent at midcentury fell roughly into two groupings. Toward the top were professions based on science, principally engineering, medicine, and the natural and biological sciences. Here the brightest students congregated in disproportionate numbers. Distinctly lower in aptitude were the social professions and quasi professions, such as teaching, management, and law. In 1950, candidates earning master's degrees for these three professions were almost equal in tested ability. B.A.'s majoring in education were clearly a cut below the master's students and were not even at the average for all college graduates. Still, one-third of them ranked in the top 40 percent of all college graduates, and they differed very little in academic ability from their college classmates seeking careers in business and law.

Until the end of World War II, of course, great pools of academic talent lay untapped. Countless young men lacked the money or the encouragement needed to enter college. Many were barred because of the color of their skin. Young women were held back by social convention and discrimination as well as by lack of funds. Doubly handicapped, one young black woman recalls her interview with the dean of the Cornell Medical School in the 1920s: "The dean said that there had been a number of meetings of the Admissions Committee about me, that my application had been carefully considered, that I was a very good student and a promising physician, but that I would *not* be admitted. . . . 'You know,' he said, 'twenty-five years ago there was a Negro man admitted to Cornell Medical School and it didn't work out. . . . He got tuberculosis.' "[32]

After the war, however, the GI Bill, the demands of a growing economy, and the development of generous financial aid programs succeeded in bringing masses of new students into colleges and graduate schools. Eventually, even the barriers of racial and gender discrimination began to disappear. Interestingly, colleges did not increase their enrollments primarily by reaching down to students with lower levels of ability; most of the new students were talented young people previously unable to progress beyond high school. As a result, the huge growth in student populations up to 1970 did not cause any reduction in academic quality. What it did do was virtually eliminate the reserve army of academically gifted young people who had previously been unable or unwilling to go to college.

Prior to the war, of the top tenth of all high school students in intellectual ability, only 60 percent attended college and less than half managed to graduate. By 1960, over 90 percent of the top tenth entered college, and by 1970, 85 to 90 percent were receiving a degree.[33] Thereafter, the nation could no longer count on expanding the pool of academically gifted students simply by building more dormitories and giving more financial aid. As the need for talent continued to grow, the task of finding enough people to meet the demand threatened to be difficult for the first time in our history.

Before this problem could become acute, however, help providentially arrived from two quarters. Huge numbers of baby boom children began to graduate from universities and seek employment in business and the professions. In addition, women and minorities started to prepare themselves for careers in law, medicine, and management, aided by a new national policy to prohibit discrimination based on race or gender. These developments promised to postpone for at least a generation any insufficiency of talent to fill demanding jobs. As society continued to grow in complexity, however, it seemed unlikely that such shortages could be avoided indefinitely.

COMPENSATION AS AN INCENTIVE

The practice of rewarding those who perform well dates back to very early times when kings allowed their nobles and chiefs to keep the spoils of the battles they won. Shortly before the birth of Christ, Julius Caesar is said to have instituted a more elaborate system to supply bonuses to loyal soldiers participating in successful campaigns—50 dinari for every legionnaire and 500 for each centurion.

In America, financial incentives began to be used in factories and mills after the Industrial Revolution. As the gospel of "scientific management" spread throughout American industry, more and more firms paid their employees according to the units they produced to encourage them to work harder. Prior to World War I, however, the use of such incentives was much less common among professionals and managers. Only 5 percent of large companies paid a bonus to their top executives from 1904 to 1914, even though most European firms routinely gave extra payments to their managers when earnings were strong.[34]

By the 1920s, American practices had changed completely. A majority of corporations were now giving bonuses to their executives in amounts that often reached 50 percent of base salary.[35] Later on, after World War II, stock options also grew popular, primarily as a means of avoiding the effects of high income tax rates. By the 1960s, only one-third of a typical CEO's compensation was fixed—i.e., base salary and pension—with the rest coming in bonuses and stock options that were supposed to vary according to the company's performance.[36]

Trial lawyers were the only other professionals whose earnings were shaped in such a way that a large fraction of their income depended on performance. In personal injury cases, attorneys for the complaining party normally tried their cases for a contingent fee, which allowed them to pocket a substantial fraction of any damages they won for their clients but to receive nothing if the case failed. This practice—virtually unknown in the rest of the world—was introduced not only to give poor people access to the courts but to encourage attorneys to pursue their client's cause with proper zeal.

Elsewhere in the professions, performance incentives made little headway before World War II or even after. Few universities tried to vary compensation substantially to reflect differences in faculty performance. In the case of teachers, a brief flurry of interest in merit pay emerged after World War I and again after Sputnik in the late 1950s. But the movement quickly died when teachers resisted the idea, fearing favoritism and arbitrariness in deciding who should receive bonuses. Large law firms—the elite of the profession—were generally content to distribute profits among their partners according to age and length of service in the firm. Federal officials were likewise paid by seniority and not on the basis of their performance. Doctors charged for services rendered, often billing their patients according to their ability to pay. But the fees physicians earned did not vary depending on how successful they were in curing their patients.

Amid these many variations in pay practices, professions in the 1960s were enjoying a period of relative prosperity and stability. Earnings in all of the callings in this study were rising steadily at about the same rate. The supply of talented young university graduates entering each occupation seemed to stay reasonably related to demand. The public gave every sign of being tolerably satisfied with the performance of its managers and professionals. Nevertheless, tendencies were beginning to emerge that would soon disturb this tranquil state. The growing numbers of young men and women starting their professional careers threatened to intensify competition for jobs and depress compensation. Only temporarily obscured by the flood of new graduates was the longer-term issue of how intellectual ability should be distributed to meet the constantly growing needs of business and the professions now that the nation could no longer call so easily on untapped reservoirs of talent. Just beginning to be visible through the frustrations over Vietnam and the Great Society was a mounting concern over the effectiveness of American institutions and an urgent desire to improve their performance. All of these challenges promised to have important effects on American managers and professionals and on the rewards and incentives they received.

CHAPTER 3

WHAT HAPPENED AFTER 1970

Each of the management and professional groups we have described was destined to encounter the changes that swept over America during the 1970s and 80s. In one way or another, all of them would cope with a new generation of workers more numerous, more diverse in race and gender, more questioning, and less obedient and loyal than any other generation within memory. All would experience the massive erosion of confidence in our institutions and their leaders that occurred after Watergate and Vietnam. All would endure the inflation of the 1970s and witness the swing to conservatism capped by Ronald Reagan's election in 1980. And yet, despite these common challenges, each profession and calling had its own peculiarities and problems that caused it to react in a special and distinctive way.

BUSINESS EXECUTIVES

The quarter century ending in 1970 was a time of unparalleled success for American business. The United States was the only major nation to emerge from World War II with its industrial base intact. It continued to profit from abundant natural resources to complement the most advanced manufacturing plant ever known. In 1950, America alone accounted for more than 40 percent of the entire world output. For the next twenty years, productivity grew even faster than it did during earlier decades when the United States first rose to industrial prominence. With the economies of so many other countries still ravaged by the war, American corporations were well insulated from foreign competition. Indeed, throughout the 1950s, neither exports nor imports ever exceeded 4 percent of the gross national product.

Toward the end of the 1960s, America's dominance still seemed secure to the casual observer. In 1967, Jacques Servan-Schreiber published a best-selling book entitled *The American Challenge*, in which he spoke of America's growing economic dominance in Europe and the rest of the world, attributing it in large part to the skill of the managers who captained our great corporations. "Considering the extraordinary lead enjoyed by American industry in the key sectors of our economy," he observed, "some economists have asked whether the fastest path to development might not lie in letting Americans manage our industries." By 1980, he warned, "The United States will have entered another world, and if we fail to catch up, the Americans will have a monopoly on know-how, science, and power."[1]

Even as Servan-Schreiber wrote, there were telltale signs that all was not well in the flagship of capitalism. Annual productivity growth had dwindled to 2 percent. For the first time since the war, trade with Japan and Germany recorded a deficit in 1970. Automobiles were just starting to show a negative trade balance; the same was true of consumer electronics. Machine tools and semiconductors were still narrowly in surplus, but their market shares were eroding in the face of foreign competition. The steel industry, once the largest and most efficient in the world, was already losing substantial amounts of business to lower-priced competitors abroad.

By the end of the next decade, complacency would turn to anxiety, even alarm. Productivity growth sagged to less than 1 percent per year. America's trade balance began to tip into deficit. Virtually all of the consumer electronic industry had been lost to foreign competitors; imported cars were starting to cut significantly into domestic markets; even semiconductors seemed in danger of being lost irrevocably to the Japanese. Suddenly, foreign trade was moving up toward 10 percent of our gross national product, and America began to feel vulnerable on many fronts to more efficient rivals overseas.

Beginning in 1970, therefore, American business executives moved swiftly from an era of confidence, approbation, and acknowledged leadership to one of crisis and anxiety. Before the end of the decade, they would be widely accused of complacency, excessive preoccupation with short-term profits, parochialism, indifference to quality, unimaginative, authoritarian behavior toward their employees, and rigid adherence to outmoded policies of mass-producing standardized products. From their own inner temple, the Harvard Business School, they stood condemned by Professors Robert Hayes and William Abernathy for having lost touch with the realities of manufacturing in their misguided fixation on financial manipulation and analytical models.[2] In little more than a decade, "the American challenge" had been transformed from a saga of superiority to a grim struggle for survival.

One might have expected that American business would respond to this predicament with a determined strategy to attract and reward the talent needed to meet the competition from abroad. The actual response, however, was rather puzzling. Compensation rose dramatically, but only for top executives. The trend started slowly in the 1970s with paychecks growing by a modest 25 percent in real dollars throughout the decade. The pace picked up rapidly in the 1980s. CEOs in the top five hundred corporations saw their salaries and bonuses advance over the decade by 50 percent in real dollars.[3] In addition, stock options came into widespread use, giving bonanzas to many executives as the Dow-Jones average tripled in value. Total real compensation for CEOs, therefore, may well have risen by more than 100 percent over the decade.

Middle managers, on the other hand, did much less well. According to one well-known private survey, the compensation of experienced middle managers for a large sample of companies remained flat during the 1970s but then rose by almost 25 percent during the 1980s.[4]

Starting pay for MBAs followed a much less prosperous course. Although nominal salaries rose from $12,528 in 1969–70 to $36,175 in 1989–90, the cost of living rose even faster. Over the entire two decades, therefore, real starting salaries declined by slightly more than 15 percent.[5]

Graduates of the leading business schools fared considerably better. Real starting salaries for Harvard MBAs, for example, began the 1970s at a level more than 15 percent above the national average. Instead of falling in the 1970s, they held their own and actually advanced slightly. During the 1980s, they performed even better, rising by 1990 to a point roughly 15 percent above the 1970 level and approximately 40 percent above the average for MBAs nationwide.[6]

Amid the ebb and flow of starting salaries, the 1970s and 1980s witnessed a large increase in the number of students opting for a career in business. During that period, the proportion of all undergraduates majoring in management climbed from 13.68 percent to almost 25 percent.[7] While male undergraduates shared in this growth, the driving force was clearly the shift in the ambitions of women. From 1970 to 1990, the number of women graduates with BAs in business and management grew more than tenfold, from 10,461 to 116,377.[8]

Enrollments in MBA programs also grew massively. Over the two decades, the total number of students taking the standardized business school admission test (GMAT) almost tripled.[9] Although universities could not expand rapidly enough to accommodate more than a fraction of these applicants, the number of MBAs awarded grew at roughly the same pace, rising from 26,481 to over 74,000 by the end of the period.[10]

The huge influx of students seeking the MBA did not bring any loss of intellectual ability. On the contrary, average scores on the GMAT rose through the two decades.[11] Moderate increases also took place in the share of the most successful students opting for business careers. The share of straight A students bound for business from leading private liberal arts colleges rose from 2.8 percent in 1966 to 6.1 percent in 1976, and a similar senior survey from another group of elite colleges showed further growth from 7.2 percent to 14 percent from 1982 to 1989.[12]

The results of these talent shifts were particularly marked for leading business schools. With much larger applicant pools to choose from, the quality of their student bodies rose steadily through the twenty years. By 1990, they had closed most of the gap traditionally separating their students from those enrolling in medical school and Ph.D. programs in the social sciences. No longer accessible to students of modest academic achievements, the best business schools were now a major claimant for the ablest young college graduates in the nation.

THE LEGAL PROFESSION

In retrospect, the years from 1950 to 1970 were as much of a golden age for lawyers as they were for corporate executives. The amount of money spent on legal services in America trebled in real dollars as the economy prospered and the population grew. With the help of stiffer educational requirements and bar exams, however, the growth of practitioners continued at a gratifyingly deliberate pace until the mid-1960s, just as it had in the two preceding decades.

In this world of stable expansion, competition for business was moderate and civilized. Most corporations gave all their legal work to a single law firm. In return, they typically received a bill once or twice a year, which they paid obediently, seldom fussing over the petty details of why the charges were what they were. Able young men (there were very few young women) went to the best law schools, joined a law firm when they graduated, struggled to achieve partner status, and then looked forward to a lifetime of steadily rising income in the company of respected colleagues.

Eventually, this legal paradise was disrupted by the pressures of mounting competition. In the mid-1960s, the number of new lawyers began to accelerate as the first wave of baby boomers, clutching their new J.D. degrees, descended on Wall Street and other business centers. From 1970 to 1988, the total number of lawyers would virtually treble, from 274,000 to 757,000.[13] The volume of lawsuits filed also began to rise, especially in the federal courts, as a result of environmental rules, affirmative action regulations, and other legislation of the 1960s and early 1970s. Talk of a litigation explosion began to fill the air, reawakening long-smoldering hostilities toward the profession.

In this environment, legal bills began to seem large enough to embattled corporations to call for closer scrutiny than they had previously received. Companies strengthened their general counsel's office and instructed it to determine whether legal work could be purchased more cheaply elsewhere or done more efficiently within corporate headquarters. Suddenly, established law firms found themselves haggling over charges and dividing the business of longtime corporate clients with other firms on a competitive basis.

In order to please their demanding patrons, many partnerships started to grow and diversify to equip themselves to handle all kinds of cases wherever their clients did business. Growth had to proceed quickly, and firms often lacked the time to expand by gradually training young associates. Instead, they sought to acquire instant credibility in new localities and new specialties by bidding away attorneys from other firms or absorbing entire partnerships through merger. The pace of expansion was remarkable, especially in the 1980s. As late as 1978, there were only 15 firms in the country with more than 200 lawyers; ten years later, the number had risen to 115.[14]

As law firms grew at this dizzy pace—acquiring new offices, new specialties, new groups of lawyers—the effort to steer these organizations became ever more difficult. In the old days, management was entrusted to a respected senior member working part-time at the task. "Law firms are administered in only two ways," quipped a managing partner of that era, "badly, and worse." Such casual habits could be tolerated no longer. More and more firms began to hire professional administrators to analyze their budgets, develop marketing plans to sell their services, and create long-term strategies for future growth.

In the other world of private practice—the world of individual clients, of tiny firms and solo practitioners, of personal injury, real estate, and divorce cases—competition was also leaving an imprint. This sector took the brunt of the vast expansion in law graduates and the frantic hunt for business that ensued. Competition had long existed in this segment of the bar; the familiar image of the ambulance chaser gives vivid testimony to that. But the struggle for business began to take new forms. In 1977, the Supreme Court struck down the profession's long-time ban on advertising, opening up a new world of aggressive marketing.[15] Publicly funded law firms created to serve poor clients threatened the private practitioner from a new quarter, as did the growth of chains of legal offices, such as Hyatt Legal Services, with over 180 locations in shopping centers and business districts in more than a dozen states.

As competition intensified, rewards for the fortunate grew impressively. By relaxing requirements for charging contingent fees, judges made it easier for lawyers to use this device more broadly. By liberalizing the rules for joining hundreds of plaintiffs in class action suits, the Supreme Court opened vistas of lucrative rewards for attorneys lucky enough to participate or enterprising enough to help organize such proceedings. Regulatory laws enacted in the 1960s created new causes of action against large corporations, raising the possibility of huge damage awards in fields such as the environment, race and gender discrimination, health and safety, and consumer protection. Vinson and Elkins pocketed more than $220 million as their share of a billion-dollar treble-damage award against the Atchison, Topeka and Santa Fe Railway. Lawsuits arising from the asbestos litigation alone led to more than $2 billion in damages.

What happened to lawyers' earnings in this newly competitive environment? Total income for legal services more than trebled in real value over the twenty-year period.[16] But costs rose rapidly too, and there were many more lawyers at the end of the period to share the larger pie. As a result, earnings per lawyer declined by 20 to 30 percent during the first ten years, when the increase in practitioners was especially rapid, and did not fully recover even in the second decade when business grew faster than the supply of lawyers.

These broad trends masked considerable differences among different sectors of the bar. The largest twenty firms—the elite of the profession—did well throughout the entire twenty years, especially at the end when fees from corporate takeovers and other huge mergers helped to increase real profits per partner by over 50 percent between 1985 and 1990.[17] Other large firms had a harder time keeping their revenues ahead of rapidly rising costs. For them, net profits per partner rose only a little, if at all, over the two decades.[18]

Small firms performed at least as well as their larger counterparts, though not nearly as well as the elite firms. After having their earnings decline by more than 10 percent in the 1970s, partners saw their incomes rise smartly in the 1980s to finish 10 to 15 percent above the levels of the early 1970s.[19]

Much harder hit were the solo practitioners, who bore the brunt of the large increases of new lawyers entering the profession in the 1970s. During that decade alone, they suffered a staggering loss in real income of close to 45 percent.[20] The 1980s were considerably better, but real income was still down by 10 to 20 percent from 1970 levels by the end of the decade.

Because the success of a law firm depends above all on the quality of its attorneys, competition was vigorous, especially for the best young graduates from leading law schools. Even so, as new J.D.'s poured forth in growing numbers, average starting salaries at large and medium-sized firms gradually declined, both in real terms and in relation to starting salaries for college graduates and MBAs, until about 1983.[21] At this point, they began to rise in real dollars (and relative to other callings) so as to end the decade a few percentage points above their 1970 levels.[22]

The most prestigious firms did much better by their new recruits.

Starting salaries on Wall Street not only held their own; they actually increased by 20 percent in the 1970s and by another 40 percent or more in the following decade.[23] But what the leading firms actually offered was a Faustian bargain. In the 1980s, the number of hours each associate billed to clients increased on average from 1,820 a year to 2,200; the number of months associates waited until becoming partner grew by 20 percent; and the odds of being elevated to partnership in a Wall Street firm shrank from one-in-four to one-in-five.[24]

These changes reflected the new realities of maximizing profits in a competitive world. As law partners analyzed their business, they realized that the money to be made came largely from the margin between what they paid their associates and what they could bill their corporate clients for the work of these young attorneys. The more associates a firm could maintain for every partner, and the more hours they worked, the larger the pool of profits would become. The only limit was the necessity to keep working conditions from deteriorating to the point that even lavish salaries would not attract new recruits.

How did students respond to these varying trends in earnings? As incomes for most attorneys started to decline in the early 1970s, male undergraduates reacted quickly by turning to other lines of work. The number of men taking the Law School Admissions Test peaked in 1972 and then declined until the mid-1980s.[25] For a decade, however, these defections were almost offset by a flood of women applicants, whose numbers continued to rise throughout the 1970s.[26] Overall, therefore, applications to law school fell only gradually from 1974 until 1985–86, and then jumped by a remarkable 50 percent in the last four years of the decade when starting salaries were growing strongly.[27]

These swings in applications were muted by the actions of law schools, which expanded and contracted much more slowly. Although the number of students taking the Law School Admissions Test more than trebled from 1964 to 1974, enrollments only doubled.[28] When applications fell by 16 percent in the early 1980s, enrollments dropped by less than 4 percent and then rose by only 8 percent during the huge increase in applications at the end of the decade.[29]

In conclusion, then, despite the economic problems of the profession during the 1970s, the impact on law school applications was never severe, and massive increases in the late 1980s brought them to a point almost 30 percent higher than they had been twenty years before. Even more impressive was the change in the intellectual quality of the pool. One might have thought that new applications would come primarily from students who previously lacked the ability to go to law school or feared they would not succeed in the profession. In that case, the quality of the pool would have gone down as the size increased. Instead, the college grade averages and test scores of applicants rose through the 1970s, declined only when the pool itself shrunk in the early 1980s, and then rose sharply again at the end of the decade to reach its highest level ever.[30]

Law schools also did particularly well in increasing their share of the most academically talented students. From 1966 to 1976, the proportion of top students from elite private colleges choosing legal careers rose from 13.7 percent to 21.6 percent.[31] By 1980, law schools of medium reputation were enrolling a student body of greater ability than the best schools had managed to recruit only twenty years before.[32] Overall, law students were now the intellectual equal of medical students and Ph.D. candidates in the humanities and social sciences and were beginning to challenge doctoral students in some of the scientific disciplines as well. For a profession that had attracted undergraduates of only average ability as late as the 1950s, this was no small achievement.

PHYSICIANS

Having turned back President Truman's proposals for national health insurance after the most expensive publicity campaign in history, the medical profession stood primed to share fully in the prosperity of the 1950s and 60s. And so they did. Doctors' incomes rose by approximately 7 percent per year during those decades, a rate faster than that of any other profession.[33] The health sector also grew rapidly in size. Although the number of doctors rose very slowly—a tribute to the earlier labors of the American Medical Association (AMA)—the entire medical work force grew more than threefold. New hospitals sprouted with the help of generous federal subsidies. By 1970, total medical costs were consuming 7.3 percent of GNP, up from only 4.5 percent just two decades before.[34]

Amid this growth and prosperity, however, changes occurred during the 1960s that would create new problems for doctors in the decades to follow. One critical event was the passage of Medicare and Medicaid in 1964, which completely altered the manner in which most doctors would be paid. Prior to these laws, many physicians charged what patients could afford to pay and used high fees from wealthy patients to make up for the care they gave to the poor. By having the government pay the bills of indigent and elderly patients, Congress altered these practices profoundly.

In one sense, Medicare and Medicaid gave a windfall to doctors by guaranteeing them payments from millions of patients who previously were unable to afford the cost of their care. But the new laws proved to be a mixed blessing. The price of government funding was a steady increase in the paperwork and red tape associated with taking care of patients. In addition, by bankrolling the health costs of a significant share of the population, the government suddenly became a major stakeholder, along with insurance companies, employers, and health maintenance organizations, in the effort to hold down the costs of medical care.

With the nation's health bill rising constantly at rates well above inflation, physicians became more and more vulnerable to criticism. By 1969, the president of the United States was declaring a "massive crisis" in health care.[35] Three-quarters of the public agreed. In 1970, *Fortune* magazine helped to usher in a new decade by observing pointedly, "The doctors created the system. They ran it. And they are the most formidable obstacle to its improvement."[36]

The other great change for the profession was the sudden growth in the number of physicians. In 1965, there were 135 M.D.'s per 100,000 Americans, only 12 more than in 1930, despite the massive improvements in the quality of medicine and the growing access to health services that had occurred in the intervening years.[37] After various commissions had documented the existence of a serious doctor shortage, even the AMA did not oppose increasing the number of practitioners. With financial assistance from Congress, the supply of new doctors soon began to mount rapidly. From 1964 to 1980, the number of students graduating each year from medical school jumped from 7,409 to 15,135.[38]

These changes had a dampening effect on physicians' earnings during the 1970s. For the first time since the Depression, earnings per doctor barely advanced at all in real terms. In fact, average income actually declined slightly, although the drop is probably due to the influx of women, who tended to choose less remunerative specialties and to be paid less well than their male classmates. Sluggish earnings continued into the early years of the 1980s. At this point, incomes suddenly began to rise again in real terms, growing by an average of 2.5 percent a year until the end of the decade.[39]

These overall trends conceal important differences in the fortunes of the various medical specialties. Some of them, such as general and family practice, psychiatry, and pediatrics, yielded average real incomes that were hardly greater in 1990 than they had been in 1970. Others, such as surgery, anesthesiology, and radiology, saw average real incomes rise over the period by 30 to 50 percent. In general, it was in specialties requiring sophisticated procedures, hospitalization, and little patient contact that earnings grew most handsomely.[40]

Student response to all these trends went through several different stages in the years from 1970 to 1990. Boosted by large increases in the number of women, applications to medical schools surged ahead for a time, increasing by more than 70 percent from 1970 to 1974. Thereafter, despite continuing increases in the number of women, applications drifted steadily downward to a low point of 26,721 in 1988, fully 40 percent below the 1974 peak. At this point, interest began to pick up again, and applications grew slightly to 27,563 in 1990.[41] After 1990, applications rebounded even more strongly over the next three years, climbing to a point 30 percent above the 1988 low.[42]

As in the law, the wide fluctuations in applications were moderated by the admissions policies of medical schools. The total number of new M.D.'s did grow by over 70 percent in the 1970s, reflecting the results of a national effort to increase the supply of doctors. In the 1980s, however, the number of new graduates remained virtually the same despite the large falloff in applicants.

Unlike law and business, the medical profession failed to increase its share of exceptionally talented students during the 1970s and 1980s. Overall, scores on the standardized admissions tests even fell slightly. Among Phi Beta Kappas, the fraction entering medicine declined gradually, moving from 23 percent in the early 1970s to 18 percent in the early 1980s.[43] The share of top students from elite private colleges also dropped somewhat in the 1970s and in the 1980s.[44] By 1990, therefore, medicine still attracted academically able students, but the gap between them and their counterparts entering law and business had narrowed appreciably. In fact, by the end of the period, law schools were doing better than medical schools in attracting top students from elite liberal arts colleges—a marked change from the situation only twenty years before.[45]

UNIVERSITY PROFESSORS

Along with the rest of America, universities enjoyed a halcyon period in the 1950s and 60s. World War II had taught the country that science was important to a great nation; Washington now committed itself to building the finest research capability the world had ever seen. At the same time, returning veterans gave Congress the impetus to expand opportunities to attend colleges and universities. As time went on, these two goals were bolstered by new forces. The baby boom stimulated another massive expansion of the higher education system. Sputnik reaffirmed the importance of maintaining scientific preeminence at any cost. Antipolio vaccine, chemotherapy, and other medical breakthroughs fueled a massive rise in funding for health research. The rapid growth of the electronics industry and the entrepreneurial frenzy of Silicon Valley and Route 128 dramatized the potential of an alliance between university-trained scientists and American industry.

The partnership of government, business, and universities in pursuit of wider access and better research produced levels of financial support never before experienced by colleges and universities. The results were dramatic. In twenty years, the number of students graduating from college doubled,[46] while federal support for research in real dollars rose more than twentyfold.[47]

During these years, academic careers seemed more attractive than ever to young people of talent. It was not simply that salaries were outpacing other professions (for the first time in the twentieth century). Professors had become more prominent in American life and had more opportunities to do exciting things. Faculty members were prowling the corridors of power—consulting in corporate boardrooms, advising international bodies, serving on government task forces. Even humanists, who had little to say to Washington or Wall Street, learned to enjoy a more eventful life spiced with foundation-backed projects and conferences in exotic places.

In this environment, it is small wonder that enrollments in Ph.D. programs began to soar. Federal funding helped to ease the financial burdens of long years of graduate training. Jobs were plentiful as universities frantically expanded in an effort to stay abreast of rising enrollments. Draft deferments gave graduate education an added boost. From 1960 to 1970, the number of new Ph.D.'s climbed from ten thousand per year to more than thirty thousand.[48]

This euphoric era came to an abrupt end in the late 1960s under the strain of Vietnam, racial tension, and radical protest. While campus turmoil distracted the attention of campus officials, other changes were occurring that would have much more lasting effects on the nation's colleges and universities. After twenty-five years of rapid growth, government research funding leveled off. Enrollment increases slowed markedly as the baby boom generation crested. When President Johnson elected to fight the Vietnam War by trying to have guns *and* butter, inflation quickly began to drive up costs. At the same time, endowments languished as the stock market entered a period of stagnation from which it would not emerge for fifteen years. To cap these financial problems, many people were angered by universities with their continuing riots and their seeming disregard for America and its traditional values.

Under these conditions, campus growth soon slowed and budgets grew tighter through the 1970s. Faculty hiring was quickly curtailed. Real earnings for professors started to lag behind inflation. By the end of the decade, salaries had shrunk significantly in real terms; the total drop would approximate 20 percent from its peak in 1973 to its low point eight years later. Only a few disciplines escaped this decline, all of them in subjects such as business administration, computer sciences, and engineering, where universities were in direct competition for talent with industry.

Fortunately, the 1980s proved entirely different, as a measure of prosperity returned to universities. At last, stock prices rose rapidly and inflation slackened. Salaries for full professors turned upward and began to rise modestly but steadily in real terms. By the end of the decade, they had virtually equaled their 1970 levels or even surpassed them in some universities by a few percentage points.[49]

Salaries for new (assistant) professors closely followed the trends for senior faculty. In the 1970s, they fell by 20 percent in constant dollars, only to recover in the 1980s to a level slightly above the 1970 figure.[50]

How did these fortunes affect the flow of talent into academic careers? Predictably, as real salaries declined and job opportunities dwindled, the production of Ph.D.'s began to stabilize and fall, beginning in 1972. As with the legal profession, a sharp drop in the number of men was moderated by a growth in the cohort of women, who had begun flocking to graduate programs toward the end of the preceding decade. By 1977–78, though the total number of men receiving doctorates had dropped by over 20 percent, the overall decline was only 7 percent.[51]

During the 1980s, the number of Ph.D.'s began to increase and eventually surpassed the 1970 level. But this growth was entirely due to the steady rise in the number of foreign students, who accounted for almost one-third of all doctorates awarded in 1990. The total of Ph.D.'s awarded to U.S. residents continued to slide and finished the decade at 4 percent below the 1980 figure.[52]

With enrollments declining only slowly, the number of new Ph.D.'s greatly exceeded the academic demand throughout the 1970s, forcing many aspiring professors to look for jobs outside the universities. When prosperity returned in the 1980s, however, job prospects began to revive along with salaries. Before too long, the large cohorts of professors hired in the 1950s would begin to retire, starting in the late 1990s. As a result, undergraduates thinking about academic careers could look forward to something on the order of twice as many new jobs by the end of the century as were available during the 1980s.[53]

Eventually, these trends began to have an effect. The total number of applications to graduate schools appeared to pick up by the middle of the decade, at least in certain disciplines. From 1985 to 1990, the number of students taking the Graduate Record Examination (GRE) in history rose by almost 40 percent, in physics, by 20 percent, in literature by a remarkable 60 percent, in psychology, by over 25 percent.[54]

Yet a nagging question remained. Could interest in academic careers ever revive to anything like the levels achieved in the 1960s? The early indications were not favorable. By 1990, the percentage of college freshmen expressing an interest in becoming a professor had risen from a low of .02 to only .04 percent, well below the level of 2.1 recorded in 1966.[55] Despite the large increases in some fields, the number of students taking the GRE exams in 1990 was still below the levels for 1980 and 1985 in chemistry, biology, economics, geology, music, and political science.[56] Reviewing these trends, experts were projecting substantial shortages of Ph.D.'s in all major fields by the end of the century, not only in science but in the humanities and social sciences as well.[57]

These raw numbers tell only a part of the story of the 1970s and 1980s. Important shifts also occurred in the flow of exceptional talent into the professoriate. The attractions of academic life in the 1960s were especially great for intellectually gifted students. As enrollments in graduate school grew, average GRE scores also rose, suggesting that Ph.D. programs were rapidly expanding their share of exceptional academic talent.[58] Through the 1960s, graduate schools claimed 23 percent of all Phi Beta Kappas,[59] while a survey of the top students from fourteen elite colleges in 1966 showed an astounding 46 percent planning to enter Ph.D. programs.[60]

The altered climate of the 1970s reversed these trends completely. Not only were there declines in the number of applicants to graduate school; GRE scores fell in most disciplines.[61] The percentage of Phi Beta Kappas seeking Ph.D.'s dropped to 16 percent in the early 1970s before climbing back to 19 percent in the early 1980s.[62] The share of top students from the elite colleges intending to earn a doctorate fell from 46 to 23 percent, a figure far below the percentage planning to enter the major professions.[63]

This loss of exceptional talent did not affect the quality of new faculty hired during the 1970s and 1980s. Because there were fewer jobs to fill, departments could become more selective in choosing from the smaller cohort of new Ph.D.'s. Hence, surveys of department chairs in leading universities produced few complaints that assistant professors were any less able than those hired during the boom years of the 1960s.[64]

Eventually, however, the number of new jobs will begin to rise sharply. The question for leading graduate schools is whether the supply of exceptional talent will rise with it. The evidence on this point is mixed. Among Phi Beta Kappas from the most highly rated colleges and universities, twice as many entered Ph.D. programs during the 1980s as the number choosing either law or medicine. Even so, the numbers electing graduate study were only slightly above those of a decade earlier. Similarly, among the highest-achieving seniors from a sample of elite private colleges and universities, the proportion planning on Ph.D. programs remained at a robust 24 percent throughout the 1980s; but this was only a slight improvement over the preceding decade and far below the level of a decade earlier.[65] In short, though universities claimed an impressive share of the very best students, they showed no sign of returning to the halcyon days of the late 1950s and early 1960s.

TEACHERS

In 1970, public schools found themselves at a critical moment of choice. After many years of growth, student enrollments were beginning to decline as the baby boom generation passed through the schools on its way to adulthood. By 1984, total enrollments would drop to 39 million children from a high of 46 million in 1971. This shift seemed destined to produce a hefty surplus of teachers. But other changes promised to make deep inroads into two groups that had long furnished the public schools with ample supplies of cheap labor. Suddenly, minorities and women could perceive new opportunities in interesting, lucrative professions, such as business, law, and medicine, which had previously seemed all but closed to them.

As more and more women and minorities began to move into other callings, it should have been apparent that the corps of public school teachers stood to suffer permanent losses of quality. In theory, school boards could have met this challenge by raising salaries and choosing the best from a surplus of applicants in order to maintain, or even improve, the intellectual caliber of their staff. A decade earlier, this strategy might have been viable. By 1970, however, the mood of the public made such a policy impossible.

After a decade of the New Frontier and the Great Society, the country was disillusioned with its schools and their constantly swelling budgets. In the years that passed since the launching of Sputnik, the public had heard about the wonders of the open classroom, the New Math, bilingual education, the reform of science teaching. The nation had launched a massive but divisive effort to integrate its classrooms. Hundreds of millions of dollars had gone into federal initiatives to aid disadvantaged children, expand education research, create magnet schools, bus children from one neighborhood to another. Yet the results of these efforts seemed marginal at best. Newspapers reported that College Board scores were steadily declining across the country. Reports had filtered through from publishing houses that classroom texts had to be "dumbed down" because they seemed too difficult for grades they had previously served satisfactorily. Amid such publicity, James Coleman had issued the findings from his massive empirical study, which appeared to claim that the quality of schools had little impact on student learning.[66] To a public weary of raising taxes, the gloomy news about the nation's schools seemed to give ample reason to balk at further investments in public education.

Rather than aggressively recruiting teachers, therefore, school boards took the opposite tack. With fewer openings to fill, officials capitalized on the surplus of applicants to let salaries fall. During the 1970s, average earnings dropped by almost 25 percent in real dollars, and starting salaries fell even further.[67] Compensation for teachers declined more than in any other profession save accounting.

While paychecks were growing slimmer, working conditions in the public schools were deteriorating as well. After World War II, when teachers were asked to identify their principal problems with students, they listed such aggravations as running in the halls, chewing gum, and whispering in class. By the 1980s, the list had changed dramatically to include such items as carrying guns to school, taking drugs, and assaulting other students. In 1982, 25 percent of high school teachers reported that they had been physically attacked during the previous year, 12 percent stated that they would have something stolen from them in a typical month; 48 percent said that students had insulted them with obscene gestures during the past thirty days.[68]

With their salaries falling and their environment growing worse, the status of teachers dropped by more than that of any other major profession. In 1969, 75 percent of all parents agreed that they "would like to have a child of [theirs] take up teaching in the public schools." By 1980, the figure had fallen to 48 percent.[69]

Beset by all these problems, teachers' morale suffered badly. At the end of the 1960s, barely 2 percent of all public school teachers said that they would "definitely" choose another profession if they were starting over; only 7.1 percent indicated that they would "probably" look elsewhere.[70] By 1981, 12 percent would "definitely" choose another profession, and 24 percent would "probably" seek other employment.[71] Even in 1990, after several years of real increases in salary, 17 percent strongly agreed that they would not become a teacher if they had to choose all over again, and 21 percent agreed with reservations.[72]

Predictably, the effect of these trends on the supply of teachers was dramatic. The number of undergraduates majoring in education dropped by more than 50 percent from its best year in 1972–73 to the late 1980s. The number of master's students peaked somewhat later, in 1976–77, but then fell by over 40 percent.[73] The declines were especially severe for students planning to teach science, where the numbers dropped by 64 percent, and for students preparing to teach mathematics, where the total plunged by 79 percent.[74]

The loss of interest in teaching was particularly great among minorities. In the 1960s, 60 percent of all black B.A.'s in North Carolina chose to become teachers, a fraction far greater than that of whites. By the 1980s, the percentage of blacks going into teaching had actually dipped below the level of whites.[75]

Such declines might not have been particularly worrisome if those turning away from careers in the public schools were entirely representative of the entire pool. After all, demand for new teachers had dropped, and it was only natural for the supply to fall as well. Unfortunately, the losses came where they could be least afforded. By every known measure of intellectual ability, teachers were already below the average for all undergraduates even before the 1970s began. The exodus that occurred in that decade made matters worse. In 1970, Graduate Record Examination scores for education majors were only seven points below the national average for the verbal test and thirty-nine points below average on the quantitative portion. Just five years later, education majors had slipped to twenty-five points below average in verbal ability and fifty-one points below in quantitative reasoning.[76]

Long-term trends were even more discouraging. At midcentury, scores on standardized tests of ability given to all male undergraduates had revealed that master's students in education were only slightly below the average for all graduate students and roughly equal to students in law and business schools.[77] By 1980, the comparisons would no longer be even close.

These trends were especially noticeable among the most intellectually gifted students. In the late 1960s, an undergraduate with an IQ of 130 was almost as likely to enter teaching as a student with an IQ of only 100. By 1980, the chances that someone scoring 130 would become a teacher were only one-fourth as great.[78] Among top students from elite liberal arts colleges, the fraction planning to become teachers dropped below 2 percent.[79] Phi Beta Kappas taking jobs as teachers fell from 10 percent in the 1950s and early 1960s to slightly more than 8 percent in the 1970s to 6 percent in the 1980s (with many of these leaving within a few years).[80] Moreover, Phi

Beta Kappas from top-ranked colleges and universities were much less likely to choose teaching than their counterparts from other institutions and much more likely to leave within a few years.

In important respects, even these gloomy statistics do not reveal the full extent of the decline in academic ability among teachers. Numerous surveys show that a substantial fraction of education majors never actually teach and that the academically ablest students are the least likely to do so.[81] Further studies reveal that the most successful students who do move into the public schools leave after only one or two years at twice the normal rate, especially if they teach science or math.[82] Worse yet, although one-third of all teachers who leave the profession return to it after a few years, the most talented—especially in science and math—are the least likely ever to teach again.[83] As a result of all these tendencies, one study in 1980 found that among college graduates who had actually begun teaching and expected to remain in the profession, only 2 percent ranked in the top 20 percent of their college classes in academic ability.[84]

These trends threatened to grow worse as the 1980s drew to a close. With the children of the baby boom generation beginning to enter the schools, the demand for new teachers promised to rise dramatically in the coming decade. Over a million new hires were projected for the decade as a whole, enough to replace half of the entire current teaching force.

Where all of the new recruits would come from was still not clear. The numbers of B.A.'s majoring in education had recovered by only 10 percent by the end of the 1980s, despite the large increases in teachers' salaries, and the number of master's students had grown even less.[85] By 1989, the proportion of college freshmen expressing an interest in teaching had risen to only 8.9 percent from a level of 6.4 percent a decade earlier—hardly adequate to meet anticipated needs.[86] Meanwhile, the number of college seniors taking the Graduate Record Examination for education was 36 percent lower in 1990 than it had been in 1980.[87] In short, as the nation grew increasingly concerned about the quality of education, the prospects for hiring sufficient numbers of able teachers seemed discouraging indeed.

FEDERAL GOVERNMENT EMPLOYEES

The federal government is the nation's largest employer of professional and managerial personnel, with 22,000 Ph.D.'s, 100,000 engineers, 15,500 lawyers, and 50,000 computer specialists on its payroll. At the beginning of the 1970s, however, neither these employees nor the agencies they worked for stood in high repute with the American people. The middle class had grown impatient with the seeming failure of many Great Society programs. The public was agitated by the partisan furies of the Vietnam War and disillusioned over the lies and cover-ups of Watergate. In the wake of these frustrations, the fraction of the public expressing "great confidence in the people running the executive branch" fell from 39 percent in 1966 to 15 percent after Watergate, and wavered between 15 percent and 24 percent throughout the next decade. Meanwhile, the proportion agreeing that "you cannot trust the government to do right most of the time" rose from a modest 22 percent in 1964 to 44 percent in 1970, 62 percent in 1974, and 70 percent in 1980.[88]

The conflicts and disappointments that spawned these sentiments also fed the long-standing suspicion that Washington was ineffective and profligate. The number of Americans who believed that the government "wastes a lot of money" rose from 47 percent in 1964 to 59 percent in 1968, up again to 74 percent in 1974 and then to a record 78 percent in 1980.[89] These attitudes, coupled with an inflation that swept many working people into progressively higher tax brackets, produced a growing resistance to all efforts to extract more revenue to finance government programs. With such feelings running strong, the climate for maintaining pay scales for bureaucrats could scarcely have been chillier.

The reckoning was not long in coming. From the early 1970s to 1990, salaries for high-level career managers and professionals (GS-17 and 18) declined by 25 percent in real dollars.[90] By 1987, the National Commission on the Public Service (the Volcker Commission) reported that the gap between the highest-ranking career civil servants (the Senior Executive Service, or SES) and the pay of corresponding officials in the private sector had grown to 65 percent.[91]

The salaries offered to college seniors by federal agencies suffered at least as much. From the early 1970s to 1990, graduating students saw the government's starting pay erode by more than 30 percent in real dollars,[92] even as the salaries offered them by banks, investment companies, and consulting firms were rising by almost the same amount. Salaries for new recruits with master's degrees dropped by almost 25 percent, while Ph.D.'s suffered nearly as much. Doctors and dentists entering federal service fared even worse, losing 30 percent in real starting pay.[93]

The lure of government jobs was also declining for reasons other than money. Politicians were quick to capitalize on the antigovernment mood. Jimmy Carter openly ran against Washington and its bureaucracy. Ronald Reagan loudly proclaimed his intention to lead a crusade to the Capitol "to drain the swamp." Clearly the image of public service had been badly tarnished since the glory days of John F. Kennedy with his call to "ask not what your country can do for you; ask what you can do for your country."

In the wake of these difficulties, the morale of senior career officials suffered badly. By the late 1980s, a majority of officials in the Senior Executive Service (SES) responded in a survey that they would no longer recommend a career in government to their own children.[94] It was clear that compensation had much to do with these dissatisfactions. In 1990, 84 percent of SES officials pronounced themselves "not satisfied" with their pay, while 83 percent affirmed that the government's goal of "providing a compensation system designed to attract and retain highly competent senior executives" was not being met.[95]

In the face of these developments, applications by college graduates to the federal government appeared to decline significantly. Although accurate records are not kept by the government, figures are available for the numbers of people taking the Civil Service Examination in the 1980s. Most categories of college and professional school graduates experienced severe declines during that decade.[96] For example, the number of life scientists taking the exam appeared to drop by 50 percent, as did the number of engineers. Only one-third as many physical science majors took the test in 1990 as in 1980. The number of computer science specialists taking the exam plummeted to only 25 percent of the 1980 levels.

It is impossible to determine what effect these developments had on the quality of the civil service. Until recently, the federal government has not tried to keep track of the abilities of its recruits. Nevertheless, impressionistic accounts abound. They are almost invariably gloomy. A 1989 survey of installation heads and personnel officers found that much larger percentages reported greater difficulty in hiring and retaining good employees than was true only five years before.[97] Another survey found that 73 percent of the federal executives polled felt that the quality of new hires was either "marginally worse" (59 percent) or "much worse" (14 percent) than in the past.[98]

At the end of the 1980s, the government responded to these concerns by trying to inquire more deeply into the charge that the quality of the federal work force had declined. Studies of certain categories of highly educated personnel—such as scientists, engineers, and computer specialists—yielded conflicting results. On the one hand, tabulations of the academic records of recently hired federal employees did not reveal any marked decline from the achievement levels of employees entering the government two or three decades earlier. On the other hand, questionnaires revealed increasing numbers of supervisors who believed that the quality of recent hires *had* eroded.[99]

A study of Phi Beta Kappas entering federal service suggests how these differences might be reconciled. The proportion of Phi Beta Kappas currently working in the federal government actually increases slightly over the decades—from 5.42 percent in the classes of 1971–75, to 5.03 percent in 1976–80, 5.71 percent in 1981–85, and 6.89 percent in 1986–90.[100] What these figures omit, however, is the number of Phi Beta Kappas who joined the government earlier but subsequently left. When these figures are added in, the percentage of all Phi Beta Kappas who have served in the federal government turns out to have declined from 10.5 percent in the classes of 1971–75 to 7.5 percent in the classes of 1986–90.

A closer look at these figures suggests how the passage of time affects the government's effort to maintain a first-rate civil service. Of the 10.5 percent of all Phi Beta Kappas in the classes of 1970–75 who have worked regularly for the federal government at one time or another, almost half (5 percent) have left, and another 1 percent plan to leave. Only 4 percent still work for the government and have no plans to leave, while only half of 1 percent of Phi Beta Kappas from other sectors have plans to join the government.

The gradual seeping away of talent threatens to be at least as pronounced for recent classes (1986–90) of Phi Beta Kappas. Of the 7.5 percent who have worked full-time in the federal government, .63 percent have already left and another 2.5 percent plan to leave. No one in the sample currently working in other sectors intends to take a job with the federal government.

The outlook for the government, then, is far from promising. Taking note of repeated complaints from government officials, the

Volcker Commission declared in 1989 that "many agencies report that, in the absence of the ability to make external hires, they are promoting staff who have previously been passed over for promotion. Still others report that they are able to make quality hires only by raiding other federal agencies."[101] In summing up, the commission concluded, "the nation is now spending only enough to recruit in the lowest quartile of the labor market, far below the average or the median required."[102]

Evidence from the colleges and universities seemed to bear out these gloomy assessments. A 1988 survey of placement officers showed that in most fields, university officials rated the government's prospects of hiring high-quality graduates as only fair or poor; low pay and the poor image of the federal government were by far the most commonly cited reasons.[103] Enrollments in schools of public administration fell by 25 percent from their peak in the mid-1970s. Meanwhile, the percentage of graduates from these schools taking jobs in government dropped from 76 percent to 51 percent, while the proportion accepting jobs in the federal government fell to 16 percent.[104]

More troubling still are the findings from a survey conducted for the Volcker Commission in 1989 involving 1,800 college seniors belonging to national honor societies.[105] The federal government employs approximately 8 percent of all newly graduated lawyers in the country, 7.5 percent of all scientists and engineers, and more than 15 percent of new doctors. Yet among the 1,800 outstanding students, only 3 percent ranked the federal government as their "most preferred" career choice, and most of those who did were members of the public administration honor society (which made up 20 percent of the sample). Overall, the honor students ranked government jobs below those in large corporations, small businesses, and higher education not only in terms of compensation but also on grounds such as challenge of the work and opportunities for personal growth. The only characteristics on which government careers fared well were job security and service to society.

These results should scarcely come as a surprise. Of all the groups reviewed in this study, no other institution suffered the losses of pay, prestige, and public confidence that the federal government endured in the 1970s and 1980s. After all these setbacks, the wonder is that erosion in the quality of the civil service was not much more pronounced.

CHAPTER 4

THE 1970s AND 1980s IN PERSPECTIVE

The fortunes of the six professional groups we have considered varied widely over the two decades from 1970 to 1990. Figure 4–1 tells the story. The big winners, unquestionably, were corporate CEOs, who saw their real salaries and bonuses rise by 100 percent without even counting the huge bonanzas they reaped from stock options and other forms of deferred compensation. Young associates in the most prestigious law firms took home real starting salaries in 1990 that were virtually twice what they were in 1970. Their partners enjoyed only slightly less success. Surgeons, radiologists, and anesthesiologists all saw their real incomes rise by 40 to 50 percent, while middle managers posted gains on the order of 20 to 25 percent. Even teachers, having seen their salaries decline by 20 percent in the 1970s, bounced back in the 1980s and ended the decade approximately 10 percent ahead of where they were twenty years before.

Other professionals were less fortunate. University professors lost heavily in the 1970s, gained back their losses in the 1980s, and finished the two decades with approximately the same real income as they were earning at the beginning. Family doctors and other general practitioners also fell back in the 1970s, gaining only enough ground in the 1980s to end the two decades about where they had started. Much the same was true of partners in medium-sized law firms. Much harder hit were managers and professionals in the federal government, along with solo law practitioners, who lost approximately 20 to 30 percent of their real income over the course of the entire period.

Overall, professionals in the past two decades saw their earnings

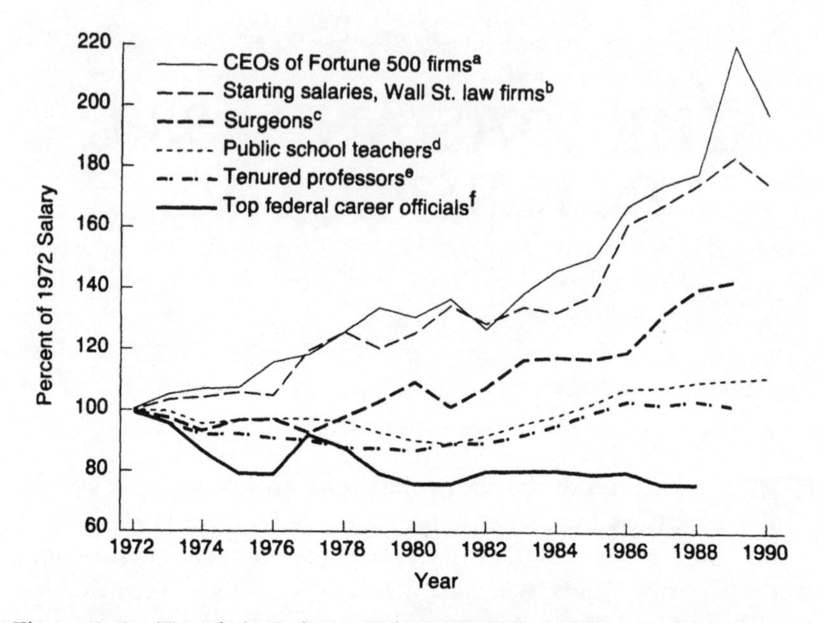

Figure 4–1 Trends in Relative Salaries (1972 = 100)

Sources: (a) *Forbes*; (b) Harvard Law School Placement Office; (c) American Medical Association, *Socioeconomic Characteristics of Medical Practice*; (d) American Federation of Teachers, *Survey and Analysis of Salary Trends*; (e) *Bulletin* of the American Association of University Professors (category I schools); (f) U.S. Office of Personnel Management, *Pay Structure of the Federal Civil Service.*

diverge in surprising ways from those of other segments of the work force. In every country, doctors, lawyers, civil servants, and corporate executives have traditionally earned much more than the average worker. Their pay advantage, however, has gradually declined through most of this century. In 1966, the Stanford economist Tibor Scitovsky documented this trend and predicted that it would continue.[1] Ten years later, labor economists, especially in England, were still confirming this forecast.[2] As educational opportunities increased throughout the population, they opined, the supply of professionals would grow and grow, driving down their earnings premium. Egalitarian sentiments, which had increased in the West during the twentieth century, would bring added pressure to erode the privileged position of the learned professions and narrow their advantage still further.

The 1970s and 1980s were an ideal time to demonstrate the

accuracy of these predictions. By 1974, the number of students graduating from college was more than three times as large as it had been only twenty years before. Professional school enrollments were rising almost as rapidly. From the mid-1960s to the mid-1970s, the number of medical students doubled, while the number of law and business school students grew threefold. Surely, such increases would drive professional earnings even closer to the levels in other segments of the work force.

As we now know, although the stage seemed perfectly set, the last act turned out very differently from what the labor economists had envisaged. During the 1970s, earnings did stop growing or declined in most professions for all but the most successful members. By the end of the 1980s, however, the premiums earned by law partners, doctors, and business executives in the private sector had not only gained back the lost ground; their advantage over ordinary workers had climbed to the highest levels in many years. What could have upset the earlier predictions?

The most obvious flaw in the analysis was the tendency to concentrate on changes in the supply of professionals and to ignore what might happen to the demand for their services. As matters turned out, earnings in the professions rose strongly in the 1980s because a series of events caused the demand for professional services to grow at an unusually rapid pace. In medicine, it was the passage of Medicare and Medicaid, which made health care affordable for millions of poor and elderly people. In law, it was the flood of new government regulations in the 1960s and early 1970s in such areas as the environment, affirmative action, and consumer protection, not to mention new causes of action and opportunities for private suits created by judges. In business, continued economic growth in the 1980s, fueled by the birth of new enterprises and corporate expansion overseas, created jobs for professional managers and caused American companies to hire executives at a faster pace than their counterparts abroad.[3]

In addition to benefiting from a growing demand for their services, each of the professions was fortunate to escape the powerful currents eroding the jobs and paychecks of less educated workers, especially in the manufacturing sector. Foreign competition did not threaten the jobs of doctors and attorneys. Physicians were beyond the reach of doctors abroad, while lawyers actually gained employment by moving to open new offices overseas. Even business executives found that foreign trade, on balance, expanded their opportunities until the end of the 1980s, when corporations facing stiff competition from abroad started to trim their large cadres of managers to save money. Technology likewise had a different effect on professionals than on ordinary workers. Although computers and fax machines may have increased the speed and thoroughness of lawyers' work, they did not take away lawyers' jobs. Similarly, technology may have given powerful new tools to physicians, but it undoubtedly did more to expand services than it did to restrict employment in the medical (and allied health) professions.

Another surprising development in the last two decades was the ability of leading private-sector professionals to widen the gap between their own earnings and those of other members of their calling. In prior decades, differences in income within several of the professions had gradually diminished. In the 1980s, however, the incomes of CEOs advanced much more rapidly than those of newly graduated MBAs or middle managers. Surgeons—already the most highly paid members of their profession—increased their earnings by 30 to 50 percent, while family doctors, pediatricians, general internists, and other lower-paid specialists gained very little ground. Partners in elite law firms prospered—the very best even doubled their incomes—while solo-practitioner firms suffered a decline in real earnings. Even in academe, while professors as a whole barely maintained their incomes, the top salaries in leading private universities rose faster than the pay of the average faculty member.

It is hard to explain this tendency simply by looking to the interplay of supply and demand. Eventually, the finite stock of exceptional talent will encounter a steadily mounting need for able professionals and generate powerful pressures to push up the earnings of leading practitioners. In the period from 1970 to 1990, however, the supply of talent in many of these professions was growing steadily. Certainly, this was true of business and academe, where the number and quality of Ph.D.'s, MBAs, and business majors had increased substantially since the 1950s, and in law, where the supply of attorneys had been rising rapidly since the 1960s.

Just why leading professionals fared so well, therefore, calls for a deeper explanation than one can glean from figures of the sort we have discussed thus far. Satisfactory answers require a careful look at the particular institutions and procedures for determining compensation in each professional field. Such an account is the work of chapters still to come.

A final noteworthy trend in professional earnings is the widening gap between government salaries and private-sector compensation. Lifetime earnings have long been higher in corporations, law firms, and private medical practice than in the civil service. In 1970, however, a newly graduated MBA or J.D. or M.D. could still expect approximately the same starting salary in the federal government as in the private sector. By 1990, the outlook for recent graduates was entirely different. Starting salaries in the federal government had declined by 20 to 30 percent. Meanwhile, new MBAs from the better schools were earning 15 percent more than they did in 1970, beginning associates in large law firms were being offered anywhere from 10 to 100 percent more, and young doctors were making at least as much as their predecessors two decades earlier and, in several specialties, substantially more.

Teachers fared much better than federal civil servants, especially in the 1980s. By the end of that decade, their starting salaries were approximately 10 percent above the 1970 levels. But even they did not keep up with the more successful segments of the private sector. Associates in large law firms, MBAs from the better schools, and young doctors in the more technically sophisticated, hospital-based specialties all saw their incomes rise more rapidly than teachers over the two decades.

For the ablest young people, therefore, opportunities in the private sector seemed much more lucrative in 1990, compared with public-sector careers, than they did in 1970. Once again, this tendency does not seem to have resulted simply from market forces or from some objective change in the relative needs of the public and private sectors for highly educated professionals. Although teaching and public service both lost ground over the past two decades in their effort to recruit highly talented university graduates, it would be difficult to argue that either the public schools or the federal government grew relatively less important to the nation. Rather, the explanation must be rooted in other causes that await consideration in subsequent chapters.

INTERNATIONAL COMPARISONS

Are the patterns of compensation in this country common to most advanced, industrial nations or are they unique to the United States? This is not an easy question to answer. Precise analysis is impossible, because the data are fragmentary and hard to compare across national boundaries. Nevertheless, some broad differences do emerge that are substantial enough to warrant mention.

On the whole, our private-sector professionals seem to do quite well in comparison with their colleagues abroad. American doctors occupy a particularly enviable position. Their average annual compensation has been estimated at more than five times the earnings of the average member of the work force. In contrast, German and Canadian doctors earn about four times the pay of the average employee, while British doctors enjoy a modest premium of 2.5.[4] Only Japanese physicians seem to be able to earn as much as (perhaps even more than) physicians in this country.

To illustrate the advantage American physicians have over their counterparts in Europe, consider the following comparison between the average net incomes of different categories of doctors in France and the United States in 1982.[5]

	France	United States
General practitioners	$33,174	$71,400
Pediatricians	24,876	70,500
Obstetricians/Gynecologists	44,773	112,300
Cardiologists	42,524	128,600

If anything, recent trends tend to favor American doctors even more. In 1989–90, the average income of physicians was $84,819 in Canada, $53,405 in France, $45,021 in Japan, $39,991 in Sweden, and $51,118 in Great Britain. During the same period (1989), the average income of American doctors was $155,800, three times the figure of any of the other nations except Canada.[6] Although most physicians abroad pay much less than Americans to attend medical school, this difference does not come close to accounting for such large disparities in earnings.

Comparisons between the pay of American executives and corporate managers abroad show more mixed results. While top executives in large companies have much larger paychecks than their counterparts overseas, CEOs of small firms typically earn only 33 to 50 percent more, and middle managers fare even less well.[7] Scattered data available suggest that midlevel executives in America actually tend to earn slightly less than their opposite numbers in several other countries.

Information about lawyers' incomes is much more fragmentary than it is for other professionals.[8] From the limited data available, German lawyers seem to receive, on average, at least as much as their American counterparts. Japanese and British attorneys appear to earn somewhat less. Published earnings for the average French or Italian attorney are much lower still, so much so that one must question the accuracy of the reporting.

What stands out most vividly in comparing the incomes of private-sector professionals in various countries is not the differences in *average* earnings but how much more the most successful American practitioners receive. In 1990, for example, the average compensation for chief executives of large companies in France, Germany, England, and other European countries was less than $1 million.[9] In Japan, top executives barely earned half that sum.[10] During the same year, however, American CEOs of the two hundred largest companies were taking home an average of $2.8 million in all forms of compensation. According to one analyst, our chief executives in 1990 earned more than one hundred times the pay of an average worker compared with ratios of thirty-five in Great Britain, twenty-three to twenty-five in France and Germany, and only seventeen in Japan.[11]

American lawyers enjoyed a comparable success. There is no counterpart abroad to the most successful personal injury lawyers in America, because there is no other country that allows a contingent fee. On the other hand, large law firms do exist in major cities overseas, and they are becoming more lucrative. Stimulated, perhaps, by frequent contact with leading American lawyers, partners of firms in Paris, Frankfurt, and London earned profits in 1990 averaging $250,000, $300,000, occasionally even $500,000 per year. By and large, however, these figures were still only one-half or one-third the average profit per partner in the top American law firms.[12] Moreover, the differences in scale are substantial. Although the total population of Western Europe exceeds that of the United States, the twenty most profitable law firms in Europe had a combined total of barely 150 partners in 1990.[13] In contrast, the twenty leading American firms totaled more than *two thousand* partners.[14]

There are no reliable data to compare the earnings of leading American physicians with their counterparts overseas. It is likely, however, that the patterns observed for lawyers and executives are equally evident in the medical profession. The dispersion of earnings for American doctors is strikingly wide. Neurosurgeons, for example, earned *on average* more than $340,000 in 1990 compared with only $95,000 for family doctors. According to their income tax returns, American physicians taking home more than $500,000 per year must have numbered in the thousands in 1990. It is inconceivable that a substantial number of doctors could earn amounts of this size under the more heavily state-controlled health care systems in Europe.

Even university faculties show a similar pattern of earnings in America, albeit at a much more modest level. The average salary in 1990 for full professors in American universities was just under $60,000.[15] This figure is, if anything, below the amount paid to German, French, or Italian professors (especially if fringe benefits are counted), although it is still above the average pay of English faculties. On the other hand, the top salaries at the best private universities in America are probably 50 percent higher than the salary of a leading German or Italian professor and further still above the salaries of prominent faculty members in Great Britain.

In contrast to the earnings of private-sector professionals, teachers and federal officials compare much less favorably with their opposite numbers abroad. In the civil service, for example, top-ranked career officials in the United States earned approximately $120,000 per year in 1992 (up from less than $90,000 in 1990). By mid-1992, according to *The Economist,* a permanent cabinet secretary in Great Britain earned close to $170,000, and a pay commission was on the point of recommending a substantial increase.[16] A comparable official in Germany could reasonably expect over $140,000 including normal bonuses.[17] Compared with other advanced industrial nations, the United States still ranks in the top half absolutely but probably falls in the bottom half if top civil service salaries are compared with average earnings for other professions and occupations in the society. Moreover, few industrial countries have experienced the erosion that has occurred in the United States over the past twenty years in the pay of high civil servants relative to their counterparts in the private sector.

Public school salaries show a similar pattern. Because teachers have been studied more than almost any other profession, it is possible not only to compare salaries in absolute terms (the United States ranks in the upper third of industrialized nations) but also to see how teachers' pay compares with that of other professions and with average per capita incomes in various countries.[18]

	Teachers' Salaries as % of Average per Capita Personal Consumption, 1985	Middle Managers' Salaries as % of Teachers' Salary, 1985
France	172	305
Belgium	236	155
United States	241	204
Italy	258	159
Great Britain	279	138
West Germany	288	180
Japan	339	248
Canada	357	159
Spain	362	127

As these figures make clear, relative to the rest of the working population, teachers' salaries in America fall somewhere in the bottom third of industrialized countries.*

In sum, compensation for highly educated professionals in America differs in two important respects from the practice in other industrialized democracies. The most successful professionals in the private sector tend to earn two or three times as much in the United States as they do in other countries. In contrast, public-sector professionals, such as teachers and government officials, do not earn as much as their counterparts in some countries, at least, and the relative standing of their salaries ranks only in the middle or below the median for all highly developed nations.

The modest earnings of teachers and government officials in the United States reflect broader problems in the way young people look at careers in the public sector. For example, Ronald Sanders' study of honor students in American colleges reveals the low regard

* In fairness, however, we must remember that teachers in many other countries have a longer school year.

most of those young people have toward careers in public service.[19] By almost every criterion, working for the government—federal, state, or local—was consistently rated as inferior to working in large companies, in small companies, or on a university faculty.

In contrast, several other countries have a strong tradition of recruiting an elite civil service. In these nations, good students believe that government careers enjoy high status and offer opportunities to exercise significant influence over the affairs of state. Consequently, the most successful students compete vigorously for positions in the national ministries. As Ezra Vogel describes the process in Japan:

> Leading bureaucrats have invariably attended the best universities. . . . Within Tokyo University, the ablest students enter the Law Faculty, which in fact provides broad training for public administration, with secondary emphasis on political science and law. The top graduates of the Law Faculty enter the most prestigious ministries . . . and agencies . . . providing they pass the ministerial written examination and demonstrate poise, breadth and commitment in interviews. . . . This selection procedure ensures that elite bureaucrats are not only extremely able but are also protected by an aura of respect, rivaled perhaps only by the elite bureaucrats of France.[20]

As Vogel implies, much the same account could be given of the French bureaucracy, which recruits its high civil servants from elite *grandes écoles* where the competition to enter is ferocious. England too recruits the bulk of its "fast streamer" civil servants from Oxford and Cambridge and regularly attracts several times as many applicants as there are places to fill.[21]

In other countries, the status of civil servants is somewhat less exalted than in France and Japan, though still above the United States. In Germany, for example, one experienced observer reports that "the prestige of higher civil servants is in general not superior to that of other academically trained groups."[22] Recent recruits do not come disproportionately from the best universities, and increasingly, the top students go not to the government but to the banks and large corporations.

Only rarely in Europe, however, does the higher civil service seem to receive little respect and attract indifferent candidates. The Italian bureaucracy is unusual in seeming to settle for security and relative autonomy at the cost of exerting any significant influence over events.[23] Interestingly, Italy is the only major country in which the bureaucracy's reputation for waste and inefficiency is even worse than in the United States.[24] In this environment, as one might expect, government is not a favored occupation for the ablest, most promising young Italians.

THE INFLUENCE OF MONEY ON THE DISTRIBUTION OF TALENT AMONG THE PROFESSIONS

The pay and prestige of public-sector jobs in America have declined markedly in the last quarter century. Not surprisingly, then, the 1970s and 1980s witnessed a massive shift of young people out of teaching and government employ into the private professions, especially corporate management and law. While business school graduates trebled and law school enrollments rose by 100 percent, education majors dropped by 50 percent, Ph.D.'s (American citizens) fell by 15 percent, and applications for civil service jobs plummeted by 50 and 60 percent or more. What caused these changes in the career aspirations of highly educated young Americans? Was money a critical factor, as economists would have us believe? Or were other forces at work that proved more powerful?

Business

If money is important in choosing a career, the results should be especially clear in business, for many studies show that compensation matters more to corporate executives than to members of other professions. At first glance, it would appear that money was indeed a major influence on career choices in the 1970s and 1980s. As we know, earnings for executives rose substantially over the two decades, especially for CEOs, and students flocked to business majors and management schools in rapidly increasing numbers.

Standing alone, however, these facts are too crude to support any conclusions about the role of money in influencing students in their choice of careers. For one thing, much of the growth in the number of students seeking business careers resulted from a huge surge of interest among women. Although money may have played a role in causing this unusual increase, the immediate cause was not compensation but the lowering of barriers that had long made management careers the almost exclusive preserve of men. As a result, if we wish to isolate the influence of compensation on career choice during this period, we would do better to confine our attention to men.

We would also be wise not to look simply at changes in the total number of men majoring in business or applying to schools of management. Such changes could be partly due not to movements in salaries but simply to fluctuations in the number of students attending college. To filter out these fluctuations, we should confine our attention to shifts in the *percentage* of male undergraduates majoring in business and the *percentage* of male B.A.'s applying to business school.

Figure 4–2 portrays these changes in relation to movements in the real starting salaries of MBAs from 1970 to 1990. Even a cursory glance at this table reveals a surprising fact. During the 1970s, when real starting salaries were steadily drifting downward, stu-

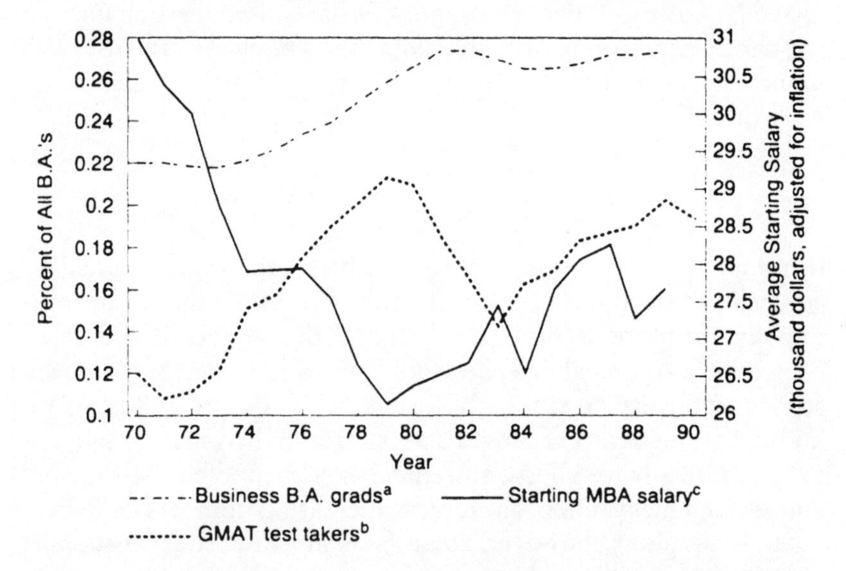

Figure 4–2 Trends in Business: Starting Salaries of Male Graduates

Sources: (a) *Digest of Educational Statistics*; (b) Graduate Management Admissions Council (note: figures for 1970–75 are estimated from data for total test takers, foreign as well as U.S.); (c) College Placement Council.

dent interest in business careers rose very rapidly. This is exactly the reverse of what one would expect to find if changes in salaries were truly a major factor influencing career choice. One could explain this puzzling result if business salaries had done better in the 1970s than pay in other occupations of interest to college students. But this does not appear to have been the case.*

Could students have been influenced by the pay of more experienced managers and not by starting salaries alone? To test this possibility, Figure 4–3 depicts the same trends in student interest contrasted with the pattern of middle-manager salaries. Here, the fit is somewhat better. Still, the critical fact remains that salaries

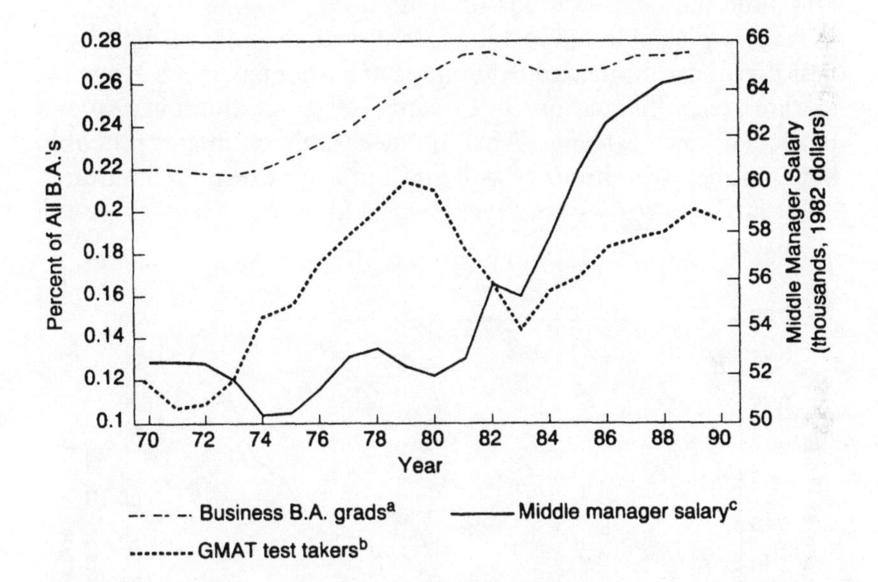

Figure 4–3 Trends in Business: Middle Manager Salaries of Male Graduates

Sources: (a) College Placement Council; (b) Graduate Management Admissions Council (note: figures for 1970–75 are estimated from data for total test takers, foreign as well as U.S.); (c) Hay Management Consultants.

* The average beginning salary for college graduates taking jobs in business lost ground in the 1970s against beginning pay for other graduates with more than a college education. Nevertheless, the number of undergraduate business majors rose sharply. In the case of MBAs, starting salaries had only a mixed success, faring better than beginning pay for all lawyers and for economics Ph.D.'s but less well than the pay for engineers and lawyers in large firms.

stagnated in the 1970s just as student interest surged, while pay rose smartly in the 1980s only to have student interest taper off or decline.

Figure 4–4 substitutes the salaries of CEOs from Fortune 500 companies. The fit improves for the 1970s but not for the 1980s. The greatest increases in compensation occur just when interest in business careers lags most perceptibly. Moreover, one can hardly suppose that tens of thousands of undergraduates made their career choices by looking, not to the starting salaries for MBAs nor to the earnings of moderately successful managers, but to trends in the compensation given to chief executives of the nation's largest corporations. Even Adam Smith would be startled to see undergraduates pitch their expectations so high.

A more plausible supposition is that students considering a business career *are* motivated by money but do not pay much attention to short-term fluctuations in earnings, let alone shifts in any one particular set of earnings. After all, most undergraduates probably have no idea whether they will end up as an executive in a large corporation, a real estate developer, an investment banker, or the

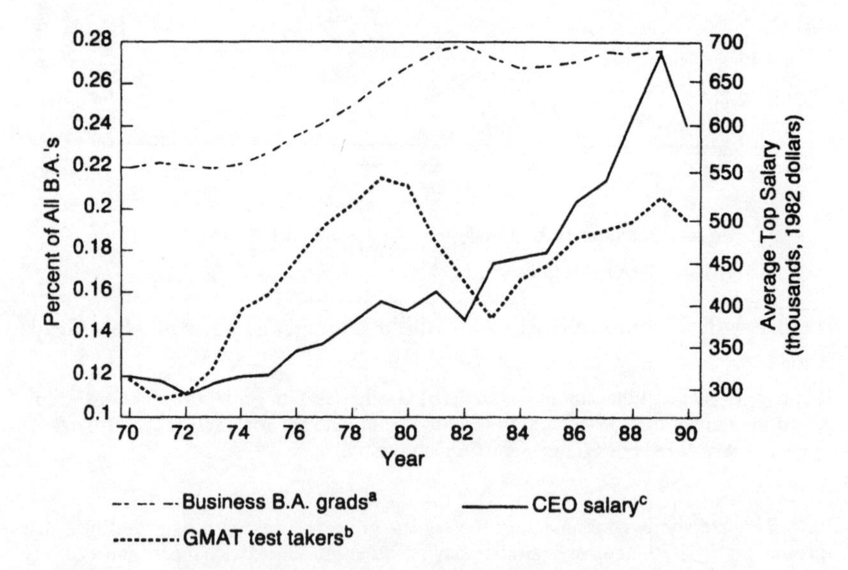

Figure 4–4 Trends in Business: CEO Salaries of Male Graduates

Sources: (a) *Digest of Educational Statistics*; (b) Graduate Management Admissions Council; (c) *Forbes*.

owner of a small firm. They cannot even predict their starting salary, because they probably do not know what field of business they will enter. As a result, they can scarcely make so much as a crude estimate of their lifetime returns from a management career.

What they *do* know is that business is a good field to enter for people who are interested in earning money. For this reason, the number of students who decide to seek a business career is likely to change, not so much because of fluctuations in the starting salary for MBAs or in the pay received by CEOs, but because of changes in the value students attach to being well-to-do. The more important money becomes to undergraduates, the more their minds will turn to the possibility of a management career.

Fortunately, for the past quarter century, a national survey has recorded the percentage of college freshmen who feel that being "very well off financially" is a "very important goal." Figure 4–5 portrays the growing importance of this value and compares it with the shifts in the number of students majoring in business or apply-

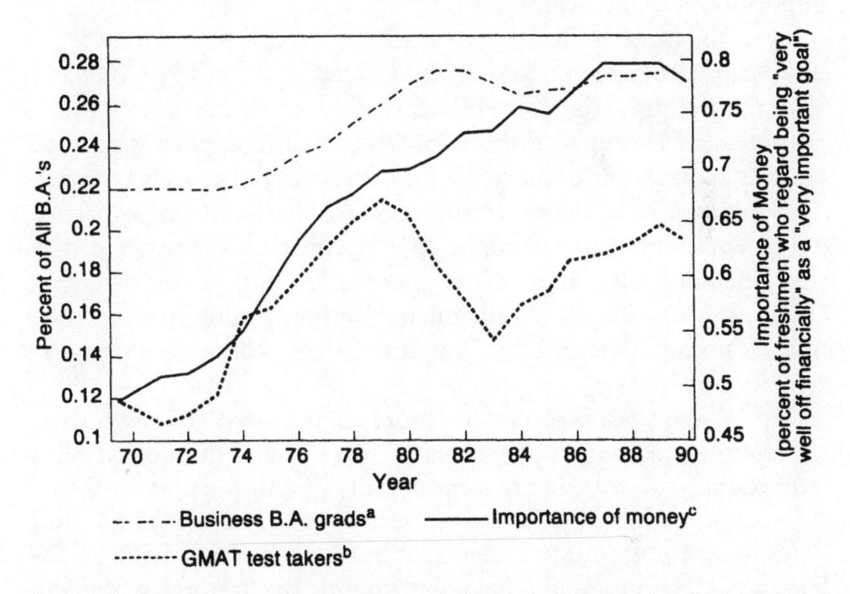

Figure 4–5 Trends in Business: Importance of Money to Male Graduates

Sources: (a) *Digest of Educational Statistics;* (b) Graduate Management Admissions Council; (c) Eric Dey, Alexander Astin, and William S. Korn, *The American Freshman: Twenty-Five-Year Trends, 1966–1990.*

ing to business school. As the graph reveals, the interest in financial well-being began to rise very rapidly in the 1970s, presumably because this period marked the end of postwar optimism about continuous growth and prosperity. In the 1980s, however, the growth in student aspirations to be very well-to-do slackened appreciably, as did student interest in pursuing a business career.

Although the fit is not perfect, the rise in students' desire for wealth comes much closer than changes in compensation to accounting for trends in career choice. In particular, it suggests why the number of male students interested in business rose so much more rapidly in the 1970s than in the 1980s, even though real salaries for executives increased much faster in the latter decade than in the former.

Medicine

The case of medicine differs sharply from that of business. Figure 4–6 contrasts the trends in physicians' earnings with those of male applications to medical school.

Even the most skillful use of statistics cannot hide the fact that applications declined seriously and steadily from 1974 onward, whereas average salaries were reasonably stable in the 1970s and rose steadily throughout the 1980s. The fall in applications is especially remarkable because doctors' incomes did as well as or better than those of any major profession over the twenty-year period. To be sure, applications might have declined even further if doctors' incomes had fallen. Nevertheless, looking at the divergent trends, one can hardly avoid concluding that future earnings were not a significant factor in shaping the career decisions of prospective doctors.

In fact, the truth is somewhat more complicated. To begin with, the sharp increase in applications up to 1974 and the steep decline over the next few years are undoubtedly due to the unusual situation brought about by Congress' decision in 1968 to end all draft deferments for graduate students except for those preparing for the health professions. When medicine became one of the few remaining safe havens from possible combat duty in Vietnam, applications soared, doubling in size from 1968 to 1974. Predictably, when the war ended, the tidal wave of applicants quickly began to recede, although its momentum took several years to dissipate as some of

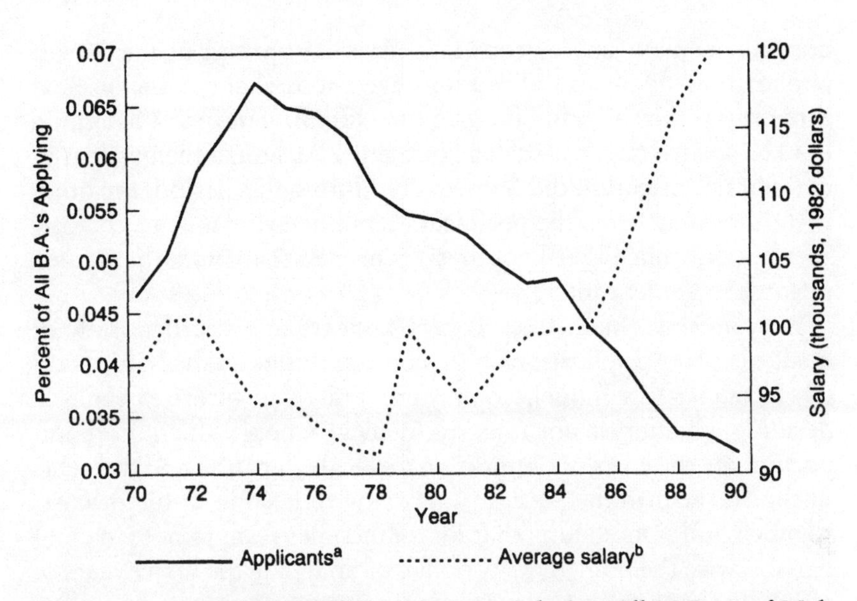

Figure 4–6 Trends in Medicine: Average Salaries (All M.D.'s) of Male Medical School Applicants

Sources: (a) "Annual Report: Medical Education in the United States," *Journal of the American Medical Association*; (b) American Medical Association, *Socioeconomic Characteristics of Medical Practice.*

the undergraduates who had become premeds during the draft years kept on applying to medical school.[25]

Still unexplained, however, is the continued drop in applications during the late 1970s and 1980s in the face of steadily rising incomes for physicians. A common explanation for this decline is the growing dissatisfaction of the medical profession over malpractice litigation, red tape, and the efforts of corporations and insurance companies to hold down health costs by overruling doctors who ordered tests or hospital procedures that seemed unnecessary to those who ultimately paid the bills. Harassed by litigation and challenged by insurers, physicians grew angry and upset. At the beginning of the 1970s, 95 percent of all doctors reported that they were either "very satisfied" or "satisfied" with their careers.[26] By the late 1980s, almost 40 percent declared that they would not become doctors if they had to choose all over again, nor would they recommend such a career to their friends and children.[27]

This striking turnabout undoubtedly had some effect in discouraging students from applying to medical school.[28] Nevertheless, it does not explain one curious fact. At the very end of the 1980s, applications finally stabilized and even rose slightly. In the next three years, they actually jumped by a full 30 percent. What could have happened to cause such a large shift? Although the burdens of malpractice litigation did lighten a bit during this period, the other irritations that vexed the profession remained very much as before. As a result, some other hypothesis is needed to explain the sudden upsurge in student interest.

A promising clue to the mystery appears in an earlier study of medical school applications.[29] According to this analysis, prospective physicians are influenced only moderately by future earnings in deciding whether or not to go to medical school. Much more important are the costs of obtaining a medical education and the debts one must incur in the process. Preparing to become a doctor costs so much and lasts so long that future incomes seem remote in comparison with the immediate problem of financing the many years of medical school and postgraduate training.

In view of these findings, it is significant that medical school tuition and fees have risen much more slowly in recent years than they did during the previous decade. From 1977 to 1982, private medical school tuitions increased by over 60 percent in real dollars while public school tuitions rose only slightly less rapidly. In the next five years, private tuitions rose by another 33 percent in real dollars while public tuitions advanced at about the same rate. In the last five years, however, private tuitions have risen by only 5 percent, and public tuitions have gone up by less than 15 percent. More important still, in 1987, for the first time in many years, student scholarships increased at a rate equal to that of tuitions and loans. By 1989, scholarship funds were rising even more rapidly than loans and much more rapidly than tuitions, so that the net cost of attending medical school actually began to fall for needy students.[30]

It seems very likely, then, that slower growth in educational costs is the principal cause of the recent upsurge in student interest, just as the rapidly rising costs in the prior decade must have been a major reason for the steady decline in applications. In all probability, the robust increases in doctors' incomes during the late 1980s also helped to explain the recent increases in applications. Conceivably, the recession in the early 1990s, punctuated by reports of layoffs of managers and professionals from large corporations, may have made medicine seem more attractive to students concerned with finding a secure niche in an uncertain and threatening world. In all these ways, therefore, financial considerations seem to have played a more important role in guiding applicants to medical school than the trends in Figure 4–6 would initially suggest.

Law

One might suppose that potential law students would be more susceptible to changes in their prospective incomes than students considering medical school. The latter tend to conceive a strong desire to be a doctor in their early teens, presumably for reasons quite apart from money. In contrast, most law students have much weaker commitments to a legal career, and many decide to go to law school only late in their college career after failing to discover any alternative that attracts them more.

Lacking strong independent reasons for choosing a career in law, such students should be especially receptive to the influence of money in making their decision. At the same time, prospective lawyers must have difficulty estimating what their future earnings are likely to be. Like business, the legal profession is divided into many segments, each with its own earnings trajectory. These trajectories follow widely different paths. In the 1970s and 1980s, partners in the very best firms enjoyed a virtual doubling of their real incomes; partners in medium-sized firms gained very little, while most solo practitioners saw their compensation shrink by more than 40 percent in the 1970s and by 10 to 20 percent from 1970 to 90. Figure 4–7 portrays these divergent results.

Confronted by such differing trends, can students even make the roughest guess of what their lifetime earnings will be? Fortunately, the picture is not as confusing as this figure might suggest. For better or worse, the legal profession is quite stratified so that different groups of students will be sensitive to earnings in different segments of the bar. Undergraduates with high grades and test scores who plan to attend one of the leading law schools will presumably pay attention to starting salaries and partners' earnings in large firms, because that is where most of these students will seek employment. Conversely, most seniors with relatively low college grades and test scores are more likely to be sensitive to trends in the earnings of solo practitioners and very small partnerships. In all these modes of

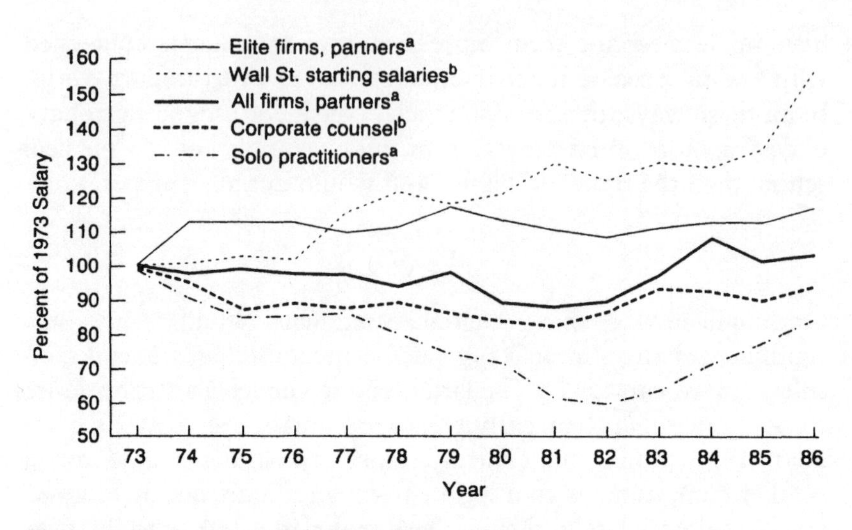

Figure 4–7 Lawyers' Salaries (1973 = 100)

Sources: Altman and Weil, *Surveys of Law Firm Economics*; (b) Richard Sander and E. Douglas Williams, "Why Are There So Many Lawyers? Perspectives on a Turbulent Market," *Law & Social Inquiry* 14 (1989): 431, 466.

practice, moreover, despite the differences in earnings among them, there are some important similarities. By and large, earnings in every sector of the bar tended to stagnate or do worse from the early 1970s to the early 1980s and to rise substantially from that point onward.

If compensation is a major factor affecting career decisions, one would expect to see a similar trend in applications to law school. In fact, just such a trend seems to have occurred. The number of students taking the Law School Admissions Test peaked in the early 1970s, just after lawyers' incomes began to decline. Thereafter, the number of students taking the test dropped almost continuously until the mid-1980s and then turned up and rose sharply through the last five years of the decade. These trends are reasonably responsive to the path of earnings. Apparently, then, changes in income did play a role in the minds of college seniors thinking of applying to law school.

Academic Careers

Most people would suppose that students contemplating a Ph.D. would be much akin to medical students in regarding money as a distinctly secondary consideration. Love of learning, interest in young people, freedom to pursue one's own intellectual interests all seem more vital to prospective scholars than how much money they expect to make. Nevertheless, economists continue to look closely at changes in expected earnings to explain the ebb and flow of doctoral students.

At first glance, the data seem consistent with the economists' assumptions that changes in earnings have important effects on career choice. Salaries for new Ph.D.'s and for tenured professors started to fall in the early 1970s and continued on a downward path until about 1981, when they began to rise once again. Like clockwork, the number of male students taking the Graduate Record Examination (required by most Ph.D. programs) likewise fell until 1982, only to rise thereafter through 1990. Figure 4–8 reveals these trends.

The trend in the number of would-be Ph.D.'s, however, does not follow academic salaries exactly. The drop in the number of stu-

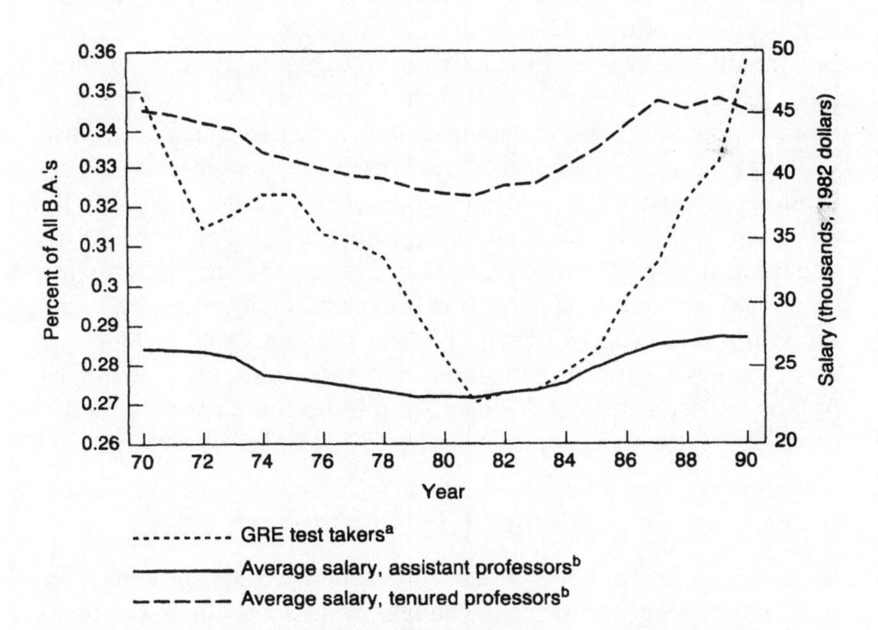

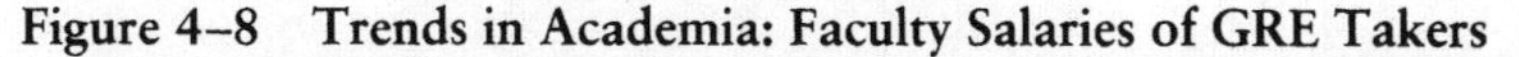

Figure 4–8 Trends in Academia: Faculty Salaries of GRE Takers

Sources: (a) Educational Testing Service; (b) *Bulletin of the American Association of University Professors* (category I universities).

dents taking the Graduate Record Examination seems steeper in the 1970s than the decline in faculty salaries. Moreover, toward the end of the 1980s, real starting salaries for assistant professors began to level off while tenured professors actually suffered a slight decline in pay. Nevertheless, the numbers taking the Graduate Record Examination continued to rise rapidly, as did applications to most leading graduate programs.

These aberrations suggest that other factors may be at work to help explain fluctuations in the number of Ph.D. applicants. The obvious possibility is that potential Ph.D.'s react more to the prospects of obtaining a job in a college or university than to the salary that they can expect to earn. Most graduate students choose an academic career because they are strongly attracted to the peculiar advantages of university life. For them, one would suppose, the greatest deterrent would not be a slight dip in the relative standing of academic salaries but the fear of spending years of study earning a Ph.D., only to find that there are no prospects for a permanent academic career.

The job market in the 1970s and 1980s behaved quite consistently with this thesis. During the 1970s, prospects for gaining tenure in a university were distinctly unfavorable. By the early 1980s, however, alert students (and their advisers) could predict that the number of tenured posts opening up would be rising again (because of increased retirements) at about the time when entering Ph.D. candidates reached the point of competing for a permanent job. By 1986 and 1987, word of a coming shortage of faculty began to appear in newspaper articles, followed by book-length treatments of the subject not long thereafter. It seems likely, then, that the mounting realization of favorable job prospects did as much as money to sustain the growing interest in obtaining a Ph.D. throughout the 1980s, just as the drying up of jobs helped cause the number of Ph.D. students to drop during the 1970s and early 1980s.

School Teaching

Several economists have published detailed studies showing that teachers are highly sensitive to changes in salary.[31] On first impression, these findings are surprising, because one does not imagine that young college students decide to become teachers to make money. What seems to happen is that many persons considering teaching feel that they must have a good chance of earning enough to live a decent life and make adequate provision for their families. As salaries rise, therefore, more and more would-be teachers believe that they can reach this threshold and afford to enter such a career.

The events of the 1970s and 1980s appear to bear out these suppositions. Teachers' salaries fell steadily throughout the 1970s until 1981, when they began to rise again, continuing upward through 1990. Interest in teaching on the part of college freshmen traveled almost the same trajectory, falling steadily through the 1970s, stabilizing in the early 1980s, and increasing throughout the rest of the decade. Trends in the number of education majors graduating from college and students receiving an M.A. in education followed suit (with an appropriate lag of several years to reflect the time students took to complete their degree). Thus, the number of B.A.'s in education began to fall in 1973, while M.A.'s peaked in 1976. After dropping for more than a decade, the totals started to rise again in 1987 and moved up sharply in succeeding years. Figures 4–9 and 4–10 record these trends.

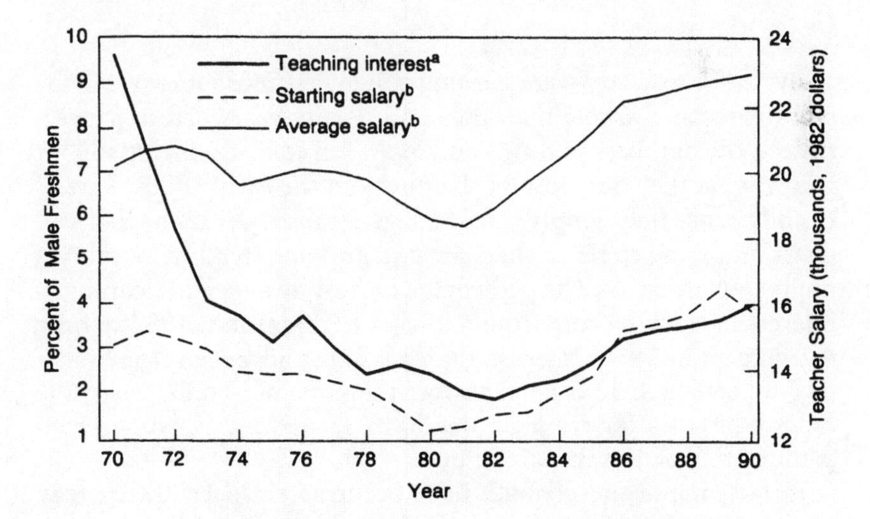

Figure 4–9 Trends in Teaching: Freshman Interest in Teaching

Sources: (a) Eric Dey, Alexander Astin, and William S. Korn, *The American Freshman: Twenty-Five-Year Trends, 1966–1990*; (b) American Federation of Teachers, *Survey and Analysis of Salary Trends.*

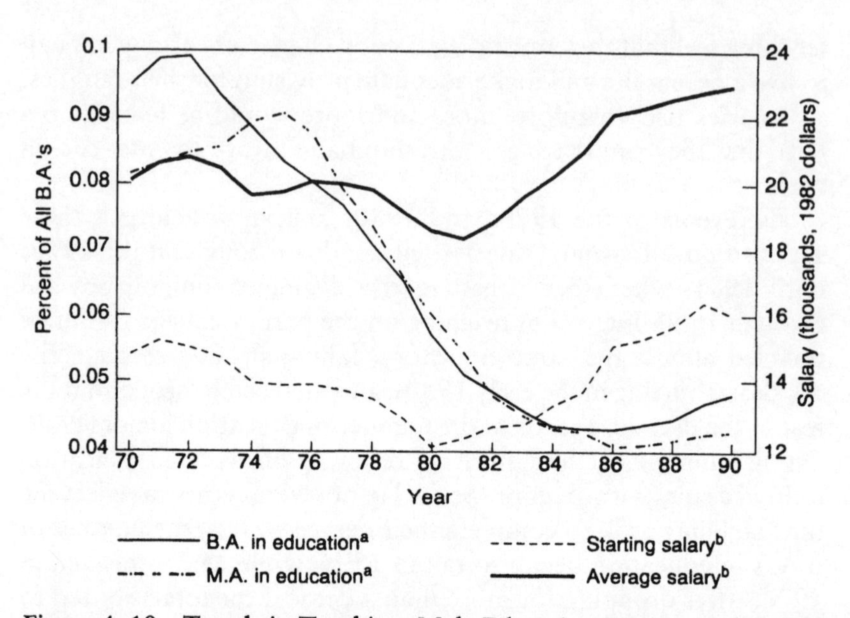

Figure 4–10 Trends in Teaching: Male Education Degrees and Teachers' Salaries

Sources: (a) *Digest of Educational Statistics*; (b) American Federation of Teachers, *Survey and Analysis of Salary Trends.*

By 1990, teachers were earning somewhat more relative to the work force as a whole than they had twenty years before. Nevertheless, the numbers of B.A.'s and M.A.'s in education were still far below what they had been at their peak in the early 1970s. Part of the difference may simply reflect a lag, because the numbers of students preparing to be teachers are still growing steadily. But this is not the whole story. The percentage of freshmen men indicating an interest in teaching rose from a low of 1.9 percent in 1982 to only 4.1 percent in 1990. Interest among women advanced from a low of 7.6 percent to 13.8 percent over the same period, but even the latter figure is a far cry from the 30 to 35 percent of women who planned to teach in the late 1960s.

In fact, important changes have occurred since 1970 that may account for this lagging interest in teaching. Women now have much greater prospects in professions such as law, business, and medicine that seemed so inhospitable a quarter century ago. The value attached to earning a lot of money has risen enormously, which must make a career in the public schools less attractive to members of both sexes. Morale has declined throughout the 1980s as teachers have felt unfairly criticized for the failings of the schools and burdened with new regulations adopted in the spirit of reform. These factors have apparently combined to depress the flow of students choosing a teaching career. They may prove to be serious obstacles in the coming decade, when the public schools will need to recruit much larger numbers of teachers and the nation's expectations for the quality of education will be higher than at any other time in our history.

CONCLUSION

Looking back on the varied experience of these professions over the past twenty years, what can we make of the role of money in student choices about their careers? Examining the evidence, few people would deny that earning a comfortable living is a major factor in the minds of most college seniors. Undergraduates may indicate in surveys that financial considerations are relatively unimportant, but that is undoubtedly because, more often than not, *all* the choices they are considering promise to yield a decent income. If they had to choose between practicing law and digging ditches, we can be reasonably sure that compensation would count for much more in their decision.

Money also seems to have contributed to the most important set of career changes that took place in the past twenty-five years: the movement of tens of thousands of highly educated students away from teaching and government service into more highly paid jobs in private business law practice. As we have observed, not only did the numbers of young people entering schools of law and business double and treble; their intellectual level also rose significantly. In 1950, law and MBA students were only of average ability; their test scores were far below those of classmates in medical schools, engineering, or graduate (Ph.D.) studies. By 1990, the situation had changed; the quality of students seeking admission to schools of law and business now rivaled that of applicants to any other graduate or professional school. Conversely, the grades and test scores of students entering teaching moved sharply downward in the 1970s and still have not returned to 1970 levels.

Although many factors helped to produce this shift of talent, the value students attached to money was undoubtedly a major influence. The easing of discrimination may have been the immediate cause of the sudden movement of women into law, business, and medicine, but when the opportunity arose, a powerful reason for choosing these professions over others was that they paid so much more than teaching school, taking shorthand, or working as a nurse. Similarly, at a time when "being very well off financially" became much more important to college students, the handsome incomes earned by successful business executives and lawyers must have impressed many talented young people and helped to move them into these professions.

It is one thing to say that money is an important factor, however, and quite another to imply that large numbers of students actually choose their careers on the basis of fine calculations of expected lifetime earnings or temporary shifts in the starting salaries of one profession relative to others. Such estimates hardly seem possible, save in a few professions, such as teaching, where most salaries vary within a fairly narrow range and job prospects depend on demographic trends that are quite easy to chart in advance. In other callings, the career possibilities are so numerous and their earnings so varied that it is all but impossible to estimate future earnings with reasonable accuracy. Can a college senior contemplating business school really guess where he will fall on the long continuum from bankrupt developers to run-of-the-mill vice presidents to successful entrepreneurs and chief executives of large corporations? Can prospective trial lawyers truly calculate whether their career will resemble that of the successful litigator taking home half a million dollars a year or the struggling attorney making a modest living representing employees in workmen's compensation cases or defending insurance companies against routine accident claims? Even in a more structured vocation such as college teaching, undergraduates rarely have a clear sense of what the relative earnings of professors will be in seven or eight years, when they finish their Ph.D.'s—let alone in fourteen years, when they are finally reviewed for tenure.

Common sense suggests not only that such calculations are impossible but that they will often be outweighed by other considerations of more immediate importance. The past twenty years offer numerous illustrations. In the 1960s, as William Bowen and Neil Rudenstine have pointed out, the end of draft deferments for graduate students was apparently the dominant factor in causing the share of male undergraduates entering Ph.D. programs to fall even though academic salaries and job prospects were still highly favorable.[32] Conversely, continued draft deferments for health professionals caused male students to apply to medical schools in record numbers during the early 1970s. Even in business, the growing desire to earn a handsome income seems to have had more influence than current salary trends in causing rapid increases in the numbers of males seeking business degrees in the 1970s. More striking still, the breaking down of traditional barriers of discrimination in law, medicine, and business was undoubtedly the precipitating cause of the huge influx of women into all three professions at the end of the 1960s and the early years of the 1970s.

In sum, many factors enter into the choice of a career. Among them, however, large, persistent differences in earnings play a substantial part, especially during a period when changing values in the society and an uncertain economy cause many young people to attach more importance to making money. Such differences do much to explain the substantial shifts that occurred over the past twenty years away from teaching and government service toward law and business. In this way, compensation has an important effect in determining which sectors of society claim the largest shares from the finite pool of intellectual talent available to meet the nation's growing needs.

Apart from their impact on the career choices of college graduates, the patterns of professional earnings we have considered raise a number of other issues. What should we make of the fact that leading practitioners in this country receive so much more money than their counterparts in other industrialized nations? Are we all better off because such lavish rewards go to those who reach the top of their profession? And should we be glad or sorry to see so many of our most talented young people turning from teachers colleges, government offices, and Ph.D. programs to schools of management and law? These questions await consideration in the chapters to follow.

PART II

CHAPTER 5

CORPORATE EXECUTIVES

"Mind-numbing," "eye-popping," "breathtaking," "scandalous"—these are but a few of the adjectives recently heaped on chief executives—or rather, on their paychecks—by editorial writers, politicians, and almost everyone else. By 1990, almost everyone seemed to agree that executive pay had reached unseemly heights. Of the one million taxpayers with incomes in the top 1 percent, approximately three hundred thousand (or 31 percent) were business leaders. The select group of CEOs heading Fortune 500 companies averaged $1.4 million per year in salaries and bonuses (and another $1.4 million in stock options and other long-term incentive payments).[1] As individual chief executives cashed in their stock options, the most successful CEOs reported spectacular one-year incomes of $10 million, $20 million, $40 million, even $78 million for Steve Ross of Time-Warner Communications.

The subject of executive compensation boiled over and became a public issue only after automobile executives traveled to Tokyo on a trade mission with President Bush. The sight of Lee Iacocca complaining to leading Japanese executives making only a fraction of his pay was a spectacle that no reporter could resist. The stories that ensued provoked an angry reaction. The business press has repeatedly condemned large corporations for their lavish earnings.[2] Over 75 percent of the American people now believe that top executives are paid too much.[3] President Clinton has proposed legislation to disallow tax deductions for salaries over one million dollars per year, and the Securities and Exchange Commission has ruled that questions of executive pay can come before the shareholders for a vote.

However merited they may seem, these disapproving views are only opinions, and they are not unanimous. According to Kevin Murphy of the Harvard Business School, "top executives are worth every nickel they get."[4] Leon Hirsch, who took home $118 million in 1991 as head of U.S. Surgical Corporation, insists that "I'm not paid enough," dismissing doubting consultants as "a bunch of self-appointed pseudoexperts who thrive on sensationalism and pure hokum."[5] In view of these differences, it is worth taking a more measured look at the problem to see whether the earnings of top executives and professionals are justified and, if they are not, what level of compensation might be defensible.

THE MARKET FOR EXECUTIVES

In the perfectly competitive world so dear to classical economists, all chief executives would receive amounts approximating what they added to the net profits of their company. Firms that could benefit the most from inspired leadership would pay the most money to the CEO of their choice. Because everyone in this world is perfectly informed, such companies would proceed unerringly to identify the best chief executives and offer them more than they were currently earning. The latter, being motivated primarily by love of money, would happily agree to serve. In this way, the greatest talent would move automatically to the firms in which it could do the most good, resources would be utilized more productively, and everyone would benefit as a result.

In the real world, matters do not work out quite so felicitously. One annoying problem is that both executives and boards of directors lack the knowledge they need to make informed decisions about compensation. Executives rarely know what opportunities exist for them in other companies or what such jobs might pay. Similarly, directors do not have perfect knowledge even about their own CEO. If the firm is prospering, no one can be sure how much of the credit belongs to the leadership and how much to favorable economic conditions, changes in tax laws or government regulations, outstanding subordinates, or wise investments made in some earlier regime. If the company is performing sluggishly, directors cannot always know how much blame should be heaped upon the current CEO and how much belongs to onerous government regulations, bad luck, or the mistakes of a previous chief executive.

Because of imperfect knowledge, there will normally be a substantial gap between the lowest pay that a CEO would accept and the best offer that directors could bring themselves to approve. A new chief executive, typically promoted from within, will probably agree to serve for only a modest increase in pay, because the promotion itself brings such added prestige and authority and because managers just appointed know little about what offers they could command from other firms. On the other hand, unless there are alternative candidates of virtually equal promise, the directors will be quite generous, if need be, because they will wish to end the search successfully and not antagonize their chosen candidate, or God forbid, have to start again because of a squabble over salary.

As time goes on, the gap between minimum and maximum compensation will tend to widen even further. Most CEOs might have to settle for modest pay increases, if they were pressed hard to do so, because they will be reaching an age at which they have fewer opportunities to jump to other firms. At the same time, they will have accumulated more and more knowledge about the firm they head so that the cost of replacing them will tend to grow. Directors will not wish to risk damaging the enterprise by making the CEO feel disgruntled over pay or, worse yet, leave and force them to search for a successor with the risk of learning years later that they have replaced their leader with someone less effective.

The process just described works in much the same way even if the company is performing in an undistinguished manner. Once again, the range of possible outcomes is very wide. Although some boards will force their CEOs to accept a pay cut, others will continue to authorize handsome increases in pay. In theory, this should not happen; numerous individuals should be capable of improving the performance of a lackluster company, and their availability should depress the pay offered to incumbent CEOs and even lead to their departure. The problem is that boards of directors have no way of being certain just who these other individuals are. At best, they can learn of a few outsiders by hearsay or from search firms, but they can only guess how well these individuals would actually perform in a different company. Even inside candidates are unknown quantities in taking ultimate responsibility for the firm. As a result, unless incumbent CEOs are clearly doing a poor job, the board is likely to stick with them, even give them a generous increase, although they are in fact performing only adequately. That is one reason why many top executives, such as Ross Johnson of RJR Nabisco, were able to continue with munificent pay in the 1970s, although the assets of their companies were performing far below their true potential, as subsequent takeovers made clear.

If a company is performing well, the ceiling in negotiating a CEO's compensation is virtually unlimited, because firms of substantial size can so easily afford even the most munificent paychecks. According to Michael Jensen of the Harvard Business School, "in 1988, the 1000 largest public companies (by sales) generated total funds of $1.6 trillion. Yet they distributed only $108 billion as dividends and another $51 billion through share repurchases."[6] With such sums at their disposal, companies can easily pay their top executives extremely generously. Granted, directors must pay some attention to their shareholders. They may also be reluctant to run the risk of provoking adverse publicity. But there are so many examples of pay packages running into tens of millions of dollars that boards can usually offer very substantial amounts with little risk of serious opposition, provided that the company's shares are appreciating in value.

The process of fixing executive compensation, then, is unusual because of the vast range of possible outcomes. In the face of such uncertainty, most top executives are in an unusually strong position to strike a favorable bargain, because they exert such influence over the process. CEOs almost always serve as chairman of the board. They typically have a good deal to say about the choice of new board members. They are the key people who decide on the fees paid to the directors, fees that average over $40,000 for only a few days of work each year. They often choose the consultant who presents recommendations on their next pay increase to the board—and most consultants are only too aware that candor, restraint, frugality, and other Puritan virtues may not be warmly remembered when it comes to picking a successor for the following year. In this environment, the task of fixing the compensation of top executives is hardly an arms-length transaction comparable to setting the salaries of middle managers and other kinds of employees.

Because of the peculiar characteristics of executive pay, competition often pushes compensation up rather than holds it down. A few grasping CEOs will use their influence to persuade their directors to grant very generous increases. Other top executives, who might otherwise have been more restrained, will then feel justified in asking for higher raises as well. Eventually, even the most responsible boards will conclude that it is only fair to offer their own CEO a hefty increase. Because few directors will wish to incur the burdens and risks of searching for a new leader, and because they cannot be sure how well potential replacements would perform, the easiest course is simply to recommend increases that are comfortably within the upwardly spiraling norm for top executives.

The amounts of discretionary money available to large corporations also benefit professionals who happen to be strategically placed in transactions involving large transfers of funds. As Kurt Vonnegut has observed:

> In every big transaction, there is a magic moment during which a man has surrendered a treasure, and during which the man who is due to receive it has not yet done so. An alert lawyer will make that moment his own, possessing the treasure for a magic microsecond, taking a little of it, passing it on.[7]

Lawyers are not the only ones to profit from these precious microseconds. Brokers, investment bankers, and consultants of various kinds are among the fortunate ones who are similarly situated. These professionals are commonly involved in transactions where the amounts at stake are so large in relation to their compensation that they encounter little resistance to their fees. When hundreds of millions of dollars change hands, even a tiny percentage fee yields handsome returns, but who is to complain?

Rarely have these opportunities been so stunningly lucrative as they were during the wave of mergers and takeovers in the 1980s. As Bryan Burroughs and John Helyer describe the leveraged buyout of RJR Nabisco, Drexel Burnham pocketed $227 million in fees for arranging a bridge loan; Merrill Lynch took home $109 million for its role in the bridge financing; Kohlberg, Kravis and Roberts netted $75 million in fees for masterminding the acquisition; Morgan Stanley received $25 million for giving advice.[8] According to the authors, Wasserstein-Perella also took home $25 million although they were not hired to give advice or render service but were engaged chiefly to keep them from serving opposing parties. Oh, yes. In addition to these fees, golden parachutes were bestowed upon a number of RJR Nabisco executives, such as the $53 million awarded to Ross Johnson, the retiring CEO, and the $45.7 million paid to his second-in-command. These parting gifts were given despite the fact that the same top executives had allowed RJR Nabisco's assets to underperform so grossly as to make such a huge buyout possible.

The RJR Nabisco takeover, while exceptional in size, was only one in a wave of mergers that took place during the 1980s. The ease with which new owners drew added earnings from the assets of the companies they bought suggests how readily firms can find the money to pay inflated salaries to a few strategically placed executives. Such payments bear little relation to the ideal prices for professional services that would emerge if markets were filled with hundreds of competing firms and all participants were fully enlightened. Nor is there reason to suppose that the pay executives receive is closely linked to the contribution they make to social welfare or economic growth. It is impossible to calculate how much CEOs have contributed to their own firm's bottom line, let alone how much they have accomplished for the economy. The entire process of fixing compensation is shrouded in uncertainty, and the CEO typically exerts more influence than any other individual over the final outcome. This procedure differs so much from any market for services that Adam Smith ever imagined that it cannot conceivably sanctify the amounts currently earned by corporate leaders.

FURTHER ARGUMENTS

As Groucho Marx once said, "If you don't like my principles, . . . I have others." In much the same way, those who defend the earnings of top executives conjure up other arguments to calm the skeptics who remain unmoved by appeals to market principles. With such large sums at stake, it is hardly surprising that so much ingenuity has been expended on the search for justifications.

Economists have contributed one of the most intriguing reasons for encouraging huge earnings in corporations and other hierarchical institutions.[9] Reaching the highest rank in such organizations, it is said, can be likened to a tournament. By giving very attractive prizes to the winner—i.e., the CEO—a company can induce would-be successors at lower levels in the hierarchy to work even harder. With commendable imagination, economists have turned to sport to test their theory by observing the effects of large prizes on the play of professional golfers. Sure enough, bigger prizes seem to improve scores, especially in the late rounds of the tournament when players are tired and need every bit of motivation they can get.

Despite the inventiveness of this theory, it may not provide an accurate account of why large companies pay such high salaries and bonuses. If it did, one would expect to find bigger paychecks for CEOs in companies with larger numbers of vice presidents competing for the top spot in order to compensate them for the smaller chance they have of winning. As yet, however, those who have compared the practices of varying kinds of corporations have found no evidence that boards of directors act in this way in setting the CEO's compensation.[10]

It is also far from clear that larger prizes will have a positive effect on the performance of ambitious young executives. Working for organizations is not like playing golf. In contrast to competitors on the PGA tour, corporations are enterprises in which teamwork is important to success. Such cooperation is especially likely to suffer if colleagues are competing fiercely with one another. Vice presidents mesmerized by the hope of vast rewards may not only refrain from helping competitors but may even resort to petty stratagems to sabotage their leading rivals.*

Such concerns help to explain the reluctance of Japanese corporations to pay their chief executives anything like the amounts common in America. The Japanese seem convinced that huge paychecks will not motivate subordinates but only undermine teamwork and destroy morale. That is why the gap between what their executives earn and the pay of other employees has been gradually narrowing over many years. Just the opposite, of course, has been true in most

* Curiously, there is also evidence that competition is not a particularly effective way of obtaining better performance *within* organizations. In an interesting series of experiments, psychologists have identified highly competitive people and compared their progress in business, science, and undergraduate course work. In each case, those who are strongly motivated by competition have done less well than those who rank low on competitiveness. What correlates best with successful performance in all these fields of endeavor is not competitiveness but a capacity for hard work and a taste for mastering challenging problems. These attributes seem to have nothing to do with the value that the individuals involved place on material rewards. See Janet Spence and Robert Helmreich, "Achievement-Related Motives and Behavior," in Janet Spence (ed.), *Achievement and Achievement Motives: Psychological and Sociological Approaches* (New York: W.H. Freeman 1983), 10.

American corporations, where compensation for CEOs, which averaged forty-three times the pay of an average worker in 1960, jumped to more than one hundred times the average wage in 1990.[11]

Another rationale for multimillion-dollar paychecks stresses the weighty responsibilities of top executives and the need to pay them huge rewards to inspire them to exert every ounce of energy and ability at their command. This justification is even flimsier than the last. One can argue that corporate leaders will work harder if a substantial part of their paycheck depends on how well they perform (although we will question even that hypothesis later on). But there is no reason to suppose that American executives would work less hard if they were paid several hundred thousand dollars a year instead of several million. It is at least as plausible to assume that executives who were paid less would value a raise much more and hence might be motivated to work even harder.

One can argue that executives making $1 million a year have more to lose if they are fired than CEOs making only $200,000. But higher-paid executives will also have less to fear from losing their jobs because they will probably have saved more to protect against such an eventuality. Besides, the threat of being fired is hardly an ideal way to motivate CEOs. Executives who are moved chiefly by a desire to keep their jobs are likely to avoid risk and spend too much time cultivating their boards of directors or trying to make themselves indispensable. Hence, the basic point still stands. Even if the *terms* on which executives are paid affect their motivation, there is no basis for believing that the *size* of their paycheck has any demonstrable effect on their performance. (If it did, of course, we would all be well advised to add a zero or two to the salaries of top government officials, Supreme Court justices, and many more.)

Seasoned observers of the corporate scene are likely to make a different argument to defend the pay of business leaders. They will stress the importance of the decisions that top executives make and the huge amounts of money that are often at stake. If CEOs and investment bankers manage their mega-transactions well, are they not entitled to a small fraction of the proceeds? Granted, their earnings may run into the millions. As Michael Novak points out, however, "one single good executive decision can make a difference to a firm of far more than that."[12] Without the benefit of exceptional leadership, clients and shareholders could well end up losing much greater sums than anything spent on salaries and fees. That is why Warren Buffett exclaims, "You'll never pay a really top-notch executive . . . as much as they are worth. A million, $3 million, or $10 million, it's still peanuts."[13]

What does Mr. Buffett mean? Surely not that it is necessary to pay millions of dollars per year to induce able executives to do their best. There is no evidence whatsoever that sums of this magnitude are needed to motivate CEOs. Rather, Mr. Buffett seems to be saying that top executives *deserve* such big salaries, provided they are "really top-notch," because they make a greater contribution to their companies than any conceivable salary they could be paid.

With all due deference to Mr. Buffett, it is not a simple matter to know whether a corporate leader is truly "top-notch." The very executives who were lauded for their leadership in the 1950s and 1960s turned out to be reckless expansionists whose acquisitions forced the painful corporate restructuring of the 1980s. Moreover, although a company may have prospered, no one has yet found a way of proving how much of the credit is properly due to the CEO and how much belongs to luck, a favoring environment, or the inspired work of able subordinates.

Even if we can tell that certain leaders are "top-notch" by Mr. Buffett's standards, it is still not self-evident that they "deserve" a share of the benefits resulting from their labors. When a night watchman discovers a fire in company headquarters and goes to exceptional lengths to rescue valuable files, he will rarely receive a percentage of the losses he has saved his employer. Nor does anyone feel the slightest inclination to pay our public officials in accordance with the value of their accomplishments. Imagine giving President Bush a few percentage points of the estimated total savings for keeping Saddam Hussein out of Saudi Arabia. Or paying Secretary of State James Baker a portion of the gains from helping to bring about a lasting peace between Russia and the United States. The very idea of such payments seems preposterous. So long as we can attract able people to compete for high public office and motivate them to do their best, there is no reason to add to their pay simply because they make decisions that benefit the public handsomely.

There is another problem with arguing that top executives deserve a share of their companies' successes. If they "deserve" a portion of the gains when their firms do well, they presumably ought to assume part of the losses when their companies do badly. Yet cuts of this kind occur even less frequently than cuts in blue-collar wages. In bad times, executives may forgo bonuses or opportunities to cash in on appreciated stock, but they still receive base salaries that far exceed those of anyone else in the company. At most, they lose the chance to participate in gains; they are not asked to help defray a portion of any losses. True, they can always lose their jobs. But this fate befalls them only rarely and is generally accompanied by large amounts of severance pay even if they are asked to leave for performing inadequatetly.

Despite these arguments, Mr. Buffett clearly speaks for many business leaders and economists when he asserts that the size of a CEO's paycheck is relatively unimportant and that what counts is whether the compensation has been properly based on company performance. According to the prevailing wisdom, so long as share prices are rising smartly, no corporate leaders need apologize nor do the shareholders have any reason to complain.[14]

This is an exceedingly blinkered view. It reduces executive compensation to a private matter between stockholders and CEOs—"a simple principal-agent problem," in the language of economists. One might just as well argue that there was no reason for all the fuss about the salary paid to the head of United Way, William Aramony, because total donations to the organization rose steadily under his leadership. In fact, executive compensation has ramifications that extend well beyond the shareholders. The entire country has an interest in whether earnings are above what is needed to attract and motivate corporate leaders. After all, the distribution of income affects the degree of justice in the society, the public's confidence in the economic system, even the balance of political power and influence in the nation.

The size of a CEO's paycheck may also affect the morale and incentives of others who work for the corporation. It is axiomatic that leaders lead by example. Even if huge salaries and bonuses rest on solid company performance, they may set a poor standard that will ultimately weaken the loyalty of others in the organization. As one prominent pay consultant has observed, "One of the sad things about the evolution of compensation in this country is that the gap between executives' and line workers' salaries has widened dramatically over the past decade. We are close to convincing this generation of workers that 'it's every man for himself.' "[15]

In truth, we are still some way from proving just what impact a huge paycheck has on the performance of subordinates. Lavish executive earnings have already complicated union negotiations in more than one corporation. In an intriguing recent article, two investigators found that firms with unusually high executive salaries produced goods of lower quality than companies that paid their top officials more modestly.[16] But these are only straws in the wind. Much more work will be needed to determine whether paying so much to top executives actually weakens morale down the line.

Whatever the truth may be on this point, the Japanese have apparently acted on the assumption that very high pay for top management does in fact have harmful effects on the work force. For several decades, Japanese corporations have made a conscious effort to narrow the difference between the pay of workers and executives. This policy is not a matter of social ideals. It results from a conviction that keeping executive compensation closer to the pay of ordinary workers will increase loyalty, cohesion, and ultimately productivity for Japanese firms.[17] Because Japanese business methods have provoked so much interest in this country, one might have thought that their example would provoke some debate over our prevailing theories of executive compensation. Yet Japanese methods hardly figure in scholarly conferences and corporate discussions on how best to pay corporate leaders.

Of all the arguments used in defense of executive compensation, the only one that occasionally has substance is that a board may have to pay extremely well to keep an able CEO from being pirated by another company. How many CEOs would actually be bid away if their salaries were lower is an interesting question that we will not pursue at length. Suffice it to say that more than 70 percent of all CEOs are hired from within and that most are not many years from retirement. As a result, it is doubtful that the threat of losing an able leader will occur frequently or that it accounts for the high level of executive pay in this country.* Even if corporate leaders were more

* If competition for talent were responsible for driving up the pay of CEOs, one would expect to find that comparably high rates of pay had existed for many years, because the market for executives presumably did not only become a potent force in the 1980s. One would also expect to find at least the same rate of increase in the pay given to key younger executives, because the competition for their services would presumably be even more brisk than the market for CEOs, who are often too close to retirement to

mobile, the fear of losing a CEO can only explain the action of a particular board in approving a huge pay package. *It does not mean that the entire system of executive compensation can be justified as a matter of social policy.* As we have previously pointed out, ignorance, ample supplies of corporate funds, influence from chief executives, and other distortions cause the "market" for CEOs to stray much too far from the competitive ideal to vindicate the paychecks that result when rivals vie for an executive's services.

TYING PAY TO PERFORMANCE

American companies have been particularly fond of motivating executives by linking their compensation to performance on the job. Such practices fit naturally with the results-oriented ethos of the modern corporation. Surveys show that those who choose to become corporate managers are more concerned with making money than members of any of the other major professions and hence are likely to respond well to monetary incentives.[18] It is not surprising, then, that 95 percent of all large corporations favor bonuses, merit pay, or similar devices. By now, the idea of performance pay is rarely questioned in business circles; its value is simply taken for granted.

Despite this widespread support, performance-based pay has had its share of problems in actual practice. At the root of these difficulties is the challenge of measuring performance reliably. Most managers do not work independently like an automobile salesperson. They function as members of a group. As a result, trying to isolate the specific contributions of each individual is usually a subjective, arbitrary task. That would not be an insurmountable problem if everyone involved had confidence in the fairness and objectivity of the process. But such is often not the case.

In some instances, corporate managers do not fully trust the superiors who evaluate their performance. On other occasions, they

---

be attractive candidates and disinclined, in any event, to leave the companies they head. In fact, neither of these suppositions seems to fit the facts. There have been only two periods of unusually rapid increases in top executive salaries during the past seventy-five years—the 1920s and the 1980s. The reasons have more to do with the prevailing ideology of these decades than with the competition for chief executives and will be explained in Chapter Thirteen. As for pay rates for younger executives, they seem to have risen at a significantly slower rate than the compensation for chief executives.

suspect that rival colleagues are currying favor or manipulating the system to achieve higher ratings than they deserve. Even if these pathologies are not present, the odds of building confidence in the system are diminished by the well-nigh universal tendency of human beings to evaluate themselves more favorably than the facts allow. A common rule of thumb is that average people will rate themselves at the eightieth percentile of their peers.[19] In the can-do world of corporate management, where self-confidence counts so heavily, one survey of hundreds of managers and professionals actually found that almost half of the respondents placed themselves in the top 5 percent.[20] With such high expectations, many of those being judged are bound to resent their evaluations and distrust the system even if the ratings are scrupulously fair.

Because of the delicacy of the task and the resentments it can provoke, many companies fail to carry out executive evaluations or give them perfunctory treatment. In a study of sixty higher-level managers, over 40 percent replied that they had not had a performance appraisal of any kind in over a year.[21] Many others spoke of cursory evaluations containing little specific information. "Your boss knows he should do the appraisal, so he takes the easy way out . . . like having you fill out the rating form on yourself, then just signing it and turning it in so you get your raise."[22] Or, as another executive put it, "when I do get an appraisal, most of the time it is like kissing your sister . . . It looks good but there isn't much substance."[23] To quote yet another, "There are a lot of 'FUD' managers around . . . those who manage by fear, uncertainty, and doubt. They intentionally withhold information, feedback, and performance reviews on their people, believing in their ignorance that they are improving performance."[24]

According to specialists on compensation, the record of performance-based pay is generally discouraging. One text makes the assertion that fewer than 20 percent of all performance appraisals are done effectively.[25] Several studies of performance-based pay in a variety of companies have found that up to 80 percent of managers are dissatisfied with their compensation plans.[26] According to a recent report from the National Research Council, "less than one-third (of employees) rate their organization's performance appraisal plans as 'effective' in tying pay to performance or in communicating organizational expectations about work."[27]

In addition to these negative appraisals, there is no solid empirical evidence that performance pay actually motivates managers to do better work. Experts are divided on the subject. Businesses in Japan, Germany, and other advanced economies rarely pay individual bonuses and still manage to compete effectively against us. No matter. American managers seem to feel no need of evidence to prove that paying people for good performance will motivate them to work harder. The proposition is simply too obvious to require demonstration.

PERFORMANCE PAY FOR CEOs

The problems of paying lower-level executives pale before the difficulties of rewarding top corporate officials. At this level, the amounts of performance pay reach monumental proportions. Chief executive officers of Fortune 500 companies often receive approximately 75 percent of their total yearly compensation—at least $1 million or more—in bonuses, stock options, restricted stock, and other forms of performance-related pay. In recent years, some CEOs have cashed in stock options worth tens of millions of dollars to reward them for the strong performance of their firm.

It is harder than one might think to pin down the theory underlying performance pay for CEOs. The rationale seems to have changed subtly over the years to accord with shifting perceptions of the quality of business leadership in this country. In the early 1970s, the most common reason for tying executive compensation to performance was to create attractive rewards that would motivate able CEOs to do their best. Toward the end of the 1970s, the emphasis shifted slightly as the abilities of American business leaders began to be called in question by corporate raiders and foreign competitors. Economists began to advance the idea that top executives were more risk-averse than their shareholders, because the CEO's reputation and career are linked almost entirely to the fortunes of one firm while shareholders have diversified their portfolios and thus can afford more venturesomeness in their leaders.[28] It followed that shareholders should create special rewards for superior performance to induce their CEOs to behave more boldly. By the late 1980s, after repeated tales of scandal, mismanagement, and waste, new voices began to emanate from the academy urging that pay packages be structured so that CEOs might share in corporate losses as well as corporate gains to force them to take greater care to protect the interests of their shareholders and not engage in self-aggrandizing ventures harmful to the firm.[29]

All these theories rest on a remarkably unflattering view of corporate leaders. Citing little or no evidence, the authors assume that all CEOs are hugely self-interested individuals who will not exert their best efforts unless they are showered with large sums of money.[30] Why directors should choose such people to head their corporations is hardly obvious, nor is it clear how these leaders could ever set an example that would motivate their employees. Rather than tarry over such questions, however, theorists hurry on to the real challenge: how to use monetary rewards to "align the interests of the chief executive with those of the shareholders." By artfully shaping the compensation package, they argue, directors can construct a series of financial incentives that will transform a cautious, self-serving manager into the decisive, venturesome leader who will maximize value for the stockholders.

Whether monetary rewards can actually change behavior in this fashion is by no means clear, and proponents have not marshaled much evidence to test the proposition. As one student of compensation points out, "We do not know, for example, whether offering higher salary levels in order to attract and retain key executives really pays, whether promoting executives from within really pays, whether different risk-return trade-offs in pay-for-performance plans really do attract executives who are more (or less) prone to take risks. And we do not know if any of these subsequently affect performance."[31]

Digging deeper into these theories only gives rise to further questions. How do we know that CEOs are risk-averse? Is this a good description of the corporate leaders in the 1960s whose adventures in buying unrelated businesses led to all of the turbulent acquisitions and restructuring of the 1980s? Why must we assume that executives who have already made enough millions to make them secure for life will respond so energetically to the prospect of making still more millions? The answers to these questions are not self-evident, yet the economists who pronounce on executive pay do not trouble to supply us with an explanation.

Another problem with these theories is that they are not consistent. If we mean to reward top executives for what they accomplish, then the board should not pay them in accordance with the appreciation in the company's stock, because stock prices can increase in value for many reasons unrelated to the CEO's decisions. On the other hand, if we simply wish to align the CEO's interests with those of the shareholders, payment in appreciated stock may be appropriate. Similarly, if we are trying to increase the CEO's willingness to take risks, we will want to reward successful performance yet shield the chief executive from the possibility of loss. But if we wish to make CEOs more sensitive to shareholders and more careful about squandering the assets of the company, then chief executives should share in corporate losses as well as participate in the gains. It is difficult to use the theories intelligently without straightening out these inconsistencies. As yet, however, there is no convincing evidence to resolve the matter.

Apart from its other weaknesses, the prevailing theory of performance-based executive compensation is highly questionable as a matter of sound public policy. By assuming that the problem to be solved is simply to align the interests of the CEO with those of the shareholders, the theory ignores a generations-old debate about which constituencies corporate managers should try to serve. Until recently, the accepted view seemed to be that management ought to balance the interests of its employees, its customers, and the public at large as well as those of its shareholders. As the Business Roundtable put it in its 1981 Statement on Corporate Objectives, "Balancing the shareholders' expectations of maximum return against other priorities is one of the fundamental problems confronting corporate management. The shareholder must receive a good return, but the legitimate concerns of other constituencies also must have the appropriate attention."[32]

Most of the pay packages currently in use proceed from a different premise. They create huge financial incentives for CEOs to prefer the interests of the stockholders whenever they conflict with the concerns of the employees or the public. Such conflicts are not unusual. Companies can react to a recession by emphasizing layoffs or by absorbing temporary losses. They can take risks that shareholders may approve or avoid them in deference to the more conservative interests of creditors and bondholders. They can cut research and development budgets to increase short-term profits and jeopardize the long-term viability of the firm. When problems of this kind arise, it is not obvious that management should automatically favor the interests of shareholders.

These problems are especially troubling in an economy such as ours where shareholders typically hold their stock for short periods in an effort to realize immediate gains. Since 1960, the average length of time that shareholders held stock has shrunk from seven years to two. In this environment, aligning the interests of management with those of the shareholders promises to encourage chief executives to adopt excessively limited time horizons. A long series of commentators have criticized the short-term outlook of American business and pointed to the threat it poses not merely to local or employee interests but to the continuing growth of productivity and the long-term health of the economy.[33] Binding management behavior even more closely to shareholder interests through lavish stock options tends only to exacerrbate these problems.

Those who defend the primacy of shareholder interests argue that corporate managers are not trained to balance constituency needs or to weigh matters of public interest and have no mandate to play this role.[34] Perhaps so. But there are potent arguments on the other side. Japanese corporations do not prefer shareholder interests to all others.[35] Nor do German companies.[36] Nor does a majority of the American people want its corporations to behave in this way.[37] At the very least, there are questions here that are worth considering carefully before offering huge rewards to CEOs to concentrate so heavily on the interests of stockholders.

Any difficulties with the theory of executive compensation pale in comparison with the problems that have arisen in putting the theory into practice. Under the glare of publicity and scholarly analysis, performance pay for top executives has turned out to be a sham and an embarrassment that has undermined the public's confidence in business leadership. A series of studies have now shown that the compensation actually paid to CEOs bears very little relation to the record of their companies. A typical analysis recently published by two Harvard Business School professors found that "in most publicly held companies, the compensation of top executives is virtually independent of performance."[38] Similarly, CEOs have been much less likely than their workers to suffer a pay cut when hard times come.[39] Apparently, many top executives of poorly performing firms have persuaded their boards that they are entitled to lavish rewards even when earnings sag—presumably by arguing that disappointing results are due to problems quite beyond their control with which they have struggled heroically. (One must look far to find a board that will do away with bonuses and other performance-based rewards when positive results occur for reasons beyond the CEO's control.)

A closer look at the record documents these problems in vivid detail. Far from rewarding executives only for above-average performance, most stock option plans allow CEOs to profit from *any* appreciation of the shares they receive, even if the gains are no greater than those obtainable from risk-free Treasury bonds. Compensation packages are also adjusted frequently. (From 1955 to 1983, the incentive plans of the two hundred largest industrial companies in the United States had an average life-span of fewer than eighteen months.)[40] Most of the changes helped to increase the rewards or made them easier to obtain. In particular, when share prices declined, so that executives could not cash in on their stock options, the "strike price" was often reduced, allegedly to make sure that the option stayed sufficiently within reach to encourage the CEO to keep trying. (Again, the reverse rarely occurs after stock prices *rise* for extraneous reasons.) After many years of experience, one prominent pay consultant–turned professor describes the process as follows:

> If you go to a track meet and watch the high jump, you'll notice that each time a contestant clears the bar, it is raised to a higher level. And if a contestant knocks the bar over, he or she is eliminated from competition. Would that the world of executive compensation ran the same way. Instead, we have a different kind of game going on. If you knock the bar over, the bar is simply lowered. And if you still knock the bar over, it is lowered still further. Indeed, should it become necessary, a trench will be dug and the bar buried.[41]

Many incentive plans lend themselves to manipulation by top executives seeking to increase their rewards. If pay varies with the size of the corporation, CEOs may be tempted to acquire other firms even though the merger makes little long-term sense for their company. If bonuses depend on annual earnings, inventories may be depleted at the end of the year or expenses may be deferred. As a leading consultant, Lester Korn, once observed, "We have seen all too many instances of chief executive officers retiring after 15 straight quarters of record earnings. We cover these executives with glory for their stupendous achievements. Then, two years later, the companies they left are on the rocks. Only then do we learn that they achieved their goals by slashing R&D budgets, for example, or by closing down operations—decisions that were expedient at the time but disastrous for the long run."[42]

The typical response to such criticisms is that they merely reflect problems of execution that can be ironed out with time and care. What other reply would one expect from business executives and their consultants who have such a large personal stake in perpetuating the current system? And yet, if performance-based compensation remains so weakly related to actual performance after more than fifty years of experience, it is a sure sign that flaws exist that go far beyond technical details of implementation. In fact, the problems are not difficult to find.

In the best of circumstances, it will be hard to measure the performance of a chief executive or to create a set of financial incentives to match the shifting mix of interests that a large, complicated organization should respond to over time. Trying to overcome these problems would be difficult even for disinterested judges acting with complete objectivity. As we have seen, however, the process of fixing executive compensation is anything but impartial, because the typical CEO has so much to do with choosing the directors, picking a pay consultant, and shaping the information that comes before the board.

The consequences of such a flawed process are predictable. It is hardly surprising that companies almost always introduce incentive pay as a supplement rather than a substitute for base compensation, that CEOs are rewarded when their company does well but are rarely penalized (truly penalized) when it does poorly, that the chief executive's pay is typically pegged at least at the median of the peer group and never below it, that stock option plans are frequently readjusted and almost always in the CEO's favor, that surveys are often conducted by looking to peer groups carefully selected to include too many high-paying companies.

A recent study of large companies reached the interesting conclusion that executive pay correlates much more closely to the salaries of members of the compensation committee than it does to the company's actual performance.[43] Such findings are not unexpected;

they are the natural result of a badly biased process. So long as that process remains more or less intact, one must expect that abuses will continue.

SEEKING A REMEDY

It is far easier to demonstrate that many executives are overpaid than to devise a remedy. While everyone can point to serious flaws in the market for executive services, no one knows exactly what a truly competitive paycheck would be. Hence, any proposal to make things better must be something of an improvisation, an invention designed not for perfection but merely to bring executive compensation closer than it currently is to defensible levels. In pondering such suggestions, one should not ask whether the patient will fully recover but only whether the cure will be better than the disease.

The mildest, least expensive remedy is simply to turn the spotlight of publicity on the issue of executive compensation and expose the excesses and perverse results that have been brought to light so frequently in recent years. Notoriety of this kind will help to inhibit directors from rubber-stamping enormous salaries and bonuses or approving fat increases unrelated to the firm's performance. The deterrent effects of publicity may become even stronger now that the government will require more complete, understandable disclosure of all the details of executive pay packages, including the arcane minutiae of stock option plans.

These advantages are plainly worth having, the more so because the cost is so low. But they are far from a complete remedy. Publicity works erratically. It comes and goes and focuses only on egregious cases. Its effects are unpredictable. Years of adverse publicity on the business pages did not prevent the huge pay increases of the late 1980s. Even the storm of criticism in early 1992 that moved the subject to the front page of almost every newspaper in the land did not keep executive pay from rising to record levels or prevent the announcement that Roberto Goizueta of Coca-Cola had taken home a tidy $86 million for the year. At best, therefore, publicity is only a first step. If it is not buttressed by more effective remedies, its effects will be haphazard and will eventually subside.

Stronger medicine may come with the recent decision of the Securities and Exchange Commission to require a much more detailed explanation of executive pay packages and to allow the issue of executive compensation to appear on the ballot for a nonbinding vote by the shareholders.[44] In today's world, few directors will choose to disregard an adverse vote of the shareholders or run the risk of provoking such expressions of disapproval. As a result, the action of the commission will surely strengthen the pressure on directors to avoid outlandish pay packages that bear little or no relation to performance.

A further step in encouraging closer scrutiny of executive pay would be to strengthen the hand of the directors in deciding on issues of compensation. Under such proposals, directors would be chosen by shareholders—especially large institutional shareholders—rather than being handpicked by the CEO. The compensation committee would be wholly composed of independent directors and would have access to their own pay consultants and their own stock of information. In this way, setting the compensation for top executives would be a genuinely arms-length negotiation in which the interests of the shareholders would be paramount.

Experience in the field of laber relations should warn us that regulating negotiations over pay can easily lead to a daunting tangle of rules and litigation. The same fate could overtake discussions over executive compensation. To ensure arms-length bargaining throughout American business, the government would have to enact detailed rules to make certain that outside members of the board were truly independent, that management had no power to determine their selection or their fees, that the directors had adequate independent advice, that shareholders were properly and adequately informed, and so on.

Even if boards of directors do become more independent and negotiate at arms length with adequate information, it is still not clear that the consequences will be altogether benign. We can be reasonably sure that boards of directors will take greater pains to tie compensation more closely to performance. No independent director will want to risk giving handsome pay increases to CEOs in the face of sagging profits and declining stock prices. The effect on the *amount* of compensation, however, is much more problematic. It is far from clear that directors will object to having their CEOs reap handsome rewards so long as the company has greatly increased in value to the owners. The stockholders themselves are unlikely to object. There will be other chief executives with conveniently high salaries to whom the directors can point for vindication. Finally, independent though they may seem, most directors will develop a close, friendly relationship with a reasonably successful CEO. They will not want to take the risk of replacing such a person with an untried substitute. Nor will they wish to leave the company in the hands of someone who feels disgruntled and ill-used, so they will end by paying handsomely—so long as the company performs well.

The ultimate problem with efforts to strengthen the hand of the stockholders is that CEOs may feel more strongly pressed to adopt the short-term outlook of most present-day investors. Prof. Michael Porter of the Harvard Business School has argued eloquently and convincingly how oriented shareholders have become to immediate gains and how unrestricted stock options can cause corporate leaders to adopt the same narrow perspective at the expense of the nation's long-run economic interests.[45] Unless something is done to encourage the growth of stable, long-term investors, giving more power to shareholder-directors and subjecting compensation packages to shareholder approval may only make these problems worse.

The last available cure for excessive paychecks, of course, is direct government intervention. As usual, the medicine can come in stronger or milder doses. The mildest version is simply to put a ceiling on executive compensation for corporate tax purposes. Such a ceiling would not fix compentation but merely set a limit on the amount a firm could deduct as a business expense.

President Clinton has urged Congress to prohibit tax deductions for compensation in excess of $1 million per year. Unfortunately, the practical effect of this proposal is likely to prove disappointing to its sponsors. There was a time, in the 1970s, when such a limit might have created a psychological barrier to restrain executive paychecks. In that era, few CEOs earned more than $1 million a year. Today, however, this barrier has long since been breached. Hundreds of chief executives now receive seven-figure salaries, and it is most unlikely that limiting tax deductions will cause boards of directors to scale back their earnings. Faced with a choice between cutting the CEO's paycheck by many hundreds of thousands of dollars per year or simply paying taxes on the excess, what board will urge a cut? The tax involved is a tiny fraction of total earnings, and stockholders are unlikely to mutiny and risk the defection of the chief executive to some other, more permissive corporation.

Thus, the limit is likely to do very little to restrain the huge pay packages currently given to CEOs of large companies. At best, it is a symbolic gesture to express official concern and to reassure taxpayers that the government is not subsidizing paychecks that most people would consider excessive.

If the Congress should become more ambitious and try to set a *mandatory* ceiling on executive compensation, added complications would quickly arise. For example, if compensation were limited to a fixed multiple of average employee earnings, firms would be much more likely to offer homes, yachts, and other expensive perks that the government would have to review to decide whether they should be classified as income. In addition, tiny companies filled with highly educated, well-paid personnel would be able to pay their chief executive much more than huge corporations that happened to have a less skilled work force. Because such a result would be hard to defend, pressure would quickly build to incorporate more and more complicating factors into the maximum—sales volume, size of work force, absolute and relative performance, and so forth. In these ways, the government would be quickly drawn into an intricate process generating intense political pressure and threatening to produce arbitrary, rigid results. Nothing in our experience suggests that public officials are capable of carrying out such a task except for limited periods in time of war or grave national emergeny.

In fact, it would be hazardous to put a ceiling on top executives' earnings even if one could find an administratively feasible way of doing so. Any remedy that limits pay in a single occupation threatens to drive talented people to other lines of work where similar restrictions do not exist. Prospective executives might shun established companies and start their own firm, or even go to law school and become corporate lawyers. In this way, limits on earnings tailored to particular professions could distort the flow of talent in ways that did more harm than good. If incomes are to be trimmed, better to do so across the board and not risk misallocating valuable human resources. Such a strategy calls for remedies that transcend corporate executives and can best be considered after our review of earnings in other lucrative professions.

In the end, therefore, no remedy yet proposed promises to cure all the ailments that afflict executive compensation. Granted, the worst abuses may mercifully come to an end. There will be fewer

CEOs taking home millions of dollars as their companies wallow in substandard performance. But none of the measures currently under review is likely to force leading executives to accept paychecks under $1 million a year as their counterparts abroad regularly do. Nor is there an end in sight to CEOs who benefit handsomely from increases in the price of company stock that come about for reasons having little to do with their own actions. American companies may face daunting competition overseas and increasing scrutiny from shareholders at home. But their leaders are in no serious danger yet of relinquishing their position as the best-paid executives in the world.

CHAPTER 6
DOCTORS

Of all the private professions, medicine has been the most successful in shielding its compensation from the chill winds of competition. As the president of a local medical society once remarked, "Our mentor has always been Hippocrates, not Adam Smith."[1] In seeking to avoid competition, doctors have profited much from the special characteristics of their calling. The fact is that medicine does not lend itself well to a free market. Health care is too expensive for all citizens to afford. At the same time, it is too important to leave anyone unprovided for and too complex for most people to decide by themselves just what services they need.

To protect consumers from the hazards of competition, governments invariably come forward with a heavy dose of regulations, subsidies, and controls. In no country has the medical profession resisted these intrusions as tenaciously as in the United States. Rather than have the government intervene, our doctors have traditionally sought to regulate the market themselves in ways that served their private interests. Ironically, however, whenever the government has insisted on acting, the medical profession has been more successful in America than in any other country in shaping official policy to ensure that physicians receive higher compensation than free, competitive markets would allow. In a nation in which total health care expenditures exceed $900 billion per year and doctors receive roughly 10 percent of the total, this is not a trivial accomplishment.

THE CAUSES OF HIGH EARNINGS

Over seventy-five years ago, American doctors managed to capitalize on the desire for quality in medicine to blunt the forces of competition. Following the Flexner Report in 1911, the American Medical Association (AMA) worked tirelessly to discourage proprietary medical schools and thereby helped to restrict the number of doctors to levels well below what a free market would allow. The result, as Simon Kuznets and Milton Friedman concluded in a massive study, was to push doctors' earnings well above competitive levels by 1929.[2]

In the early 1960s, even the AMA agreed that the number of physicians was not large enough to meet the nation's needs. With government funding, new medical schools sprang up, and enrollments of medical students started to increase. Nevertheless, physicians continued to keep their earnings high, thanks to the willingness of the government and private insurance plans to approve their fees and reimburse them accordingly.

Today, the vast majority of people in the United States are covered by Medicare or by some sort of private insurance plan. Because a third party is paying most of the cost, consumers have little reason to shop for better prices, nor do doctors have an incentive to lower their charges to gain more business. If anything, the reverse is true. Until recently, the federal government and most private health plans have paid doctors an amount based on the fee they actually charged for the treatment in question, or on the fees they customarily charge in such matters, or on the prevailing rates in the local area, whichever was the lowest. Under each of these alternatives, keeping prices up leads to higher approved rates with little or no loss of business.

In this environment, what doctors charge bears little relation to what they would receive in a truly competitive market. Instead of having to cut prices to meet competition, American physicians have managed for decades to boost their earnings more rapidly than any other major profession. Only in the 1970s, when the number of physicians rose by one-third, did per capita incomes pause in their upward march. As conditions improved during the 1980s, earnings began to rise again, exceeding inflation by an average of approximately 2.5 percent per year.[3]

To be sure, the work of doctors has grown steadily more demanding as their earnings have risen. With the passage of time, physicians have gradually come to direct larger teams of assistants and technicians and to use more expensive, sophisticated equipment. As a result, rising fees might merely seem to reflect increasing levels of responsibility. Yet larger responsibilities afford a shaky foundation on which to build a claim for greater compensation. Although they may make a job more wearing and burdensome, they also make it more attractive to many talented people. There is no method of weighing these conflicting attributes. Instead, the market is supposed to resolve such uncertainties by letting compensation reach whatever level is required to attract the necessary numbers of people to each occupation. By every indication, current rates of compensation are well above what they need to be to attract sufficient numbers of doctors, despite the responsibilities they bear.[4] That is why applications to medical school have consistently been far in excess of what the nation's medical schools can accommodate.

Other scraps of information also belie the notion that current salaries simply reflect the complexities of modern practice. As Kuznets and Friedman demonstrated, doctors were already charging much more than competitive rates in the 1920s, before technology began to make their duties more complex and demanding.[5] Moreover, while doctors have taken on greater responsibility in all Western countries, American physicians have outdistanced their counterparts abroad in boosting their incomes. Today, the average doctor in the United States earns more than 5.4 times the pay of a typical American worker (compared with a multiple of 4.3 in Germany, 3.8 in Canada, and 2.5 in Great Britain).[6] By every plausible measure, then, most American physicians seem to be overpaid, receiving substantially more in earnings than a competitive market would allow.

Amid this general prosperity, a fortunate minority have fared spectacularly well. A few of these doctors attract wealthy patients willing to pay above the normal rates. But most of the highest-paid physicians are practitioners who have managed to capitalize on imperfections in Medicare and other systems of payment.

Under prevailing practices, fees are set for new procedures when they first come into use and are seldom adjusted downward as doctors learn to use the technique more efficiently. For some of these procedures, the profit margins have grown very large indeed. For example, over three hundred thousand coronary bypass operations are performed each year at a fee to the surgeon ranging from $2,000 to $10,000 per procedure. The basis for this rate was set when the operation was new and very time-consuming. Now that the procedure has become more common, surgeons can perform a bypass in roughly half the time required twenty years ago and at less risk to the patient.[7] Nevertheless, the fees for each operation did not fall over this period. As a result, by the mid-1980s, surgeons were able to make over $500,000 per year simply by performing three bypass operations (or twelve hours of work) each week.[8]

Other doctors have earned extravagant incomes by using assistants in such a way that they can perform more procedures each week than were envisaged when the rates were originally set. Thus, anesthesiologists have profited handsomely from using a resident (student) to do much of the less-skilled work, enabling them to complete many more procedures at the same high rates. Residents also do much of the preoperative and postoperative work of surgeons, thus freeing them to perform more operations. By such methods, the peculiarities of the payment system help to boost earnings far above competitive levels in several specialties, such as orthopedic surgery, anesthesiology, and ophthalmology.

Still other physicians have earned extremely large incomes by establishing their own facilities for certain types of services, such as orthopedic surgery. By performing more efficiently (and by avoiding federal rules on payments to hospitals), physician-owners can reap greater rewards than they could obtain by simply operating in a hospital and charging a fee for their services. As in the previous examples, the physicians involved have done a commendable job of figuring out how to perform medical procedures more efficiently. The problem in each case is that the inflexible price system in the health care field allows doctors to continue pocketing the savings instead of being forced by competition to pass them on to the consumer.

More dubious ethically is the practice of investing in ancillary facilities, such as diagnostic laboratories, kidney dialysis centers, ambulatory surgical units, and other lucrative health care enterprises. A General Accounting Office report found that at least 40 percent of the doctors in Florida who see patients directly referred them routinely to entities in which they have a financial interest.[9] These facilities frequently set their prices well above the rates commonly charged for the services involved. Doctors also tend to prescribe tests and medical procedures much more often when they are performed at facilities in which the physicians have a financial stake. Thus, Florida doctors who had an interest in radiation therapy units sent patients there for treatment over 50 percent more frequently than the average for all American patients, and the charges for such services were more than 40 percent higher than the average rates elsewhere in the nation.[10] Similarly, the average markups for physical therapy and comprehensive rehabilitation were found to be two to three times greater when the services were performed in facilities in which physicians held an interest.[11] The same pattern occurs when doctors bring expensive testing procedures into their own offices. For example, a recent study revealed that physicians who operate diagnostic imaging equipment in their own offices utilize these machines far more often than doctors who do not own their own equipment and charge from 1.6 to 6.2 times as much for such tests as independent radiologists.[12]

In principle, of course, there is nothing wrong with investing in medical facilities and equipment. A problem arises only when physicians stand to gain financially by referring their own patients to facilities or products with which they have a financial relationship. This is a clear conflict of interest that allows many doctors to prescribe unnecessary tests and services while further padding their earnings by charging excessive prices. After much internal struggle, the American Medical Association has recently declared such practices unethical. State legislatures would do well to prohibit them by law.

THE EFFECTS OF EARNINGS ON THE SUPPLY OF TALENT

If everyone who wanted to go to medical school could enroll, the United States would be training many more doctors than we need. As we have seen, however, medical schools admit only a fraction of those who apply. After a concerted effort to increase the supply of doctors, beginning in 1963, the number of physicians per 100,000 people rose from 141 to more than 230 in 1990. This growth has prompted many doctors and health care experts to complain about a glut of physicians. Nevertheless, doctors in America still make up only about the same proportion of the total population as in Germany, Canada, and Sweden. As a result, there is no clear evidence yet that the number of doctors in America is excessive, although many people worry that it is fast becoming so.

More serious problems arise from the distribution of physicians among the various specialties and subspecialties of medical practice. By the late 1980s, only 33 percent of all American doctors were engaged in primary care, and the percentage of medical students interested in such a practice had declined by more than one-third since the beginning of the decade. If present trends continue, fewer than 25 percent of all physicians will be generalists by the early years of the next century.[13]

In contrast, primary care physicians make up 45 percent of all doctors in West Germany, 52 percent in Canada, 70 percent in Great Britain, and 73 percent in Australia. These differences have important effects on health care costs. Not only do specialists charge much higher fees; according to studies of the treatment given to patients with the same severity of illness, specialists tend to recommend hospitalization more frequently, they are more likely to use expensive tests and procedures, and they are less inclined to suggest preventive measures.[14] These findings have led health economists to conclude that the high proportion of specialists in America is a contributing factor to our exceptionally high health care costs.[15]

The strong preference of medical students for specialty practice is undoubtedly influenced by the fact that many specialists in the United States earn so much more than primary care physicians. In 1991, doctors in family practice and general internal medicine earned $102,000 and $110,000, respectively. Meanwhile, anesthesiologists received $221,000; radiologists $246,000; neurosurgeons, $339,000; and cardiovascular surgeons, $420,000.

Although differences in income may be one reason why so many American doctors choose specialty practice, other causes are even more important. For example, medical students seem increasingly interested in an aspect of practice referred to in the trade as "controllable life-style." To physicians with small children or diverse interests, it is better to perform cataract operations on a 9-to-5 schedule from Monday to Friday than to be a general practitioner on call at all hours to take care of emergencies.

Medical students also respond to role models, perceived differences of prestige and status, and other messages subtly transmitted during their years of training. In most American medical schools, these cues are plainly slanted in favor of specialty practice. The most powerful faculty members, who do the most interesting research and use the most advanced equipment and techniques, are typically specialists who enjoy having able young people follow in their footsteps. Successful students who manifest an interest in primary care are often told by professors in leading schools that they are simply "too good" for such a career. Medical schools themselves have a clear stake in having students flock to the specialty residencies, because specialties generate more hospital revenue than primary care. Now that medical schools derive over 37 percent of their revenues from medical services (up from 12 percent in 1970), such considerations are no longer trifling.

The type of student admitted to medical school may also contribute to the bias in favor of specialty practice. Admissions committees tend to favor candidates with strong science backgrounds and require all applicants to take a heavy dose of undergraduate science courses as a prerequisite to admission. By and large, such students are more inclined to value the intellectual challenge of some of the specialized fields and less likely to be attracted by the prospect of human interaction and social service that characterize primary care practice. All in all, therefore, higher incomes undoubtedly play a part in attracting students to specialty practice, but they are imbedded in a larger complex of interrelated factors involving status, intellectual challenge, and the medical school environment that exert a powerful influence over the shape of the profession and its costs to the American people.[16]

PERVERSE INCENTIVES

High earnings not only attract students to lucrative specialties; they are structured in ways that create very curious incentives for practicing physicians. Almost three-quarters of all doctors are paid a fee for each service they perform. This method has the advantage of encouraging them to work hard, because the more patients they attract and the more services they provide, the more money they will make. If patients were well informed in the arcane mysteries of medical care, the results might even be acceptable. But most patients know next to nothing about such matters and have little incentive to find out. In this atmosphere of ignorance, a fee-for-service system can reward doctors for acting in ways quite contrary to the public interest.

Because most physicians are paid according to the number of services they perform, they can increase their income by recommending more operations, tests, and other procedures than their patients really need. Such procedures are increasingly easy to justify now that malpractice suits have become so common and doctors must defend themselves against charges of failing to do all they could for their patients.

In addition, because doctors make a much larger net return on certain procedures than on others, they have a strong incentive in doubtful cases to recommend the more expensive treatment. As one president of a state medical society put it,

> Suppose a patient comes in complaining of diarrhea. If I do a colonoscopy examination, many third-party payers will readily pay nearly $400. That is ten times the forty dollars I might receive if I just talked with the patient to find out what he was doing that was causing the diarrhea. Yet, from the point of view of his health, listening might be a better way for me to spend the hour.[17]

Under prevailing reimbursement practices, even primary care physicians can increase their incomes substantially by recommending more tests and diagnostic procedures than their patients need.[18]

A final set of perverse incentives exists because so few states prohibit physicians from engaging in obvious conflicts of interest. Most states do not prevent doctors from referring their patients to laboratories, diagnostic facilities, or even hospitals in which they have a financial interest. Some states do not yet bar kickbacks from hospitals or from other physicians in return for referring patients for treatment. Pharmaceutical firms routinely offer physicians gifts or trips to exotic vacation spas in the hope that they will prescribe the company's products. In almost all states, companies can offer doctors the chance to sell drugs to their patients at a tidy markup and thus increase their incomes by $50,000, $60,000, or even more.[19]

Most doctors undoubtedly have a sincere desire to serve their patients and will not deliberately recommend needless tests, prescribe expensive drugs, or perform unnecessary work simply to make money. But even conscientious physicians are constantly faced with situations where medical opinion is divided and the proper treatment is unclear. In such situations, it is plainly unwise to surround them with choices that are artificially skewed so that some alternatives are much more lucrative than others.

Considerable evidence suggests that these loaded choices have in fact resulted in unneeded or excessively expensive treatment. That is undoubtedly one reason why many kinds of operations—such as coronary bypass surgery, hysterectomies, and prostatectomies—are performed much more frequently in America than in Europe (with no demonstrable effect on longevity or good health).[20] It likewise has something to do with the fact that health care organizations that pay their doctors in ways that avoid these perverse incentives have achieved savings amounting to 25 percent or more.[21] In these circumstances, there is good reason to look for other ways of paying doctors that reinforce rather than undermine sound, cost-effective medical practice.

SEARCHING FOR REFORM

By now, the system of health care in the United States has achieved the dubious distinction of arousing almost everyone's displeasure. Our expenditures have grown to consume over 14 percent of the gross national product, up from only 5.2 percent in 1960. By comparison, health care costs in 1990 amounted to only 9.3 percent of GNP in Canada, 8.6 percent in Germany, 6.7 percent in Japan, and 6 percent in Great Britain. Spiraling costs have severely burdened the treasuries of the federal as well as state governments. Medical expenses, and who should pay for them, have become a leading cause of strikes and labor disputes. Doctors are annoyed by all the administrative burdens and intrusions that result as hospitals, insurance companies, and employers struggle to hold down costs, avoid improper charges, and decide who should pay the bill. The public suffers because America spends more money on health care than other countries but still leaves over 35 million of its citizens uninsured. With all these problems, the search for a better system has become increasingly urgent. Americans now consider health care reform among the most important issues facing the country, and President Clinton is making an all-out effort to perform radical surgery on our current system.

In casting about for ways to improve upon the status quo, most authorities on the subject devote little time to the subject of doctors' incomes. If the topic is mentioned at all, commentators tend to dismiss it as having only minor significance. Because doctors' total net earnings amount to only $90 billion per year in a $900 billion industry, they can seem rather insignificant. Even if physicians' incomes could be cut by one-third, experts observe, the savings would be swallowed up by a single year's increase in the nation's health bill.

Such reasoning is vulnerable on several grounds. Although the gains from reducing doctors' incomes are limited, lowering the relative earnings of physicians to the levels commonly found in other industrialized societies could lead to savings of up to $20 billion per year, and $20 billion is no paltry sum. Unlike most other reductions, these savings are not a one-shot affair, for doctors' incomes under our fee-for-service system keep on rising faster than the cost of living year after year. Moreover, these direct gains are not the only reason for paying attention to doctors' earnings. Perverse incentives created by fee-for-service billing lead to unnecessary procedures and hence unnecessary costs. To the extent that large differences in earnings contribute to the high proportion of medical specialists, they add still more to our total health bill.

It is true, of course, that advances in technology and the aging of the population are more significant factors than doctors' fees in causing health costs to rise.[22] But aging is an inexorable process for which no one can be blamed, and many technological improvements are well worth having despite their added cost. Hence, excessive earnings constitute a much larger portion of the *unjustified* costs of medical care.

In the end, we must remember that the causes of bloated costs are multiple. In all likelihood, a successful strategy to contain health care bills will require efforts to curb a long list of different items. If we pass too lightly over problems as substantial as doctors' incomes, we are unlikely ever to get the job done.

One obvious way to try to restrain physicians' earnings is to limit the fees they charge. In fact, the federal government has been moving for several years to assume greater control over Medicare fees and has recently taken a major step in that direction. No longer will Washington base its payments on the usual and appropriate fee for the doctor and the area in question. Instead, Congress has approved a Medicare fee schedule that fixes the maximum amounts doctors can bill for their services. The new schedule is based on the nature and amount of work doctors perform in each medical service and procedure relative to others. The net result is a considerable shift in the overall fee structure. If all goes according to plan, primary care physicians and others who spend much of their time with patients will earn relatively more per procedure, while surgeons and others who specialize in hospital-based procedures will receive considerably less.

The new policy continues a trend toward placing specific limits on physicians' fees under Medicare. One can appreciate the motives behind the government's action. If Washington pays most of the medical bills for the elderly, setting maximum prices must seem better than leaving doctors free to charge their customary amounts. Yet fixing prices, whatever form it takes, is an extremely difficult process. The new fee schedule is no exception to the rule. A Harvard team worked on the problem for years, investigating scores of separate procedures.[23] With the help of interviews backed by advisory panels of doctors, the Harvard investigators inquired into the training, time, technical skill, mental effort, judgment, physical labor, and stress involved in carrying out each procedure. The team then assigned relative weights to these disparate items and converted them into a total number of points. Thereafter, government officials decided how to translate the points into overall dollar amounts. Overhead costs—office, equipment, malpractice premiums, and the like—were subsequently added to produce a total allowable fee.*

This intricate task does not come to an end when the government (or private insurer) has announced its fee schedule. Technology, experience, and new knowledge constantly change the ways in which doctors perform their work and often affect the amount of time and skill required. It is the failure to take account of such changes that has allowed many doctors to earn a fortune doing procedures at prices set years before, when the work was much more difficult and time-consuming. Hence, fee schedules need constant review and adaptation. Such revisions require much time and effort. Moreover, they must take place not in quiet rooms filled with experts but in a politically charged environment where efforts

* Even this complicated procedure left out much information that should ideally enter into an estimate of how much a procedure is worth. For example, how to account for the quality of work performed. Or the value of the service performed. How to reflect unusual complications that arise in carrying out an operation. In addition, the government did not correctly measure practice costs, with the result that specialists continue to receive more than their actual expenses while primary care physicians receive less. See Hsiao, Dunn, and Verrilli, "Assessing the Implementation of Physician-Payment Reform," *New England Journal of Medicine,* 328 (1993): 928.

are constantly made to influence the outcome for the benefit of one interested group after another.

Once the fees are set, many doctors will try hard to manipulate them to their financial advantage. Medical societies regularly present seminars on how to "unbundle" procedures by charging separately for different parts to increase total Medicare fees. Another common topic is the fine art of reclassifying procedures into categories that allow higher charges. These tactics have become so intricate that hundreds of consultants offer their services to doctors for a percentage of any added amounts they can extract from the government. Not all of this maneuvering may even be legal. Already, a Pennsylvania investigation found that 20 percent of all doctors billing the government for Medicare payments under the new fee schedule had inflated their charges improperly.[24]

Another way doctors can get around fee limits is to perform more tests and more operations when their need is debatable. This is what critics allege took place in 1973 and 1974 after President Nixon imposed a freeze on Medicare payments. In fixing the current fee schedule, therefore, the government anticipated this reaction by deliberately reducing its authorized fees to offset the added services that doctors were expected to perform. As a further restraint on the growth of services, Washington will set a target amount each year that it plans to spend on doctors' fees under Medicare. If the amount is exceeded, the target figure for the following year will be reduced accordingly. In this way, the government hopes that medical societies will be moved to persuade their members not to perform unnecessary services, because those who do so will reduce the total sum available for doctors as a whole. In addition, the government plans to develop and publicize protocols of appropriate care that will help to identify individual practitioners who seem to be giving more services, or more expensive services, than their patients actually require.

How the new policy will work in practice is still unknown. It will clearly lead to more bureaucracy and will provoke all of the political pressures that arise whenever the government acts directly to limit anything as sensitive as compensation. More important, its potential as a strategy for curbing costs will be limited by the fact that Medicare is only a piece of the larger patchwork of plans and programs that make up the American health care system. If private health insurers do not adopt the government's fees, doctors may react to substantial cuts by shifting costs to the private sector or even by refusing to accept Medicare patients, as some have already done in New York City in response to the new schedule. Whatever health plans do, physicians may perform more services for patients who are not covered by Medicare and hence are not subject to the cap on total expenditures. Because these compensatory tactics are available, it is not yet clear how much the government will accomplish in holding down the total cost of doctors' services, even if it manages to insulate its own programs from debilitating political compromises.

The government could avoid many of these problems if it were to establish a national system in which the state paid for all health care and subjected doctors to fee schedules for all or most of their work. Under such a system, the government could either negotiate a schedule directly with doctors and their specialty groups or delegate this task to some other organization, as Germany and Holland have done.[25] In either case, Congress could determine each year how much money the nation would spend on health care and how much of that total would go to compensate doctors. Negotiations could then take place to adjust the fees for different procedures and specialties within this overall limit. Congress would reduce appropriations in subsequent years to offset any overruns caused by a greater-than-anticipated volume of services.

By organizing the health care system in this fashion, the government could limit costs more effectively, at least in theory. If fees were carefully set and periodically updated, doctors would no longer have an incentive to favor lucrative procedures. Expenditure caps would keep practitioners from pushing up costs by performing unnecessary services. If the government managed to stick to its guns and insist upon a moderate yearly growth in total expenditures, it would force the medical profession to curb its fees and find some way to prevent individual members from padding their incomes with unnecessary work. In these ways, a national system of health care, however cumbersome, would seek to address all the shortcomings of our current methods of compensation.

A national system, of course, is not a likely possibility for the United States, at least for the time being. Skeptics are not convinced that the government is strong enough to resist the powerful pressures for expanded services and new technology that work to drive up costs. Insurance companies would not take kindly to the loss of an important part of their business. Much popular resistance might develop once voters realized how much their taxes would have to rise to finance the new program (even though the increases would be largely offset by reductions in the payments made to private insurance plans). For all these reasons, despite the enthusiasm of Canadians for their more centralized system, similar proposals have received little attention in the current debate over health care reform. Instead, advocates of change have been more inclined to look for other remedies that rely more on competition and market forces to restrain costs.

MANAGED COMPETITION

In recent years, growing numbers of people have enrolled in prepaid plans or health maintenance organizations (HMOs) to take care of their medical needs. Many of these entities pay doctors on a fee-for-service basis but closely monitor the work of participating physicians to keep them from performing unnecessary services. Other prepaid plans do not use fee-for-service but simply employ physicians on a salaried basis. In either case, the incentives shift radically. No longer can the physician count on earning more money by performing more work; any inclination on the part of traditional fee-for-service doctors to order too much care is now substantially restrained.

It has become reasonably clear that HMOs do indeed manage to keep down costs by changing the manner of compensating their physicians. On average, plans that pay their doctors on a salary basis manage to lower expenses by anywhere from 10 percent to 40 percent, mainly by reducing the amount of hospitalization.*[26] A careful experiment to ensure that the HMO patient population was equivalent to that of traditional fee-for-service providers found that overall costs were still 25 percent lower in the health maintenance organization.[27]

Whatever the precise method that HMOs use to pay their physicians, competition among rival plans forces them to try to keep

* Once these economies have been made, however, HMO costs move up at approximately the same rates as expenditures made under other forms of organization and payment.

their physicians from providing unnecessary services. Some critics even worry that HMOs may be *too* successful in this respect. Having removed the temptation to perform too many services, competition may substitute a new pressure to perform too few. Instead of worrying over the excessive sums they pay for medical care, HMO members may begin to fear that doctors are skimping on important tests or avoiding needed procedures to allow their health plans to save money.

Fortunately, a number of forces help to counteract this danger. Most doctors are far too conscientious to take chances with their patients' health by failing to perform needed services. In the setting of a prepaid plan, peer pressures will also help to keep such neglect from occurring. A specialist who fails to order a necessary test may hear about it from the primary care physician in charge of the patient. A general practitioner who does not take proper precautions with an expectant mother may be questioned by an obstetrician colleague. In addition, because most members will remain in the same plan for a period of years, prepaid plans also have a built-in incentive not to overlook procedures now that could lead to health problems with greater costs at a later time. Beyond these safeguards, the ever-present threat of a malpractice suit serves as an ultimate check against irresponsible behavior by physicians.

For these or other reasons, careful studies of HMOs have not revealed any tendency to offer a lesser quality of health care than patients receive in other settings.[28] To cut costs still further, however, many HMOs have devised additional incentives to encourage frugality on the part of their medical staff. Some of these techniques have nothing to do with money. For example, an HMO may organize itself so that a primary care physician acts as gatekeeper and must approve the referral of any patient to a specialist. Other HMOs have regular staff meetings to discuss individual cases or require second opinions whenever a member physician recommends an expensive treatment, especially one involving hospitalization.[29]

Increasingly, however, HMOs have also introduced financial incentives to hold down costs.[30] At times, the incentives are constructed on a group basis. The entire staff, or some subgroup within it, will have a portion of their compensation withheld until the end of the year and will forfeit all or part of this amount if the plan runs a deficit. In other HMOs, individual physicians pay a penalty if their performance (in terms of tests ordered or the hospitalization rates of their patients) exceeds group norms. Conversely, bonuses may go either to the entire staff or to individual members if their performance exceeds expectations.

Financial inducements of this kind raise troubling questions. If such incentives actually affect physician behavior, as HMO administrators seem to believe, it is not clear that they will be beneficial.* We do not yet know how frugal we wish to be in treating patients—or, to be more precise, where we would ideally strike the balance between too many services and too few. As a result, there is a risk that health maintenance organizations may eventually go so far in creating incentives to reduce care that they will threaten the well-being of their patients.

In view of these uncertainties, Congress has probably acted wisely in prohibiting such incentives by HMOs that accept Medicare patients. If we are not sure about the proper level of service to provide, it is no more prudent to give bonuses for reducing care than it is to allow doctors to earn additional fees for carrying out more procedures. The best course would be to encourage a process in which physicians can work together with the aid of relevant information to reach a more enlightened understanding of how much care is appropriate.

All things considered, the prepaid plan (without bonuses for cutting costs) seems to offer the most promising setting in which to nurture such a process. Groups of physicians working together can pool experience and learn from one another. Informed by data culled from a fixed patient population, they would seem to have the greatest chance of learning from experience how to strike the appropriate balance between too much care and too little.

Heartened by these prospects, some experts have urged the government to reform the entire health care system by organizing it

* At least one study failed to discover any significant reduction in hospitalization or in the number of patient visits when doctors faced the possibility of paying penalties or earning bonuses for their performance. Alan Hillman, Mark Pauly, and Joseph Kerstein, "How Do Financial Incentives Affect Physicians' Clinical Decisions and the Performance of Health Maintenance Organizations?" *New England Journal of Medicine*, 321 (1989): 93. Still, the growth of these incentive schemes suggests that many managers of HMOs at least *think* they are effective.

around a broad array of HMOs and other health plans.[31] Under such schemes, all families and single individuals would be assigned to one of a number of newly created purchasing organizations that would negotiate with existing health plans to select a set of providers with suitable plans at reasonable prices from which their members could choose. The power of large, well-financed purchasing agents, coupled with competition among the plans, would generate the necessary pressure to hold down costs.

Various features would be added to protect individual patients. To ensure universal coverage, the government would subsidize the premiums for those who could not afford to join. To avoid inadequate coverage, each plan would have to offer a minimum array of services and observe a limit on the dollar amount of deductibles their members would be required to pay. To aid individuals and their purchasing representatives in choosing an appropriate plan, each provider would have to publish adequate information about its services, benefits, and past record.

What effect would a system of managed competition have on physicians' earnings? No one really knows. Proponents insist that competition among rival health plans will exert pressure to hold down compensation. How effective this process will actually be, however, is far from certain. In some respects, managed competition resembles the situation in corporate law where large firms compete for the business of major companies. Thus far, though such competition has doubtless helped to hold down legal fees, it has not yet prevented established firms and their partners from continuing to earn very large sums each year.

Will managed competition help to restore a healthier balance between the earnings of specialists and the incomes of primary care physicians? In principle, if costs can be kept down by hiring more primary care doctors and fewer specialists, competition will cause the health plans to bid up the salaries of the former while reducing the numbers and the incomes of the latter. How well this process will work in practice is again uncertain, because earnings are only one factor—and probably not the most important one at that—in causing so many medical students to choose a specialty other than family practice or general internal medicine.

As this book went to press, President Clinton was completing a massive review of the health care system that seemed likely to culminate in proposals for a national program of managed competition. Proposals of this kind raise a number of questions that are difficult to answer. Will competition suffice to hold down total health care costs without some sort of mandatory cap on total expenditures? If not, will such a cap lead eventually to more and more elaborate price controls? Can managed competition succeed without finding a way to control the spread of costly technology? Can it work in rural areas that cannot support more than a single health care provider? Armed with such questions, opponents will counter with a host of objections on behalf of doctors fearful of losing their autonomy, patients fearful of losing their personal physician, and small business owners fearful of being required to assume new costs on behalf of their employees.

At this juncture, it is anyone's guess whether managed competition will provide a permanent solution to the nation's health care woes or whether America will eventually move to a national plan similar to Canada's. Regardless of which method ultimately prevails, both approaches attack the central problems of compensation, and either would represent a distinct improvement over the status quo. As we have observed, our current system is seriously flawed. Many doctors continue to be grossly overpaid, while most receive substantially more than one would expect under conditions of genuine competition. The large, persistent oversupply of medical school applicants and the ability of other nations to attract enough physicians with income levels well below ours suggest that most doctors earn much more than the market can justify. Existing patterns of compensation further inflate medical costs by helping to attract too many specialists and by creating perverse incentives that encourage unnecessary services and favor more expensive over less expensive medical procedures.

The present system of compensation is so deeply rooted and its effects so deeply ingrained that the results will not be eradicated for decades, if ever. The practical question, therefore, is not whether we can achieve perfection but whether Washington can begin to move in the right direction by taking steps to restrain the most excessive incomes while giving physicians a more rational set of incentives. On this score, there is room for guarded optimism, if only because the defects of our current system are so glaring and so burdensome that the public (including business) is crying for relief.

The fate of President Clinton's plan is still unknown, and even if it prevails, its eventual success in solving the problems of the health care system is impossible to predict. Still, the odds of making some significant progress seem considerably brighter now than they have been for many years.

CHAPTER 7
LAWYERS

The universe of lawyers is made up of several worlds—the world of large firms, of corporate legal staffs, of public interest advocates, of government law offices, of small partnerships and lawyers practicing on their own. The most populous of these domains is the preserve of solo practitioners and tiny firms. There, attorneys representing individuals or small businesses devote their skills to resolving the innumerable controversies that crop up in families, work places, hospitals, roadways, and every other location in which human beings interact.[1]

EARNINGS IN THE REALM OF PLAINTIFFS' LITIGATION

Many of the practitioners in this world make their living representing individuals with a claim against another person, a government agency, or a business firm. Their cases may involve allegations of negligence in an automobile accident, a charge of employment discrimination, a wrongful eviction by a landlord, a claim of carelessness on the part of a doctor, a possible violation of occupational health and safety laws, or a defective product that causes injury. Many of the claimants seeking redress have little money to pay lawyers' fees and litigation costs. Without some form of aid, they would have no means of gaining access to the courts.

Different countries have solved this problem in different ways. The United States is virtually unique in adopting a device known as the contingent fee. Under the typical contingent fee arrangement, lawyers will agree to take a promising case on the understanding that they will charge nothing for their services if the case is lost but will take one-third or even one-half of any sums they gain for their client by negotiating a voluntary settlement from the offending party or by winning a damage award through litigation in court. In this way, claimants of modest means can avoid any risk of losing money in the event that their legal proceeding fails. At the same time, they can keep at least a substantial share of any damages they win if their suit prevails.

Although the contingent fee was originally designed to help people of limited means, its uses have spread more widely. As judges have allowed punitive damages and created new remedies for such injuries as "pain and suffering," the sums of money retrievable in personal injury cases have grown significantly. Even more lucrative are class action suits where hundreds or even thousands of potential claimants join in a single proceeding with the possibility of cumulative damage awards of awesome proportions. The lure of obtaining a fraction of such handsome sums has caused most trial lawyers to insist on contingent fee arrangements, even if their clients can afford to pay the normal hourly rate. In recent years, major law firms have also begun to accept cases on a contingent basis, something almost unheard of only a few years ago.

The world of plaintiffs' litigation would seem competitive enough to satisfy the most zealous of free market economists. In most cities, the yellow pages are packed with the names of lawyers eager to take any promising claim that comes along. On freeways such as the road from Santa Fe to Albuquerque, billboard after billboard flashes the names and pictures of smiling attorneys specializing in personal injury work, criminal cases, or divorce proceedings. Curiously, however, the crowded market for legal services turns out to work quite differently from anything described in an economics textbook.

Under the classic conditions of perfect competition, individuals ready to bring suit would know everything about the abilities of all the lawyers who might represent them. Attorneys would not be able to insist on a standard percentage of all moneys gained from taking such cases. Instead, they would bargain with potential clients and arrive at a percentage arrangement that would vary with the strength of the complaint and the size of the potential settlement or court award. Claimants with a powerful case for winning a large amount of money could demand that a lawyer accept a small percentage of the award, while plaintiffs with weaker claims and smaller sums at stake would have to share more equally.

This is not what occurs in real life. Most potential clients know very few lawyers and have no way of judging their abilities. They seek out particular attorneys either because they happen to know them or have a friend who knows them or because they have heard their advertisements over the radio or read about them in the newspaper. There is little bargaining over the terms of the contingent fee. Most plaintiffs do not know whether they have a strong case, and rare is the lawyer who will inform them (and agree to a lower percentage of the take) when they happen to have an extremely high probability of winning. In most instances, therefore, the contingent fee is a standard rate that seldom varies with the size of a likely settlement or the odds of prevailing in court.

In these circumstances, the earnings of trial attorneys hardly correspond with what one would expect from a normal competitive market. Some do extremely well because they are lucky enough to fall heir to a few strong cases with large amounts at stake. Some may be adept at ignoring the code of ethics by organizing ambulance chasers who swarm around accidents and line up potential clients for a small fee. Still others succeed because they can find a client willing to bring a class action on behalf of a large group of people who have a legal claim but have not yet tried to bring suit. Many attorneys labor endless hours and do a skillful job only to lose a closely contested case that was not strong enough to begin with. Others win a large settlement with little effort either because the opposing counsel is inept, or because it is cheaper to settle than to litigate, or because the company they are suing fears that the facts involved may tempt a judge to establish an awkward precedent. Instead of perfect competition, then, the world of plaintiffs' litigation is a much more haphazard place where ignorance and luck play prominent roles in shaping the fortunes of attorneys.

Of course, there are famous plaintiffs' lawyers who preside over a stable of associates and succeed, year in and year out, in earning incomes of more than $1 million. Because of their reputation, these attorneys are asked to take many more cases than they can handle. As a result, they can pick and choose more carefully and hence confine their efforts to claims that are likely to produce big verdicts or generous settlements. In this way, they can exploit the rigid contingent fee structure and reap huge rewards for the effort they expend.

Exactly what kind of ability they possess to achieve this enviable position is a difficult question to answer. Energy, intelligence, ingenuity, and negotiating skills presumably play a role. According to one trial lawyer, "Personal injury trial work involves a sixth sense, an intuitive 'feel' of the emotion in a courtroom, which transcends logic and legal research. The really big stars are those who have that sensitivity to an extraordinary degree, and no years of school can ever teach it."[2]

It is impossible to prove how important these skills really are, because no one knows how much they affect the outcome of a trial. There are no box scores that record the batting averages of personal injury lawyers. Such statistics would be meaningless anyway, as a good record may reflect the power to choose strong cases rather than a capacity to win claims that other attorneys would lose. Even if some successful lawyers do have a special talent for coming out on top, it is not clear how much society should wish to reward this capacity. The aim of the law is to do justice by arriving at the truth, not to organize forensic duels in which the prizes go to those most skillful in playing on the emotions of lay juries. For all these reasons, the lavish earnings of successful plaintiffs' lawyers find but a tenuous and uncertain justification either in the marketplace or in public policy.

THE CONTINGENT FEE AS AN INCENTIVE

The contingent fee is one of the oldest forms of performance pay in America. The reason for permitting lawyers to charge plaintiffs only when they win is not merely to open the courts to people of modest means but to inspire attorneys to do their utmost for their client in order to share in a settlement or award. Unlike the corporate CEO, plaintiffs' lawyers do not earn a handsome salary when they lose. At times, they even have to pay out-of-pocket costs.

Attorneys are not the only professionals compensated in this manner. Unless they are famous enough to be paid simply for showing up, golf and tennis pros must do well or leave tournaments empty-handed. Unlike Jack Nicklaus or Jennifer Capriati, however, lawyers who are too strongly motivated to win can do a lot of mischief. They may bring insubstantial suits if there is a chance of sharing a large award. They may harass defendants with endless requests for documents and interrogatories to extract a settlement. They may indulge in questionable tactics to manipulate juries, or even manufacture evidence to inflate the amount of damages. As Deborah Rhode observes, "Reported cases and surveys reveal a striking incidence of overly zealous representation ranging from garden variety discovery abuse to suppression of evidence and complicity in fraud or perjury."[3] Granted such conduct can occur without contingent fees. Nevertheless, when lawyers get paid only if they win, the incentives to behave unprofessionally, if that is what it takes to succeed, are clearly very strong.

The pathologies of unbridled motivation sometimes reach extraordinary levels. After serious accidents, insurance adjusters often hurry to settle claims for modest sums before the victims know their rights, while ambulance chasers try to get there first to persuade the injured party to seek an attorney. In the words of law professor Jeffrey O'Connell, "Adjusters, trying to get a settlement, and chasers trying to sign-up the victim for their lawyers, work frantically, using stratagems and spoiler tactics, even to the point of climbing hospital fire escapes or otherwise sneaking into the hospital rooms to a patient's bedside as soon as he has recovered sufficiently to write his name."[4] Even fraudulent claims are not unknown. According to Charles Ward, a former Regional Director of the Insurance Crime Prevention Institute, lawyers have been the "masterminds behind schemes to stage phony accidents and inflate or falsify outright medical bills or other claims."[5]

In addition to encouraging questionable practices, contingent fees create incentives that do not necessarily match the needs of the client. Occasionally, it will serve a lawyer's interest to talk clients into continuing a suit in hopes of a larger reward even though they would be better advised to settle immediately for a definite amount. More often, it is the lawyer who wants to accept a quick settlement after a minimum of effort even though the client might do better by persevering in search of a larger recovery.[6]

Although contingent fees help many clients of modest means to bring a lawsuit, the process hardly succeeds in providing a just, effective way of compensating the victims of negligence. One study of medical malpractice revealed that half of the lawsuits leading to a monetary recovery were probably without merit.[7] It is even more striking how few individuals with deserving claims receive anything at all. A major investigation of malpractice cases discovered that only one in every eight or ten meritorious claims ever reaches a lawyer, and only half of these result in any payment of money to the victim.[8] Still another report, this one a study by the Rand Corporation of disabling injuries, found that 81 percent of the injured parties took no action at all while only 7 percent ever filed a lawsuit.[9] Of the settlements and damage awards actually paid, moreover, little more than half the money, if that, typically goes to the plaintiff; the remainder is eaten up by legal fees and other costs.

POSSIBLE REMEDIES

Because the current system of compensating accident victims seems so cumbersome, costly, and erratic, many reformers have urged greater use of no-fault plans similar to those that some states have enacted in the field of automobile accidents.[10] Under these schemes, insurance companies make prompt payments to all accident victims, without having to litigate issues of fault, in amounts sufficient to cover tangible losses such as medical care, property damage, and lost wages. Typically, the victim cannot recover for intangible losses such as pain and suffering. The money saved by avoiding litigation costs, lawyers' fees, and pain and suffering awards enables no-fault plans to pay all victims at a cost lower than that of conventional insurance plans operating within a traditional tort law system. By offering speedy payments to all injured parties without the expense and delay of litigation, no-fault insurance promises to benefit victims, premium-payers, and insurance companies as well.

The group that stands to lose the most from no-fault legislation is the trial bar (which earns more than $1 billion a year in automobile accident fees alone). Over the years, therefore, trial lawyers have fought tenaciously and successfully against the no-fault system. They have managed to persuade legislators to limit and dilute most no-fault plans in the auto accident field by such devices as allowing lawsuits for claims over a modest amount or by making the purchase of no-fault insurance optional. By now their determined opposition has dimmed much of the enthusiasm for trying adaptations of the no-fault concept in new areas, such as medical malpractice or product liability cases.

Even if no-fault were to spread, it is suitable only for certain types of accidents. Some other method would be needed to curb excessive contingent fees in other fields of litigation. The obvious alternative would be to impose some sort of direct control over contingent fees to limit the amount lawyers could receive. Some jurisdictions have already moved in this direction by imposing a sliding scale in which the percentage of the damages lawyers can collect diminishes as the size of the award increases. While superficially attractive, such methods suffer from difficulties similar to those that result from all attempts to place a ceiling on excessive incomes. For example, most studies of accident litigation have concluded, contrary to popular impressions, that the existing system overcompensates those who suffer minor accidents but undercompensates the seriously injured. If this is so, reducing lawyers' incentives to prosecute big cases vigorously will hardly improve matters.

Moreover, sliding scales only strike at one cause of lucrative fees. They do nothing to prevent lawyers with strong cases from pocketing their share of a large settlement without having to devote much time or skill. To prevent these windfalls would require much more extensive judicial oversight of the fee system and might embroil judges in detailed inquiries into the amounts of work actually performed in winning large awards. It is far from clear that avoiding excessive fees would be worth the added time and cost of forcing heavily burdened judges to conduct such investigations.

Because the compelling virtue of the contingent fee is to make legal services available to those who cannot afford a lawyer, a more ambitious possibility would be to substitute some better means of providing legal representation to persons of modest means. Enterprising lawyers or entrepreneurs could establish prepaid legal plans for people of moderate incomes. In order to reach individuals too poor to afford such a plan, Congress could increase the funding for poverty law offices so that all indigent people could obtain legal help. With these reforms in place, the justification for contingent fees would disappear.

Such remedies are intriguing. In the long run, they may provide a desirable solution. In the short run, however, neither of them seems realistic. Prepaid legal plans have not proved widely popular with the public. As for increased funding for legal services, the prospects are impossibly bleak in this chilly fiscal climate. For the time being, then, the lawsuit lottery seems destined to continue, making some lawyers rich while holding forth to all attorneys the glittering prospect of a jackpot gained from falling heir to a big class-action suit or a lucrative personal injury case.

EARNINGS IN LARGE LAW FIRMS

Of the many worlds of legal practice, the most prosperous by far is the world of large elite firms that serve the highly specialized needs of corporations and other important institutions. Here are to be found the more successful graduates from the better law schools spending their days (and many nights) working on complex proceedings involving commercial law, the federal tax code, antitrust, securities regulation, environmental litigation, and other forms of legal ordering.

In the past twenty years, large law firms have become as competitive and meritocratic as professional organizations anywhere. They vie relentlessly with one another for business and work very hard at trying to persuade the best students from the leading law schools to join them as associates. Only rarely does one encounter the blatant prejudices that once caused leading firms to refuse to hire Jews and blacks and to refrain from even interviewing women. Good law firms prosper by selling their services to corporate legal staffs. In that market, success usually requires more than graduating from the right prep school or joining the proper clubs.

In view of the keen competition for new business, one might think that the incomes partners earn must be close to the competitive ideal. Like personal injury lawyers, however, leading firms benefit from unusual circumstances that cause their earnings to rise above the levels one would expect from a truly competitive market.

Such firms sell their services under a special set of conditions. The amounts they charge are typically only a tiny fraction of the annual budget of a medium to large company. They are also very small in relation to the amounts of money at stake in the kinds of big cases in which large elite law firms specialize. Moreover, when they negotiate a fee, neither the lawyers nor their clients can estimate precisely how much the total charge will be. Firms can quote hourly *rates* for the services of their members. But they will rarely know how many hours of lawyers' work will be needed to defend a lawsuit or conduct a complex negotiation.

Most corporations employ their own legal staff to take care of routine cases. They turn to the elite firms principally to deal with important or highly specialized cases. When a corporation chooses a law firm, therefore, price is seldom the dominant consideration. Much more important is the quality of the legal work. Once a company decides on the best lawyer and firm for its purpose, it will seldom look elsewhere because of a failure to agree on the hourly fee.

When times are good in such a market, elite firms can find plenty of opportunities to work continuously at rates ample enough to provide a handsome living for the partners. On occasion, a firm may be fortunate enough to attract cases in which the stakes are so high that even outlandish rates go unquestioned. The wave of mergers and acquisitions in the 1980s offered just such an opportunity, and the firms that managed to capture a share of this business did extraordinarily well. Fees of several millions of dollars for a few weeks of work were not unknown.

When business slows, partners have a more difficult time maintaining their earnings. Corporations become more aggressive in trying to control costs. Even so, the best response may not be to lower rates. Because price is not the prime consideration for companies choosing a law firm, cutting hourly rates may not win new clients. Instead, it may signal inferior quality and ultimately scare away more business than it attracts.

Eventually, of course, if hard times persist, a law firm will have to do something. It may even agree to lower its rates if important clients insist. But there are other ways to respond when the volume of work diminishes. Lawyers can keep busy by taking the time to research legal issues a bit more thoroughly or by deciding to interview a few more witnesses in preparing a case. Because these are matters of professional judgment, it will be difficult for clients to protest as long as the work performed remains within reasonable limits. Alternatively, a firm may intensify its efforts to gain new business, perhaps by impressing prospective clients with its commitment to minimize the total number of billable hours. Even if all these strategies fail and business continues to sag, a firm may well respond not by reducing hourly rates but by letting people go—younger associates and paralegals first, then less productive partners, if need be. For the remaining partners, therefore, earnings may well remain high despite a decline in the amount of work.

Partners also benefit from being able to charge much more for the work of their experienced associates than the cost of the salary they pay these younger colleagues (plus a proportionate share of the overhead). This is not what one would expect in a truly competitive market. According to the theory of marginal productivity, employees should receive up to the full value of the added output they produce. Under truly competitive conditions, therefore, law firms would hire more and more associates until the salaries they had to pay equaled the net incremental revenues that their young lawyers gained for the firm. Yet that is not what seems to occur. Salaries for associates did move up more rapidly in the 1980s than the profits-per-partner in most large firms. In exchange, however, firms required their younger colleagues to work much harder and thereby charge more billable hours. As a result, total billings for experienced associates remained far above the salaries these younger attorneys earned for their services, even after making full allowance for overhead costs.

It is not entirely clear why firms do not bid up the price of new associates even further in an effort to take the ablest candidates away from their competitors. Probably, hiring partners in the same city know that any one firm would have to raise its starting salary substantially to sway potential recruits and that such tactics would be swiftly matched by competitors so that all firms would be worse off. As a result, competition for the best young lawyers usually takes the form of aggressive recruiting and attractive summer programs for law students rather than a rapid escalation of salary offers. Sharp increases in starting salaries do occasionally take place. But these jumps typically occur when leading firms begin to face competition for the best recent graduates from sources outside the legal profession. Thus, when Cravath, Swaine & Moore shocked its fellow firms by a very large increase in starting salaries in 1986, it gave as a reason the fear that more and more of the most outstanding law school students were taking jobs with consulting organizations and investment banking firms. Because threats of this kind seem to occur infrequently, law firms can hold salaries well below billing rates to clients, leaving a handsome margin of profit for the partners.

One final question remains in seeking to understand why law firm incomes behave as they do. A remarkable feature of the 1970s and 1980s was the ability of elite firms to prosper while other segments of the bar saw their earnings stagnate or decline. How did these firms manage to boost their incomes so handsomely without attracting the competition that could force them to price their services more competitively?

One can only speculate about the answer. The most likely explanation is that the elite were partially insulated from competition because of the problems new firms encounter in becoming sufficiently well known and trusted to gain the business they need to survive. In theory, ambitious lawyers in less prosperous firms would take note of the high hourly rates and profits of the leading firms and begin to offer their services at substantially reduced rates. With the growing influx of talent entering the legal profession since the late 1960s, many of these lawyers would presumably have the raw ability to serve corporate clients well. Nevertheless, it would be extremely difficult for the new entrants to obtain enough corporate business to sustain a highly specialized elite practice. How could prospective clients judge their abilities? What track record would they have on which to make an adequate appraisal? In this way, ignorance and lack of experience narrow the field and create barriers that prevent competition from attacking established firms with full force.

New firms do emerge periodically (just as old ones disappear through merger). Almost invariably, however, such partnerships are created by lawyers from leading firms who are disgruntled with their situation and anxious to strike out on their own. These new entrants do add to the competition. But accustomed as they are to the ways of large firms, they are unlikely to enter the field by offering their services at cut-rate prices. Tactics of this sort might signal a lack of quality and would hardly satisfy the ambitions of most attorneys who leave established firms. Rather, lawyers who break away will typically rely on taking with them a number of clients with whom they already have close relations and who will continue to pay the customary fees. As a result, new firms do not pose the same kind of threat to prevailing rates that economists have in mind when they describe the impact of an influx of blue collar workers on an industry with unusually high wages. That is why the largest law firms managed to boost their real incomes by anywhere from 20 to 100 percent in the 1970s and 1980s even as the earnings of most other lawyers hardly increased at all.

INCENTIVES IN LARGE LAW FIRMS

In almost every large firm, the normal way to bill for services is to charge according to the time spent on each client's case. Typically, lawyers keep track of billable time in units of 15 minutes or less and charge their clients for the number of units they spend at the hourly rates agreed to in advance. In most firms, everyone is under pressure to log impressive numbers of billable hours each year. The share of profits partners receive is typically influenced by the total hours they have billed. Associates are urged to meet targets that often exceed 2,000 hours per year; they doubtless realize that their annual bonus and prospects for promotion will depend to a significant degree on the figures they submit.

Whatever other merits it may have, this system of compensation is hardly calculated to produce optimum efficiency in rendering legal services. As Chief Justice Rehnquist once observed, "If one is expected to bill more than two thousand hours per year, there are bound to be temptations to exaggerate the hours actually put in."[11] To be sure, attorneys with more business than they can handle may have no reason to claim more hours than they actually need to do their work. When business lags, however, temptations arise to pad legal charges.

Some lawyers deliberately inflate their billable hours. At worst, they simply claim more time than they actually spend on the client's case. More often, the techniques are subtler. Attorneys flying across the country may bill one client for travel time even though they spent the hours in flight working on the case of another client, who will also be charged for the same block of time. Lawyers may bill a client for relevant research that was already performed (and charged for) on behalf of a previous client with a similar case. Others may cheat in pettier ways by charging a full quarter-hour unit for a telephone call lasting less than two minutes.[12]

Surveys suggest that only a minority of lawyers will resort to the tactics just described. But greater waste may result, especially in slack periods, from the decisions lawyers make about how much time to spend on their cases. Law practice is filled with judgments of this kind: how many witnesses to interrogate, how much research to perform, how many lawyers to bring to an important meeting, how long to continue discovery proceedings to find information for a possible trial. There are no clear answers to these questions. Unless a firm is overloaded with work, charging by the hour will weight the scales in favor of more exhaustive research, more elaborate discovery, and more attorneys attending meetings. Lawyers themselves concede as much. More than half of the respondents in one survey admitted that hourly billing occasionally or frequently influences lawyers to render services they might not otherwise have performed.[13]

In addition to encouraging too much work, charging by the hour also reduces the incentive to cut costs. It is often possible to perform legal work more efficiently by utilizing computers more extensively or by making more effective use of paralegal personnel. If lawyers stand to gain from increasing the hours they spend, however, their efforts to seek labor-saving devices will hardly rival those of the Ford Motor Company or Xerox.

In recent years, corporations have begun to strike back by making greater efforts to curb unnecessary legal costs. Companies are hiring more and better lawyers of their own to monitor outside counsel. Corporations are scrutinizing legal bills with greater care, even to the point of reviewing expenses during litigation and calling in auditors to examine charges after the fact.

Efforts of this kind are doubtless helping to curb flagrant abuses. They have caused law firms to bill more carefully to avoid the risk of embarrassment or confrontation with a valued client. Firms are less likely today to bring several lawyers to meetings where one would suffice or to spend more time on interrogatories and depositions than they can readily defend. Still, it is difficult for corporate officials to second-guess a litigating attorney on how much research to carry out or how many witnesses to interview. Efforts to monitor expenses too closely run obvious risks of demoralizing outside counsel or costing more in auditor's fees than any savings achieved. In short, cost-conscious clients can do only so much. Despite their efforts, the practice of hourly billing will continue to deter lawyers from performing efficiently. Now that law firms are taking in receipts totaling more than $80 billion per year, the perverse effects of time-based charges will increasingly create a significant problem.

In addition to billing clients, law firms must decide how to distribute their net earnings among their partners. Only recently have large firms come to recognize that the way in which profits are distributed can affect the incentives, and hence the performance, of their members. In the 1960s, and for as long as anyone could remember, most large firms distributed profits among the partners largely on the basis of seniority. Younger members settled for modest returns, secure in the realization that their opportunity for greater rewards would surely come. The new competitive environment of the 1970s put this policy under severe strain.

When aggressive firms sought to expand by hiring young lawyers from other organizations, rigid, seniority-based systems left established partnerships highly vulnerable. As one ambitious associate described the problem, "I earned basically the same as every other associate at my age level. I was doing better work, I had much more responsibility, and much more pressure. I was overworked and I was exploited. Then I looked at the young partners. They weren't earning a hell of a lot more than I was; you had to wait 25 years to see a real share of the money. And I thought, why not take some risks?"[14] Soon after, he jumped ship and joined another firm.

Seniority-based compensation had the further disadvantage of failing to penalize those who preferred not to work quite as hard as their colleagues. In the stable world of the 1950s and 1960s, this problem could be safely ignored to preserve good feeling among the partners. But when aggressive firms began to raid their competitors, and everyone struggled to maximize profits, such tolerance proved too costly. Gradually, more and more firms began to consider changing over to a system that gave greater rewards to the "rainmakers" who brought in new business and to the hardest-working partners who kept the clients satisfied and loyal.[15]

The old ways did not pass without challenge from partners who feared the impact of performance plans on collegiality and morale. No one spoke more eloquently for tradition than Larry Nelson of Milbank, Tweed when he sought to persuade his partners not to abandon the seniority system. "Let me assure you" he said, "reducing the compensation of a [less successful] partner to motivate him does not have the intended effect. Instead, it humiliates him. It destroys his ego and self-confidence. It depresses him. It causes him to brood. It makes it hard for him to concentrate on his work." But, added Nelson, "the greatest loss will be Milbank's willingness to support its partners in fulfilling the special responsibility that I believe lawyers have to the community at large. As our obsession with the almighty dollar grows (an obsession that is mystifying since I am not aware of any partner who could be described as poor), I believe that it will become more and more difficult for partners to fulfill that social responsibility."[16]

Arguments of this kind rarely prevailed for very long. Eventually, compensation by seniority gave way to performance-based rewards, affectionately described in the trade as "You eat what you kill." By 1990, only a handful of firms still clung to the older, more mechanical way of distributing profits.

Despite their popularity, however, performance-based rewards have not fully lived up to expectations. Whereas the new plans were supposed to help firms counter attempts to bid away younger partners, the number of defections appeared to increase. Many of the departures have occurred after squabbles over the proper way to divide the profits.[17] For even if everyone agrees to slice the pie according to performance, there is still room for dispute over what performance means, who really was responsible for bringing in a lucrative new client, and how much to credit the ability to attract business as opposed to successful work with existing clients or time spent mentoring young associates or serving the profession.

Performance-based plans can also weaken loyalty to the firm by making it clear that rewards come chiefly from one's own efforts rather than membership in the organization. Partners soon learn that under a performance plan they do better by enhancing their own reputation rather than promoting the interests of the firm. Often, they will "hoard" clients, avoiding asking other partners to help in ways that might entitle them to a share of the profits. As a result, clients do not always get the attention of the lawyers best qualified to help them. Meanwhile, morale may suffer when partners squabble over money, and legal skill comes to matter less than the entrepreneurial talents of attracting business.

It is not easy to find a way of avoiding these problems while still protecting one's firm from losing especially productive partners to the lure of lucrative offers from rival organizations. One or two firms, such as Cravath, Swaine & Moore, have managed to avoid performance pay and to continue distributing their profits in accordance with seniority. But Cravath has succeeded, at least in part, by its formidable ability to attract business and its practice of hiring an unusually large body of associates relative to the number of partners. In this way, it can give each partner an average income of well over $1 million per year. Such elevated earnings enable the firm to pay by seniority without much risk of having partners defect to other firms for more money. Few firms, however, can earn enough to employ this strategy, and even Cravath can succeed only by making its associates work extremely hard for an exceptionally small chance of ever becoming a partner.

TRYING TO REPAIR THE DAMAGE

The alternatives for trying to curb the earnings of partners in large firms are not dissimilar to those suggested for cutting the pay of CEOs. Their effectiveness, however, is not quite the same. Publicity is likely to work less well for law firms than it does for corporate executives, because earnings, even for the best-known partners, will not come close to the spectacular incomes of a Michael Eisner or a Steve Ross. Placing maximum limits on legal earnings is also awkward. Judges are accustomed to passing upon the appropriateness of legal fees, but only in certain types of cases. The last thing they want is to move aggressively to expand their jurisdiction in this area where the guidelines are murky and the subject highly controversial.

The most promising remedy by far, therefore, is more aggressive bargaining by corporations over the fees they will pay their outside lawyers. Many companies are now taking this route. Not only are they scrutinizing bills more closely and asking for discounts on hourly rates; they are trying hard to induce firms to set a fixed fee in advance of taking a case.

There is still much room for progress in curbing fees through corporate bargaining. Companies could press harder for lower hourly rates, especially at times when business is slack. Even greater benefits might accrue if law firms could be persuaded to agree on a total bill in advance of taking a case, with the understanding that the fee would be reopened if the case turned out to require more time and effort than anyone could reasonably have anticipated. Without some limit of this kind, law firms will never have a strong incentive to keep costs to a minimum. Granted there will always be a risk that the remedy will work too well and cause firms to do less work than the case actually requires. But law firms have a strong desire to perform well in order to preserve their reputations, just as corporations have an obvious need to avoid prejudicing their case by refusing to increase the fee when added services are required. As a result, there is reason to believe that law firms and their clients could set fixed fees in most cases without undue risk to either party if companies were strongly inclined to press in this direction.

For the time being, however, the effects of corporate bargaining are still unclear. Despite the recession, total receipts for large firms continued to rise in 1991, albeit slightly, and profits per partner declined a bit only because there were more partners on board to divide the pie. When the economy revives and legal business is brisk, the leverage of corporate clients will diminish. All in all, therefore, hard bargaining seems to have some restraining effect but continues to fall short of providing an ideal remedy.

As for how to divide the law firm's profits, there is again scant prospect of a perfect solution. Almost all firms are likely to continue giving differing rewards according to performance. But most firms no longer believe they are doing so primarily to motivate sluggish partners to work harder. Rather, paying partners by performance is chiefly viewed as a way of giving more to partners who bring in most of the business so that they will not defect to other firms for more money. If this danger were removed, many firms might well abandon differential rewards to avoid the discomfort of evaluating one another's performance and haggling over which criteria to use.

In these circumstances, the most attractive compromise is likely to involve retaining performance-based pay but keeping the differences as small as possible and making the criteria for these distinctions as clear as circumstances will allow. Achieving even this limited goal will not be easy. In most cases, success will turn on building a strong firm culture based on mutual respect that motivates all the partners to work hard and accept smaller differentials in exchange for greater collegiality and relief from having to argue over who deserves the credit for bringing in new business.

Almost invariably, building such a culture will depend on having key members of the firm transmit the desired values to their colleagues by personal example. In other words, success in keeping loyalty high and pay differentials low requires a kind of leadership that values a strong, cohesive organization above the desire to maximize personal rewards. Interestingly, a reporter investigating firms with unusually clear cultures and high morale concluded, "At just about every firm where I found strong, credible leadership, I also found . . . a pervasive feeling that the leaders were taking out less than they were really worth by any commonsense standard."[18] Reading about these partnerships, one comes away with a suspicion that their members are more satisfied with their work than lawyers in firms where pay differentials are large and key partners continuously judge their colleagues in order to decide what share of the profits they deserve.

CHAPTER 8

UNIVERSITY PROFESSORS

In comparison with successful lawyers, doctors, and business executives, professors are a poorly compensated lot. There are no academic incomes of $1 million, or even $250,000 per year*; the average annual salary for full professors at research universities was still under $60,000 in 1990.[1] While scholars in America are adequately compensated by international standards, they are no longer ahead of their counterparts in Europe. In a few countries, such as Switzerland and Germany, average salaries and benefits are actually higher.

COULD PROFESSORS NEVERTHELESS BE OVERPAID?

Not everyone is convinced that university faculties are modestly paid. Occasionally, some carping legislator complains that professors earn a lot of money, considering that they teach only a few hours per week and have their summers to themselves. Such remarks reveal a lack of knowledge about the true nature of work in a modern university. The number of "contact hours" of classroom teaching takes no account of the time required to prepare courses, do research, keep up with new scholarship in one's field, perform administrative chores, and attend to all the other student encounters and small tasks that crowd a professor's day. According to the National Science Foundation (NSF), the average faculty work load in all colleges and universities is forty-six hours per week.[2] The

* Professors in medical school may seem to represent exceptions to this rule, but those that are highly paid receive the bulk of their income from patient care and not from their strictly academic duties.

figure is two hours greater for universities alone and is slightly higher for full professors (with tenure) than for assistant professors. Moreover, the figures given are *year-round;* they rise to fifty hours per week or more during the academic year and fall to thirty-five hours in the summer. The overall averages are not markedly less than those recorded for lawyers and physicians and hence give little sign that professors are a specially pampered or indolent lot.

Informed skeptics may raise a question about outside income, because many faculty members earn extra money consulting for companies and government agencies, collecting royalties, giving lectures, or teaching in summer school. Approximately four of every five professors earn added income of this sort.[3] But the total sums involved amount to only 20 to 25 percent of base salaries—hardly enough to affect the overall impression of faculty compensation as sufficient to provide a comfortable but not luxurious standard of living.

Even the top professors at leading universities typically received no more than $150,000 in academic salary during 1992. Because such individuals may well have won a Nobel prize (or its equivalent) and made great contributions to society, it is worth asking why they should earn so much less than successful professionals in other fields. Universities could surely afford to pay them a much larger salary. Many institutions spend millions of dollars simply to provide adequate laboratories for scientists recruited to their faculties. If universities are willing to pay so much to attract outstanding professors who will add luster to their reputations, why do they not bid up the salaries of the best scientists and scholars to amounts far above their present level?

Part of the answer probably lies in the traditions of academic life. Over the years, a clear impression has taken hold that professors have chosen to forgo high incomes for the greater satisfactions of teaching students and searching for truth. Because of this perception, proposals to pay huge salaries even to famous professors would be jarring to trustees, legislators, and other significant constituencies.

One may still ask why such attitudes have not gradually given way before the constant pressures to compete for outstanding professors. In fact, top salaries did move up a bit more rapidly than average faculty compensation in the 1980s, and it is conceivable that "star" professors will receive even more favorable treatment in the future. Yet the nature and organization of universities militate against dramatic movements in this direction.

Universities are not hierarchical institutions, like corporations, in which a few members are promoted to positions of special responsibility where they can claim much higher levels of compensation. Nor are universities affluent enough to behave like major law firms and distribute large sums to all their professionals. Instead, they are collegial institutions with limited resources. They cannot afford to pay lavish salaries to all or even a large portion of their faculties, nor are they free to offer great sums to a few professors, no matter how distinguished, without creating tensions and resentments that could easily damage faculty morale. As a result, although the competition for outstanding professors is probably keener than it is for law partners or chief executives, and although offers to move elsewhere for higher pay may come more frequently in academe, top salaries are kept much lower to preserve collegiality.

The same constraints do not apply so clearly to certain other figures within an academic institution, such as the president, the football coach, or the director of the university hospital. Fixing the compensation of these individuals is beset by ambiguity. Hospital directors are in the anomalous position of holding a university appointment while presiding over a corps of practicing physicians, many of whom earn several hundreds of thousands of dollars each year. Successful coaches can bring much added revenue to the university, and there is a brisk market for their services. Accordingly, any university that wishes an excellent coach and a winning program (with the added ticket sales and TV revenues that go with it) must pay a sum several times greater than the salary of a senior professor—a decision that hardly fits easily with the values of an academic institution.

Successful university presidents can also bring much wealth and fame to their institution. Because they preside over large, complex organizations with budgets that often exceed one billion dollars per year, their job rivals the task of leading a major corporation. For these reasons, one can understand why the business executives and corporate lawyers that dominate many boards of trustees might consider it proper to raise the president's salary to approximate the compensation given to the football coach, the hospital director—or even their own earnings, for that matter. Over the past decade, some boards appear to be moving in precisely this direction.

Although understandable, such a policy carries great risks. In the end, the most critical task for a university president is to motivate the faculty to address the principal challenges facing the institution. That is why boards of trustees still choose professors to be university presidents instead of selecting candidates with extensive backgrounds and training in management. At present, however, presidents are finding it more and more difficult to build close relationships with their faculties, because they are strongly pressed to devote most of their time to fund-raising and financial administration. These duties are doubtless essential to meet the needs of the institution. But they will not suffice when the time comes to rally the faculty to meet some crisis in the university or to make imaginative reforms to improve the quality of education. To accomplish these acts of leadership, a president must enjoy a high level of trust and credibility within the faculty and not appear as a distant administrative figure out of touch with the intellectual life of the institution. It is difficult enough to maintain such trust in the best of circumstances. Receiving a huge salary is likely to make the task even harder.

In a large university, most professors will form an impression of their president from a few symbolic actions and key decisions. Earning a salary many times that of the average professor does not convey the image of an academic leader deeply engaged in the intellectual affairs of the university. Rather, it threatens to widen a gulf between faculty and administration that has already undermined effective academic leadership on many campuses.

ARE LOW SALARIES HARMING OUR UNIVERSITIES?

If few people wonder whether faculty salaries are too high, many have worried that they are too meager to attract enough talented young people into academic careers. Professors are not the only ones who should take an interest in this question. Universities, and their scientists and scholars, have come to play a critical role in America's future, because they are the principal source of three ingredients essential to the progress and prosperity of nations: new discoveries, expert knowledge, and highly trained people. Universities and their faculties also perform other vital functions. They interpret and transmit our traditions and our culture. They help us to understand the world and our place within it. They play an important role in assessing and criticizing our government, our public policies, and our institutions.

There is no doubt that unusual powers of mind are needed to carry out these tasks. Of all the occupations we have considered, that of the professor calls most clearly for intellectual talent of a high order. For this reason, it is important to universities and to the nation that the academy continue to attract a substantial share of the nation's most gifted students.

Are universities able to recruit all of the exceptional intellectual talent they need? At first glance, the answer to this would appear to be no. Whatever measure one uses—Phi Beta Kappas, top graduating seniors from selective private colleges, summa cum laude graduates of Harvard—the percentage of outstanding students choosing academic careers dropped by 50 percent or more from the 1960s to the 1970s and 1980s.

Although these figures seem disturbing, it would be unrealistic to expect that universities could attract as many exceptional students to their doctoral programs as they did in the 1960s when higher education was enjoying an unprecedented boom and graduate school enrollments were swollen by young men fleeing the draft. It is also unclear what universities could do to change matters. Top Ph.D. candidates already receive much better student aid packages than their classmates in schools of law or business, and still there is no way that universities can compete with law firms and corporations for students interested in earning large incomes. The Harvard Business School has recently tried to lure a few of its best recent graduates into its Ph.D. program by offering a financial aid package more than twice as generous as arts and sciences faculties can afford. Yet the school continues to have great difficulty persuading its alumni to forsake business for an academic career.

Fortunately, there is some evidence that the intangible advantages of academic life matter more than money to most exceptional students contemplating a university position. So long as salaries exceed the minimum needed to persuade prospective scholars that they and their families can have a decent life, their decision whether to enter academic life will rarely turn on modest fluctuations in earnings. What is likely to matter more is the outlook for finding a job at a decent university. As a result, applications to graduate school began to rise once again in the mid-1980s as prospects for finding an academic post turned brighter after more than a decade of gloom. More important, after losing ground in the 1970s, graduate schools in the 1980s began to attract twice as many Phi Beta Kappas from top-rated colleges and universities as either law or medicine and four times as many as business schools.

Should academe do even better? Who knows how the best students should ideally distribute themselves among the various occupations and professions. Only a rabid partisan could be confident that the nation will suffer if universities fail to increase their share much beyond the current level. Most of the rare students capable of truly important contributions to knowledge have strong intellectual commitments and will probably enter academic life in any case. Others, who might be lured by higher faculty salaries, may make equally important contributions if they move instead into business, medicine, or some other challenging calling.

American universities also have an important advantage of a different sort that helps them to find outstanding talent. At present, and in the foreseeable future, English will be the lingua franca of the scientific and scholarly community, and most of the best young scientists and scholars around the globe will speak it. While German universities will be restricted to hiring faculty from the German-speaking world and the Japanese will have to recruit from their own country, our institutions will be able to search for talent everywhere. Because they still offer a highly attractive setting both for graduate study and for a scholarly career, they have a unique ability to attract talent from all parts of the globe.

In the future, other nations may improve their competitive position by raising salaries and improving their academic facilities. Still, it will be difficult to overcome our advantage in recruiting throughout the world. The primacy of the English language is not likely to disappear, at least not for several generations. Moreover, universities are much harder to reform than industrial enterprises. While other nations have been gaining rapidly on the United States in industrial output and productivity, they have not closed ground in higher education. As a result, our universities should continue to have a considerable edge in searching for talent worldwide so long as they maintain their salaries and facilities at competitive levels.

The more immediate problem for American colleges and universities is whether they will attract enough Ph.D.'s to meet all their staffing needs over the next two decades. The slump in academic jobs that has prevailed for the past twenty years will soon end. But students respond slowly to changes in the academic labor market, and when they do, it takes another six or eight years for them to finish their graduate studies and begin their careers as faculty members. As a result, it is doubtful that the supply of Ph.D.'s will rise rapidly enough to meet the sharp increase in demand that will occur at the end of the 1990s, when large cohorts of faculty hired after World War II begin to retire and need to be replaced.[4] Instead, William Bowen and Julie Ann Sosa project that even under optimistic assumptions, new Ph.D.'s could fall 30 percent short of the demand in the humanities and social sciences between 1997 and 2007 unless compensatory steps are taken.[5]

Fortunately, universities can do a number of things to adjust to these impending shortages.[6] They can raise academic salaries to wean a larger share of Ph.D.'s away from other occupations. They can try to shorten the time to obtain a degree, which has slowly crept up to consume more years than most thoughtful observers think wise. They can recruit more foreign scholars and graduate students. They can increase the proportion of graduate students who actually obtain a Ph.D. (bearing in mind that completion rates in the humanities and social sciences often hover around 50 percent, far lower than in the better law schools, business schools, and medical schools, where 80 to 90 percent or more of entering students typically finish). As a last resort, colleges and universities can reduce their need for new professors either by decreasing faculty-student ratios modestly or by decreasing the fraction of their faculty holding the Ph.D. degree.

Although measures of this kind could conceivably eliminate the projected shortfall of Ph.D.'s, it is hard to predict just how successful many of the remedies will be. As a result, universities have been urging for years that the federal government put new resources into fellowships to induce more students to enter graduate study. The most thoughtful proposal has asked for approximately three thousand new fellowships per year at a total annual cost in steady state of $180 million.[7]

The outlook for such support in these deficit-ridden times is hardly favorable. Moreover, the case for new resources is weak. No one can be sure how much of a shortage will develop or in what fields it will occur if universities take sensible steps to protect themselves. Nor can anyone be certain how many additional Ph.D.'s will result from awarding more federal fellowships, because many recipients would presumably go to graduate school in any case, while others will never graduate.

If a shortage of Ph.D.'s does develop, it is unlikely to affect the so-called Class I universities that produce almost all of the nation's Ph.D.'s and receive almost all of the federal research funds. Rather, the pinch will occur at comprehensive universities and nonselective four-year colleges.[8] No one knows just what the effect will be on the quality of education if there are fewer Ph.D.'s at these institutions. On the face of it, however, it seems odd to spend millions of tax dollars training Ph.D. candidates in research methods (with little careful preparation for teaching) so they can move to institutions featuring heavy teaching loads and relatively little scholarly publication.

Sending more Ph.D.'s to teach in comprehensive universities may also deflect these institutions from developing an appropriate mission for the needs of their students. One of the principal problems in American higher education is the failure to find models of excellence other than that of the research university. Although there are vitally important functions for comprehensive universities and four-year colleges to perform, trying to become a research university is not one of them. Yet in the past, much emulation of this kind has occurred. The result has been that many faculty members have spent too much time on scholarly work and too little on creating programs of education appropriate for their students. It is hard to imagine how this problem will be overcome by populating such institutions with new, young professors steeped in the values of the research university.* Instead, federally funded fellowships would

* If the federal government does provide fellowships, it would do well to use a substantial part of the funds to reduce attrition rates in existing programs by granting dissertation awards that would allow advanced graduate students to concentrate on finishing their thesis without being distracted by the necessity of having to work many hours a week to make ends meet. It might also be wise to limit fellowships to universities that agree to publish their requirements for a Ph.D., the extent of attrition in each of their departments over the past several years, the average time taken to complete a degree in each department, and other data to help fellowship holders decide which institution to attend. Such information will not only allow students to make more intelligent choices; it will also put gentle pressure on universities to take appropriate

probably do more good attracting talented students into fields such as school teaching and government service rather than increasing the number of Ph.D.'s.

A SMALL QUESTION OF INCENTIVES

Like doctors, professors in research universities are compensated without much thought of trying to reward them to improve their performance. But this does not mean there are no financial incentives that affect faculty behavior. Although universities may be disinclined to give special payments for particular services, the outside world has no such scruples. Government agencies offer extra stipends to professors who work on approved research projects during the summer. Other campuses provide generous honoraria that lure scholars from distant places to give speeches and guest lectures. Corporations give handsome fees to faculty members who consult or help to conduct training sessions for their executives.

Unfortunately, this cornucopia of financial opportunities offers few rewards for teaching conscientiously or working individually with students. Several studies have found that salaries are actually slightly lower than average for professors with heavy classroom loads.[9] At most institutions, it is more likely that professors will receive higher pay if they are prolific scholars than if they are dedicated teachers.

These differences are probably not intended. Deans often raise the salaries of professors who have offers from other universities to persuade them not to leave, and professors with such offers are typically those who publish abundantly. Similarly, it is the more productive scholars who receive the lion's share of royalties, summer stipends, and invitations to consult. Once again, no one is consciously favoring research over teaching. It is simply that research attracts attention outside the university, while inspired teaching lives on only in the minds of students.

There are also few rewards for good citizenship on campus. Most institutions do offer added stipends for performing certain admin-

steps to decrease the time students spend completing their studies and to increase the proportion who eventually earn a degree. Such reforms are long overdue. It is hardly fair to expect the federal government to expend more resources on fellowships if only half of the recipients ever emerge with a Ph.D.

istrative duties. By and large, however, those sums are available only for unusually onerous assignments, such as a deanship. They are rarely given for work on committees and often do not exist even for service as a department chair.

Such patterns of compensation create obvious risks that faculty members will neglect teaching and administration and concentrate too much on research and consulting. Yet few universities take adequate steps to avoid these dangers. Professors are supposed to teach a "full" load of courses, but even this requirement is seldom closely monitored. Still less common are official efforts to determine how conscientiously professors teach their courses or guide their students.

To guard against excessive consulting, most institutions do have a rule that faculty members cannot work more than one day per week on outside activities. But this is a vague standard at best. Does it include weekends, unpaid service for professional organizations, government consulting at the urgent request of a high official? Because no one knows, no one asks, and professors interpret the rule to suit their own convenience. Systems for ensuring compliance are usually inadequate. Many institutions do not even ask their professors for regular reports on outside activities or take action against offenders.

In this atmosphere of indifference, one would suppose that the attractions of research and outside consulting must lead most professors to neglect their teaching duties and ignore their students. Indeed, many critics have talked of a golden age of teaching and excoriated faculties for slighting their classes in favor of writing books and advising corporations.[10] Yet those who make this claim offer no data to back up their charges, and the record offers them scant support. Far from revealing a golden age, a closer look at history suggests that complaints about teaching were common long before research and consulting became prevalent on university campuses.

At Harvard, for example, protests about the equality of instruction go back almost to the founding of the institution. According to Samuel Eliot Morison, the university's official chronicler, "almost every graduate of the period 1825–1860 has left on record his detestation of the system of instruction at Harvard."[11] In the words of a faculty committee on instruction in 1901, "Certain lecturers failed to interest, some were inaudible, and some wasted time dictating data or having it copied from the blackboard."[12] In 1939, before the flood of federal research money reached the campus, an undergraduate committee (including a future Nobel laureate in economics, a dean of the Chicago Law School, and the first director of the Harvard-MIT Program in Health Science and Technology) wrote that "the difficulty with Harvard teaching is that the personnel is not selected or advanced with teaching ability as a major consideration; and since it is not believed by instructors to be a major criterion, they do not devote sufficient time and thought to teaching."[13]

Since World War II, investigators have looked more carefully at whether long hours in the laboratory or other kinds of scholarly work actually impair classroom instruction. Surprisingly, those studies have consistently failed to reveal any negative effects.[14] If anything, productive scholars receive higher student ratings than those who do little research, although the differences are generally too small to have statistical significance.

Other inquiries have likewise failed to prove that consulting is getting out of hand. Outside earnings do not seem to make up a larger fraction of faculty salaries today than they did in the 1970s or in the 1960s. In each of these decades, extensive surveys have disclosed that the average tenured professor at a research university earned between 15 and 20 percent of base salary from outside sources.[15] Further studies have shown that professors who consult a lot also publish more than their colleagues and are no less active in campus affairs.[16] Apparently, those who do more outside work often take the time from their families and leisure hours, not from their teaching and research.

These findings testify to the strong intrinsic motivation to teach and perform other academic duties conscientiously. Most people who instruct students try to do a reasonable job because they love their subject, because it is satisfying to help students learn, or simply because it is embarrassing to seem incompetent or boring in front of others. Similarly, productive scholars work hard not only because the process of inquiry is so absorbing but because it is uncomfortable to live among active researchers without producing good work oneself. Until now, these intangible forces seem to have kept the lure of money and excitement from cutting too deep an inroad into the time professors devote to campus chores. The question remains whether they can continue to do so.

ADJUSTING THE INCENTIVES

Although the intrinsic motivations are strong, universities are probably unwise in acting as though financial incentives do not matter. As things now stand, professors on many campuses are among the least accountable professions in America. Although most faculty members are still quite conscientious, every campus has professors who devote much time to outside activities that could be better spent on teaching and other academic duties. Carnegie surveys show that scheduled office hours for students are declining.[17] There is also a worrisome growth of anecdotal talk about the difficulty of finding faculty to take on committee assignments and other normal administrative tasks.[18] Fax machines, E-mail, and personal computers make it easier for professors to work at home, where they are much less accessible to students. As attractive opportunities continue to multiply—for consulting, attending conferences in exotic places, even running lucrative businesses—the temptations to travel will surely increase. All these signs suggest that keeping faculties committed to their institution and to the needs of their students will be a major challenge on many campuses. It would be a great shame to allow the sense of academic responsibility to erode seriously, because it will be much harder to repair the damage than to take preventive measures. Any prudent university, therefore, should be thinking about ways to improve incentives and safeguards to protect the central functions of the institution.

Could universities solve the problem by adjusting their financial rewards? One can imagine a campus with a series of special payments to induce professors to concentrate more on their teaching and administrative duties. Faculty members would receive bonuses for earning high student ratings or for teaching extra classes. Added stipends might be awarded for serving on committees, advising student organizations, or chairing departments and directing institutes. Deans would adjust these payments periodically according to experience so as to increase the bonuses for administrative posts that seemed to be unusually hard to fill while reducing them for popular assignments.

How effective would this policy be? Chances are that it would result only in large outlays of money in exchange for small changes in behavior. Most faculty members already teach conscientiously and do their fair share of campus chores. For them, giving bonuses would simply pay them for work they would do in any case. As for the rest, it would be expensive, if not impossible, for a university to match the consulting fees that companies routinely offer. Many professors would not change their behavior, because their reasons for devoting lots of time to research or outside activity have less to do with making money than with taking on interesting assignments or enhancing their reputations.[19]

The worst casualty of such a system, however, would be its effect on the faculty's sense of responsibility for the welfare of the institution and the education of its students. If every extra effort must be specially compensated, the university signals that it does not expect its professors to feel such obligations spontaneously. No longer are the faculty joint participants in a common enterprise; they are simply employees working for their own account who perform institutional tasks for money.

Trying to use money to motivate professors calls to mind a story, perhaps apocryphal, about President Eisenhower when he served as president of Columbia University after World War II. At his first faculty meeting, Eisenhower spoke of his desire to work harmoniously with the university's employees. Having listened to several more references to "employees," Isidore Rabi, a Nobel prize–winning physicist, raised his hand. On being recognized by Eisenhower, Rabi rose to his feet and said, "Mr. President, I would like to make one point. We are not employees of Columbia University, we *are* Columbia University."

No system of payments can ever substitute for the genuine interest and concern of scholars, nor can it anticipate all the special efforts that a healthy university needs to elicit from its faculty. For this, one must rely on a strong, spontaneous commitment to the academic enterprise. In trying to strengthen faculty motivation, universities would make a grave mistake to respond by appealing to private gain only to weaken commitment to the institution and the traditions it stands for.

If monetary incentives are inadequate, could competition be made to do the trick? Suppose that we could devise measures of how much students learn at college, measures reliable enough that even professors would acknowledge their validity. Imagine that these measures were used by *U.S. News and World Report* as the basis for ranking America's colleges and universities. Every year, each institution's "learning index" would be disclosed for all to see, and the college in which students learned the most would go to the top of the list.

Publicizing such measures would have immediate effects on the priorities of college and university faculties. As students began to respond to the annual rankings by moving to the institutions in which they could learn the most, presidents, deans, and professors would all begin to pay much greater attention to how they could encourage more effective teaching on their campuses. Visiting committees and boards of trustees would start to ask pointed questions of the faculty and administration at universities that ranked low on the learning scale. Campus officials would soon undertake research to try to find out why certain professors and departments seemed more successful than others. Student evaluations would begin to include measures of how much progress students made in each course. As the evaluations were published, individual faculty members would quickly feel greater pressure to figure out how to teach in ways that encouraged students to learn more.

Inspired by visions of this kind, state governments are starting to consider whether to require certain measures of student achievement to hold their universities more accountable. A few states have even imposed such requirements.

As one might expect, faculty members and administrators have reacted to these initiatives with dismay. In some states, campus officials have pretended not to notice, hoping that the "assessment" movement will mercifully disappear. In other states, where legislative interest seems more determined, university representatives have openly expressed their disapproval of the whole idea.

This chilly response is inspired by more than a natural human desire to avoid stricter accountability. The problem with state assessments of student achievement is that the available tools are much too crude for the task. It may be possible to develop reasonable measures of achievement in subjects such as mathematics and foreign languages. It is much harder to do so in subjects such as philosophy, literary criticism, or political science. Standardized tests for subjects of this kind are likely to emphasize the recall of facts and simple concepts rather than the subtler forms of understanding and analysis that thoughtful professors seek to convey.

The problem is not simply that existing measures may give an inadequate picture of how much learning is going on in a university. If test results begin to affect state appropriations or to influence student decisions about where to go to college, pressures will mount to alter campus teaching to improve the results on the state-mandated tests. In this way, the attempt to introduce accountability will end by trivializing and distorting the quality of education.

If state examinations cannot provide the needed incentives, can institutions take other steps to improve teaching and strengthen concern for learning on the campus? Clearly, building incentives for better teaching is a subtle, complicated enterprise. Some professors will always insist that nothing useful can be done along these lines, that no one can be taught to teach well, that teaching is an art, a wholly personal endeavor, a fragile process that must be protected from outside meddling by the shield of academic freedom. Although these statements all have an element of truth, universities can take a host of initiatives to strengthen incentives for good teaching.[20]

A useful start is to try to keep inept instructors out of the classroom. College deans can arrange for all graduate student instructors to receive suitable training before they begin teaching sections of large lecture courses. Those who experience unusual difficulty can be asked to take more intensive work with experienced mentors, using videotaping and other proven techniques. Programs can also be designed to help prepare incoming junior faculty for the typical classroom problems they will face, such as how to organize a course, select appropriate teaching strategies, effectively use computers and other new teaching methods, and cope with recurring issues such as domineering students, racial tensions, gender questions, and the like.

There are also various measures that will encourage existing faculty members to work harder at teaching. Carefully designed student evaluations can provide useful feedback to professors. If published, such assessments will exert gentle pressure on instructors to make efforts to avoid the embarrassment of low ratings. Professors wishing to improve their teaching can have ready access to videotaping and other forms of help. Modest grants from the administration will allow instructors to defray the cost of revising their course extensively, experimenting with new teaching methods, or utilizing computers or other equipment in novel ways. Deans can offer added teaching credit to faculty members who meet regularly with their graduate assistants to discuss the planning of the course and how to teach sections most appropriately to complement the professor's lectures.

To make more fundamental improvements in the quality of education, universities can encourage faculty members to undertake research projects with the administration to discover ways of helping students learn more effectively. Such projects may evaluate the use of technology and other innovative methods of instruction. They may explore a variety of other issues such as why certain concepts of science and mathematics seem unusually hard to grasp, whether students learn more by studying individually or in groups, when active discussion is more effective than lectures, or why students work harder and read much more in some courses than in others. Today, neither faculty nor administrators conduct serious research on the process of teaching and learning on their own campus. As a result, college instruction remains among the small cluster of human activities that do not grow demonstrably better over time. Only by treating student learning as a subject worthy of serious inquiry can institutions speed the improvement of education on their campuses.

Even more powerful incentives could be created if institutions agreed among themselves on certain common measures to emphasize teaching (provided that the federal government refrained from treating such benign arrangements as violations of the antitrust laws). For example, universities could take an important step by not offering to reduce the teaching loads of professors they are trying to recruit. Such arrangements set a poor example and deprive students of opportunities to learn from exceptional scholars. Nevertheless, in the relentless competition to attract outstanding new faculty members, such offers are already common. As one university spokesman put it, "Unfortunately, the blue chip we play in the poker game these days is to offer our best scholars less time with students."[21] With the prospect of growing shortages of Ph.D.'s in the next two decades, competition for professors will intensify, and offers to reduce teaching loads are sure to multiply if some understanding of this kind is not reached.

Universities could also prepare teaching portfolios for all their graduate students and junior faculty that they would make available to prospective employers (other universities) on request. Such portfolios could include a list of the classes the candidate has taught, any student evaluations received, written assessments by faculty observers, course outlines or syllabi, perhaps a videotape of the candidate teaching, and any other relevant information. These materials would make it much easier for universities to arrive at an informed judgment of a candidate's teaching abilities before deciding whether to offer employment. More important, the mere knowledge that such a dossier was being assembled for use in hiring would be a potent stimulus to all graduate students and young faculty members to work at their teaching to present themselves to future employers in the best possible light.

Similarly, every university could agree to collect carefully designed student evaluations and make them readily available to other institutions on request. In this way, any university thinking of making offers to professors at another institution could obtain information to evaluate their teaching as well as their research. From a narrow point of view, such an arrangement might seem to invite universities to cooperate in their own destruction by helping other institutions to raid their faculty. But raiding goes on constantly in any event. By making it easier for other institutions to obtain such information, universities would signal to their faculties that the quality of their teaching would henceforth play a more significant role in their future careers.

Finally, universities could agree to make clear that the *quality* of a candidate's work, rather than the *quantity,* will be the principal factor in making appointments decisions. To emphasize this, universities might even limit the number of books and articles they will consider in their hiring and promotion reviews. To some, such a step may seem pointless, because the emphasis on quality is self-evident. Yet surveys consistently show that a majority of faculty members believe, even in selective research universities, that the number of articles and books published, rather than the quality, is the principal criterion for awarding tenure.[22] So long as this belief persists, many faculty members are likely to devote more time than they should to research simply to compile longer lists of publications to impress appointments committees.

Among these many initiatives, no mention has been made of cash prizes for outstanding teachers even though such awards are probably the most common method universities have used in recent years to demonstrate concern for undergraduate education. The omission is not entirely accidental. By themselves, cash awards are too few to affect more than a tiny fraction of the faculty. If they are offered, therefore, they should be only one of many measures, not the principal means by which a university manifests its commitment to good teaching. Otherwise, prizes may not only prove ineffective but harmful, for many will see them simply as easy tokens, public relations gimmicks that evoke cynicism and suggest the lack of a truly serious desire to improve the quality of instruction.

THE PROBLEM OF BURNOUT

Because the outside world offers so many rewards for consulting and research, professors in major universities may not always divide their energies appropriately among the several tasks they are supposed to perform. But faculty members on these campuses are rarely lacking in motivation. Although most scholars at leading institutions receive tenure at an early age and although few serious efforts are made to link their compensation to performance, there are more than enough incentives to keep them active and engaged for the rest of their careers. Aside from the attraction of teaching bright students and exploring challenging subjects, many university professors must compete for the grants they need to pursue their research and support their graduate students. They know that writing good books and articles will bring them many rewards—recognition, offers to move to other universities at higher salaries, opportunities to consult or attend interesting conferences. Sensitive to the views of colleagues, they have a strong desire to avoid being looked upon as a disappointment or a has-been. With this array of incentives, most members of research faculties are keenly anxious to excel, at least in their scholarly work.[23] The variety of tasks open to most university professors also helps to sustain their interest and enthusiasm. Those few who still lose their zest for academic work probably suffer from deeper problems of motivation beyond the reach of crude incentives such as money or the loss of tenure.

A radically different situation exists at the vast majority of colleges and universities that are *not* noted for research. At many of these institutions, faculty members have little hope of obtaining much recognition beyond their campus or of receiving attractive offers of employment elsewhere. They do not compete for research grants or hope to win prizes or see their work described in the book review sections of major newspapers. Their students are likely to know considerably less, have lower levels of interest in their courses, and need more remedial instruction than their counterparts in leading research universities.

For these professors, academic careers will often seem narrower, less stimulating, and more repetitive than they are in more scholarly institutions. As a result, tenured faculty outside of research universities are much more likely to lose interest and put more and more of their energies into hobbies, family activities, and other pursuits beyond the campus. In many institutions, quite sizable fractions of the faculty fall into this category. Experts on the subject have estimated that 15 to 20 percent of all professors in America are "burned-out."[24]

Could universities overcome this problem by paying higher salaries to successful instructors to induce faculty members to work harder at teaching? Probably not. Intellectual enthusiasm is not readily manipulated by external stimuli. Its roots lie deeper in the minds and feelings of teachers, beyond the reach of monetary rewards.

It would also be difficult to rate the teaching abilities of the faculty to determine which members deserved a bonus. The easiest method would be to look to student evaluations. But paying professors according to the reactions of their students is a dubious practice. The validity of such ratings is still a matter of dispute. Moreover, if student opinion came to affect academic salaries, the effects on the faculty could be unfortunate. Some instructors might go to excessive lengths to entertain their classes, while others might stop giving low grades or heavy reading assignments in order not to antagonize their students. To avoid these problems, colleges could de-emphasize student evaluations and ask professors to review the course materials and attend the classes of other faculty members. But few professors would wish to sit in judgment on their fellows or visit enough classes to make reliable judgments. If they did participate, they would tend to be too generous in their appraisals, recognizing that the colleague they judge today could be judging them tomorrow.

Rather than invite these problems, the wiser course would be to look to institutions that have succeeded in building high faculty morale without having a strong research mission. Such institutions do not rely on financial incentives but seek ways of infusing greater meaning into the work of their professors. The key lies in finding a central purpose that commands respect and arouses the interest and enthusiasm of the faculty.

In part, such meaning comes from linking teaching to human needs that matter—equipping disadvantaged youths with skills to succeed in satisfying careers, preparing students to help revitalize a depressed local economy, or developing the values that underlie constructive citizenship. But identifying a compelling purpose is not enough. By itself, education is highly intangible, its contributions hard to measure. If teachers are to feel that their efforts count and if they are to keep on trying to improve their skills, there must be some way of measuring results, of testing and evaluating new methods to guide further experiments. Without such an evaluation process, faculty members may gradually grow disheartened by the thought that their efforts, however well intended, have no lasting effect.

A number of institutions have succeeded in building unusual commitment and faculty morale by creating such an educational environment. Alverno College, for example, has dedicated itself to inquiring systematically into what students learn and how they can learn more effectively. The entire faculty has become deeply engaged in defining the knowledge and competencies that students should acquire and in searching for better ways to help them progress toward these goals. Through elaborate assessments carried out with the aid of outside evaluators, Alverno provides a way of obtaining feedback and measuring results that in itself motivates the faculty and sustains their interest.

Miami-Dade Community College has taken a similar path by devoting itself to admitting disadvantaged and poorly educated students and preparing them for satisfying jobs. The entire institution seems committed to continuous experimentation with technology and new pedagogic methods in order to find better ways of diagnosing the learning needs and problems of its students and helping them gain the skills and knowledge they require. A student body that might discourage many faculties is viewed at Miami-Dade as a challenge, and teaching well seems a matter of great importance to the lives of the undergraduates and the vitality of the surrounding community. As one faculty member put it, "I get my satisfaction nurturing students who have not been perceived as college material. I save lives. Just like a doctor. That's why I'm here."[25]

In each of these cases (and there are many more), active leadership has managed to transform work that might grow repetitive and uninspiring into something of continuous interest and importance. Evaluation and feedback help to guide faculty efforts and make them purposeful and deliberate rather than haphazard and blind. Various forms of recognition and support are then available to reinforce the mission. Varied assignments can help to refresh faculty interest, as can carefully planned sabbaticals.[26] The real achievement, however, lies in persuading others that there is an interesting and important educational challenge for the institution, even though it differs from the research and graduate training that command so much prestige throughout American higher education.

MAKING THE EFFORT

The most important question facing American universities today is whether they can transform themselves from institutions in which individual professors teach classes to communities joined in a common effort to find better ways to help students learn. For generations, teaching has been the private preserve of each instructor. Faculties can discuss the curriculum and arrive at institutional decisions on how many units of this or that subject will be required of students to graduate. But the process of teaching and learning within each classroom has rarely been the subject of much collective inquiry. As a result, universities are in the uneasy position of eagerly encouraging research into every institution and activity in the society except their own.

To be sure, there is much about teaching in universities that cannot be investigated fruitfully—at least, not yet. How students develop good judgment, how their character changes, and whether they can learn to be more imaginative are only a few examples of questions that have seemed well-nigh impenetrable. But many other subjects are clearly open to fruitful investigation. Foreign language teaching is one of the few subjects that did undergo careful research (because of the exigencies of war), and the effects on student learning were substantial. There is every reason to expect that sustained inquiry and experimentation directed at mathematics, science, and other subjects could eventually yield similar results.

The question that remains is whether universities can summon the will to make the required effort. Unfortunately, there is no reason to expect such a process to spring up naturally. At leading universities, the prevailing incentives are heavily weighted toward research. For all such institutions, the prospect of inquiring deeply into student learning is troubling, because professors fear that their teaching may turn out to be much less effective than they would like to believe. Worse yet, there is the worrisome possibility that investigating teaching will bring problems to light that may either take a great deal of work or even turn out to be impossible to correct.

What might persuade academic leaders to make a determined attempt to overcome this resistance and improve the level of instruction? The most likely force to move them in this direction is the pressure of public opinion. In recent years, criticism of universities has become unusually shrill. The bill of particulars is varied, and not every item involves the quality of education. The most intriguing question, however, is not about the content of the criticism but why the public has become so sympathetic to the attacks. All the complaints—not just about teaching and curriculum but about excessive tuitions, political conformity on campus, and accountability for the use of research funds—are old. Most of them were more deserved twenty or thirty years ago than they are today. Yet it is now, not then, that crude polemics against universities appear on best-seller lists, that politicians find it attractive to hold well-publicized hearings on the use of research funds, that the Justice Department considers it expedient to sue private universities over long-standing tuition and financial aid practices.

The mood of the public appears to reflect a growing realization that teaching students does not receive as high a priority at many universities, especially research universities, as most people feel it should. This perception is especially jarring at a time of national concern over the performance of all American institutions. If companies and other organizations throughout the country are committing themselves to improve the "total quality" of their work, then surely universities should do no less. If tuitions continue to rise more rapidly than family incomes, such sentiments are likely to increase.

This is not to say that the current criticism of universities is entirely fair. Much of it is highly exaggerated and one-sided. But the concerns about teaching have more than a grain of truth. There is no justification for letting graduate students instruct undergraduates with no prior training of any sort, no excuse for allowing foreign teaching fellows with limited English to inflict themselves on students, no reason to appoint professors with only the scantiest evidence of their teaching abilities and then give them little or no feedback about the quality of their instruction. Most of all, there is no justification for continuing to do so little to discover how to make the process of learning more effective. If education is as important as university leaders claim when they speak to their alumni or prospective students, such careless practices ought to stop. There are plenty of practical steps that can correct these problems and strengthen the incentives for good teaching. University presidents should emphasize these reforms, and boards of trustees should urge them vigorously to do so. Few initiatives would accomplish more to regain the confidence of the public and rebuild the understanding and support that universities need to prosper and progress.

CHAPTER 9

TEACHERS

In this decade, more than half of America's 2.2 million public school teachers will leave or retire. Their successors will face challenges more formidable than any that have ever confronted our public schools. Concerned about America's ability to compete in the world economy, the president of the United States and the nation's governors have set ambitious goals to improve the knowledge and skills of our students. At the same time, the reluctance of young people to vote and their growing disinterest in public affairs underscore the need to imbue them with a keener sense of civic responsibility. As if these aims were not challenging enough, the increasing diversity of our population makes it more important than ever to provide an education that combines a respect for different backgrounds with an appreciation of our common culture that will bind the society closer together.

The talents teachers will need to achieve these ends are plainly substantial. For the first time in memory, the public is united in believing that the first priority of our schools should be the development of intellectual skills—not basic skills alone but higher-order analytic abilities as well. If students are to function in a more demanding world, teachers will have to prepare them not merely to read texts but to interpret them, not simply to memorize the rules of mathematics but to use them to solve new problems, not just to express their own opinions but to argue logically and evaluate opposing points of view.[1]

These goals make greater intellectual demands on instructors than imparting basic skills, socializing immigrant children, instilling citizenship, helping students adjust to society, integrating the races, and other aims that have preoccupied our public schools in the past. Teachers will need to know their subjects more thoroughly and be able to stimulate their students to think actively and solve problems rather than passively absorb information. Their efforts will be all the more difficult in a society where more and more students come from broken homes, where parents spend less time than ever with their children, where young people are heavily distracted by television, drugs, and urban violence and come to school in growing numbers speaking different languages and needing special tutoring.

Teaching in such an environment is a daunting challenge. At present, it is a challenge too rarely met. As one experienced school official has observed,

> The bulk of instructional time [in the nation's schools] finds students listening to teachers talk, working on tasks that require little application of concepts, imagination, or serious inquiry. Description after description documents the Sahara of instruction demanding little thought from students beyond information already learned. What emerges unblurred is what Theodore Sizer calls a "conspiracy of the least," a tacit agreement between teachers and students to do just enough to get by.[2]

To move beyond this drab reality to a more active process of learning and problem-solving, teachers will need more than the traditional intellectual qualifications. We cannot expect our schools to raise student proficiency in algebra or biology when the American Academy for the Advancement of Science can declare that "few elementary school teachers have even rudimentary education in science and mathematics and many junior and senior high school teachers of science and mathematics do not meet reasonable standards of preparation."[3] Whatever the defects of standardized tests, only blind optimists would expect our teachers to succeed in conveying higher-order skills if their average College Board scores continue to fall close to the bottom third of all takers.[4] No magic formula defines the threshold of academic talent needed to teach the nation's children. But schools can hardly begin to meet our expectations unless they muster a corps of teachers that is at least equal in ability to the college student population as a whole.

We are also unlikely to accomplish what we seek unless our schools attract enough exceptionally talented people to muster the kinds of intellectual leadership that any first-rate educational system requires. Everyone who has visited classrooms, even in the most forbidding urban environments, knows how important it is to have one or two teachers in every school who have an infectious enthusiasm for their subject and the ability to challenge the best students to do their utmost. Many states are also planning for "master teachers" who help younger colleagues and play more substantial roles in developing curricula and improving educational programs. Above all, effective schools will need gifted principals, not just to discipline students and manage the facilities but to give academic leadership to the staff.[5] Filling these critical positions will require a pool of teachers with intellectual (and other) abilities that are well above the average.

ARE TEACHERS UNDERPAID?

In the sixteenth century, Sir Thomas Elyot observed that many "well lerned" men would become teachers "if the name of a schole meister were not so muche had in contempte, and also if thyr labours with abundant salaries mought be requited."[6] These words remind us that neither the difficulty of finding able teachers nor the remedies currently proposed are new to our age. Only the urgency of the problem has changed.

There are many reasons for believing that we will have to pay teachers more if we wish to attract candidates of the necessary quality. The test scores of education majors today are lower than they were in 1970. One-quarter to one-third of all new math and science teachers in the United States are not qualified to offer instruction, and this for subjects in which the nation's official goal is to have American students rank number one in the world by the year 2000.[7] Disproportionate numbers of the academically ablest teachers leave the profession, often after a single year, giving as their principal reason the need to earn more money.[8] With what they currently earn, approximately one-third of our current teachers feel compelled to "moonlight" to make ends meet, although most of them believe that it interferes with their classroom work.[9] Relative to other jobs in the society, salaries for teachers in America still rank well below the median for industrialized nations.[10]

Fortunately, teachers received substantial pay increases in the 1980s. By 1990, they were actually earning more in real dollars than they did twenty years before. But the pool of talent available to the schools is far from what it was in 1970, for women and minorities now have greater opportunities to pursue careers in many lucrative professions such as law, business, and medicine. Hence, it is unlikely that schools can ever succeed in getting back even to 1970 levels of quality merely by offering 1970 salaries.

These arguments have not persuaded everyone. Of all the critics, Charles Murray has presented the case against raising teachers' pay in the most elaborate detail.[11] In his opinion, states will not be willing to lift salaries very much, because even modest raises spread over two million teachers cost a lot of money. As a result, the likely pay increases will simply be too small to attract able recruits and hence will waste resources without improving the quality of instruction.

This argument is belied by a series of studies on the effects of higher starting salaries on teacher recruitment. Although few people enter the profession to make money, prospective teachers need to earn a minimum amount to support their families and live a life they consider adequate. As salaries rise, more people find that this threshold has been reached. Several studies have found that the most talented candidates are especially responsive to higher pay.[12] Other researchers have determined that a raise of only $1,000 per year will increase the supply of teachers by 10 percent.[13] Building on these results, Charles Manski has recently concluded that by raising teachers' salaries (relative to other professions), by only 10 percent (and by increasing minimum entry standards), school districts could hire enough teachers to meet their staffing needs and still lift the average test scores of new recruits to a level equal to that of all college graduates.[14]

Murray's case does not rest entirely on his belief that salary increases will be too modest to solve our problem. Far from it. He is even more concerned that rising salaries will bring to the schools a group of recruits who come not for the love of teaching but from a desire to make money. "Introducing into [the public school] environment people who are in it for the money is like introducing a virus into a system with no immunity."[15] As Murray sees it, these teachers will not be satisfied with the initial increases in salary; they will agitate for further pay raises and infect their colleagues with greed. Because their motives are impure, they will be less dedicated in their teaching. As parents come to understand their true motives, confidence and trust in the schools will erode. In the end, morale will suffer and the quality of education along with it.

Murray does not say why the higher salaries that wealthy suburbs pay their teachers have not long since corrupted the staff, produced more strikes, disillusioned the parents, and undermined the quality of instruction. Far from having these effects, suburban schools seem to hire better teachers and satisfy parents more than their inner-city counterparts. In a massive study of Texas schools, Harvard professor Ronald Ferguson found that districts that paid more attracted teachers with higher test scores and that higher test scores were by far the most important factor in explaining differences in student achievement, especially in the early grades.[16]

Murray also fails to tell us why he worries so about teachers starting at $22,000 per year but is not beside himself at the thought of lawyers and doctors who begin their professional careers earning three or four times as much. If parents distrust a new instructor who will come only for an extra $2,000 a year, their feelings toward their stockbrokers and internists must border on paranoia. Yet Murray does not mention these incongruities or give any reasons to explain them away.

Of course, even if we put aside Murray's more exotic arguments, raising teachers' salaries may still strike many people as too costly a step for America in its present state. Because school boards cannot expect to raise the salaries of new recruits without raising them for existing teachers as well, even modest pay increases will require heavy expenditures. For example, adding $1,000 to the pay of every public school teacher would cost over $2 billion per year, a formidable sum for a nation burdened with huge deficits and populated by citizens incensed at the thought of higher taxes. Worse yet, much of the extra money could go to ineffective teachers and cause them to stay longer in the profession. If so, the pay increases would cut down opportunities for talented young instructors and make the quality of teaching worse rather than better.

Although these arguments must be taken seriously, they are not as formidable as they might seem. Because half of all current teachers will be replaced in a decade, much of the added wage bill will go to the new recruits for whom it is primarily intended. Some significant fraction of those who remain will presumably be competent, dedicated teachers (many of whom will leave if they don't get substantial pay increases). Moreover, there are ways of rewarding good teachers properly without having to spend a lot of money on their less successful colleagues. For example, school districts can introduce career ladders, which reserve higher salaries and broader responsibilities for instructors who master added skills and demonstrate genuine competence in the classroom.[17] Such methods are already being introduced in states such as Tennessee, Indiana, and Texas and are likely to spread in the next decade.

There are also ways of raising salaries without having to pass along the entire cost to the taxpayer. School districts should be able to offset part of the burden by trimming their administrative costs. Granted, making these savings will be harder than many critics claim, because the bulk of what is commonly called "administrative costs" does not go to bureaucrats in the central office but to academic advisers, teachers' aides, and instructors serving in bilingual education courses, classes for the handicapped, and other mandated instructional programs that no one seems willing to cut.[18] Even so, some savings seem feasible. Enterprising superintendents could probably pare their maintenance costs somewhat. Further economies might be possible if states and school districts repealed unnecessary rules and regulations that stifle local initiative and force schools to spend money on useless paperwork and other efforts to ensure compliance.

Added savings might come from trading salary increases for other improvements that yield only questionable benefits. For example, teachers and parents have long fought with some success for smaller and smaller class sizes. Any suggestion that this effort is misguided will be looked upon in some quarters as akin to an attack on motherhood. Yet study after study has failed to show any positive effect on student achievement from reducing class size, at least at the high school level.[19] As a result, school districts that are not already overcrowded might do well to increase high school class sizes modestly, hire fewer instructors, and use the savings to offer higher salaries to their teachers. Through measures such as these, on top of administrative savings, an enterprising school district could lift salaries enough to attract candidates with undergraduate records that are at least average while still incurring only a modest increase in total costs.

MAKING TEACHING MORE ATTRACTIVE

Schools must not only recruit better teachers; they must retain them for longer periods of time. This goal cannot be achieved by relying on salaries alone. Although college students need to feel that they can count on an adequate income if they are to choose teaching as a career, few of them seek employment in the public schools to make money. What they want most is to work with young people and help them learn.[20] Unfortunately, many schools seem intent on making it hard for teachers to achieve this goal. For example, surprising numbers of teachers complain of having no space of their own in which to do their work. Most schools do not even provide offices for their staff, and many do not supply a desk, a typewriter, or a telephone. Conditions in the classroom are hardly any better. As one teacher put it,

> I sometimes wonder how we're able to teach at all. A lot of times there aren't enough textbooks to go around; the library here is totally inadequate; and the science teachers complain that the labs aren't equipped and are out of date. We're always running short on supplies. Last year we were out of mimeograph paper for a month, and once we even ran out of chalk.[21]

These are frustrating problems. As the Carnegie Foundation for the Advancement of Teaching discovered after polling over twenty thousand teachers, "The conclusion is clear: improved working conditions are essential if we hope to attract and hold outstanding teachers."[22]

Another way of helping public schools become more attractive places to work would be to make teachers participants in setting educational goals, formulating plans, and developing new programs. More and more corporations are involving their blue-collar workers in finding ways to improve methods of production. Yet many schools still keep their teachers out of discussions of academic policy. Reflecting on a recent Carnegie study, the foundation's president, Ernest Boyer, observed; "Perhaps the most significant [finding] in this survey is the frustration teachers feel about their powerlessness in teaching. We found that the majority of teachers are not involved in selecting teachers and administrators at their school, nor are they asked to participate in such crucial matters as teacher evaluation, staff development, school budgets, and student promotion and retention policies."[23]

Career development is another area in urgent need of overhaul. In many public schools, teachers see little prospect for the future save the chance to go on meeting their classes year after year. Many teachers lack opportunities to acquire important skills, such as computer literacy, or to learn more about their primary subjects, even though 18 percent admit to teaching subjects for which they are unqualified.[24] Fortunately, more school districts are beginning to expand opportunities for instructors to receive further training. Other systems are developing career ladders that allow teachers to take on added duties to guide new colleagues and help to shape curricula. Now that many states are giving more power to individual schools to manage their own affairs, possibilities for able teachers to assume greater responsibility should be still more abundant in the future.

MORE EFFECTIVE RECRUITMENT

Even if salaries rise and working conditions improve, school systems will not upgrade the quality of their teaching staff unless they search energetically for the best new teachers they can find.[25] Unfortunately, current hiring practices leave much to be desired. Although some districts do work hard to find able candidates, others hardly bestir themselves at all. As one superintendent remarked, "We just wait for applicants to come to us." Many school committees do not pay for sending teams to observe candidates teach, although this is acknowledged to be one of the best ways to judge future performance. Often, potential recruits cannot receive an offer until every existing teacher has had a chance to bid on the open positions. When they are finally contacted, they frequently cannot find out what they will be teaching or where. Uncertainties over budgets and enrollments can postpone final hiring decisions even longer. As a result, offers may not go out until late summer or even September, after all the choice assignments have been taken. By this time, many of the best applicants will have long since accepted other jobs.

School districts also make poor hiring decisions because they often ignore academic records or other evidence of intellectual talent in deciding whom to employ. One study showed that rejected applicants in a sample of school districts had as high grades and test scores and as positive letters of recommendation as those who were offered jobs.[26] Apparently, many districts regard intelligence as a relatively unimportant qualification. Some school officials even admit to discriminating against smarter candidates on the ground that they are likely to be less "empathetic" toward students and more inclined to leave the classroom for other lines of work.[27] These attitudes help to explain why teaching is one of the few professions in which members with the least intellectual ability are paid just as much and promoted just as fast as their most gifted colleagues.[28]

There is a simple way for states to remedy this problem. They have merely to change the requirements for certification and insist that new teachers have higher college grades or test scores to qualify. Over half the states have taken this route in recent years. One problem with such a remedy, however, is that it will probably screen out a high proportion of minority candidates.[29] If test scores were an accurate measure of teaching ability, this price might be worth paying. But tests are an imperfect index at best, and we can hardly afford to disqualify large numbers of capable black and Hispanic teachers at a time when minority youth will make up a majority of the entire student population in several states, not to mention in almost all major cities.

This problem reveals the dilemma that many school authorities face in searching for talented teachers.[30] On the one hand, states cannot allow candidates to be hired who lack the ability to perform well in the classroom. On the other hand, because so many new recruits must be found, officials cannot safeguard quality by using tests that screen out large numbers of candidates who could actually become effective teachers.

The obvious way around this dilemma is to develop better means of evaluating candidates. At present, the method typically used is a standardized short-answer exam emphasizing basic reading and writing skills and substantive knowledge in the applicant's field of interest. Even proponents of these tests agree that they offer a crude measure of teaching ability. Fortunately, many people are working hard to make improvements. Some are developing ways to evaluate applicants in real or simulated teaching situations. Others are emphasizing open-ended questions that are more relevant to teaching and do not reward test takers for the petty stratagems and trivial knowledge that many believe can boost scores on more traditional multiple-choice exams. In time, these efforts should succeed in producing assessments that will bar incompetent candidates without screening out large numbers of promising recruits as well.

NEW SOURCES OF TALENT

In addition to prescribing licensing exams, most state authorities require prospective teachers to complete a minimum program of training that includes mandatory courses on pedagogy, curriculum, educational psychology, and practice teaching. These requirements ensure that every new teacher will begin with a body of relevant information. Unfortunately, they also discourage large numbers of able young people who refuse to spend part of their undergraduate years sitting in classes that often seem irrelevant and stupefyingly boring. At a time when half the teaching force must be replaced, the loss of these potential recruits is a sacrifice we can ill afford.

This problem is not unique to teaching. Licensing statutes also keep talented people from becoming doctors if they do not graduate from medical school. But there is a difference. We feel reasonably sure that students must attend medical school to become competent physicians. The same is not true in the field of education. Private school teachers rarely take education courses, yet their students typically perform at least as well as public school students of equal ability. Repeated studies have even failed to show that graduates of master's programs in education are any more effective in the classroom than liberal arts B.A.'s or that their students learn more.[31]

Such findings have encouraged a number of states to try to lure new groups of people into teaching by experimenting with alternative paths to careers in the public schools. New Jersey, for example, has had a Provisional Teaching Program for graduates without education degrees since 1984. Participants in this program must have a bachelor's degree with a major in the field in which they will teach, and each must pass a basic standardized test. Applicants admitted through this program spend a year of in-service training where they are carefully evaluated to determine whether they can receive a permanent teaching license.

After eight years, the program has proved its worth. Not only has it produced a significant fraction of New Jersey's beginning teachers (over one-fourth); its graduates have done much better than conventionally trained recruits on the standardized tests and have provided most of the state's new science and math teachers. Better yet, the program has yielded twice the proportion of minority teachers as the traditional sources.

The New Jersey experience is only one way of opening doors to new sources of talent. Several states have cooperated with universities in allowing undergraduates to gain a teaching certificate provided they do some supervised practice teaching and take a minimum of courses related to education. Another possibility is to reach out to midcareer professionals who would like to move into teaching but do not wish to take a traditional preparatory program. Harvard's School of Education has started such a course for engineers, military officers, and others with math and science backgrounds. Because the participants can often take early retirement and receive half pensions to supplement their teaching salaries, they need not abandon their hopes of teaching because the pay is too low. With proper preparation, they can provide precious new blood to augment the meager supply of qualified math and science teachers.

Such innovations offer promising ways of finding added recruits for the nation's classrooms. But even these methods may not attract enough candidates to meet all the needs of our public schools. For example, improvements in salary and working conditions may still not lure enough applicants with exceptional talents to build an adequate pool of potential master teachers, principals, and superintendents to offer leadership in the future. Nor will it be easy to find enough candidates who are properly trained to teach science or mathematics or sufficiently committed to devote their energies to inner-city schools. Individuals with these qualities will be especially hard to find now that law, medicine, and business have opened their doors to women and minorities and attractive opportunities for scientists and engineers remain plentiful. To attract such applicants in sufficient numbers may well require special inducements of some kind.

Over the past several decades, the federal government has offered a variety of rewards to lure people into hard-to-fill jobs. The armed forces give four-year scholarships to those who enroll in ROTC programs and commit themselves to four years of active duty thereafter. The Department of Health and Human Services has offered refundable loans to medical students who agree to practice in undeserved areas. The Congress has agreed to forgive college loans for undergraduates who teach in public schools after receiving their degrees.

In practice, these schemes have not been uniformly successful.[32] Particularly disappointing are programs that allow graduates to discharge part of their student loans for each year of service as a teacher or a rural doctor. Interest in such programs has been modest at best, and later studies have shown that most of the participants would have taught or worked in underserved areas in any event.

Congress has had more success when it provides funds up front through generous scholarships that students must repay at stiff rates of interest if they later decide not to take one of the jobs that the government is trying to fill. Although there is no real difference between giving students a grant that must be repaid if they do not teach and giving them a loan that is forgiven if they do, the psychological effect of offering grants seems considerably greater. That has been the experience under the National Health Service Corps and the ROTC, where scholarships seem to have worked quite effectively. A similar program could well help the public schools attract the special talents they must have to perform according to our expectations.

MOTIVATING TEACHERS

To satisfy the country's needs, the public schools must have teachers who are not only intellectually talented but highly motivated as well. This point has not escaped the notice of education planners. Over the past decade, much thought has been given to strengthening incentives and various experiments have been tried.

As the nation grew concerned in the 1980s over "the rising tide of mediocrity" in our schools, a flurry of interest arose over finding a way to pay teachers according to their performance. Two reasons underlay this interest. One was the familiar hope of using money to motivate people to work harder. The other was an unspoken suspicion that many teachers were neither talented nor effective. The trick, therefore, was to find a way of raising salaries to reward the better teachers and attract able recruits without spending a lot on mediocre people and encouraging them to keep on teaching. Merit pay seemed to offer a plausible way to accomplish exactly what was desired. As President Reagan declared, "Teachers should be paid on the basis of their merit and competence. Hard earned tax dollars . . . have no business rewarding incompetence and mediocrity."[33]

At first, the outlook for merit pay seemed promising. The general public approved the idea overwhelmingly. A national poll even disclosed that 62 percent of all teachers favored basing pay on performance.[34] But feelings shifted quickly after the concept was put into practice. Florida pioneered with a merit pay plan but quickly backed down under pressure from its teachers. In Tennessee, 90 percent of the teachers under a statewide merit plan felt that the new method affected morale adversely, while 60 percent reported that it diminished their own commitment to teaching.[35] Having heard these reactions from the rank and file, teachers' unions were not backward about conveying the feelings of their members. In many cases, teachers took it upon themselves to tease and harass colleagues who were unlucky enough to win merit awards.

What accounts for this hostile reaction? An initial problem is that money does not seem to be a particularly potent incentive for teachers. True, potential recruits will not enter the profession unless the compensation is great enough to meet their basic needs. Once this threshold is passed, however, teachers are more likely to be motivated by their desire to help students learn and grow than by the prospect of taking home more money. This, at least, is the view of those who have studied the matter most closely.[36]

A further obstacle to bringing merit pay into the schools is the problem of judging how effective individual teachers are in the classroom. It is difficult to define good teaching and even harder to measure it. One can observe instructors in the classroom, but that is an arbitrary process; even experienced judges often differ on which pedagogic styles are best, and the few classes observers attended may not be representative. One can ask students for their opinion, but youngsters may not be able to give reliable evaluations. In an effort to make more precise assessments, schools can test their students at the beginning and end of each year to see how much they have learned. But teachers may respond by spending too much time coaching their pupils to score well on the tests. Besides, student progress is influenced by natural intelligence, parental interest, problems at home, and many other factors quite beyond a teacher's power to control.

Lacking reliable ways of defining and measuring good instruction, principals will find it hard to make merit evaluations that win the confidence of their staff. Worse yet, they will often be unable to advise their teachers what to do to perform better. As a result, their efforts to motivate the staff may end only by causing more frustration.

Like business executives (and other professionals), most teachers also overestimate their own performance. In one typical study, fully half of the teachers surveyed rated themselves in the top 10 percent.[37] With such inflated expectations, many are bound to resent the evaluations they receive from their principal. Because there is no objective way to verify the assessments, those who do poorly are likely to blame the administration and suspect that ratings are being manipulated to reward favorites and penalize those who speak their mind or openly support the union. Relations among the staff can also suffer as teachers come to feel that they are competing with one another for bonuses rather than cooperating to improve their school.

To counter these problems, some administrators will go to added lengths to impress teachers with the fairness and thoroughness of the evaluations. Supervisors will visit more classes, use multiple methods of assessment, and consult more with the teachers. With all the goodwill in the world, however, such efforts may only boost the cost of administration while failing to remove the distrust created by an inherently subjective and contentious process. In almost every case where they have been tried, therefore, merit-based plans have eventually been abandoned, except where they have been transformed into something quite different, such as giving bonuses to those who take on added duties coaching athletic teams, teaching remedial classes, or performing some other special task.[38] By 1990, only 4 percent of the nation's teachers reported that they were working under a merit system. Probably, most of the so-called merit-based systems were paying bonuses to teachers only for taking on extra assignments.

For many reasons, then, merit pay is not a promising way to strengthen incentives in our schools. Before endorsing such a plan, we should take more care to understand the challenge we have given our teachers by asking them to raise the academic competence of students to higher levels than ever before. This assignment calls for creative responses to a series of daunting problems. How to motivate students who perceive no relationship between their performance in school and their success in finding a job or gaining admission to college? How to teach them to think clearly and solve problems rather than simply fill their minds with information? How to keep students from dropping out? How to make up for a lack of parental interest and support?

At present, there are no clear solutions to these problems, nor are we likely to find all the answers we need in the state house or the Congress. Instead, good ideas will have to come from teachers and principals working together to share their experiences, discuss novel ideas, and experiment with new methods. To foster such collaboration, the incentives required are not those of a widget factory where the problem is to motivate each employee to work separately at a familiar task. We do not need a competition for merit bonuses that turns teachers into rivals and engenders suspicion toward the very principals whose job is to lead their staffs to higher levels of performance. The challenge in education is to find incentives that do not divide but bring about a collaborative search for better ways of coping with an extremely difficult set of problems.

At present, our entire system of public education seems almost perverse in its capacity to frustrate this kind of collective effort. Programs to train teachers are widely acknowledged to be inadequate, especially for preparing instructors to teach the higher analytic skills that students will need to succeed in the work force they are about to enter. Once employed, teachers have such heavy schedules that they find little time to prepare for their classes. (On average, they work forty-seven hours per week, yet over 90 percent can find only an hour or less per day to spend on class preparation.)[39] They seldom have a chance to meet with colleagues to discuss common problems or to explore new ideas for enlivening their classes. (Almost 60 percent report that such opportunities are "not readily available" or "poor.")[40] In the words of one teacher, "it just seems that in teaching . . . you do your thing in your class, and you leave, and you don't talk to anyone about it."[41]

As we have already discovered, many teachers play no role in shaping educational policies such as curriculum, teaching materials, or rules relating to student conduct. Academic leadership in the schools is often mediocre, because principals are often casually chosen and receive a training that emphasizes management skills rather than educational leadership. As if these problems were not enough, many enterprising principals and teachers who do wish to innovate find themselves blocked by a maze of rules and restrictions emanating from Washington, the state house, and the district superintendent's office.

The hard truth is that attracting abler people to such an environment will bring little improvement by itself. A whole series of reforms must be made to give teachers a chance to make real progress in improving the quality of education.[42]

The first essential step is to set standards that define what students are supposed to learn and then to develop the best possible methods for assessing the progress of each school in attaining these objectives. Without such measures, parents will have no reliable way of knowing how well their school is performing, principals and teachers will not know whether their efforts are succeeding, and school authorities will have no way of telling which schools are lagging and need special attention. Of equal importance is the development of curricula and grading methods that employers and admissions committees will respect enough to consider seriously when they decide whom to hire or whom to admit to college. Only when students feel that the quality of their schoolwork can affect their future will they feel strongly motivated to learn.

Once this framework for evaluation is created, a number of other changes must take place. Having set appropriate goals and standards, higher authorities should leave much discretion to principals and teachers to decide how to achieve the desired ends. Only in the case of schools that are clearly failing to make reasonable progress should superintendents intervene, and then they should act decisively by replacing the principal, supplying added funds, and giving the new leadership power to bring in at least a few new teachers and other key personnel.[43] School boards should take greater care in choosing principals, and universities should provide much stronger programs to prepare them for educational leadership. Once in office, principals must engage the interest of parents and community leaders, hire the best possible teachers, and support them by protecting them from petty distractions and by supplying them with the resources and opportunities for development that will help them perform effectively. Above all, principals must treat the staff as professionals. Teachers should have more time to meet and discuss their work. As professionals, they should be full participants in deliberations over curriculum, teaching methods, and other questions of academic policy.

Changing the system in this way would do a lot to improve the motivation of teachers simply by attacking many of the obstacles that frustrate them currently. All available evidence suggests that most teachers enter the profession with a genuine desire to help children. Any reforms that empower them to try new methods of instruction, free them from annoying administrative burdens, and allow them to collaborate in seeking educational improvements will help them achieve their personal goals and make their work more rewarding and challenging.

To strengthen motivation further, state officials could consider incentives that offer rewards not to individual teachers who excel but to all the teachers in schools that perform especially well. Incentives of this kind encourage teachers to work together to improve their institution. Instead of competition and rivalry, they foster collaboration and teamwork. South Carolina has already initiated a particularly interesting plan of this type. Schools that succeed in helping their students make exceptional gains in achievement receive a bonus based on the size of their student body. Some 25 percent of the schools in the state receive such bonuses each year and approximately 60 percent have earned a bonus at least once in the past four years. An intriguing addition to the plan is a policy of allowing successful schools to free themselves from a number of regulations and reporting requirements. In this way, schools that show that they can function effectively no longer have to comply with rules designed to force lagging institutions to achieve minimum standards.

The only danger with incentives of this kind is that the criteria for success may be crudely designed so that teachers neglect more important forms of instruction in their effort to boost test scores and win the desired reward. Fortunately, several states have been working to develop better measures, and some—such as Vermont and California—have made considerable progress. With sufficient care, it should be possible to reward superior schools without undue risk that teachers will alter the content of their classes inappropriately.

If school authorities feel that they must strengthen individual incentives even further, they would do well to avoid merit pay and move instead to create a career ladder that allows teachers who demonstrate sufficient proficiency to move to higher levels of responsibility.[44] Using new methods currently being developed by

Lee Shulman and the National Board for Professional Teaching Standards, principals should be able to judge qualifications for promotion more reliably than they can rate the quality of classroom instruction by each teacher every year under a merit pay plan. In a well-designed career ladder program, promotions will bring recognition and carry a higher salary. They will also give welcome variety to teachers' lives by adding new responsibilities, such as helping younger colleagues, devising in-service programs, or heading a curriculum committee. Properly administered, they may increase motivation without risking all the resentments and rivalries that seem to accompany conventional incentive pay plans.*

GETTING THE JOB DONE

The program just described represents a massive shift in the way power and responsibility are distributed among the layers of public education stretching from Washington to the neighborhood schoolhouse. To succeed, however, piecemeal changes will not suffice, for real progress requires the entire package of complementary reforms. Higher salaries for teachers will not bring able recruits to the classroom unless school authorities improve their methods of selection. Improved hiring procedures will not bring better instruction unless teachers have more opportunities to work together to plan the academic program. Better teaching will not bring greater learning unless businesses and universities cooperate with schools to provide stronger incentives for students to work hard at their studies.

It is the need to make so many innovations simultaneously that makes the job of school reform so hard. Conversely, it is the failure to make all the necessary changes that has caused so many piecemeal reforms to fail and has led many observers to wonder whether any improvement is possible. The ultimate question, then, is how to summon the will to break through the thick crust of tradition and bring about such an ambitious set of changes.

* If school systems initiate career ladders, they must take care not to push teachers into vying with one another for advancement. All who can demonstrate sufficient proficiency should qualify for promotion, if not at their own schools, then at some other school with a need for a master teacher. In this way, career ladders can motivate teachers without interfering with the collaboration and collegiality so important to building better schools.

At the moment, the strategy that has attracted the most attention is "parental choice"—a proposal that would allow parents to choose among several schools for their children. Under such plans, schools would vie with one another for students. The more successful institutions would drive the others to reform to avoid declining enrollments that would cut their funds and endanger the jobs of their staff. In this way, competition would bring about innovation and improvement much as it does in industry and trade. This, at least, is the theory.[45]

In fact, many problems can arise in trying to introduce competition into public education. Schools do not behave like corporations. Those that are successful in competing for students (most likely suburban schools) will not expand to increase "market share." At most, a popular school may take a few applicants from outside its neighborhood, either because they are bright and interesting to teach or because they add to the diversity of the student body. Losing these few students will hardly place enough pressure on other schools to force them to make fundamental reforms.

Anticipating this problem, many advocates of parental choice are counting on new schools to spring up that will expand the range of options and threaten to draw enough students from existing schools to shake up the system. Whether enough new institutions will appear, however, remains very much in doubt. Private schools have never managed to enroll more than a small fraction of the nation's students. The reason is obvious: starting a school is an expensive, arduous proposition; to break even, tuitions must exceed what most parents are willing to pay. If this is to change, the government will have to offer enough financial help to new schools to enable them to keep tuition low and still offer quality education. That is why most parental choice plans call for giving parents vouchers worth substantial sums that they will give to the schools of their choice to help cover the cost of operation.

Voucher plans are expensive; most schemes require the government to distribute enough money to support the basic costs of all schools, including private schools (which currently enroll over 10 percent of the nation's students). An adequately funded plan, therefore, could cost many billions of dollars. Moreover, such a change, once made, cannot realistically be reversed. Hence, it is critical not to start down this path without being reasonably sure that vouchers will succeed as advertised.

Several troublesome problems suggest that voucher plans might *not* succeed.[46] If the government were to give all parents a few thousand dollars for the school of their choice, the immediate result would be to bring private school education within reach of middle-class families who would otherwise be unwilling to pay the full tuition. This is the market that new for-profit schools would try to attract. The result would be to segregate schools according to parental income even more than is currently the case.

Some choice proposals would forestall this possibility by preventing schools from charging more than the vouchers given to parents. Even under such a plan, however, profit-making schools would still be likely to choose locations in which they can attract bright, middle-class students, because these students are the most enjoyable to teach and the most likely to help a fledgling institution succeed academically and establish a good reputation. Restricted or not, therefore, vouchers to aid for-profit schools could widen the gap between rich and poor. In neither case would market forces do much to improve the kinds of schools most in need of reform.

It is possible, of course, that churches, civic organizations, and enterprising parents might also take advantage of vouchers to found nonprofit schools of quality in neighborhoods where the level of education is poor. Whether enough of these new institutions will arise to shake up moribund school systems is highly conjectural. Because we have had little or no experience with voucher plans, we cannot predict how many organizations will undertake the considerable effort of finding suitable buildings, hiring teachers, developing a curriculum, and doing all the other things required to start a new school.

We also do not know how many parents will actually take advantage of new opportunities that emerge. In Minnesota, where all students were given a right to attend schools outside their district (with partially subsidized transportation), less than 1 percent of eligible children sought to transfer. It will take much larger shifts to force lackluster schools to initiate significant changes.

School reformers are likewise quick to assume that parents hunger for the same kind of education for their children that the nation needs in order to progress. It is far from clear that this supposition is correct. As Chester Finn has remarked, "Sating millions of individual appetites may not add up to a society that is well-prepared for the twenty-first century."[47] In the 1960s, after all, when schools relaxed their curricula and created long lists of electives, the competition in course offerings did not cause students to flock toward meatier classes and more demanding teachers. Quite the opposite occurred. Critics were rightly dismayed as schools diluted their academic programs with soft but popular subjects. Yet many of these same critics are now ardent proponents of choice without troubling to explain why students (and their parents) will do a better job of selecting schools than they did in choosing courses.

Furthermore, proponents of choice assume too quickly that outside groups, if given a chance, can readily create new schools that are much more effective than the ones we now have. The evidence for this proposition is shaky at best. Recent results on national tests reveal that private schools yield only slightly higher levels of achievement than public schools. And even these small differences may be due to the fact that parents who go to the trouble and expense of placing their children in private school encourage their offspring to study and give them more intellectual stimulation than their counterparts in the public schools.[48] In view of these findings, it is far from clear how much improvement new schools will bring to the students who enroll.

Finally, even if viable new schools were to emerge in substantial numbers, we must consider the fate of the public schools that would remain after motivated students with caring parents moved to greener pastures. In the marketplace, firms that suffer competitively either go bankrupt or attract new capital and new leadership to become more efficient. Public schools do not work in the same way. Twenty years ago, forced busing caused a mass exodus of white students in many cities but still failed to produce major improvements in the public schools. Voucher plans may have the same result, leaving public schools demoralized, short of funds, and bereft of their most active, concerned parents. In this event, parental choice will simply be one more step toward enlarging the gulf that already separates the poor from the middle class, the skilled from the unskilled, the educated from the uneducated.

In the end, therefore, as we evaluate parental choice, we need to ask ourselves just what problem we are trying to solve. If the task is simply to bring about a modest increase in the number of able, motivated students who can attend good schools, parental choice will offer some help. Still, subsidizing the entire private school system with federal vouchers is a very expensive way of achieving this limited improvement, which will do little to enhance America's competitiveness, let alone increase the cohesiveness or civic commitment of the society. If the goal is the more ambitious aim of improving the quality of education for all or most of our students, parental choice is a gamble at best. Because it might conceivably do some good, it deserves a chance to prove itself through carefully crafted experiments in communities willing to cooperate. Because it may fail—and widen the gap between the able and affluent and the rest of the student population—it would be folly to commit billions of dollars to a national voucher system until we know much more about how the reform will actually work.

Whatever the ultimate fate of voucher plans, parental choice seems unlikely anytime soon to generate enough pressure to bring about comprehensive school reform. After all, the required changes are fundamental, extending far beyond giving teachers higher salaries or recruiting them more vigorously. Real reform calls for a major shift in authority from higher levels of government to the school level as well as a series of steps to improve the quality of teachers and principals, the training they receive, the means by which they are held accountable, and their opportunities to work together in pursuit of more effective methods of teaching and learning.

Attacking this massive agenda is not a job we should leave to school boards and superintendents alone. Nor is it a process that will be carried out automatically by voucher plans, merit pay, or other devices to adjust incentives. Rather, it will require an active coalition of school officials, corporations, mayors, universities, foundations, and other local groups working together to bring about major change. Models for such a process exist in a few cities, such as Los Angeles and Louisville. By joining many important forces within the community, such coalitions not only gain added clout; they also guarantee that schools will have the cooperation of all the institutions that help to determine how far public education can progress. Only such an alliance can strike the grand bargain that will trade improved teacher salaries and greater school autonomy for higher standards and real accountability. Only a coalition of this kind can provide the framework for asking educators to widen the discussion of curriculum in exchange for cooperation from business in improving the transition from school to work to tie schoolwork more closely to the future of countless students. In short, serious reform must wait until the leaders from all important organizations in the community join together and decide that the need for better education has finally become urgent enough to demand their sustained and determined attention.

CHAPTER 10

FEDERAL OFFICIALS

As we pointed out earlier, the 1970s and 1980s were not a happy time for federal officials. Salaries for the upper grades of the civil service lost approximately 30 percent of their purchasing power and continued losing ground even in the 1980s, when starting salaries in most professions were rising steadily. The image of government was tainted by repeated scandals, while successive presidents loudly criticized federal bureaucracies to an approving public.

Gradually, a consensus emerged among knowledgeable people that a quiet crisis was brewing in the civil service. In 1988 a report of the President's Commission on Compensation for Career Executives found that pay levels for the Senior Executive Service had fallen as much as 65 percent below comparable jobs in the private sector.[1] Agency after agency complained of difficulty in recruiting professionals. Prominent columnists such as George Will observed that "the hemorrhaging of the government's lifeblood of talent is making the government dumber, not leaner."[2] Capping a long series of dire pronouncements by task forces and official bodies, the Volcker Commission concluded its labors in 1989 by declaring in its final report,

> Many young Americans feel that they can no longer afford to take a government job, while many civil servants can no longer ignore the call of private pay. If this trend continues, the result could be mediocrity in carrying out the essential tasks of government.[3]

After an abortive effort in 1990, Congress eventually approved substantial increases in compensation for the civil service with the expectation of further annual raises to eliminate much of the gap between public- and private-sector pay. It took considerable backbone to pass this measure in the teeth of public opposition. Where the initiative will end, however, remains very much in doubt. There are the usual escape clauses allowing the president to suspend the planned increases in the event of war or serious budgetary problems. Already, in 1991, President Bush found it necessary to delay expected pay raises for several months. A year later, he recommended a cut of 10 percent as a campaign pledge to trim government expenses. In 1993, President Clinton urged a temporary pay freeze followed by several years of holding increases below the cost of living. Today as in the past, therefore, occasional efforts to improve the lot of the civil service seem destined to give way to further periods of an austerity.

THE IMPORTANCE OF THE FEDERAL CIVIL SERVICE

The warnings of the Volcker Commission and the reports that preceded it did not convince everyone by any means. The opposing point of view was stated with disarming candor by one of President Reagan's own appointees, Terry Culler, associate director for Workforce Effectiveness in the Office of Personnel Management. Writing in 1986, Mr. Culler explained,

> The most important argument against seeking out the highest quality employee for the federal government seems to me, however, to be an argument that recognizes the private sector as the true vehicle for prosperity, social cohesiveness, and national welfare and as the place where we ought to encourage our best and brightest to migrate.[4]

This point of view, though rarely put so bluntly, is undoubtedly held by a significant share of the public. Even so, it is dangerously misguided, not in recognizing the vital role of the private sector but in denying one to the government as well.

Federal expenditures now make up more than 20 percent of the gross national product. Even Ronald Reagan, committed as he was to giving more authority to the states and to the private sector, could not cut the federal payroll or shrink the federal budget in real terms. It is unlikely that his successors will have any better luck. With a federal budget in excess of a trillion dollars per year, everyone has a stake in managing government agencies, efficiently and effectively.

In the vast enterprise of government, career public officials play an indispensable role. Granted the president chooses many hundreds of outsiders to fill the principal positions in the executive branch. These political appointees fashion broad policies and try to make sure they are administered in ways that conform to White House priorities and desires. But political appointees serve an average of less than two years. Most of them are not familiar with government when they arrive and must spend much of their brief tenure learning the intricate details of the policies they help to shape and the agencies over which they preside. To the extent that experience, expertise, and continuity count for anything in forming and executing policy, they must be supplied primarily by career public officials.

Moreover, the federal government is so large that even the thousands of political appointees cannot fill nearly all of the important management positions. During the Bush administration, civil servants were in direct charge of tasks as substantial as spending tens of millions of dollars to clean up hazardous waste sites across the country, developing and administering policies to regulate fishing and preserve marine life throughout the huge expanse of waters controlled by the federal government, managing chains of veterans' hospitals responsible for thousands of patients, and representing the United States as ambassadors in scores of foreign nations. These tasks demand much more than mechanically executing policies laid down by political superiors. To serve the public imaginatively and efficiently calls for the same creativity, organizational skills, and leadership abilities required of responsible executives in the private sector.

In some ways, government managers face challenges more formidable than those arising in the private sector. Unlike executives in industry, public officials are pulled by conflicting pressures from Congress and the executive branch. They serve under political appointees who come and go with uncommon frequency. They must contend with civil service rules and congressional restrictions that are frequently rigid, confusing, and out of date. With these handicaps, managing a large federal enterprise often calls for more managerial ability than executives need in guiding private corporations.

A high degree of skill is also required to carry out the regulatory responsibilities of the federal government. Congress has made it abundantly clear that it wishes private-sector competition to proceed within a network of regulations and restraints to protect the growing number of interests that the public holds dear—the environment, occupational health and safety, equal treatment among the races and sexes, truthful advertising, and many more. Much of the success or failure of these safeguards depends on how they are administered by career officials at the plant and local level. The public shares an obvious stake in having this task competently performed. Even companies do not gain by having lazy, incompetent bureaucrats enforcing regulatory laws. The government's activities are so pervasive that clumsy administrators can cause more damage than any relief they provide through ignorance and inertia.

Finally, there are important functions that private enterprise cannot carry out—defense, foreign policy, administration of justice, and many more. These tasks may not create new products or enrich our culture, but they are essential if the economy is to prosper and the quality of life improve. Carrying out such responsibilities is difficult, and high standards of performance are required. No sensible person would want to have lawyers representing the government who are less capable than counsel defending individuals and corporations accused of violating the law. Nor is it desirable for our trade negotiators to be less skillful than their opposite numbers from other nations.

RESISTANCE TO PAY INCREASES

Despite these arguments, opposition to federal pay raises comes from many quarters. In 1990, a Gallup poll reported that 59 percent of the public believed that federal officials were overpaid, while only 10 percent felt that they were paid too little.[5] Ralph Nader led the opposition to proposed raises, declaring that "more money has not and will not buy more integrity, dedication, and competence." As he put it, "mountains of resumes . . . reflect the reservoir of talent, inside and outside government, that awaits top officials who lead by example rather than by the restless envy of top corporate salaries."[6]

The passages just quoted reflect Mr. Nader's personal beliefs. Closer to the mood of the general public is his statement that "in the many letters and calls which we have received from Americans from diverse persuasions against salary increases, there is a central theme of deep disquiet about the gall of higher pay for federal officials presiding over a $180 billion a year deficit, lots of waste, proposed further cutbacks in critical housing, food, health, safety, mass transit, education, medicare and medicaid programs and a repeated refusal to defend the common citizens against the predations for the powerful."[7]

These remarks reveal much about the plight of the federal career official. Because civil service pay is linked to that of Congress and the cabinet, its fortunes are hostage to all the resentments and frustrations voters feel toward elected and appointed officials. As the different segments of government blur together in the public mind, career officials are blamed for unpopular policies that they had no hand in making. Because "bureaucracy" is a convenient whipping boy for every politician, the civil service is regularly accused of waste and condemned for being unresponsive and unimaginative.

Although some of these criticisms may be amply deserved, the civil service is often the victim of half-truths and serious misperceptions. For example, a 1982 survey found that 70 percent of the public felt that government employees were paid more than comparable workers in the private sector.[8] While this is true for lower-level employees, it is certainly not the case for professionals and managers. More knowledgeable critics concede that federal salaries lag the private sector at higher levels but claim that civil service fringe benefits are superior. Again, as the Volcker Commission found, "the perception that the federal government is a leading employer in terms of benefits is not accurate."[9] (After the pension reforms of 1984, which eliminated full indexing of federal pensions, the value of total benefits fell several percentage points behind average private-sector levels.)

The public also harbors a conviction that federal employees are much more wasteful and lazy than private-sector workers. Such impressions seem exaggerated, although the truth is hard to demonstrate. In one poll, which asked people how much of every federal tax dollar was wasted, the median response was 48 cents.[10] Yet one high-level inquiry after another has failed to establish waste on anything approaching this scale. According to another survey, a majority of the public believes that 52 cents of every dollar collected for Social Security goes to administration.[11] The true figure at the time of the poll was 1.3 cents.

Such examples could be repeated many times. Every study that compares general impressions of efficiency and responsiveness in the government with reactions from those who have dealt directly with federal agencies finds that officials make a much better impression on those who experience them firsthand than their general reputation would imply.[12] As a result, while popular disapproval undoubtedly helps to keep down government pay, it is hard to credit public opinion on this issue as either wise or well informed. Moreover, even if the public were correct, lowering salaries would scarcely be a good way to increase the efficiency of the government. Rather, it would drive good people out of the civil service and erode its performance even further.

A different argument against higher federal compensation comes from more conservative sources. According to this view, attracting smarter people to the federal government will only lead to more zealous enforcement of the laws and make it harder to live comfortably under our regulatory system. As one top corporate leader put it, "the government is full of bright, long-haired arrogant young lawyers right out of Harvard Law School whose main goal in life is to harass us."[13]

Understandably, executives who feel this way will be reluctant to support higher salaries to attract even brighter, more arrogant Harvard lawyers to make their lives miserable. But this is surely a wrong-headed view. If there is opposition to regulation in a democratic society, the proper remedy is to work through political processes to change the regulations, not to hobble the execution of the laws with inept public officials.

Some conservatives offer a more sophisticated version of the same argument. Recruiting abler people into federal agencies, they assert, is bound to produce an activist, interventionist bias in Washington; after all, such people find government attractive precisely because they believe in its capacity to improve society. For those who favor a more limited role for government, therefore, it is folly to spend money improving the quality of the civil service.

But is it true that only interventionist liberals are interested in public service? Certainly, conservative administrations in the 1980s did not seem to have much difficulty finding recruits of their persuasion to bring to Washington in appointive positions. Nor did these recruits lack challenge in seeking ways to cut back government services, introduce more competition, and bring about greater administrative efficiency. Moreover, even if the premise were valid, the conclusion would still not follow. The proper means of imposing a philosophy of government on a democratic society is by prevailing at the polls. Because the winning party fills all the key executive posts in Washington it can appoint hundreds of people to policy-making posts throughout the government. These loyal supporters should be able to restrain career officials from playing too ambitious a role.

Skeptics may fear, nevertheless, that able, activist career officials will somehow manage to subvert the conservative policies of their superiors. Yet there is little evidence to support this view. One of the striking facts to emerge in both Republican and Democratic administrations is the respect that political appointees gradually acquired for the civil servants working under them. In the mid-1980s, 84 percent of presidential appointees, past and present, rated the senior career civil servants in their agency as either 4 or 5 on a 5-point scale, where 5 was the highest possible rating.[14] As James Q. Wilson has observed, "What is surprising is not that bureaucrats sometimes defy the President but that they support his programs as much as they do."[15]

After all the contrary arguments have been made, therefore, the fact remains that the federal government must attract a large number of highly talented career officials to uphold the interests of society. Any policy of settling for mediocrity in the executive branch could be ruinously expensive and damage the national interest. As a result, even if the criticisms of the civil service are correct, as some of them doubtless are, the sensible response is hardly to reduce federal salaries and allow the quality of civil servants to decline. Instead, Congress and the executive branch should surely work together to attract able candidates by insisting on some sort of comparability with average rates of pay for corresponding jobs in the private sector.

MAKING GOVERNMENT SERVICE MORE ATTRACTIVE

Higher salaries alone will not suffice to bring outstanding individuals to the public service. At best, federal pay scales will approximate the average for the vast private sector; they will never come close to the salaries offered to promising candidates by major corporations and law firms. Indeed, if experience is any guide, government pay scales will often fall far short of even equaling the private-sector average. Since World War I, certainly, earnings for higher-level federal officials have failed to rise as fast as those of the work force as a whole in every decade but one.

Happily, there are other attractions of public service that few private organizations can match. In particular, the opportunity to further the public interest and to "make a difference" is also a significant factor to many students in choosing a career.[16] Clearly, federal agencies need to capitalize on this idealism as effectively as they can. In the words of Astrid Merged, dean of the Ohio State School of Public Policy and Management, "For students who want to serve and make a difference, offering careers as managers or analysts will not do the trick. We need to demonstrate the link between those careers and the lofty missions of government: cleaning the air, making the streets safe, unlocking a cure for AIDS, internationalizing the economy, bringing the underclass into the American mainstream."[17]

In contrast with these attractions, however, other aspects of government service are distinctly unappealing. For our most successful college seniors, the federal government scores well below universities, large corporations, and small businesses on a whole series of important dimensions: opportunities for challenging work, prospects for personal growth, pleasant working conditions, good collegial relations, autonomy in one's work, professional recognition, and possibilities for advancement.[18] Not all these characteristics are easily changed. Yet some of them are—and without spending large amounts of money.

A useful place to start would be to improve the image of public service. This aspect of working for the government should be an asset but has been allowed to become a liability. In one recent study, college placement officers in a variety of fields ranked the poor reputation of government among the two principal reasons (along with low pay) that discourage able students from careers in public service.[19] Senior civil servants leaving the government likewise cite the lack of public respect as a significant factor in their decision.

Unfortunately, the image of government has worsened appreciably in the past thirty years. The excitement of government service that President Kennedy inspired gave way to doubts by the 1970s and then to efforts by Presidents Carter and Reagan to run against Washington by blaming the bureaucrats. "I am coming to Washington," President Reagan declared, "to clear the swamp." However attractive such messages may be to voters, they chip away at the government's most precious asset in attracting talent. Moreover, because the failings that anger the public most are usually the fault of elected and appointed officials (not civil servants), there is all the more reason for government leaders to protect the career staff instead of belittling them to curry political favor.

Like the private professions, the public sector deserves a fair share of unusually talented individuals. Because starting salaries in government have fallen so far behind the compensation given to the graduates of leading law schools and business schools, the civil service needs some special initiative to attract exceptional young people. The obvious first step would be to offer ample scholarships to college or professional school students in exchange for a commitment to serve in the federal government for a stipulated period following graduation.[20] As in the case of prospective teachers, such a program should take the form of grants, not loans, and students unwilling to fulfill their commitment to serve should have to repay their scholarships at market rates of interest.

Attracting talented young professionals will do little good if they leave after a few years for lack of opportunity to assume more responsibility. Yet a major drawback of government service is the widespread impression that the prospects for advancement are much more limited than in the private sector. This perception is shared by college students generally and even by students who serve as government interns. It is one of the principal reasons senior civil servants give for leaving the federal service.[21]

Several forces combine to limit opportunities.[22] Careers in the federal service are typically narrow and specialized, giving young professionals little chance to develop their skills to assume wider administrative responsibilities. In the private sector, top corporate managers delegate much authority to younger executives, despite the risk that errors will occur, because the flexibility and innovation that can result are more than worth the cost of an occasional mistake. In government, although creativity and flexibility may be celebrated in theory, the benefits seem minor in comparison with the political cost of errors that lead to negative publicity or hostile public hearings. As a result, top officials do not delegate much responsibility to middle management, hoping to maintain enough control to avoid misadventures that could cause political damage.

The civil service has not done much to overcome these problems by taking active measures to develop capable, broad-gauged managers. Supposedly, the Senior Executive Service was to accomplish this purpose by selecting promising administrators and offering them general management training and opportunities to move from one agency to another. Unfortunately, the government has not exploited these possibilities effectively. Federal agencies spend, on average, less than 1 percent of their payroll on training, compared with 3.3 percent by Fortune 500 companies.[23] Transfers have seldom been used to provide fresh challenges for able officials frustrated in their current jobs. Movement from one agency to another is rare, and the transfer process has been compromised by a growing sense that it was being used for partisan political purposes.

The ultimate damper on career opportunities is the practice in Washington of making far more political appointments to government agencies than is true of any other advanced, democratic nation. This tendency springs from a desire not only to reward political supporters but to secure greater political control over the administration of executive branch activities. Ironically, this goal is rarely achieved because most political appointees have little contact with the White House and often proceed to follow their own agendas. What their presence does accomplish is to limit opportunities for career advancement and subject federal agencies to an endless parade of inexperienced managers that no self-respecting corporation would allow.[24] It would be wise, therefore, to follow the recommendations of many commissions and advisory groups by cutting back sharply on the number of political appointments.

Along with increased training and better career development, government agencies need to review their methods of recruitment and make them more efficient, more responsive, and more flexible. At present, the public sector spends far less money on recruitment than private corporations and law firms. According to one recent study, 50 percent of federal agencies have no recruiting brochure, 58 percent have no money budgeted for college recruiting, and 49 percent have no advertising budget.[25] For young people interested in government service, there are complicated forms to fill out, civil service exams to take, and other intricate procedures causing such long delays that many of the best candidates have long since taken other jobs by the time their applications are finally processed. In one study, over half of those who declined a government offer said they had accepted another job while waiting for a response from a federal agency.[26] Problems of this kind are serious enough to cause a recent team from the U.S. Merit System Review Board to conclude that "Every agency contacted by the Board agreed that the Federal hiring process is a labyrinth of lengthy and confusing procedures that result in the Government losing applicants to jobs in the non-Federal sector."[27]

These problems are not accidental. They spring from the government's overweening desire to avoid embarrassing mistakes. Senior government officials take elaborate precautions to ensure that units under their authority do not engage in nepotism, favor political cronies, discriminate against women and blacks, or employ criminals, incompetents, or foreign agents. That is why recruitment procedures are kept under central control, subjected to detailed regulations, and swaddled in elaborate forms for officials to fill out to ensure conformity to the rules.

Fortunately, there are recent signs that the Office of Personnel Management is making greater efforts to improve and simplify recruitment procedures. Agencies have been delegated more power to make hiring decisions on the spot, hot lines have been installed to give immediate information to college students about job openings, and special salary supplements have been authorized when the government is significantly handicapped in recruiting or retaining qualified individuals. It is too soon to know how successful these initiatives will be or even if they will survive. Still, the outlook is more promising than it has been in the past.

Whether the public sector takes advantage of these opportunities depends as much on attitude as on resources. Government agencies calculate their futures in very different ways from their counterparts in the private sector. Law firms and corporations must either maintain the highest possible quality of personnel or risk losing business, prestige, and ultimately money. Government entities, on the other hand, have much less to fear from hiring recruits of indifferent quality unless their performance becomes so dismal as to cause corruption, waste, or public dissatisfaction that inflicts political costs. This does not mean that government leaders never insist on striving for the highest quality of civil servants in their agencies.

There are many examples of vigorous, successful recruiting. Yet these instances will remain the exception rather than the rule until there are compelling reasons for adopting high standards and making them an article of faith throughout the government. The problem of improving the quality of personnel, therefore, is ultimately a problem of incentives.

MOTIVATING THE TROOPS

As a little-known candidate in 1976, Jimmy Carter elected to run as an outsider and capitalize on the deep distrust toward Washington that had arisen over Watergate, Vietnam, and controversial programs involving poverty and race. Among Carter's concerns was the federal bureaucracy. When he took office, therefore, he set about to reform the civil service to make it function more effectively.

By hammering away on the theme of incompetence and waste, Carter succeeded in persuading Congress to pass the Civil Service Reform Act of 1978. Prominent in its provisions was a scheme to introduce merit pay to the higher reaches of the federal bureaucracy. For the first time, government managers and professionals would receive special bonuses if they did a particularly good job. In this way, Carter hoped to energize government officials and surround them with incentives that would elicit higher performance.

What followed resembled a parody on the foibles of bureaucracy.[28] Personnel offices spent months on plans to implement the new scheme only to be upset by last-minute legal opinions shifting the basic ground rules. Lacking a staff experienced in the intricacies of merit pay, the Office of Personnel Management relied on untried novices to give advice to confused agency officials. Instructions were unexpectedly changed in midstream. Directives of byzantine complexity bogged down the process of implementation, resulting in costs that were said to run as high as one billion dollars. Last-minute funding reductions were ordered by the comptroller general, forcing agencies to revise their plans yet again. Eventually, after all this travail, the government succeeded in handing out such small merit awards that they could not possibly have a positive effect on motivation.

Instead of rousing the best and brightest to ever-increasing efforts, incentive pay produced only resentment. After holding hearings on the subject, Congresswoman Oaker was moved to describe the program as a "disincentive millstone" around the neck of the federal government.

Responding to these complaints, Congress revised the system in 1984 and ordered the government to start over. The new program overcame much of the dissatisfaction engendered by its predecessor but only by allowing supervisors to rate everyone so highly that over 90 percent became eligible for some kind of award. Regrettably, those who were already at the top of their pay scale were ineligible for extra pay, thus preventing the plan from offering them any added incentive to excel. By the third year of its operation, however, bonuses were no longer correlated with performance anyway, so the potency of the incentives seemed largely irrelevant.[29]

At the root of these difficulties are problems akin to those of merit pay in the public schools. Evaluating performance is often difficult, because the goals of government are usually more nebulous than achieving production quotas or boosting profit margins. Subjective evaluations run special risks of abuse and misunderstanding in the government because of the fear that political appointees, who often evaluate high-level career officials, will be biased in their judgments and confuse partisan loyalty with professional competence. In one recent study, almost 70 percent of government managers expressed the belief that performance evaluations were influenced unfairly by higher officials.[30]

As in the private sector, many supervisors have been reluctant to give honest evaluations and risk prejudicing good relations with their subordinates. Instead, they have quietly used the new system not for its intended purpose but as a way of giving as many bonuses as possible to get around pay ceilings that are widely considered to be rigid and unfair. For these reasons, far too many people have received very high ratings, further attenuating the link between merit awards and exceptional performance.

Similar problems have cropped up in introducing performance pay into the Senior Executive Service. Shortly after the original law was passed, Congress cut the percentage eligible for bonuses each year from 50 to 25 percent. Later, the Office of Management and Budget lowered the ceiling once more, to 20 percent. Regard for the program quickly sagged. Moreover, implementation again proved difficult. Today, bonuses are widely used not to reward exceptional performance but to get around pay restrictions or to keep valued executives from leaving the government. As the Task Force on Pay and Compensation for the Volcker Commission remarked in 1989, "The idea of performance bonuses for SES members is a good one, but the current implementation of the idea amounts to little more than use of bonuses to increase the salaries of deserving executives."[31]

With this record, it is not surprising that government employees are highly critical of existing practices (although 72 percent still endorse the principle of linking pay to performance). According to recent surveys by public management associations, only 3 percent of federal administrators believe the current system should be continued in its present form, while 40 percent feel it should be completely abolished.[32] Similar results have emerged from surveys of the Senior Executive Service. According to a 1987 study, "78 percent said that the SES bonus system did not provide an effective incentive for them to meet their job objectives . . . 69 per cent said the SES bonus system is not administered fairly . . . 76 per cent said there is not a direct link between their performance and their likelihood of receiving an SES bonus."[33]

With diplomatic restraint, a 1991 report by the National Research Council concluded its comprehensive review by stating that "the reforms have by most measures fallen short of expectations, despite fairly substantial midcourse corrections."[34] Other critics have been less kind. According to one author, a federal official who frequently writes on compensation policies, "The merit pay system put a previously stable employee compensation system in shambles."[35]

BEYOND BONUSES

Are there other steps that can be taken to strengthen incentives in government agencies to provide efficient, effective service? Recent developments offer some hope. In the past few years, tax revolts and other forms of popular discontent seem to have stimulated governments, especially at the state and local levels, to look harder for opportunities to introduce the discipline of the marketplace to improve performance. Public officials have opened more government services to private competition by issuing vouchers or inviting private companies to bid. Other services have been privatized and sold to private organizations to operate.[36]

Many initiatives of this kind have been quite successful. Entire categories of service have simply been removed from government and given to private organizations stimulated by market competition. These remedies did not begin in the 1970s. But public officials have recently shown exceptional ingenuity in extending market incentives to new domains such as public schooling, fire fighting, and even the resolution of legal disputes.

Despite these successes, there are limits to market alternatives. Some public functions are inappropriate candidates for private competition. Few people, for example, would advocate contracting out such services as military operations, the administration of criminal justice, or the conduct of trade negotiations and international diplomacy. Other functions lack alternative sources of supply that can compete with one another. Rural towns are unlikely to find several organizations willing to bid on contracts for garbage removal or fire protection.

Even if services are contracted out to private organizations, the functions do not disappear from the purview of government. Public officials must still oversee the bidding process, monitor performance, and negotiate contracts with appropriate provisions to ensure fair employment practices, environmental protection, and other standards important to the public interest. These activities require a substantial number of supervisory personnel if privatization is not to collapse under a flood of complaints alleging corruption, waste, and other abuses. Thus, the Defense Department continues to employ tens of thousands of civilian professionals even though private companies supply the military equipment. The Energy Department has not gone out of business because it conducts most of its functions through outside contractors. In short, even if the government intensifies its pursuit of privatization and competition, large numbers of bureaucrats will remain with important functions to perform. Their motivation and efficiency will continue to be a matter of genuine public concern.

If merit pay has not worked well and privatization and competition can bring only limited relief, what other sources of motivation are available to inspirit public officials? Some hint of an answer may come from examples of highly dedicated agencies in the federal government. A close look at the reasons for their success suggests that the techniques required to motivate government officials are similar to those used in successful companies, schools, law firms, and other strongly committed organizations.[37] Leadership is needed to articulate appropriate goals and values and to create a sense of mission capable of inspiring enthusiasm. Members must have opportunities to contribute their ideas and to participate in finding ways to achieve the organization's goals. Candid feedback and evaluation are important, as are opportunities for training, advancement, and personal renewal, adequate facilities in which to work, and freedom to exercise initiative and responsibility.

In trying to build a highly motivated organization, government agencies start with the signal advantage of being able to call upon ideals of service that matter a lot to many people and give great meaning to their work. The opportunity to serve the public ought to provide a much more powerful source of motivation than the chance to market deodorants or manufacture garden furniture. Yet the image of public servants is not one of energized, enthusiastic people doing their utmost to carry out an important mission. Rather, the impression is that career officials, on the whole, are less likely to be highly motivated or to work hard than their counterparts in the private sector. Why?

In part, the stereotype of government is unfair. But that is not the whole story. Peculiar features of government agencies make it difficult to apply many of the lessons from other organizations about mobilizing enthusiasm and commitment.

Although many federal agencies are charged with high public purposes—cleaning up the environment, keeping the peace, enforcing justice, or exploring space—building commitment on the basis of such goals carries certain risks. Employees may become so zealous in pursuit of an agency's mission that they ignore other interests that get in their way or try to block shifts in policy that come with changes in administration. Officials in the Environmental Protection Agency may resist or lose heart when new leadership alters the priorities from cleaning polluted rivers to making sure that regulations do not hamper industry's ability to compete. Officials in antipoverty agencies may be demoralized if a new administration switches the emphasis from helping the poor to cutting costs by trimming benefits and easing people off relief rolls. Some bureaus and agencies may have goals stable enough to avoid this problem, and adjustments from one administration to another may be minor. For most, however, the proper statement of their mission is not the dedicated pursuit of a particular social goal but the subtler task of furthering the work of democracy by adjusting to changes in priority and direction transmitted through periodic elections. As always, however, there is a price to be paid. Shifting policies to conform to each new administration may be a necessary part of democracy, but it often lacks the satisfaction that comes with an unswerving commitment to cleaning up the environment, feeding undernourished children, or furthering some other vital social mission.

Creating a clear set of priorities and values can also be difficult in government because public agencies must answer to so many masters. As Martha Derthick points out, "whereas the chief executives of private, profit-making organizations can within limits define their own agendas, executives of public agencies have theirs thrust upon them."[38] Agency heads may get one set of instructions from their political superiors, another from powerful members of Congress who vote their appropriations, and still other orders from the courts, which can frustrate their efforts by redefining their powers to conform to the judges' view of congressional intent. Media reporters, interest groups, and advocacy organizations can likewise exert a powerful influence because of their ability to inflict political damage.

Some officials are sheltered from these pressures, and others skillfully manipulate them or neutralize them to maintain a fragile autonomy. All too often, however, the environment of government agencies is characterized by inconsistent goals, impossible deadlines, intrusive legislative oversight, and unrealistic administrative demands. Interest groups intent on weakening an unwelcome regulatory agency, legislators anxious to make sure that officials carry out their wishes, presidents determined to bend the bureaucracy to the White House's will all bring conflicting pressures to bear in order to achieve their separate ambitions. As a result, in contrast to private-sector organizations, which are usually constructed with the sole intent of executing institutional policy effectively, public agencies are often a hybrid built by clashing power centers with a variety of purposes in mind.

Operating in such a minefield, many public managers will hesitate to share their aims with subordinates in an open, participative process. If the goals they hope to achieve are controversial, they may find them whispered to the media or disclosed to powerful legislators with very different ideas. In view of these risks, top officials may think it necessary to keep goals hidden or ambiguous to avoid having them leaked and prematurely killed by external pressure. Yet such secretiveness can demoralize subordinates and rob their experience of much of its meaning and coherence.

In addition, public managers have much less discretion than private executives to mold an effective, dedicated unit. In an effort to improve coordination and ensure adherence to their policies, Congress and the White House will frequently impose detailed requirements on the operations of government agencies that can hamper public executives seeking to achieve greater efficiency. In trying to build a strong team, agency heads will also find it harder than their private-sector counterparts to dismiss or reassign long-term officials, even those in responsible management and professional posts. They may likewise encounter more difficulty holding subordinates accountable or evaluating their performance, because public-sector goals rarely lend themselves to precise measures comparable to profit and loss or market share.

Even if these familiar bureaucratic hurdles did not exist, another problem stands in the way of building strong cultures in public agencies. Developing a mission and nurturing commitment call for long and patient effort. Most private companies that have created a strong corporate culture built on shared purposes and values have had to spend five to ten years on the task.[39] But the average political appointee in the executive branch stays less than two years in the same post, and precious months of this brief span must be spent learning enough about the job even to think about goals and strategies. As a result, many appointed executives will simply not consider it feasible to devote their energies to building a motivated team.

The ultimate reason why many government agencies do not build a strong organization is that their political leaders do not assign a high priority to the task. Most appointed federal officials would probably agree with a former cabinet secretary, Michael Blumenthal, who remarked, "You learn very quickly that you do not go down in history as a good or bad Secretary in terms of how well you run the place."[40] The reason is not sloth or indifference. The fact is that public executives are judged not so much by the quality of their administrative skills as by the success or failure of the policies with which their names are associated. Gaining approval for new policies typically involves a long, arduous process of building support among a number of interested constituencies outside the agency. As a result, appointed officials are likely to conclude that it is impossible to push new initiatives through and still be able to worry much about the quality of internal administration.

In fairness, the outlook may not be quite as bleak as this description would suggest. There will be some new agencies, or new functions in old agencies, that allow the recruitment of an enthusiastic, committed staff and make problems of motivation seem easy. Other agencies are headed by long-term public servants with the time and anonymity to work at building a motivated team. Elmer Staats at the General Accounting Office and Robert Ball and his associates at the Social Security Administration are well-known cases in point. Still other units, like the solicitor general's office in the Justice Department, have a simple, enduring mission of compelling interest to many able attorneys. Overall, however, the obstacles to developing a shared sense of mission and commitment are undeniably greater in government than they are in the public sector.

CONCLUSION

In the end, those who would reform the civil service must come to terms with the fact that Americans want many things from their government, and efficiency and hard work are by no means the most important. Because we wish to prevent excessive concentrations of power, we have a system of divided government and checks and balances that subjects the bureaucracy to several masters who often issue contradictory commands. Because we want to avoid errors and abuses, we tolerate a complicated process of oversight, review, publicity, and investigation. Because we desire a responsive government, we open the bureaucracy to a wide variety of pressures—from citizen organizations, individual legislators, public hearings, inquiring reporters, even private lawsuits—that force public agencies to attend to the concerns of interested groups.

These conflicting demands do much to bring about the characteristic behaviors we have come to associate with bureaucracy—the timidity, lack of venturesomeness and imagination, rigid controls, cumbersome procedures, and reluctance to make exceptions even when circumstances require them. We often blame public officials for acting in this fashion even though our system of government and the demands we place upon it bear most of the responsibility.

Upset with bureaucrats, we make matters worse by opposing increases in their pay, which only makes it more difficult to attract good people to government service.

These problems complicate the lives of public officials even in the best of times. In periods of widespread disaffection with government, the work of the bureaucracy grows harder still. From 1970 to 1990, a vast array of techniques was used to try to push the executive branch to become more responsive, more responsible, more efficient, and more effective. Congress increased its oversight and issued more detailed commands. Individual legislators pressed harder for their constituents. The General Accounting Office expanded its staff and stepped up the number of its investigations. Inspectors general were installed in nineteen separate agencies. The Office of Management and Budget emerged with extensive powers to oversee and overrule individual agencies. Judges were more inclined to take a "hard look" at the exercise of administrative power. Sunset provisions, zero-based budgeting, cost-benefit analysis, and other techniques were mandated to make bureaucrats behave more rationally.[41]

In individual cases, no doubt, these methods may help to force agencies to shift priorities, attend to a neglected interest, or speed up a review process. Overall, however, subjecting the bureaucracy to so many levers of influence used coercively by a growing number of sources is draining and demoralizing. On balance, the civil service will become more cautious, more defensive, and more inclined to work by the rules to be able to justify each action taken.

In the last analysis, then, the problem of improving incentives in government cannot be separated from the attitudes of the public toward government itself. If these feelings turn negative, as they surely did after 1970, political leaders find it tempting to deflect the public's wrath by making the bureaucracy a scapegoat for the shortcomings of government. Individual legislators are quicker to search for scandal and abuse to enhance their own reputations. Congress grows less inclined to authorize increases in pay. Government leaders, intent on appearing to do something, will impose still more reorganizations, shake-ups, and review procedures. In such an atmosphere, the chances of fostering real efficiency and high morale are about as great as the prospect that the proverbial monkeys seated at their typewriters in the British Museum will reproduce the writings of William Shakespeare.

PART III

CHAPTER 11

SUMMING UP

With all that has occurred in our six fields of professional endeavor, what common threads can we find to help answer the questions posed at the outset of this study? Are certain executives and professionals significantly overpaid? Is the supply of intellectually gifted university graduates distributed among the fields in a manner that matches the nation's needs? Do current methods of compensation motivate professionals to work suitably hard for appropriate goals? As the reader will have divined, the answers to these questions are not reassuring.

ARE SOME PROFESSIONALS OVERPAID?

When Babe Ruth was asked in 1932 why he had earned twice as much as the president of the United States, he replied with characteristic bluntness, "I had a better year."[1] No doubt he did, recalling all that befell Mr. Hoover during that period. But surely it was harder for the CEOs at Ford, Chrysler, and G.M. to argue in 1990 that their year was three or four times better than that of their counterparts at Honda or Toyota. And it could not be easy for the assistant professor of neurosurgery at Cornell to explain why he earned more than nine times the salary of his own university president, who is widely regarded as one of the nation's most accomplished academic leaders. Not to mention the 60-odd law partners of Cravath, Swaine & Moore, whose earnings in 1990 averaged more than the salaries of all nine Supreme Court justices combined.

As the previous examples make clear, CEOs, sports idols, and entertainment stars are not the only ones to take home huge amounts of money. Hundreds of investment bankers, consultants, doctors, and lawyers also earn over $1 million per year. Unlike the rich and powerful in many societies past and present, relatively few professionals in America achieve success by accident of birth or by methods cruel and corrupt. The overwhelming majority are chosen for their talents and accomplishments and simply accept the rewards that seem to come naturally under the prevailing systems of compensation in this country.

Leading professionals fared especially well during the past ten to twenty years, even though the competition around them was intensifying, economic growth had slowed appreciably, and most other members of the labor force failed to increase their earnings or actually lost ground. At first glance, the good fortune of so many executives, lawyers, and physicians seems hard to comprehend. The conventional wisdom has long been that professions raise the incomes of their members by restricting the supply of qualified practitioners. While this may be true for professions as a whole, it hardly seems to apply to the more prosperous members. From 1970 to 1990, surgeons, radiologists, anesthesiologists, and other hospital-based specialists raised their earnings by 30 to 50 percent, even though the number of doctors increased more than in any other period in this century. Real profits per partner in elite law firms rose by 75 percent or more during two decades when the supply of lawyers almost trebled and competition for corporate clients grew more intense than ever before. CEOs of large firms saw their incomes more than double at a time when the numbers of MBAs jumped threefold and foreign firms challenged American business more successfully than at any other time in our history.

The reasons why leading practitioners fared so well reveal much about the special characteristics of the market for private-sector professionals. Several features of this market are particularly important.

To begin with, although employers are content merely to insist on minimum qualifications in hiring employees for most clerical and manufacturing jobs, the opposite is true in choosing a tax lawyer, an orthopedic surgeon, or a top corporate executive. The work that each of these professionals is hired to perform is typically so important that there is every reason to try to pick the very best available candidate. Unfortunately, it is extremely difficult to make such choices well. Seldom are there clear measures for evaluating a candidate's past record. Moreover, those who seek to employ a lawyer or a doctor or a business executive rarely know the identity, let alone the qualifications, of nearly all of the individuals who might in fact be able and willing to perform the work desired. Instead, ignorance narrows the field drastically, to the detriment of those who have the ability but lack the visibility and track record to reach the final list of candidates for important, highly paid opportunities.

In this uncertain world, there is much to say for choosing the professional who commands the greatest reputation. When things turn out badly, one need never apologize for having selected a leading figure in the field; it is the person who tries to save money by choosing a practitioner of uncertain quality who will have the explaining to do. There is likewise no need to spend precious time investigating the qualifications of leading figures in the field; their reputations speak for themselves. Moreover, as investigators have shown, those who enjoy a higher standing receive more credit for the same accomplishment than colleagues of lesser stature. (Sociologists call this the "Matthew effect": "Unto everyone that hath, more shall be given. . . ."). In all these ways, established figures gain advantages over other professionals who may in fact have equal abilities.

Another characteristic of the more lucrative fields of professional work is that the cost of hiring the best person, however imposing it may seem in isolation, is seldom a vital concern to those who employ such highly skilled talents. The money paid to outside lawyers is typically a tiny fraction of a corporation's budget. The same is true of the pay bestowed on top company executives. In medicine, to be sure, the fees charged by leading specialists might seem large to many of their patients. Yet patients rarely pay more than a small fraction of their medical bills; the rest is reimbursed by government agencies and insurance companies with vast financial resources.

In these circumstances, vigorous price competition is more the exception than the rule, for price is seldom a prime consideration in deciding which professional to hire. Chief executives do not win their jobs by offering to serve for less than their leading rivals. Nor do surgeons appeal to prospective patients by promising to replace their hips or remove their tumors for lower fees than are customary. Not only is money a secondary matter in choosing such executives and professionals; offering one's services for unusually low rates may signal some sort of weakness and thus repel clients rather than attract them.

In arriving at a price for their services, moreover, few professionals have to trust their fortunes to unfettered negotiations with informed and independent employers. Doctors receive much of their pay through formulas determined directly or indirectly by a government that has not been ungenerous to them in the past. Chief executives often exert great influence over the procedures for setting their own compensation. Even personal injury lawyers make their living by sharing in their clients' recoveries according to fixed percentages that bear no relation to the work and skill required to prosecute the claim.

Once the terms of compensation have been set, leading professionals can take advantage of their employer's ignorance to keep some control over their earnings and maintain them at high levels. Few clients and patients are able to judge precisely how many services they need from their lawyers and physicians. Patients rarely know whether they are being referred to laboratories or other facilities in which their doctor holds a financial interest. Boards of directors can seldom detect the balance-sheet adjustments that may have helped their president earn a bonus, nor are they well equipped to question the judgment of the consultants whom the CEO employs to recommend his pay increase for the following year.

Under these less-than-competitive conditions, market changes that would ordinarily be benign can have perverse effects. For example, efforts to publicize the earnings of chief executives in the 1980s did not stop boards of directors from authorizing large pay increases. Rather, they spurred some chief executives to press for more money in an effort to keep pace with rival CEOs and thus helped to ratchet up executive pay even further. Publishing the profits per partner of large law firms is widely thought to have had similar effects. In medicine, the growing number of doctors in the 1970s and 1980s did not foster a healthy competition to provide better work at lower prices. If anything, it pushed many physicians to render more services and order more tests to maintain their earnings.

In sum, we cannot justify the earnings of leading professionals merely by invoking the principles of market competition. Nor can we explain such high incomes by citing the need to induce able people to enter the profession and strive hard for success, or by arguing that the recipients are somehow worth every penny they receive. The thousands of applicants each year who cannot gain admission to any school of law or medicine indicate that earnings in these professions are higher than a free market would allow. The caliber of people willing to run for seats in Congress or serve as university presidents, judges, or foundation heads indicates that huge salaries are not required to persuade highly competent individuals to accept positions of great responsibility. Comparisons with other advanced countries suggest that our most successful managers and practitioners are probably paid at least two or three times the amount required to attract able people and motivate them to do their best. Because foreign professionals and executives are quite possibly overcompensated as well, the pay inflation in this country may be even greater than international comparisons indicate.

How concerned should we be by the swollen paychecks of leading doctors, lawyers, and business executives? To many people, the answer must seem obvious. Successful professionals are unusually fortunate quite apart from all the money they earn. The jobs they hold are not only well paid but exceptionally interesting and challenging—the sort of jobs that not only give great personal satisfaction but boost self-esteem, confidence, and personal growth.[2] With all these advantages, is it not grossly unfair that such favored individuals should earn fifty, one hundred, even two hundred times the average pay of working people who toil away at much less interesting jobs?

Those who ask this question may consider it only rhetorical. Yet the answer is not obvious to everyone. More than a few commentators have urged that huge salaries are but a minor problem hardly worthy of serious concern. What considerations could possibly lead them to this conclusion?

One popular argument in business magazines is that there is so much mobility in America that those who earn big money one year are likely not to earn it the next, or at least not to earn it a few years later. As a result, high incomes do not last long enough to matter. This claim may be accurate enough for some occupations—rock music, for example, or professional football. It is much less likely to be true of high earners in general. Most of the constant movement in and out of the top 1 percent of incomes occurs among individuals close to the dividing line and thus merely represents a normal fluctuation around a very elevated mean. Joel Slemrod has given an illustration of this point that reveals just how stable high incomes tend to be. According to his calculations, the average income of families that took in over $100,000 in 1983 was $176,000. The average income of these families over the entire seven-year period ending in 1985 was $153,000.[3]

Successful professionals of the kind we have been considering are especially likely to enjoy consistently high earnings. Most law partners in large firms will continue doing very well for many years. So will most leading cardiologists and neurosurgeons. Even CEOs will typically spend six or seven years in their posts earning a large salary with bonuses and stock options. And almost every chief executive will have had years of prior service as a chief operating officer or in some other job that brings a handsome paycheck to the incumbent.

Conservative writers are likely to respond that there are too few overpaid people to make much difference and that if all of them were stripped of their unjustified gains and the proceeds spread among the needy, the impact would be trivial. Michael Novak, for example, once observed that in 1978 only 354,200 taxpayers reported incomes over $100,000, while only 69,039 listed incomes over $200,000. Even if all income over $100,000 were confiscated, he concluded, the yield would amount to only $6 billion, hardly enough to make the effort worthwhile.[4]

However telling this argument may have been in 1978, it is much less persuasive now. The 1980s were exceptionally good years for the well-to-do. By the end of the decade, the number of individuals reporting incomes above $200,000 had climbed tenfold, from 69,039 to more than one million.[5] Over sixty thousand people in 1990 stated that they had received more than $1 million in that year.[6] At this point, merely taxing the incomes above $150,000 at a rate 10 percent above the current level would produce over $20 billion in added revenue. Such a sum would not be enough to solve all the problems of America, but it could surely pay for a number of worthy projects.

Still other writers have tried to ease our minds about excessive incomes by extolling the functions that rich people perform in our society. George Gilder, for example, points out that it is the wealthy who accumulate discretionary capital, and it is "discretionary capital that finances most of what is original and idiosyncratic in our culture and economy, that launches the apparently hopeless cause in business and politics, that supports the unusual invention, art or private school, that funds the institution of the future."[7] Other commentators add that rich people in the United States traditionally return much of their wealth to society through philanthropy, thus undercutting any reason one might have to begrudge them their riches.[8]

It is easy to point to splendid examples of persons who have used their fortunes imaginatively to benefit others. What is harder to prove is that private wealth is clearly superior to other ways of fostering innovation in art, education, politics, and business. Other societies have produced creative artists, great symphonies and theater, political movements of all kinds, and a dynamic economy without relying on the contributions of extremely wealthy people. Clearly, allowing professionals to earn inflated incomes is a strikingly inefficient way of making good works possible. Very few wealthy people give away more than a small fraction of their fortunes. In 1988, for example, individuals making more than $100,000 per year donated only 2.4 percent of their incomes to charity, while those making more than $1 million gave away only 2.9 percent.[9] These shares were not even as high as those reported by itemizing donors with incomes under $20,000 per year.

The average share of income that individuals earning over $1 million donated to charity in 1990 was also less than half of what it was in 1980, before their income tax rates were reduced from 70 to 28 percent. These figures suggest that limiting the earnings of the wealthiest individuals would not necessarily reduce creative philanthropy. On the contrary, if the government chose to trim incomes by raising taxes on the rich, the net cost of making a gift would decline, and the effect on charitable giving would almost certainly rise.[10] Hence, even if one believes Gilder's assertions about the creative role of accumulated wealth, it does not follow that we should do nothing about unjustified earnings.

The most intriguing argument for tolerating excessive incomes is that they do not matter much anyway, as riches do not bring real happiness to those who receive them. In Adam Smith's words, "Wealth and greatness are mere trinkets of frivolous utility, no more adapted for procuring ease of body or tranquillity of mind than the tweezer-cases of the lover of toys; and like them, too, more troublesome to the person who carries them about with him than all the advantages they can afford him."[11] Rather than eat our hearts out envying the rich, therefore, we should feel fortunate to avoid the special cares that come to those affluent enough to have to fend off fund-raisers and cope with psychoanalysts, auditors from the Internal Revenue Service, and vacation homes in exotic places. Or so the argument goes.

But is it really true that money brings no added happiness? Many psychologists have tried to answer this question. Their inquiries consistently show that rich people *are* more likely to consider themselves happy than those who have lower incomes. But the differences are not as large as some might think, and that is indeed fortunate. If happiness were distributed as unequally as money, we would long since have had a revolution. As it happens, however, happiness and contentment are divided much more evenly. The annual surveys of the National Opinion Research Corporation tell the story.[12]

EXTENT OF REPORTED HAPPINESS BY INCOME GROUPS (1973–1990)*

	Very Happy	Pretty Happy	Not Too Happy
Under $10,000	23.9	55.0	21.0
$10,000–$20,000	29.4	56.6	14.0
$20,000–$30,000	32.8	57.1	10.1
$30,000–$50,000	37.2	55.1	9.7
$50,000–$75,000	43.7	49.9	6.4
Over $75,000	44.5	50.2	5.3

* These figures are consistent with many other studies. One large-scale survey concluded that differences in wealth did not account for more than 15 percent of the differences in overall satisfaction with life. Of this, only 7 percent was attributable to actual differences in consumption, while 8 percent was due to the psychological and symbolic values of possessing more money (Andrews and Withey, *Social Indicators of Well-Being* [1976], 124). Whatever satisfaction may have resulted from affluence was dwarfed by the impact of blessings that money cannot buy, such as friends, good health, and warm family relationships.

Apparently, the reason why the rich feel somewhat more satisfied than the poor is not simply that they can buy more. If material goods were the key to lasting satisfaction, Americans would be much happier than they were in the 1950s, when their real income was much less than half what it is today. Even so, they do not declare themselves any happier today than they were then.[13] Indeed, wealthier Americans seem to feel considerably *less* satisfied.[14] These findings have led some writers to assume that much of the dissatisfaction that poor people experience results not from having fewer possessions but from illusions or feelings of envy.[15] If that is so, stripping professionals of their unjustified gains might not add much to the happiness of others. So long as any differences in income remain, those who earn less will continue to be more dissatisfied than those who have more.

Arguments of this kind plainly count for something. If happiness varied as much as income, the problem of inequality would be much more urgent. But the problem does not disappear entirely. Although greater wealth may not do much to increase the happiness of most people, the fact remains that the well-to-do are much more likely to feel happy than those at the bottom of the income scale. Many poor people suffer from deprivations so acute that we could almost certainly produce a net gain in human happiness by taking income from wealthy individuals to pay for proper care for the uninsured, adequate housing for the homeless, and decent food for the undernourished.

Beyond these economic considerations, it is troubling to hear that we need not worry about excessive incomes simply because most of the poor have learned to accept their condition. Such claims are not only exaggerated; they falsely assume that the only goal worth considering in our society is happiness. Surely, there are other important values as well. Slavery does not cease to be wrong just because the slaves grow so accustomed to their lot that they no longer realize they are grossly exploited. Nor should we forget that great inequalities of wealth tend to bring about political inequalities that undermine our democratic system.

Finally, there are subtler problems of social morale to be considered. As Irving Kristol has argued, alienation and distrust are bound to result "if the principles that organize public life seem to have little relation to those that shape private lives" and if the distribution of power, privilege and property "no longer seems in some profound sense expressive of the values that govern the lives of individuals."[16] The ultimate reason why we cannot ignore unjustified wealth is that it weakens the public's faith in the fairness of the economic system. Such faith is essential if we are to maintain support for the social order and inspire individuals to observe the laws, undertake the duties of citizenship, and extend the minimum of trust toward institutions necessary for communities to prosper.

In the years to come, the public's sense of fairness will be sorely tested. Active workers will have to bear ever greater burdens to support a growing retired population and to help repay a huge national debt they had no part in making. Global forces will continue to depress the wages and threaten the jobs of semiskilled and unskilled workers. *Their* share of the national income will decline while a growing demand for the limited supply of highly talented, educated people continues to drive up their incomes to higher and higher levels. Amid these mounting tensions, it is especially important, then, to counter those wayward forces that allow the talented minority to earn even more than their abilities deserve. To ignore unwarranted wealth perpetuates injustice and frays the bonds that hold societies together. That is the ultimate reason why excessive earnings are a genuine problem that deserves a serious search for appropriate remedies.

HOW WELL IS TALENT DISTRIBUTED?

The choices that college students make when they plan their careers are more important to society than most people believe. We have grown accustomed to look upon the supply of talented people much as we looked upon land in the nineteenth century—as an inexhaustible resource. Yet today, we can no longer conjure up fresh cohorts of bright, well-educated college graduates as we did after World War II simply by building new universities and offering more financial aid. As the demands of modern society continue to increase, we must begin thinking of talent as a finite resource and start to worry more about how it is distributed among different occupations and professions.

Because the earnings of professionals stray so widely from the ideal pattern conceived in economists' models, one would suppose that the distribution of talented people must also be far from the ideal. Unfortunately, there is no reliable way of showing what a perfect distribution would be. We have neither a viable means of agreeing on national priorities, nor an adequate measure of what individuals contribute to society, nor even an accurate way of estimating talent. These deficiencies rule out any attempt at precise demonstration. Nevertheless, the facts permit at least a few tentative observations.

One point that seems perfectly clear is that students, lured in part by the prospect of high earnings, seek to enter the predominantly private professions in much larger numbers than the system can absorb. Schools of medicine, for example, have usually attracted at least double the number of applicants as there are places available. More than twice as many students applied to law schools in the 1980s as could be accommodated. Even in business, applications to schools of management have been running far ahead of the number that can be admitted.

There are also indications that business, law, and medicine may be using more professionals than they actually need. From all accounts, American corporations seem to employ a remarkable number of executives and managers compared with other advanced countries. Prof. Gosta Esping-Andersen, for example, reports that managers and executives make up 11.5 percent of our work force compared with 5.7 percent in Germany and 2.4 percent in Sweden.[17] These differences may result in part from institutional features unique to this country. For example, some of our managers may be performing personnel and benefits functions that would be administered by the state in most European countries. Lobbying and public relations activities may also be much more prevalent in the United States. Still, the disparities remain strikingly large. The speed with which American corporations have been shedding layers of management in the face of growing foreign competition adds to the suspicion that many firms make more profligate use of executives than their businesses actually require.

In the case of medicine, America does not yet have more doctors than any other industrial nation (relative to the size of the population). Nevertheless, the expanded enrollments that began in the 1960s have pushed the number of M.D.'s in this country toward the high end of the range, and there is much talk of a glut of physicians. By the year 2020, when the number of physicians is expected to peak, there will be an estimated 288 doctors for every 100,000 people, twice as many as in 1970 and more than almost any other industrial nation now enjoys.[18] Unfortunately, a surfeit of doctors does not merely waste talent; it can needlessly push up medical costs as well. If more physicians must vie with one another to serve the same number of people, they will be tempted to recommend more services and procedures than their patients really need in the struggle to maintain their revenues. As the number of M.D.'s continues to rise, such pressures can only grow stronger.

Lawyers have become even more numerous than doctors. Over

700,000 attorneys are currently active in the profession, up from 274,000 in 1970. Although it is difficult to make comparisons with other nations (because some tasks performed by lawyers in one country may not be carried out by lawyers in another), most observers credit the United States with having a larger practicing bar relative to the size of the population than any other country.[19]

Legal professions seem to be growing rapidly in all industrialized societies. If America still holds the lead, it is chiefly because we have a more fragmented society with a more adversary, competitive culture and a higher standard of living than almost any other nation in the world.[20] That said, there are good reasons for suspecting that the United States uses more attorneys than are truly needed.*

Certainly, our legal system generates less pressure for efficiency than most other private-sector activities. Congress does not pay much attention to the impact of new laws on the volume of litigation; indeed, the susceptibility of the legislative process to interest group lobbying invites the kinds of complicated exceptions and loopholes that foster litigation. A strong and politically active trial bar tenaciously resists efforts to introduce legislative innovations such as no-fault plans, which could drastically curtail the use of lawyers in automobile accident cases and related fields of tort litigation. In the courtroom, our adversary system of justice invites dilatory and harassing tactics by attorneys that even vigilant judges cannot prevent. Except in the most routine matters, judges tend to be more concerned with doing justice in the particular case than with crafting clear rules that might minimize future litigation. And lawyers, as we have already pointed out, can scarcely have much incentive to seek more efficient ways of rendering legal services when they earn more money for every extra hour they spend.

The tendency of the leading private professions to absorb more practitioners than they need not only causes inefficiency; it also wastes valuable talent, because these professions recruit so heavily from college graduates with above-average abilities. A few figures

* Some writers have claimed that in the United States an excess of lawyers slows economic growth. This argument is based on correlations between national growth rates and variations among countries in the number of lawyers relative to population. Such studies have been criticized severely for resting on faulty data about the number of lawyers in different countries and for confusing correlation with causation. For a recent series of essays on all sides of this issue, see "Debate: Do Lawyers Impair Economic Growth?" *Law and Social Inquiry* 17 (1992):585.

tell the story clearly. In 1981, students graduating from law school received scores of 584 (verbal) and 609 (quantitative) on their College Board exams; business school students averaged 545 (verbal) and 612 (quantitative); and medical school students achieved an average of 580 (verbal) and 642 (quantitative).[21] All these scores were far above the national mean of 472 (verbal) and 431 (quantitative).

This record contrasts vividly with the performance of students planning a teaching career. At about the same time that students of law, business, and medicine were performing so well on their College Boards, education majors were receiving scores far below the average—only 429 on the verbal test and 397 on the quantitative exam.[22] Low as they are, moreover, these scores do not reveal the full extent of the problem. Repeated studies have shown that education majors with the highest scores are the least likely ever to teach in public schools and the most likely to leave the classroom within the first few years. In a retrospective survey of high school graduates from the class of 1972, therefore, those who started teaching and remained in the profession had College Board scores 42 points below those who taught for a while and then left—and a full 118 points below those who never taught at all.[23]

The predominantly private professions do especially well in attracting the most outstanding college seniors. For example, of all the Phi Beta Kappas graduating between 1970 and 1990, medicine claimed approximately 18 percent, although only 1.5 percent of all college graduates became doctors during this period.[24] Private law practice accounted for 12 percent or more of the Phi Beta Kappas, whereas only 3.5 percent of all college graduates took law degrees. In contrast, only 7 percent of the Phi Beta Kappas chose to teach in primary and secondary schools, although 10 percent or more of all college graduates took jobs in the public schools. Of the Phi Beta Kappas who did elect to teach, a significant fraction left the classroom after only a few years.

Similar results emerge from the career choices of straight A students from elite private colleges. In this group of outstanding graduates, 14 to 17 percent went to law school in the 1980s, 10 to 15 percent chose to become doctors, and 7 to 14 percent entered business. In sharp contrast, barely 1 percent of this group expressed an intent to become teachers.[25]

The record is not much more encouraging for college graduates entering the federal civil service. By the late 1980s, 7.5 percent of all Phi Beta Kappas were entering the federal government, but the numbers were dwindling, and at least one-third planned to leave the civil service in the near future. A study of honor society seniors from leading universities tells an even more discouraging story. Asked to choose their preferred employer from among the federal government, state and local governments, the military, small businesses, and large corporations, only 3 percent designated the federal government, and only 4 percent of those taking jobs after graduation chose to enter the federal civil service.[26] In contrast, 38 percent of those taking jobs chose large corporations, 21 percent moved to universities, and 18 percent went to work for a small business.

These figures will not dismay everyone who reads them. Some will say that the private sector is the key to the progress and prosperity of the nation—as it surely is—and that in consequence, the predominantly private professions deserve every able person they can get. Recall the Reagan appointee who insisted that "the private sector [is] the true vehicle for prosperity, social cohesiveness, and national welfare, and the place where we ought to encourage our best and brightest to migrate."[27]

No reasonable person would deny the importance of the private sector or dispute its claim to a generous share of exceptionally talented, creative people. The question is how large that share should be and what claims can reasonably be made by occupations, such as school teaching and government service, that lie outside the private practice of law, management, and medicine.

In medicine, so great is our concern with preserving our good health that one can scarcely say the nation could ever have too many outstanding doctors. And yet, not only are we fast accumulating more doctors than we require to meet our health needs; the ablest young physicians do not always practice the type of medicine that society most requires. With physicians in many high-tech specialties earning three or four times the income of family doctors, current patterns of compensation have helped to produce a medical profession with many more specialists and many fewer primary care practitioners than in any other advanced nation.[28] As the most talented young doctors continue to flock to these specialties, America experiences higher rates of hospitalization and heavier use of expensive procedures than would occur if there were fewer specialists and more physicians rendering primary care. The net result is to further inflate the cost of medical care in the United States, with no indication that the health of our population is any better than in other countries with much higher proportions of general practitioners.

In business, as in medicine, it is hard to object to attracting more talented young recruits into management. After all, corporations have a decisive impact on the prosperity of any country through the goods they produce, the jobs they provide, and the success they enjoy in raising productivity and contributing to economic growth. At a time when America is challenged more than ever by global competition, it is surely important to draw upon the ablest, best-trained people to lead the nation's business organizations.

If the talented students who have increasingly chosen business careers were truly gravitating to the companies that need them the most, one could scarcely quarrel with the result. It is not clear, however, that this is taking place. A careful look at the graduates of our very best business schools suggests that they are disinclined to join the companies that are most important to our struggle for global competitiveness—and when they do, they are not likely to stay very long. According to one study from the Stanford Business School, within fifteen years after receipt of an MBA, as many graduates were working for small companies of ten employees or fewer as were employed by larger corporations, and a full one-third were self-employed.[29] Harvard Business School graduates appear to follow a similar pattern, avoiding large firms and jobs in manufacturing for other, more entrepreneurial endeavors. According to *Fortune*, "the Harvard Business School is growing more remote from corporate America. Increasingly, its MBA's don't want to work there. Not in line jobs or for big companies, at any rate."[30] Added a Harvard alumnus who graduated in the top 5 percent of his class, "Having just come back from my tenth reunion, I can say that essentially nobody from my class is on the path to running a large business."[31]

Of course, no one would deny that many small firms play a vital role in pioneering new products, creating new jobs, and infusing fresh energy and dynamism into the economy. Still, a very large fraction of the jobs, the overseas trade, the research, and the investment in the economy are accounted for by large manufacturing corporations. Moreover, not all of the alternative careers selected by the ablest business school graduates seem essential to improving competitiveness, increasing productivity, and raising growth rates in the economy. For example, even after the market jolt of October 1987, 15 to 20 percent or more of the graduates of leading business schools continue to seek careers in the financial sector, where lucrative opportunities abound. Here, too, many individuals can perform valuable service helping to mobilize capital for productive uses and improving the efficient operation of capital markets. Yet much of what transpires in Wall Street seems to go beyond socially productive activity and resembles some sort of casino to accommodate clever people searching for short-term gains. Moreover, however useful financial services may be, the sheer number of highly educated professionals engaged in selling bonds, analyzing stocks, talking with clients, and looking for market anomalies to exploit seems well in excess of any contribution they make to the long-term prosperity of the nation. Such concerns prompted James Tobin, Nobel prize–winning economist, to "confess to an uneasy Physiocratic suspicion, perhaps unbecoming in an academic, that we are throwing more and more of our resources, including the cream of our youth, into financial activities that generate high private rewards disproportionate to their social productivity."[32]

Any doubts about the value of educating so many talented executives pale before the reservations most people feel on observing the hordes of able students flocking to our law schools. The popular view of lawyers—immortalized by Shakespeare but doubtless of more ancient vintage—is jaundiced enough that it is worth a moment's pause to say a word on behalf of this beleaguered, though well-compensated, profession.

In fact, if we followed the advice of Dick the Butcher and killed all the lawyers, we would soon find ourselves in an untenable position. For lawyers perform a variety of functions vital to the progress of the economy and the welfare of society. No civilization can flourish if its members cannot count on some way of setting limits and enforcing safeguards to protect individuals from the misconduct of their neighbors, the exploitation of powerful organizations, and the injustices of the state. No economy can function, let alone prosper, without a stable framework of rules and procedures that set reasonable limits on competitive behavior, ensure that promises are kept, and allow rational planning to occur. Only lawyers can give competent advice about these rules and counsel companies and private individuals how to stay out of trouble. Only persons trained in the law can staff the institutions that resolve the disputes that inevitably arise, especially in an individualistic, success-oriented economy where rivals are forever testing the legal limits to gain a competitive advantage. As a result, those who argue that lawyers are unproductive parasites that drag down economic growth are guilty of much oversimplification.[33] Perhaps lawyers do not literally "produce" anything tangible, but their services are essential if production is to occur and markets are to function.

Highly capable people are undoubtedly needed to perform these important tasks—as judges, litigators, and counselors to large organizations, not to mention other jobs that lawyers traditionally fill, including serving as appointed public officials and elected political leaders. The question, then, is not whether the law needs a reasonable share of exceptionally talented, highly educated people, but whether it deserves a share of this valuable resource that is *several times* greater than the fraction of college graduates entering the legal profession.

One cannot answer this question fully without knowing more than we do about the various functions exceptionally talented lawyers perform. We are aware that most of the ablest lawyers, unlike their counterparts from business school, gravitate to major law firms that devote the bulk of their time to serving large corporations and organizations. Presumably, most of what these firms do has considerable financial and commercial importance. Even so, there are reasons to question the social value of devoting so much talent to work of this kind.

Increasingly, lawyers in the leading firms spend their time litigating on behalf of corporate clients. Although much of this litigation may be necessary, some of it—no one knows how much—is primarily tactical, being designed to delay unfavorable actions on the part of a government agency or corporate rival or to punish and intimidate adversaries by forcing them to incur heavy legal costs. No legitimate social purpose is served by using the law in this fashion. Responsible attorneys often try to persuade their clients not to litigate in these situations. Nevertheless, as Ronald Gilson suggests, such suits may well be growing more frequent as fewer corporations seek the long-term relations with a single law firm that would enable the firm to acquire enough influence to dissuade clients from litigating irresponsibly.[34] Similarly, as law firms grow larger and litigation becomes more impersonal and more adversarial, patterns of cooperation may be eroding that help attorneys to settle cases more easily and to agree to conduct litigation more expeditiously.[35] In these various ways, increasing amounts of the work performed by leading firms has a questionable social utility.

Still another problem arises from the nature of the adversary system through which much of the legal work in this country is conducted. This process relies on competition among lawyers to ferret out all the relevant evidence and make all the pertinent arguments so that judges, juries, government officials, and other arbiters can have the facts and the reasoning they need to arrive at sound decisions. In such contests, skill presumably counts for a great deal. It follows that the ideal of arriving at truth and justice through an adversary process comes closest to realization when the advocates on both sides are roughly equal in ability.

In real life, however, such equality is more the exception than the rule. The ablest lawyers usually go to established firms where they frequently litigate and negotiate with a much less experienced government attorney or with a solo practitioner representing a private claimant.[36] At times, they lobby legislators or public officials to obtain special favors for powerful clients when other interested parties are not represented at all. In these circumstances, so long as the most promising young lawyers choose overwhelmingly to serve large corporations, continuing to add more and more exceptional talent to the profession may help to make legal encounters more unequal and to increase the odds of prevailing for reasons other than the true merits of one's case. If so, the influx of exceptional talent may succeed not in furthering justice but in magnifying the human imperfections of our legal system so as to diminish, rather than enhance, the welfare of society.

In conclusion, then, there are serious and legitimate doubts whether society is well served by having so many of our ablest college graduates enter the predominantly private professions. If we are to resolve these doubts, however, we need to look not only at the private sector but at other fields of endeavor, especially public vocations such as school teaching and government service, which tend to attract less than their proportionate share of the ablest students.

The superior attractions of the private over the public sector arguably served America's interests tolerably well for many generations. Until the New Deal, the federal government had very limited functions, and most of them—such as customs collections and the postal service—did not present problems of great complexity and challenge. To squander able people on such modest tasks might have been a waste of their talents. The role of the public schools was also limited. As Marc Tucker and Ray Marshall have documented in detail, employers were not particularly interested in a highly educated work force.[37] Instead, following the theories of scientific management made famous by Frederick Taylor, they sought to break down factory work into simple, repetitive movements that required little thought. Hard labor and obedience, not intelligence and initiative, were the priorities of the day. Responding to these needs, most schools concentrated on assimilating immigrant children and teaching students to adjust to society and become law-abiding, obedient citizens. Higher-level problem solving could be left to managers and professionals, who increasingly had university training.

In recent decades, the needs of our society have changed dramatically. By all accounts, improving the education of our work force has become essential to increasing productivity and raising wage levels throughout the economy. Japan and Germany, in particular, have shown how much a properly trained, well-educated labor force can contribute to the general prosperity of a nation. Beyond the workplace, the growing ethnic diversity in our population and the large number of citizens who do not even bother to go to the polls create a challenge to our democracy that calls for schools that can build common cultural bonds and foster a stronger sense of civic responsibility. To meet these needs, it is clear that school systems must have an abler, better-educated corps of teachers than we have had in the past.

The work of the federal government has also grown enormously in complexity and importance since 1930. Government programs and policies affect the welfare of the entire nation and touch almost every aspect of our lives. The problems that the government is called upon to address—crime, poverty, health care, and many more—are often more complicated than those facing any private-sector institution. Implementing policies through vast, cumbersome federal agencies may well be more daunting than anything that corporate executives have to confront. And yet, by making the government an unattractive place to work, we are continually forced to choose between inadequately staffed public programs and reliance on the private sector for tasks, such as health care and job training, that it has never performed effectively in the past.

Against this background, the shift of so many able students from the public to the private sector over the past two decades does not bode well for the nation. In saying this, I do not mean to fault the young men and women who choose to earn their livelihood working in a law firm, a private medical practice, or a corporation. Students should be free to pursue the calling that satisfies them the most. Nevertheless, insofar as their decisions are based on large, unwarranted differences in compensation, society suffers unjustifiably.

From this standpoint, the country has hardly been moving in the right direction. In the early 1970s, graduating students from leading schools of law and business could earn approximately the same whether they went to work for the federal government or elected to go to Wall Street. Their starting salaries were only twice that of a beginning teacher. By 1990, the situation had changed radically. Wall Street salaries had grown to more than double the starting pay in the federal government and four times the salary of a beginning teacher. These large and growing differences are considerably greater than those in most other industrialized countries. They have undoubtedly helped to cause the shift of talented young people from the public to the private sector. There is little reason to suppose that the country will be better off as a result. Although we clearly need excellent education and effective government more urgently today than we did twenty years ago, the quality of the young recruits staffing our schools and government offices seems, regrettably, to have declined.

HOW SUCCESSFUL IS MERIT PAY?

The effort to motivate executives and professionals deserves attention because of the importance of the work such people perform. The last two decades have seen much experimentation along these lines. If equality was the battle cry of the 1960s, incentives became the buzzword of the 1980s. This new preoccupation was a natural outgrowth of the nation's rising concern over lagging productivity at home and mounting competition from abroad. It is hardly surprising, therefore, that economists emerged as the chief source of wisdom on the subject and that their emphasis on financial rewards dominated the policy debates.

For generations, economists have proceeded on the assumption that human beings are motivated chiefly by a desire for money. This simple premise is extremely useful in constructing models and testing theories. Because money is quantifiable and flexible and offers a common yardstick for all kinds of goods and services, it has the virtue of encompassing the endless variety of human needs and desires in a single, unifying measure.

In keeping with this theory of motivation, organizations everywhere made renewed efforts in the 1970s and 1980s to tie the compensation of professionals to performance. Merit pay was introduced for teachers and civil servants; boards of directors fashioned elaborate and lucrative pay packages to spur CEOs to greater efforts; law firms abandoned the ancient practice of paying their partners by seniority and started to reward them according to their effort, skill, and success in attracting new clients. Even health maintenance organizations began to experiment with bonus plans to induce their salaried doctors to work harder or to cut out unnecessary lab tests and hospital procedures.

The striking fact about these attempts is that they have all either failed completely or fallen far short of expectations. Although President Reagan endorsed merit pay for teachers, virtually all school systems have abandoned such plans, just as they did in the 1920s and the 1960s. Bonus systems for the federal civil service have been a disappointment either because they were poorly administered or because the bonuses were too small to affect performance. In the private sector, despite the best efforts of boards of directors and expensive pay consultants, CEOs have manipulated the system so that the relationship between executive compensation and performance is embarrassingly weak. Law partners continue to squabble over how to divide their profits, and most firms no longer maintain their current practices to motivate their partners but simply to defend themselves against raids by other firms to steal away their most valuable members. Even in medicine, HMOs encounter a dilemma in trying to tie compensation to performance, because incentive schemes that reward doctors for working harder may induce them to perform too many services, whereas bonuses aimed at making them more cost-conscious may cause them to perform too few.

There are many reasons for this disappointing record. At the most basic level, all pay-for-performance schemes proceed from a belief that the prospect of monetary rewards will motivate people to work harder and more effectively. Although the premise seems obvious, there is surprisingly little empirical evidence to support it. Many companies have shown that financial incentives can have a positive effect on the performance of repetitive tasks, such as factory work. But very few studies of merit pay exist for the complex, creative jobs so common in management and the professions. Such findings as there are seem inconclusive. As a result, we still know very little about how much a CEO who is already a multimillionaire will be stimulated by the chance to earn millions more. Nor do we know how potent an incentive a bonus will be in callings such as teaching and public service, which members have chosen for reasons other than making money. It is quite possible that merit pay has worked badly in the federal government and the public schools precisely because its proponents have tried to use inappropriate incentives for the people they are supposed to motivate.

Even if performance pay were an effective motivator, it would be difficult to put such methods of compensation into practice. Experience reveals that performance plans must satisfy a formidable list of requirements. The principal reason why so many attempts fail is that *all* of the following specifications must be met to achieve the hoped-for results:

1. Supervisors must be able to define good performance and assess the quality of work performed. This is often a difficult task where professionals are concerned, because their work can rarely be measured quantitatively and they often engage in activities like teaching that resist clear definitions of excellence.

2. Management must create a process for evaluating performance and allocating rewards that seems objective and fair to everyone involved. This is no easy task either, because most people being evaluated overestimate their effectiveness and hence are likely to be disappointed by the results.

3. Supervisors must assess performance honestly and communicate the results clearly and fully to those being evaluated, even when the message is unpleasant. It is difficult to convey such

assessments to people with whom one works every day whose loyalty and morale are important to the well-being of the unit.

4. To gain the confidence essential to the plan's success, those whose work is evaluated must thoroughly understand the goals of the compensation system, the way in which their performance will be assessed, and the formula for fixing the amount of compensation. Otherwise, misunderstandings and resentment are sure to arise.

5. The performance goals must be set high enough to challenge individuals to make their best efforts but not so high as to frustrate and discourage even the highly motivated.

6. The rewards must be large enough to motivate effectively but not so large as to tempt people to resort to improper or even illegal behavior to qualify.

7. The incentive plan must recognize all the behaviors and objectives that the organization wishes to encourage and reward them in the right proportion according to their relative importance to the firm. Long- and short-term objectives must be balanced appropriately. Individual and group incentives must be combined to elicit the proper blend of teamwork and individual effort. The size of the bonuses and the nature of the goals and behaviors they reward must fit the values and culture of the organization. The aims and priorities of the organization must be clear and generally accepted; otherwise, there will be no agreed-upon purposes to which the incentives can be linked. Crafting an incentive package that meets all these specifications can be extremely challenging, the more so because the goals of an organization are not static but shift in accordance with changing circumstances.

8. Evaluation methods must reflect the goals of the organization so accurately and be administered so objectively that no one can benefit by manipulating the system or by taking other actions that are harmful to the institution. Countless instances of game-playing testify to the difficulty of meeting this specification.

Because failure to meet any one of these prerequisites may sink the entire program, it is not surprising that the success rate is so low. The risks involved, moreover, are not merely that the effort will fail. Performance pay can have harmful consequences that leave an organization in worse shape than before. The competition for bonuses can endanger rivalry among professionals who should cooperate for the good of the organization. In addition, as evaluating performance is always a difficult, arbitrary task, efforts to make such assessments in awarding pay can easily cause resentments that disrupt harmonious working relationships between subordinates and their superiors. More important, efforts to link pay to performance cause professionals to focus on making more money instead of doing the best possible job. Those who administer compensation do their best to make the two goals coincide, but this is rarely possible for the complex work that most executives and professionals perform. In one way or another, opportunities arise to boost one's income at the expense of the organization. Subordinates withhold unpleasant information from their superiors, plant managers deplete inventories to make their annual bonus, teachers urge their slowest learners to stay home when tests are given that affect their paychecks.

In view of all these difficulties, attempts to motivate professionals with money have reached a most unsatisfactory state. As the 1990s began, a series of media exposés described the lavish paychecks given to CEOs of poorly performing companies. These revelations provided a fitting climax to twenty years of disappointment in the use of financial incentives to improve the work of professionals. Still, the effort to tie pay to performance continues, a triumph of hope over experience. The record deserves a more searching reappraisal.

CONCLUSION

If any conclusion emerges clearly from this study, it is that no effective competitive market regulates professional compensation in this country. So widely does the real world diverge from the mythical realm of perfect competition that it is impossible even to guess what patterns of compensation would result from truly competitive conditions. (What would it mean, for example, for all clients to be perfectly informed about all conceivable sources of legal advice, and what would be the consequences of possessing such a vast store of knowledge?) Far from being fully informed about the services they need, those who employ professionals are usually hampered by ignorance, unable to judge exactly what they require or who is best equipped to provide it. In addition, professionals rarely settle their compensation through arms-length negotiations with informed and independent parties. In the private sector, executives and professionals have been able to exert great influence over their own compensation because of their political power, their superior knowledge, or their dominant position in the organization that employs them. In contrast, the pay of teachers and civil servants has been fixed by official bodies moved by political pressures that have much less to do with market forces than with the public's desire to avoid higher taxes. To appreciate how much difference these procedures make, one has only to imagine what CEOs would receive if their pay were set by elected politicians.

Under such artificial conditions, there is no reason to suppose that the process of fixing professional compensation will result in just rates of pay, or produce an optimal distribution of talent, or create a system of incentives calculated to elicit the kind of effort needed to excel in the important tasks that professionals perform in our society. Instead, many practitioners in the private sector are overpaid, some egregiously so. The distribution of talent seems heavily skewed to the benefit of the private sector even though much of the work of government and the public schools is increasingly important to the nation and cries out for able people. Incentives are often warped in ways that lead executives to take an excessively short-term view while tempting lawyers and doctors to provide more services than their clients and patients truly need.

If market forces work so imperfectly, what other factors help to determine the earnings of executives and professionals? Many influences play a part—custom, example, opportunism, political expediency, to name only a few. Through all these pressures, however, another force intrudes to leave a clear imprint on the way we compensate highly educated people. The fact that Japanese companies pay their chief executives much less than American firms, that leading professionals in the United States earn much more than their counterparts abroad, that executive compensation rose much faster than blue-collar wages during only two decades since the First World War—the 1920s and the 1980s—has much less to do with market forces than with prevailing attitudes and beliefs in the society. At every point, compensation policies in this country bear the mark of values that lie deep in our culture. Understanding this process has an importance that transcends the incomes of professionals, for values affect not only earnings but every facet of our national life and institutions. It is to this subject that we turn in the following chapter.

CHAPTER 12

THE IMPACT OF VALUES

The connections between current compensation practices and prevailing beliefs in the society are not difficult to trace. The munificent salaries of CEOs reflect the high regard Americans have for initiative and success and the importance commonly attached to leadership in explaining the fluctuating fortunes of large, prominent organizations. The vast inequalities in earnings rest on a widely shared belief that people are paid for their achievements and that this is a good and just way to cause them to work as hard and as well as they can. The tolerance for high private-sector incomes also bespeaks a faith in competitive markets as the one best way to promote free choice, select the fittest for demanding roles in our economy, and reward those who perform well. Conversely, the modest salaries paid to public officials and teachers are symptoms of a deep-seated skepticism toward government as an instrument for solving society's problems.

These attitudes are not new to America. The emphasis on the power of corporate leadership is rooted in our long-standing belief in individualism and our traditional admiration of successful entrepreneurs. For generations, students in this country have learned that the Industrial Revolution and our rise to economic preeminence are virtually synonymous with the deeds of legendary figures such as Andrew Carnegie, Henry Ford, John D. Rockefeller, and J. P. Morgan. Turn-of-the-century scholars elevated business leaders to heroic proportions and even endowed them with a pseudoscientific superiority. According to William Graham Sumner of Yale, "The millionaires are a product of natural selection. . . . They may fairly be regarded as the naturally selected agents of society for certain work. They get high wages and live in luxury, but the bargain is a good one for society."[1]

The recognition that the public gave to these industrialists and financiers was matched by its fascination with the vast fortunes they accumulated. Money had long since achieved a more overt importance in the New World than in the more settled, class-oriented societies of Europe. By the 1830s, social commentators could observe that "all classes are either striving after wealth or endeavoring to keep up its appearance."[2] Not until the Industrial Revolution, however, did the quest for large fortunes become a prominent feature of American society. After the Civil War, as Robert McCloskey once put it, "a kind of mystic veneration was accorded to the man who could 'buy and sell' his less competent contemporaries."[3] By the end of the nineteenth century, James Bryce could conclude in *The American Commonwealth* that "there are more great millionaires, as well as more with a capital of from $250,000 to $1 million in America than in any other country."[4]

The success of the "great millionaires" gained added justification from the widespread belief that opportunities to prosper in business were available to anyone willing to work hard. Tales of Horatio Alger and other rags-to-riches stories sold in the millions of copies. The conviction that free markets rewarded the worthy was a constant theme throughout the nineteenth century. As Edward Everett put it, "wealth in this country, may be traced back to industry and frugality. The paths that lead to it are open to all."[5] This belief in opportunity was linked to a faith in open competition as the guarantor of social mobility and the engine of economic growth. The confidence of ordinary Americans in free markets survived even in the Great Depression, as the Lynds discovered when they found the residents of "Middletown" believing that "competition everywhere insures everything's being done that *can* be done. . . . competition is what makes progress and has made the United States great."[6]

Just as firmly rooted in our traditions is an instinctive distaste for strong government. This distrust can be traced back to the sturdy individualists who rebelled against the British and wrote a constitution noted for its checks and balances and its elaborate safeguards to protect the individual against arbitrary rule. In Tocqueville's words, "The citizen of the United States is taught from infancy to rely upon his own exertions in order to avoid the evils and the difficulties of life. He looks upon the social authority with an eye of mistrust and anxiety and he claims its assistance only when he is unable to do without it."[7] These attitudes persisted throughout the nineteenth century. In 1907, James Bryce described the prevailing sentiment in words that Tocqueville could have written: "The fewer occasions for interfering with individual citizens are allowed to officials, and the less time citizens have to spend in looking after their officials, the more will the citizens of the community prosper."[8]

Over the years, of course, all these values have often been criticized, even bitterly attacked. Reformers and muckrakers have long condemned the acquisition of great wealth and the tactics and transgressions of leading industrialists. Media commentators and gossip writers constantly chronicle the follies and extravagances of the rich. Social scientists have repeatedly documented the plight of poor and disadvantaged groups and shown how they are hindered and handicapped in the competition to get ahead. Even government has had its staunch defenders and its periods of ascendancy. As the twentieth century wore on and wide-open competition proved incapable of providing secure employment or avoiding deep recessions, the state began to claim a more important role in economic affairs.

Beginning with the New Deal and extending through the Great Society, a different public philosophy gained the ascendancy. This new doctrine had three important themes. It looked to the national government as the principal force in managing the economy and seeking to preserve full employment. It built a welfare state to protect citizens from the consequences of joblessness, sickness, and old age. It reached out to weak and neglected segments of society by aggressively seeking equality—equality of bargaining power by the National Labor Relations Act, then equality of opportunity by expanding access to college, and later equality of political power by extending voting rights to all.

The New Deal philosophy proved remarkably successful for more than thirty years. Even Republican presidents felt obliged to respect its basic tenets and preserve its programmatic achievements. Gradually, however, problems arose that exposed contradictions in the philosophy that its liberal proponents found difficult to resolve.[9]

In trying to extend equal rights and opportunities to all groups, liberals had supposed they were furthering the traditional process of assimilation that had created America's melting pot of different races and nationalities. Contrary to expectations, however, society did not come steadily closer together in the 1960s. Different groups—defined by race, gender, sexual preference, or religion—grew more conscious of their separate identities and more zealous in pursuing their special interests. The liberal instinct was to press for reconciliation, tolerance, and understanding. As different groups pressed harder to assert their life-styles and secure their rights, this response proved deeply troubling to many people who were increasingly worried that basic moral standards and personal values were disintegrating. Faced with this concern, liberals found it difficult to confront problems such as rising crime and swelling welfare rolls for fear of seeming racist. They were reluctant to deal with questions of family values lest they seem antifeminist or homophobic. To their supporters, these attitudes bespoke a generosity of spirit. To others, they smacked of permissiveness and moral relativism.

By the end of the 1960s, a suspicion was also abroad in the land that many ambitious federal programs were not working very well. Expensive campaigns to alleviate poverty did not stop the outbreak of urban riots. Washington's efforts to improve education brought declining test scores and well-publicized reports that seemed to conclude that spending more money on schools did little to enhance educational progress. Federal job programs were often tainted by scandal and did not seem to thin the ranks of the hard-core unemployed or even find jobs for those whom the government trained. As taxes to support these programs increased, popular disaffection rose, and confidence in government waned. Yet liberals had no answer to these discontents except to call for still more federal initiatives.

Finally, federal efforts to address the problems of poverty and race were increasingly threatening to blue-collar workers, who had long been a mainstay of the Democratic coalition. To many people, affirmative action programs seemed little more than quotas that collided with deep-seated beliefs in merit and seniority. Housing initiatives and busing efforts proved disruptive and menacing to working-class neighborhoods. Once again, liberals seemed unable to find a way of responding to these fears without compromising their commitment to racial equality.

As these problems and frustrations continued to fester, traditional values of individual initiative, free markets, and limited government enjoyed a renewed popularity. Not that these values had ever disappeared entirely. Although partially eclipsed by the New Deal and the Great Society, they still survived as a force in shaping our beliefs and public policies. Critics may have lambasted the "malefactors of great wealth" and condemned outlandish fortunes, but the distribution of wealth remained about the same in the 1970s as it had been at the time of the American Revolution.[10] At capitalism's lowest ebb, during the Great Depression, America did not drift very far or very long from the principles of market competition. Even the civil rights and antipoverty movements of the 1960s respected traditional values by limiting efforts to redistribute income and relying more on education and equal opportunity than on programs to equalize results. When the New Deal philosophy seemed to falter, therefore, the foundations for a different approach lay close at hand.

THE REAGAN DOCTRINE

By the 1980s, the older values had gradually displaced the ideology of the New Deal and the Great Society. Financial incentives assumed greater importance as professional incomes reached new heights, income tax rates declined, and merit pay spread from the private sector to government agencies and public schools. The move toward deregulation and privatization gave renewed emphasis to market competition as the preferred way of organizing the economy. Meanwhile, the role of the state eroded, along with the salaries of its officials, as the public seemed less confident than ever in its government following Vietnam, Watergate, and the controversies over the Great Society.

The renaissance of the older values did not begin in the 1980s. Surveys showed that making money began to assume greater importance for college students as early as the early 1970s, when the economy started to stagnate and a bumper crop of graduates had to compete for available jobs.[11] Huge salaries were already paid to sports heroes and media stars before President Reagan ever entered the White House. Trust in government started to erode as early as the mid-1960s, and had already sunk to a low ebb long before the 1980 election. President Carter did not need Reagan to remind the American people that government could not solve their most important problems or to deplore "the complicated, confusing, overlapping and wasteful Federal Government bureaucracy."[12]

What the "Reagan revolution" did accomplish was to lift these values to the status of an official ideology for achieving economic prosperity. According to this doctrine, entrepreneurial energies would multiply under the stimulus of stronger financial incentives. Business would gain new energy from renewed competition and from lifting the heavy yoke of government regulation. "You say soak the rich. I say *get* rich," Jack Kemp declared. "I want to restore the reward for taking an entrepreneurial risk and creating jobs."[13] As Kevin Phillips points out, "Entrepreneurs, heroes again as in the days of Horatio Alger and Henry Ford, were welcomed in Congress, courted by venture capitalists, coveted by investment bankers, and even transformed into civic icons by a host of new national magazines—*Inc., Venture, Entrepreneur, Millionaire,* and *Success.*"[14] Competition and market solutions were much emphasized and approved. With occasional lapses for reasons of political expediency, official doctrine favored deregulation, free trade, and competition even in fields such as health care and education.

As private initiative waxed, the role of government waned. Though distrust of the state was already rampant before Reagan took office, no public figure trumpeted its shortcomings with greater gusto. "I have come to Washington to clean up the swamp," he declared. "The government is not the solution. The government is the problem."[15] As Paul Goldberger of the *New York Times* observed, "If there is any legacy of the Reagan years it is to have devalued completely the importance of the public realm and to have raised dramatically the value we place on the private realm, so much so that the public realm has almost ceased to have meaning."[16]

How well did this doctrine work in the 1980s? Undeniably, there were successes. Entrepreneurs like Bill Gates, Lee Iacocca, and Steven Jobs built large new companies or saved old ones. With vigorous leadership, a number of great corporations were restructured, downsized, and brought to levels of efficiency and quality that restored their ability to compete in world markets. Productivity in manufacturing rose by approximately 2.5 percent during Reagan's years in office, hardly spectacular but an improvement over the preceding decade. Inflation dropped from double digits to modest levels, and unemployment did the same. Overall, the economy grew by 2.5 percent per year in the 1980s—not very impressive by Japanese standards but better than our record in the late 1970s.

At the same time, much did not go well in the 1980s: huge deficits, the costly savings-and-loan scandals, undiminished poverty, embarrassingly low rates of saving, growing disparities between rich and poor. Despite the gains in manufacturing, overall productivity per worker rose by little more than 1 percent per year, approximately one-third of the rate in Japan. The economy grew, but most of the gains went to the wealthy, as the earnings of many blue-collar workers declined. Though employment increased, the growth was not as robust as in the 1960s and 1970s and consisted in large part of low-wage jobs in the service sector.

Whatever the merits and demerits of political leadership in the 1980s, Americans were clearly not satisfied with the results. A 1992 Gallup poll found that 74 percent of Americans were no longer confident that the next generation in this country would be able to live better than their parents.[17] By the summer of 1992, over 80 percent of the American public were dissatisfied with the way things were going in the country.[18] Large majorities continued to express little confidence in the leaders of government and other major institutions.

In short, Americans are not optimistic about the economy or the government and do not feel that either is working well. Now that we are emerging from the cold war and can plan for what we hope will be a better future, we would do well to review the ideology of the 1980s and decide whether it is adequate for our purposes. As we will discover, each of its premises suffers from problems that deserve careful thought as we decide what kind of society we wish to build to assure our future progress and prosperity.

THE FAITH IN LEADERSHIP

To a remarkable extent, Americans attribute the success of corporations to the actions of their leaders. Originally, this point of view was stimulated by the exploits of the entrepreneurial giants of the Industrial Revolution. It fitted nicely with the hierarchical system of assembly-line production and large corporations that concentrated decision making in the hands of top managers and reduced blue-collar workers to the status of regimented drones.

This form of organization no longer seems suited to the needs of modern business, which call for sharing responsibilities more broadly throughout the enterprise.[19] Nevertheless, strong forces combine to perpetuate the belief in the centrality of corporate leadership. For one thing, the public is always more interested in personalities than in the interplay of abstract forces and trends. Recognizing this, business writers dwell upon the exploits of top executives in describing the fortunes of large corporations. CEOs, who release much of the news that emanates from their companies, are likewise inclined to emphasize the role of leadership, at least when the fortunes of their firms are rising. (One study of corporate reports disclosed that CEOs were given credit for good news three times as often as any other cause but were three times *less* likely to be held responsible for corporate reverses.[20]) With those who produce the news, those who interpret it, and those who read it all tending to emphasize corporate leadership, it is hardly surprising that so many people believe that chief executives play the decisive role in shaping the fortunes of American business.

In fact, there is surprisingly little empirical evidence to confirm or deny this supposition. Much of our ignorance stems from the difficulty of disentangling the actions of the chief executive from all the other factors that affect the progress of a company. Empirical studies of leadership do exist, but most of them have dealt with professional sports, where one can easily measure the team records before and after new coaches and managers take over. By and large, these inquiries suggest that leadership shifts have no effect on the success of the team.[21] Baseball, of course, is not big business. Interestingly, however, the few studies that do attempt to measure the effects of corporate leadership also fail to show that CEOs have the impact they are commonly thought to have on the performance of their companies.[22]

The experience of the last two decades likewise cautions against putting too much stock in the prevailing assessments of corporate leaders. Many a chief executive has been touted as exceptional only to be humbled later on by error and misadventure. Companies that were rated among the best managed in America during the 1970s, such as General Motors and IBM, must even then have been developing policies and practices that would leave them in disarray only a decade later. Even the ill-starred Ross Johnson of RJR Nabisco was lauded by *Fortune* as "America's Toughest Marketing Man" who "prefers to spend money making his plants the lowest-cost producers, trimming their distribution systems till they hum, inventing products, advertising their message, and chewing up the competition."[23] Looking backward, business historians writing about the 1970s and 1980s will chronicle a long procession of Donald Burrs, Henry Guttfreunds, and Jimmy Lings who swept like meteors across the sky, starting in a blaze of glory, passing suddenly through obloquy to oblivion, but always replaced by new shooting stars to light up the business pages and the trade magazines.

Business executives are not the only leaders who assume exceptional importance in America. Political leaders do not receive anything like the lavish emoluments that corporate boards bestow upon their CEOs. Nevertheless, the public, abetted by the media, imagines that they possess a degree of influence over national events that can only be termed extraordinary. Toward the end of the Carter administration, for example, poverty had begun to rise again, inflation was rampant, the Soviets had invaded Afghanistan, unemployment was high, and America's declining competitiveness was growing ever more apparent. Political scientists were writing learned articles on the limited power of the presidency. Yet an ABC-Harris poll found that the public, by a whopping margin of seventy-three to twenty-one, agreed that "there is nothing wrong with this country that good leadership couldn't cure."[24] Once again, the media have contributed heavily to these perceptions by constantly suggesting that skillful presidents have a much greater capacity to mobilize public opinion or to sway congressional votes than careful research can verify.

To be sure, common sense suggests that leaders of large organizations do make a difference in setting goals, making critical strategic judgments, and building loyalty and commitment within an institution. No sensible organization would fail to take great care in choosing the ablest person it can find. But it is dangerous to believe, as so many Americans do, that almost any problem encountered by business and government would disappear if only the right CEOs and political leaders could be put in charge. Such attitudes lead to an endless cycle of raised expectations and frustrated hopes. They oversimplify the task of reform by slighting all the other forces that help to account for institutional success or failure. They foster a separation between top management and the rest of the organization that seems less and less in keeping with contemporary notions of effective institutions. In the end, therefore, just as excessive faith in political leadership threatens to end in disappointment, a doctrine that counts heavily on promoting prosperity by celebrating business leadership and increasing its rewards promises to repeat the 1980s by achieving only sluggish growth and bloated compensation.

REASONABLE OPPORTUNITIES

Any doctrine emphasizing monetary rewards and tolerating highly unequal incomes can be morally defensible only if it includes a commitment to give all citizens opportunities to compete and to progress to the full measure of their ability. Otherwise, there can be no assurance that those with little money deserve their lot or that those who earn large incomes are entitled to receive them. Nor can we justify existing inequalities on the ground that they are needed to maximize the welfare of the entire society.

This point is universally acknowledged. Political leaders of every party and persuasion praise America as the land of opportunity and social mobility and extol these characteristics as special virtues of our society. Just what the government should do to ensure ample possibilities for advancement, however, has never been entirely clear. Of course, no government can possibly guarantee equal opportunity for the entire population. Accidents of birth, family, schooling, and community distribute life's chances in uneven ways that no public policy can correct. What we *can* expect of the government, presumably, is to do what is reasonably possible to extend opportunities to all.

A century ago, this commitment seemed modest enough. Most careers were easier to enter than they are now, because they required less education and training. The belief that anyone could achieve wealth and advancement by pluck and hard work was widely shared throughout America. Granted, a fortunate few enjoyed educational opportunities and social connections that gave them great advantages over others. But no one at that time felt that the state's responsibility extended much beyond providing free public education to all.

Today, the educational requirements for most better-paid occupations are much greater than they were in the nineteenth century. More important, the sense of what a government can do to expand opportunities has grown enormously. Federally financed student aid programs can open doors to college for almost anyone who cares to enter. Special classes can assist the handicapped or the recent immigrant in overcoming barriers that fate has placed in their way. Job training can prepare disadvantaged youth for decent careers. Prenatal counseling, adequate nutrition, and preschool education can help youngsters succeed in school and even raise their IQ scores. Although there is still disagreement over such issues as how to overcome the disadvantages of the urban ghetto or remove the residue of racial discrimination, enough is known that any government committed to expanding and equalizing opportunity will have a broad agenda to pursue.

This agenda poses a problem for the ideology of the 1980s, because it involves the government in ambitious programs that conflict with the commitment to a more restricted role for the state. As George Will has shrewdly pointed out,

> Conservatives are . . . fond of the metaphor of a footrace: All citizens should be roughly equal at the starting line of the race of life. But much that we have learned and continue to learn—and we are learning a lot—about early childhood development suggests that "equality of opportunity" is a much more complicated matter than most conservatives can comfortably acknowledge. Prenatal care, . . . infant stimulation, childhood nutrition and especially home environment—all these and other influences affect the competence of a young "runner" as he or she approaches the academic hurdles that so heavily influence social outcomes in America. There is, of course, vast scope for intelligent disagreement as to what can and should be done to make "equality of opportunity" more than an airy abstraction. But surely it is indisputable that "equality of opportunity" can be enhanced by various forms of state action.[25]

By the 1980s, the total cost of prenatal counseling, nutrition programs, family support, day care, parental leave, college loans, and all the other methods of expanding opportunity had grown to formidable dimensions. When hard choices had to be made, therefore, many people who supported the current ideology were reluctant to spend heavily to open doors through new programs that brought so little direct benefit to themselves. It should hardly come as a surprise, therefore, that programs of this kind received little support throughout the 1980s. When the time came to assign priorities and approve a budget, cutting taxes and curtailing domestic spending usually prevailed over job training, student aid, or funding for education.

Throughout the decade, even programs that commanded general

approval were seriously underfunded. Despite a long-standing commitment to encourage access to higher education, Congress allowed federal aid to college students to decline substantially in real dollars during the 1980s.[26] Some $7 billion were cut from programs for women and children.[27] Although experts were well-nigh unanimous that Head Start would save society several dollars for every tax dollar it consumed, only 30 percent of eligible children could be enrolled by 1990.[28] Study after study confirmed that prenatal counseling and early nutrition could raise IQs and prevent mental retardation and low-birth-weight babies. By doing so, such assistance seemed to be a valuable long-term investment for society. Nevertheless, the Women and Infant Children (WIC) program, which sought to fill these nutritional needs, still reached only 50 to 60 percent of eligible mothers by 1990, while 25 percent of all expectant mothers did not receive prenatal care.[29] Even our public schools, with all the talk of crisis and competitiveness, did not attract an impressive level of support by international standards. The president of the United States may have said at the Education Summit in Charlottesville, Virginia, that "America spends more on its schools than any [other] country on earth."[30] In fact, however, by the close of the 1980s, the United States actually ranked among the bottom third of industrial nations in the percentage of GNP devoted to primary and secondary education.[31]

In the end, therefore, the ideology of the past two decades did not manage to reconcile its distaste for big government with its commitment to an open competitive society where all people have the chance to succeed or fail according to their merits. On most occasions in the 1980s, the conflict was quietly resolved by limiting government efforts to broaden opportunity. By so doing, the responsible officials undermined the very ideology they sought to promote.

COMPETITION AND MARKETS

Nothing so graphically illustrates the prevailing doctrine of the past two decades as its emphasis on the value of private competitive markets. There is much to be said for this point of view. In many ways, competition is a remarkable mechanism for organizing human activity to allocate resources, promote efficiency, and provide goods and services for consumers. Recent world events have dramatized the superiority of free markets over centralized government planning as a means of organizing the economy. The issue, therefore, is not whether competition is a sound policy but how extensively it should be used. This question has assumed exceptional importance in the past two decades as enthusiasm has grown for extending free markets to new forms of activity, such as health care, public education, and municipal services, that were heretofore organized according to very different principles.

So popular has competition become as a way of ordering human activity that one can easily lose sight of its limitations. As economics textbooks are forever pointing out, competition works well only if there are a large number of providers capable of selling the same product or service, and customers have sufficient knowledge to make informed choices. Where these preconditions are lacking, special safeguards will be required if competition is to have any hope of working as advertised. Even in areas of activity that lend themselves well to free markets, competition can create problems when it becomes too intense. In all commercial markets, reasonable rules and ethical standards are needed not only to protect each person's legitimate rights but to preserve the minimum of trust required to allow business transactions and other forms of social interaction to go forward. Yet in their effort to prevail over competitors or to avoid losing money, company officials may be tempted to ignore these restraints. A special challenge for competition, therefore, is how to ensure that everyone abides by the rules in a system that relies so heavily on self-interest and personal gain as the means of motivating people to work.

To this problem, economists respond by pointing to the power of free markets to channel selfish ambitions into socially productive efforts. As Milton Friedman points out, "The one thing you can absolutely depend on any person to do is to put his interests ahead of yours. . . . So the problem of social organization is to set up an arrangement under which greed will do the least harm. It seems to me that the great virtue of capitalism is that it's that kind of system."[32]

Alas, competition does not work perfectly to hold selfish motives in check. Price-fixing, union-busting, false advertising, environmental spoliation, and consumer fraud are only a few of the unsavory methods that companies have used to gain an advantage over competitors. Such temptations are not peculiar to the business sector; they exist wherever competition is keen. To take but one example, coaches in many universities have resorted to all sorts of illegal tactics to achieve athletic success: under-the-table payments to athletes, forged transcripts, secret out-of-season practices, and unlawful steroid use to enhance performance. The more we inflate the rewards of success and increase the penalties of failure, the more we tempt competitors to violate the rules.

The problems go beyond the performance of illegal acts. No occupation can expect to maintain the high moral standards that the public expects of business and the professions by relying primarily on laws and threats of punishment. Most ethical transgressions are either impossible for the law to detect or not important enough to justify the time and expense of a legal proceeding. As a result, every calling tries to instill a voluntary sense of restraint among its members, a discipline born of custom, nourished by tradition, and buttressed by peer pressure. Such habits are always fragile. They take a long time to develop and are quickly destroyed. Under normal market conditions, they may hold up reasonably well with proper care and attention. As competition grows keener, however, the struggle to succeed or simply to survive may cause determined rivals to ignore all manner of established norms.

Carried to extremes, competition can even diminish the satisfactions that many professionals find in their work and subject their personal lives to heavy strain. Curiously, this problem is typically overlooked in discussions of competitive markets. The premise in these deliberations is that the only topic worth pursuing is how to pay people enough to attract them in sufficient numbers and motivate them to perform effectively. Work itself is not regarded as a source of fulfillment but simply as a factor of production and a necessary burden that employees must bear to buy more goods.

This view of work is sadly incomplete. Numerous surveys and studies make clear that most people do not consider their job a burden but a central means of fulfillment in their lives.[33] That is why a large majority say they would keep on working even if they suddenly became financially independent and why most lottery winners do in fact remain in their jobs.

There is no reason to assume that competition will automatically make work more enjoyable. The name of the game is efficiency, not personal fulfillment, and the two are not always the same. On the contrary, when competition grows too intense, it can demand a level of effort out of proportion to the benefits achieved, just as it can cause people to violate the law and undermine professional norms.

THE EMPHASIS ON MONEY

The limits just described were tested repeatedly in the 1970s and 1980s as the prevailing ideology enhanced the rewards of commercial success by celebrating wealth and lowering income tax rates, especially for the well-to-do. The results were predictable. No one should be surprised that scandals erupted on such a scale in sectors such as housing, the savings and loan industry, health care, investment banking, even organized religion. Nor was it fortuitous that more doctors fattened their wallets by ordering expensive tests from laboratories they owned, or that lawyers were accused of fraud in unprecedented numbers, or that chief executives used their influence to gain lavish pay packages that rewarded them even when their companies did poorly.

Such problems were magnified by an ideology that accorded little respect to government and continuously sought to reduce its role. In the course of strenuous efforts to shrink bureaucracy, official defenses against wrongdoings are likely to weaken as well. The opportunities and temptations to engage in dubious behavior seem all the more attractive when law enforcement slackens and the risks of getting caught diminish. The results can be costly. Only mischief could come of decisions to cut government budgets in the 1980s by trimming the staff for management oversight in the Office of Management and Budget and by paring the number of auditors and investigatory personnel in other federal agencies. As the head of the General Accounting Office put it, "When you look at what happened in the S & L crisis and look at the situation at H.U.D. and things like that, if we had proper systems, if we had the right numbers of auditors to go out and check on this, we would have saved billions of dollars. In other words, we have been penny-wise and really pound foolish here. It's a very scary situation for the federal government and the American taxpayer."[34]

Professional standards also came under increasing strain as competition intensified during the past two decades. The legal profession offers abundant illustrations. Although warnings about the decline of professionalism had been made periodically over many decades, the articles and symposia on the subject grew ever more numerous in the 1970s and 1980s. For the first time in history, the American Bar Association formally acknowledged the danger by establishing a commission to study the matter.[35] The opening paragraph of the commission's report stated the issue succinctly: "Has our profession abandoned principle for profit, professionalism for commercialism?"

At about the same time, another prestigious body, the Kutak Commission, was examining the lawyer's ethical duties in the course of revising the American Bar Association's Model Rules of Professional Conduct.[36] The original drafts of the commission's report tried to clarify and strengthen the lawyer's obligation to the court by setting forth a number of explicit provisions emphasizing claims of justice over duties to clients. Among these were requirements that lawyers disclose facts adverse to their client's case if "disclosure would probably have a substantial effect on the determination of a material issue of fact" and that attorneys refrain from negotiating an agreement with terms that "a reasonable lawyer would know to be unconscionable." Another draft provision authorized a lawyer to disclose confidential information, if need be, to prevent the head of a client corporation from acting in ways "that would clearly violate the law and be likely to result in substantial injury to the organization." When these proposals came before the organized bar for debate, they quickly encountered fierce opposition. Eventually, all were either dropped or heavily amended to minimize their effect.

The Kutak Commission also sought to create a requirement that every attorney spend a minimum of forty hours each year in pro bono legal services for indigent individuals or for worthy community groups. This proposal followed a major effort by the organized bar to increase such services when President Reagan tried unsuccessfully to abolish the federally funded Legal Services Corporation. After an encouraging start, the fraction of lawyers devoting time to pro bono work seems to have declined, leading to the Kutak Commission's attempt to make such services mandatory.[37] By the end of the 1980s the profession had rejected these proposals, and the campaign for more pro bono work had pretty clearly failed. The largest law firms reported spending less than 2 percent of all billable hours on legal services for the poor.[38] Close observers concluded that the pressure to expand profits and increase billable hours was a major reason why firm members did not contribute more of their time.[39] As one writer put it, "Small wonder that associates who leave for work before their children wake up and return home hours after the au pair has tucked them into bed have no singular desire to busy themselves with law reform or pro bono activities."[40]

In other callings, increased competition and the lure of higher earnings have put similar pressure on ethical standards. In medicine, for example, improper billing, conflicts of interest, and other abuses are estimated to cost in the billions each year.[41] Acts of fraud by attorneys are reported to be at an all-time high.[42] White-collar fraud in business seems to have risen as well, and executives constantly complain of a declining willingness to honor commitments or observe ordinary standards of confidentiality.

The desire to make a lot of money has also placed greater stress on professionals than many of them expected. An intriguing case in point has arisen in large corporate law firms. During the 1970s, as we have seen, competition grew keener among these organizations and the search for higher profits became much more intense. Partners sought to link compensation more tightly to performance while keeping closer track of the number of "billable" hours logged by each partner and associate. These stimuli had the desired effect. The average number of billable hours by Wall Street firms grew by almost 30 percent from 1982 to 1989 alone.[43] Individual lawyers vied with one another to achieve greater feats of legal industry. One fabled partner even took advantage of the time changes on a long flight west to charge more than twenty-four hours of work in a single day.

The result of all this toil was a healthy jump in the earnings of many corporate lawyers. The twenty-five most profitable firms in the nation boosted their real profits per partner by 50 percent or more during a single five-year period in the late 1980s. With average billable hours per lawyer reaching 2,200, even 2,500 hours per year, however, one could legitimately ask whether raising each partner's yearly income from $400,000 to $600,000 was truly worth the sacrifice required.

Rising fees soon led to other problems as corporate clients began to question law firms more closely about the bills they submitted. Suddenly, partners accustomed to exercising their own judgment over the conduct of legal proceedings were being challenged by clients who questioned whether it was truly necessary to take so many depositions, interview so many witnesses, or bring so many lawyers to meetings. With their professional autonomy threatened and their hours of work increasing, attorneys, both in law firms and in the profession as a whole, felt a mounting discontent in the 1980s.[44] The percentage of male partners expressing dissatisfaction grew from 9 to 22 percent from 1984 to 1990, while the percentage of dissatisfied female partners rose from 15 to 42 percent. The same trends were evident among younger lawyers as well; levels of dissatisfaction for experienced associates rose from 13 to 32 percent among males and from 25 to 33 percent among females.

Similar concerns exist in other professions as well. Doctors and business executives, along with lawyers, appeared to work harder through the 1980s. Like attorneys, physicians found their professional judgment questioned by cost-conscious insurance companies and their daily work encumbered by filling out forms for agencies determined to control their medical expenses. Most practitioners were not pleased with the results. According to a survey by Juliet Schor at the end of the decade, virtually half (48.9 percent) of all professionals indicated that they would willingly trade *all* of their anticipated increases in earnings for a commensurate reduction in their working hours.[45] Doctors were so distressed about their loss of autonomy, their paperwork, and their long hours that almost 40 percent declared they would no longer enter medicine if they had the choice to make all over again.

Conceivably, competition will eventually overcome discontents of this kind. In the long run, law firms trying to retain talented members may accommodate those who want to reduce their hours and agree to take a cut in pay. Doctors who want to control their life-style may be able to find HMOs and specialty practices that will allow them to do so. These happy results, however, have not happened yet, and one should not simply assume that they will occur automatically. For the moment, the balance in many organizations appears to be out of kilter. As we have seen, in doctors' offices as well as law firms, levels of discontent seem to be rising, not falling. The reasons are not hard to discern. Longer hours may bring higher earnings. But there is no evidence that professionals will gain any lasting gratification by continuing to raise their incomes; all studies of happiness and satisfaction testify to the contrary. Indeed, as work schedules grow longer, successful practitioners must increasingly lack the time either to enjoy their earnings or even to decide how to use them fruitfully.

In pointing to the pressures that the last two decades have placed on ethical standards, professionalism, and satisfaction in work, I do not mean to condemn competition or to deny its many virtues. My point is simply that competition is a complex process. Beyond a certain point, intensifying rivalry and increasing the rewards for success are likely to do more harm than good. This hardly means that markets and financial incentives have no useful role to play, only that they are not a panacea for organizing human activity. As interest grows in extending competition to our schools, government services, and health care system, we will need to subject such proposals to greater scrutiny and introduce more imaginative safeguards to discourage undesirable behavior than today's market enthusiasts seem willing to acknowledge.

SHRINKING GOVERNMENT

Just as the doctrines of the eighties tended to rely indiscriminately on private markets and monetary incentives, so also did they err in constantly denigrating government and belittling its role. It may well be that the state should contract in size, and political leaders should surely think carefully before expanding its functions. Yet even Ronald Reagan could not gain broad support for eliminating important public programs. By the time he left office, there were more civilian employees on the federal payroll than there were when he began. In light of this experience, it seems all but inevitable that government will remain a major force in our society under any administration. That being so, political leaders would do better to concentrate on making it function well instead of publicly criticizing its efforts and questioning its legitimacy.

Efforts to restrict the government's role expose the contradictions that have emerged within the ideology of the past decade. Throughout the nineteenth century, free enterprise and state intervention were almost mutually exclusive; it was natural to favor restricting government while strongly supporting free enterprise. Today, the relationship between the state and market competition has become more complicated. As we have noted, the need to justify competition and inequality by maximizing opportunity for all entails a large and growing state effort to provide all manner of services, from prenatal care to job training and college loans. The emphasis on competition and material rewards increases temptations to violate laws and thus requires the state to devote more effort to policing the behavior of market participants. As the public comes to care about a growing number of important values—equal opportunity, environmental protection, occupational safety, consumer protection, and many more—rules proliferate, and the task of regulating competition grows ever more substantial.

Current proposals to extend competition into health care offer apt illustrations of these tendencies. The programs under consideration would give all families and single adults the chance to choose among rival health plans and HMOs. Yet most consumers lack the knowledge to choose intelligently among these alternatives, and great frustration, even personal tragedy, can result if they are forced to make unaided choices from a bewildering array of complex provisions, disclaimers, and exceptions. In addition, without some form of regulation, insurers will seek in various ways to avoid insuring bad health risks, while healthy people will try to gain a free ride by avoiding insurance until they fall ill. For these reasons, competition without much more is simply not a workable approach to providing reasonable health care for all at affordable prices. On the contrary, any competitive health care system will have to involve the government heavily to make sure that consumers are accurately informed of their options, that insurers do not "cream" the market by taking only healthy applicants, that everyone receives at least a decent minimum of care, and that the poor and elderly are covered at a cost that does not deplete the Treasury.

In much the same way, any conceivable system of parental choice in education must be modified substantially to ensure that parents can make informed choices and that competition does not widen the gap between affluent and impoverished schools. Hence, the government will have to take vigorous steps to ensure that parents are fully and accurately informed, that adequate transportation exists to make choice meaningful, that successful schools do not take only the brightest, whitest students, that all schools live up to minimum standards, and that special measures are available to rehabilitate institutions that are failing to serve their students well. It will take great skill on the part of public officials to introduce these safeguards while still leaving ample room for competition and local initiative.

Much the same is true of current efforts to "privatize" government by allowing corporations and other organizations to bid for contracts to perform such traditional public services as garbage removal, street repair, and fire protection. These experiments are among the more valuable by-products of the Reagan revolution; they promise to pump new energy into activities that once were the exclusive preserve of government. But it is wrong to assume that private enterprise will simply replace public agencies. Federal officials will have to exercise great skill in writing contracts that contain proper incentives and safeguard essential public interests in matters such as safety, equal opportunity, and environmental protection. Similarly, government agencies will have to monitor performance carefully to avoid corruption, promote effective service, and ensure full compliance with agreed-on standards. These are not simple tasks. As David Osborne and Ted Gaebler point out in their provocative book, *Reinventing Government*, "contracting is one of the most difficult methods a public organization can choose, because writing and monitoring contracts require so much skill."[46]

For these reasons, the ideology of the 1980s misleads us when it portrays competitive markets as an alternative to government regulation. Society has come to embrace a lengthening list of values that the market does not automatically serve, especially in fields such as education and health that touch upon vital public interests. As a result, introducing competition rarely does away with government; it simply changes its role by creating an intricate mix of markets and government regulation to produce the results that the public wants. Moreover, after privatization has run its course, vast responsibilities will remain in areas such as national defense and the administration of justice that cannot be contracted out or delegated away by government officials.

Because this mixed system requires highly capable public officials, Presidents Carter and Reagan ran great risks in treating government as a necessary evil and a last resort, just as politicians of every stripe commit a strategic blunder by constantly blaming bureaucrats. It is amusing to condemn national health insurance as a program that would have "all the compassion of the Internal Revenue Service and the efficiency of the Postal Service at Pentagon prices."[47] Still, however much such criticism may appeal to voters, it is a Pyrrhic strategy, because it demoralizes civil servants and makes genuine reform more difficult. If government is only a necessary evil and its officials are hopelessly rigid and inefficient, good people will be less likely to choose careers in public service. Taxpayers will not believe that decent salaries are justified for public officials. And the quality of government services will decline even as its regulatory functions continue to grow.

Beyond its effect on morale and recruitment, official skepticism toward government also weakens public trust and confidence in the political system. Such confidence is crucial to the stability and well-being of a democratic society. It is needed to induce citizens to participate wholeheartedly in civic life—to vote, pay taxes, take an interest in public affairs, and accept the responsibilities that every community must ask its members to bear to cope with common problems. Such involvement does not occur spontaneously. On the contrary, ordinary self-interest would lead individuals to act as free riders and let others shoulder the burdens of community life. The willingness to participate arises from a conviction acquired over many years that everyone's cooperation in making democracy work brings valuable benefits to all.

Once developed, such attitudes make a vital contribution to effective government. As Robert Putnam and his colleagues have recently shown, high civic participation is the principal reason why regional governments seem to work much better in some parts of Italy than in others.[48] Recent studies of reforms in American state and local government have reached a similar conclusion.[49]

Fortunately, a long tradition of democratic government and a remarkable record of economic prosperity have given Americans an unshakable faith in the prevailing economic and political order. Yet this is no guarantee that civic participation will be vigorous. Although the public may remain committed to the Constitution and the basic institutions of government, the last quarter century has shown how disenchanted people can become with the parties, the programs, and the politicians and officials who occupy positions of power within the system. Left unchecked, such attitudes can weaken the government in trying to carry out its essential functions.

There are several ways in which a government can provoke such disaffection. One way is to attempt too much, either by embarking on major policies that strike many people as unwise or unfair or by failing to overcome major problems that it commits itself to resolve. This is, in effect, what seemed to occur in the 1960s, with some of the ambitious programs of the War on Poverty and then through involvement in a disastrous and divisive conflict in Vietnam. Another way of undermining civic commitment is for officials to be embroiled in scandals, such as Watergate, that confirm the public's worst fears about government and politicians. These misadventures contributed to a steep decline in public trust in government after 1965. From the mid-1960s to the 1980s, the percentage of people declaring that they had "a great deal of confidence," in the leaders of the federal government dropped from over 40 percent to less than 20 percent. During the same period, the percentage declaring that they could not "trust government officials to do the right thing most of the time" rose from 22 to 73 percent.[50]

Such a massive erosion of trust creates serious difficulties for any administration in power, because trust and confidence are so important to the ability to govern effectively. When trust evaporates, however, it is particularly difficult to deal with the problem through an ideology that itself professes little confidence in government. To be sure, Ronald Reagan's open distaste for Congress and the bureaucracy endeared him to all who harbored similar feelings toward Washington and thus led to a temporary rise in public confidence in government. But this renewed support was fragile, and little was done to solidify it by taking steps to improve the efficiency and effectiveness of the executive branch. Nor did the administration show an interest in trying to reduce the exaggerated fears of many citizens concerning waste and inefficiency in government. As a result, when Iran-Contra and other scandals rocked Washington in the mid-1980s and were followed by recession at the end of the decade, confidence in government quickly sagged again to levels as depressed as they had been at the end of the Carter presidency.

This widespread disaffection has helped to push the extent of civic involvement to a very low ebb indeed. The proportion of eligible voters who made it to the polls declined steadily from 1960 until 1992, when it was revived largely by the entry of a candidate who symbolized a total rejection of traditional politics and government.[51] Young people display less interest in world and national affairs and know less about them than any other generation since investigators began looking into the question after World War II.[52]

Although Americans currently have a lighter tax burden than any other industrial nation, voters regularly turn down bond issues to fund new local services or to improve their schools, and resist paying more to Washington even to reduce our massive deficits.

The decline of civic support and participation has begun to have a profound effect on our capacity to govern ourselves effectively. Faced with a warning from President Nixon that America might lose the chance for lasting peace by not increasing aid to Russia, President Bush's immediate reply was that "there isn't a whole lot of money around" to help ensure the peaceful democratization of the former Soviet empire. Despite the size of the federal deficit, even candidate Clinton did not dare in his campaign to urge higher taxes for any but the wealthiest citizens. In speaking of the persistence of large-scale poverty, rampant urban violence, widespread drug use, and related social afflictions, President Bush stated in his inaugural address that America lacks "not the will but the wallet" to cope with these issues.

These are remarkable responses from a nation that is still almost the wealthiest in the world. Because taxes in this country are already low by international standards, it is hard to believe that the nation lacks the resources to act in its own best interests. The fact is that Americans simply have not had enough faith in their government and its leaders to provide what is needed to respond effectively to many of the most pressing problems facing the country. As opinion polls make clear, the public does not believe there is any inconsistency in refusing to pay more taxes while opposing the dismantling of any programs. In their eyes, it is possible to balance the budget and still accomplish everything the country needs if only politicians have the resolve to cut the waste in Washington. In this way have attacks on bureaucracy come back to haunt the authors and weaken their power to govern.

The ideology of the eighties, then, could not rescue us from the predicament reached under an earlier philosophy that was too hospitable to vast new government initiatives and too casual about their implementation. For the Democratic dogmas of the 1960s, it substituted the Republican dogmas of the 1980s, which were replete with their own inconsistencies and weaknesses. By the end of the decade, the promise of continued economic growth and prosperity seemed to be vanishing. Meanwhile, incomes had become increasingly unequal, leading professionals had pushed their earnings to unjustifiable levels, and our most talented young people were gradually deserting the government, the schools, and other public-sector posts in favor of private-sector careers that promised much more money.

In sum, the doctrines of the 1980s have not proved adequate to ensure the welfare and prosperity of America. Nor have they offered effective, convincing answers to the problems and shortcomings of the 1960s and 1970s. Indeed, even those who have profited the most from recent trends do not seem to be satisfied with the results. The question that remains is whether anything can be done to make things better.

CHAPTER 13

SEARCHING FOR REMEDIES

It is one thing to criticize excessive earnings and quite another to do something about them. On close analysis, all of the obvious remedies turn out to have serious limitations. Publicity can help build resistance to excessive compensation, but it works erratically and probably inhibits only egregious forms of pay gouging. Setting legal limits on compensation offers a tempting quick fix for bloated earnings, but it is a cumbersome process, causing such rigidities in pay and such administrative headaches that it should probably be avoided save in times of war or other emergency.

Hard bargaining over pay holds brighter possibilities. It will often help to moderate excessive compensation and has the added virtue of bringing about solutions that the participating parties can accept as workable. Nevertheless, bargaining succeeds only when both parties to the discussion are strong and well informed and only when their interests coincide with other legitimate concerns affected by the outcome. As we saw in discussing executive compensation, even powerful, independent boards of directors will not necessarily bring executive pay into proper alignment so long as the directors represent only short-term shareholder interests and not the concerns of employees, local communities, and the public as a whole.

Corporations negotiating with outside law firms and insurance companies overseeing doctors do not confront this problem, as their desire to hold down fees coincides quite closely with the public interest. But even large companies, sophisticated as they are, do not know enough to judge how much work their professionals need to do. In their ignorance, corporate overseers may either do too little to restrain costs or run the risk of monitoring expenses so zealously that they spend more money than they save and harass attorneys and physicians to the point of interfering with the quality of their work. As a result, it is still unclear how much corporate efforts to hold down legal and medical fees will actually accomplish.

ANOTHER REMEDY FOR EXCESSIVE EARNINGS

Are there no fully effective measures, then, to counteract inflated earnings? Only one serious possibility remains: a more steeply progressive income tax. Taxing the wealthy at higher rates is standard procedure in almost all advanced countries. Yet progressive rates are rarely imposed to eliminate excessive earnings, at least in the United States. They exist because most people believe the well-to-do can relinquish part of their income in taxes with less sacrifice than poor people. In other words, progressive taxation is put forward chiefly as a way of sharing the pain more equally. Even so, it also drains off undeserved income. The steeper the rates, the more complete this corrective process will be.

In some respects, the progressive tax is the ideal way to remove excessive earnings in a highly imperfect market. Because the Internal Revenue Service already exists, higher taxes for the wealthy will require little or no added administrative burden. Moreover, unlike remedies tailored to specific professions, progressive tax rates apply to all higher incomes and hence do not run the risk of driving talented people arbitrarily from one occupation to another. A government cap on executive earnings alone, on the other hand, might cause too many prospective managers to shift from business school to law school or from established companies into entrepreneurial ventures. Progressive taxes would be unlikely to have such effects.

President Clinton has recently proposed an increase in federal tax rates from 31 to 36 percent for single persons reporting incomes over $115,000 per year ($140,000 for married couples) with a 10 percent surcharge for taxable incomes over $250,000. The prospects of enacting this change into law are excellent. Nevertheless, elected officials have sharply different views about how progressive the income tax should be, and top rates will doubtless continue to change with the political tides as they have in the past. As a result, the debate on the subject is far from over.

Critics have offered a number of arguments against a steeply progressive tax.[1] For a long time, their chief concern was the fear that higher taxes on the wealthy would dull the incentive to work. After repeated studies, however, no persuasive evidence has emerged that tax increases of the magnitude President Clinton has proposed will actually have such an effect.[2] Wealthy taxpayers realize that working hard will net them less money, but they also know they must work harder to maintain their standard of living. By and large, these opposing pressures appear to cancel themselves out. Thus, doctors in the 1980s do not seem to have begun spending more time on their practice after Congress made major reductions in their marginal tax rates.[3]

Besides, incentives that cause highly compensated people to work harder are not necessarily a good thing. Not according to professionals, surely, who already work much more than a 40-hour week. Far from wanting incentives to work harder, the great majority indicate that they would happily give up all or most of any future pay increases if they could *reduce* their hours of work commensurately. As for society, it is true that everyone may gain from having entrepreneurs try harder to build new companies that create new jobs. But will we all be better off if doctors work longer hours prescribing more tests and performing more operations or if lawyers spend more time taking depositions and litigating in the courtroom?

There is also little reason to fear that higher progressivity will lower savings. If it did, Americans would have to worry; by most accounts, savings in the United States are already dangerously low. Nevertheless, although wealthy people will have less to put aside if their tax rates rise, so many factors influence savings rates that there are plenty of ways to compensate for any losses that higher taxes might bring. Either the government can strengthen incentives to save or it can use part of the revenues raised from steeper rates for this purpose. Such possibilities help to explain why Japan, Germany, and other advanced countries have had higher rates of saving than the United States while maintaining a more progressive tax structure. They also explain why the massive tax cuts in this country during the Reagan years produced no growth in private savings.

Many conservatives seem opposed to progressive taxes more on philosophic grounds than for purely economic reasons. According to Milton Friedman, "This seems a clear case of using coercion to take from some to give to others and thus to conflict head-on with individual freedom."[4] It is difficult, however, to maintain that anyone has a legitimate claim to earnings in excess of what competitive markets (or any other reasonable theory of social welfare) would allow. As we have discovered, much of the income that would be taxed away with higher rates exceeds the sums that would be earned under genuine conditions of competition. Friedman himself recognized this fact decades ago in his study of earnings in the medical profession. In opposing progressive tax rates, however, he either ignores the point or urges other remedies to improve the market without acknowledging that many of his proposals, such as increasing the number of doctors, are unworkable, unwise, or both.

Friedman also overlooks the possibility that limiting the freedom of the well-to-do may be outweighed by expanding the freedom of the less fortunate, either by lowering *their* taxes or by providing more education, job training, or other opportunities to use their talents more fully. He likewise fails to tell us why he places one particular value (i.e., freedom from higher taxes) over all the other values that progressive taxes might promote. It may be that leaving successful CEOs, corporate lawyers, and surgeons with over one million dollars of annual income is worth more than providing milk for undernourished children or medical care for an uninsured diabetic. But the answer is not obvious, and Friedman never bothers to explain.

A more troubling aspect of progressive taxes is that they are an arbitrary way of coping with excessively large earnings. Although many people in the highest brackets may have inflated incomes, some are bound to have more unjustified income than others. Michael Jordan may deserve the paychecks he has worked so hard to win much more than Ross Johnson deserves his $53 million golden parachute. Nevertheless, the same higher rates will apply to both. In this sense, progressive taxes may seem unfair.

In pondering this objection, we must remind ourselves that we will have to put up with a lot of unfairness whatever we do. The real injustice occurs because some people earn far more income than truly competitive markets would allow. So long as this is so, any level of taxation will leave some individuals with more or less than they deserve. If higher rates take too much from Michael Jordan, lower rates will leave too much with Ross Johnson. There is no reason to think we can avoid such unfairness by forgoing progressive rates or even that we will be less unfair by doing so.

It is also worth recalling how hard it is for any successful professionals to make a compelling moral case that they deserve all their earnings. Most well-paid doctors, lawyers, and executives work honestly and hard, but so do many others who are not well-to-do; the decisive difference between them almost always results from inherited ability, family upbringing, luck, and other factors beyond anyone's control. It is not obvious that highly paid people "deserve" to benefit from these fortuitous influences.* Moreover, those with large incomes also tend to have the most prestigious, interesting, and satisfying jobs (which yield a psychic income that is wholly free from tax). Because the well-to-do are doubly blessed, there is all the more reason to share with those who are not only poorly paid but may be forced to endure dull, repetitive work as well.

At some level, of course, higher tax rates cannot be justified even for the wealthiest individuals. Corporations will begin to offer their executives expensive perquisites instead of money, talented professionals may work less hard, and some may actually leave the United States for countries with lower taxes. Moreover, as rates grow higher, they are more and more likely to exceed what is needed to reduce excessive earnings and to take away money that is justly earned.

There is no way of telling exactly what the upper limits of progressivity should be. As a practical matter, however, it is probably not necessary to do so. Given the political realities of this country, effective taxes, even on the largest incomes, are unlikely to exceed the levels of other advanced democracies. Although these nations have reduced their top rates substantially over the past fifteen years, almost all tax the well-to-do at rates that are ten to twenty percentage points higher than ours.[5] For example, France has a top rate of 57 percent; Germany, 53 percent; Belgium, 55 percent; and Austria, Italy, and Japan, 50 percent. Raising taxes on the wealthy to some-

* It also bears repeating that the primary reason for progressive rates has never been to deprive wealthy taxpayers of unjustified income but to distribute the tax burden in a way that conforms more closely than a uniform rate to the public's ability to pay. The fact that large numbers of people earning more than, say, $200,000 a year have incomes that cannot be justified by the marketplace is simply an added reason for taxing them more heavily. Hence, there are arguments for progressive rates that help to justify their application even to individuals whose earnings are not excessive in any unjustified way.

thing approximating these levels should have no undesirable economic effects; several other countries with more progressive tax systems than ours have managed to exceed our rates of growth, productivity, and savings over the past thirty years.

Even this moderate change evokes a final plea from supply-side economists. They insist that imposing more progressive taxes will be a futile gesture, because it will not produce more revenue but simply cause wealthy people to find some loophole or tax shelter to keep from paying more to the government.* As a result, taxing the rich will do nothing to help the poor or to serve any other worthy cause.[6]

It is doubtful that increases such as Mr. Clinton proposes will produce much tax avoidance, especially now that the tax reforms of 1986 have swept away so many of the familiar shelters. Moreover, the proper response to this problem is not to refrain from raising taxes but to do away with questionable loopholes. Still, hardened veterans of legislative tax wars may insist that as top rates climb to 40 percent or above, the pressure on Congress to create new shelters will be irresistible. Even if this gloomy assessment is correct, however, there are other ways of increasing taxes on the well-to-do without raising marginal rates to such a point that tax shelters would become truly attractive. For example, the government could limit the amounts of mortgage payments deductible from income and stop the regressive subsidy given to wealthy purchasers of expensive houses or vacation homes. (Roughly 25 percent of the taxes forgone by exempting mortgage payments—or approximately $14 billion annually—goes to individuals who earn more than $100,000 per year.) Similarly, Congress could put an end to tax-free municipal bonds (while giving compensatory aid to cities and towns) and thus eliminate a tax shelter that provides a highly inefficient way of assisting local communities with worthy projects.

In the end, therefore, because other remedies are only partially effective, progressive taxation emerges as a necessary step in any serious effort to limit excessive earnings. The many imperfections

* Not all methods of reducing taxes allow wealthy taxpayers to retain their excess incomes. For example, if steeper rates lead wealthy individuals to give more of their income to charity, they will still have to sacrifice more of their (unjustified) earnings; the only difference is that they, and not the government, can choose which worthwhile cause to support.

of the market belie any claim by wealthy people that they should escape heavier taxes because their incomes are fully deserved or vital to maximizing economic welfare. Very high earnings are usually hard to justify on any grounds and hence threaten to undermine the public's belief in the basic fairness of the society. In this sense, more progressive rates do not represent a conspiracy against the rich but a way of maintaining enough confidence in the nation to ensure its health and preservation.

EXPANDING OPPORTUNITY

Even if tax rates rise for the wealthy and other steps are taken to reduce excessive incomes, some Americans will continue to earn a great deal more than others. As we have previously affirmed, such differences are defensible when based on ability and accomplishment in serving the public's needs, but only if all people have a reasonable chance to compete for greater rewards. Enhancing such opportunities, therefore, promotes social justice. In addition, it expands the pool of talent available to fill demanding jobs and thereby benefits society as well as helping those fortunate enough to succeed. In this sense, increasing opportunity is a doubly valuable enterprise.

With free public schools for all and the most accessible system of higher education in the world, America does quite well in providing opportunities for talented individuals to prepare themselves for remunerative careers. Nevertheless, a host of social problems—poverty, crime, discrimination, inadequate health care, and unequal school financing, among others—block these opportunities for many young people in ways quite beyond their control. Impoverished children are hardly likely to excel in class if they go to bed hungry, or study in rooms crowded with noisy siblings, or never see adults holding well-paid jobs, or walk to school in mortal fear of physical violence. In view of these obstacles, programs to improve neighborhoods, stop discrimination, fight drugs, reduce crime, and eliminate poverty could all help to expand opportunity for disadvantaged youths who are not now competing on a level playing field.

Apart from these general reforms, several specific steps to expand educational opportunity deserve special mention. The most compelling of these are efforts to benefit the very young by helping them to arrive at school in a state of readiness to learn. According to a nationwide survey of kindergarten teachers, 35 percent of all children start school unprepared to learn.[7] Although some of these youngsters are emotionally disturbed owing to family situations that are difficult to correct, many suffer from disabilities brought on by malnutrition, inadequate prenatal care, and other remediable causes. There are several promising programs to alleviate these problems. All these measures are well tested and successful, but each is currently unavailable to large fractions of the families who could benefit from them the most. Head Start is one prominent example; nutritional programs for young children is another; prenatal counseling is a third. These programs are exceptionally compelling not only because they help children get the most out of school but also because they can save society several times the cost of implementing them. The failure to extend these benefits to everyone who needs them is inexcusable. All could be fully funded with the tax receipts derived from raising taxes on the well-to-do to rates approximating those of other highly developed countries.

At the level of elementary and secondary schools, the quest for equal opportunity is significantly hampered by gross disparities in the resources devoted to different kinds of school districts. No one has described these differences as passionately as Jonathan Kozol in his recent book, *Savage Inequalities*.[8] In contrast to the carefully maintained, well-equipped classrooms in suburbs such as Westchester or Beverly Hills, dilapidated, dispirited schools abound in ghettos across the country. As Kozol describes them, "my deepest impression . . . was simply the impression that these urban schools were, by and large, extraordinarily unhappy places. With few exceptions, they reminded me of 'garrisons' or 'outposts' in a foreign land. . . . Looking around some of these inner-city schools, where filth and disrepair were worse than anything I'd seen [when I first taught disadvantaged students], I often wondered why we would agree to let our children go to school in places where no politician, school board president, or business CEO would dream of working."[9]

Distressed by such glaring inequalities, activists have fought to even the amounts of tax revenue available to urban and suburban districts. In a number of states, the courts have accepted these arguments and ordered the legislature to support all districts equally. Yet these decrees have not narrowed the difference in the quality of education provided in rich and poor communities. The reasons are not hard to fathom. Much of the gap results from unemployment, drugs, crime, and other social afflictions that lie beyond the reach of school budgets and will take many years to cure. Although part of the problem does result from inadequate schools, even this deficiency cannot be cured by money alone. A long series of interdependent reforms are needed to improve the quality of education in poor communities. Without making these changes, equal funding will not transform blighted urban schools into places capable of creating genuine opportunities through education.

Moving to our colleges and universities, we find a happier situation. America possesses the most highly developed system of higher education in the world, open to virtually all who seek to attend, diverse enough to accommodate the differing needs and aspirations of a huge student population, and able to offer enough scholarships and subsidized loans to benefit millions of needy students every year. One measure of the system's success in expanding opportunity is the fact that almost 90 percent of the most academically talented high school students do in fact go to college and up to 90 percent of them eventually graduate.

In the last decade, unfortunately, America has lost ground. Average college costs have risen by 126 percent as family incomes increased by only 73 percent.[10] Meanwhile, the maximum federal grants available for needy students have dropped by 15 percent in real dollars. These trends have forced many students to lower their aspirations by going to two-year colleges instead of four-year institutions, switching from full-time to part-time status, or halting their education altogether.[11] Reversing this decline, however, will not be hard. Although the cost of restoring federal grants to previous levels would require spending several billion dollars per year, the basic programs to secure opportunities for college are in place. Part of the money needed to return to adequate funding levels could come from reforming the expensive federal college loan program to cut subsidies to middle-class students, install direct lending to eliminate profit margins for banks and other private lenders, and introduce more efficient collection procedures to reduce losses from defaults.

Two problems remain, however, that affect access to higher education in America. The first is that many talented young people do not have an opportunity to choose the best education available to them because they cannot afford to pay more than the lowest available tuition or to defray the costs of living away from their family. As a result, a large majority of all college students attend whatever institution lies within easy driving distance of their home. The second and more serious problem is that most colleges have such minimal entrance requirements that only a small percentage of high school students feel that they must work hard to gain admission to the institution they plan to attend.

The ease of entering most colleges contributes to the lack of incentives in schools across the country. Observing this, many critics have begun to attack universities for being so permissive and have urged them to raise their entrance requirements.[12] But admissions officers will have great difficulty in following this advice. If their institutions are to survive financially, they must attract a reasonable number of entering students. For all but a small fraction of the nation's 3,500 colleges, having enough freshmen requires taking the vast majority of all who apply, whether or not they satisfy rigorous admissions standards.

Both of these problems could be addressed by creating an ambitious program of scholarships based on academic achievement. To illustrate, a state or federal government could offer additional grants of several thousand dollars per year to a substantial fraction of the most successful high school students (for example, the top 25 percent based on rank in class). These grants would continue for four years, provided the recipient remained in good academic standing. To ensure that public money did not go to well-to-do students (most of whom attend high schools where competition to enter selective colleges is already keen), the awards could be restricted to families with less than the median income. To provide some measure of comparable achievement, awards could be conditioned on attaining the median score on College Board exams (a requirement that should give less pain to critics of standardized tests as the SAT moves away from multiple-choice questions and begins to place as much emphasis on achievement as on ability).

A program of this scope would provide substantial motivation to large numbers of high school students, especially in schools in which incentives for studying hard, or even for going to college at all, are noticeably weak. At the same time, the awards would also bring a much larger range of colleges within reach of many students whose performance entitles them to choose the best education they can find.

The obvious objection to such a sizable program is its cost, especially at a time when the country is wrestling with large deficits that inhibit all manner of new domestic initiatives. My purpose here, however, is not merely to propose immediately feasible measures but to offer some indication of what sorts of programs are needed in a nation bent on maximizing educational opportunity and incentives. Besides, there are ways of creating such programs with very little added expense if public officials were prepared to rearrange the financing of higher education along more rational lines.

At present, state governments provide a college (and graduate) education to all qualified residents at a price that is far below actual cost. Because most students in state colleges and universities come from families with above-average incomes, the net effect of the current practice is to collect taxes from lower-middle-class families to subsidize upper-middle-class students. This policy is not only hard to justify; it contributes little to the motivation of high school students, as all who attend state universities receive the same subsidy regardless of the effort they have expended or the academic success they have achieved.

It would be comparatively simple to devise a scheme that would raise tuitions substantially for state colleges and universities and use the proceeds both to award financial aid to all who truly need it *and* to provide achievement grants for large numbers of students in the manner previously described. Such a scheme would be much fairer than the current system because it would reduce the subsidy currently paid to well-to-do families and provide more help to poorer households. In addition, it would create a potent new incentive for many high school students and a chance to enlarge their educational aspirations.* And all of this could come about without increasing the total outlay of public funds for higher education.[13]

Further possibilities for expanding opportunities exist at the level of graduate and professional education. At present, scholarship aid is quite limited outside of a few fields of study, notably Ph.D. pro-

* Similar incentives could be created for other high school students who have no aspirations to attend college. For example, as states increasingly experiment with apprenticeship programs linked to attractive jobs, access to these programs could be conditioned on successful completion of a substantial academic curriculum.

grams. Federally subsidized loans are widely available for graduate work, but the effect is to force students already owing large sums to pile up heavy additional debts by the time they complete two or three years (or more) of further study. It is not yet clear how often the prospect of such indebtedness deters students from pursuing graduate work or pushes them to choose more lucrative careers to be sure of being able to repay their loans. Nevertheless, as students leave professional school with ever-mounting debt burdens, one has to worry lest these obligations drive more and more talented graduates to move from government and teaching careers into the private sector, to forsake general medicine for the most highly paid specialties, or even to defer and ultimately abandon graduate study altogether.

One way of alleviating this problem would be to place a ceiling on the percentage of income students would have to pay in order to discharge their educational loans.* Those who continued in low-paid jobs would be relieved of their debts after a stipulated number of years. In this way, students would no longer be deterred by the fear of having to use a prohibitive share of their modest income to pay back their debts. Because graduates earning modest incomes would find it much easier to repay their educational loans, the number of defaults would drop, cutting the cost of the program significantly. Much of the remaining expense could be met by stopping the current practice of giving heavily subsidized loans to graduate students, such as those attending schools of law and business, who have excellent prospects of earning more than enough to repay their educational debts at market rates of interest.

A more ambitious alternative would be to install a system whereby all borrowers would be charged a fixed percentage of their income for each thousand dollars of debt.[14] Such a plan could be structured so that even the heaviest borrowers would need to pay only a modest share of their future income for a maximum number of years. Once again, therefore, no student would need to feel pressured by a heavy burden of debt to forgo a career in school teaching, social work, the ministry, or some other low-paid occupation.

* This is essentially what President Clinton would accomplish by his proposal to allow students to choose an educational loan plan that would limit their repayments to a fixed percentage of income.

Such a program would have the added advantage of consolidating the complicated array of current loan plans in a single program. If the new contingent loans were administered through the Social Security program or collected by payroll deductions administered by the Internal Revenue Service, the government could also reduce the number of loan defaults, which are currently running over $3 billion yearly.

Under an income-contingent plan, students taking high-paying jobs would have to pay back more than the total of their educational loans, while those in poorly compensated careers would pay less. The government, however, would have to limit the obligations of the more affluent borrowers, if only to keep students planning to enter the better-paid professions from refusing to take out loans under the plan. To accomplish this result, Congress could either put a cap on the total sums that highly paid graduates would be asked to repay or require students to pay back loans only on the first $50,000 of their annual earnings. Limited in this fashion, a contingent-repayment plan would not weigh unfairly on those pursuing highly paid careers. As we have discovered, no unseen hand validates the current differentials between the pay of young executives, doctors, and attorneys on the one hand, and beginning teachers, public officials, ministers, or legal-aid attorneys on the other. Properly devised, a contingent-repayment plan might help to reduce the excessive differences in earnings that currently seem to be pushing so many talented young people into higher-paid private-sector careers.

The proposals just described hardly exhaust the possibilities for expanding career opportunities for those with substantial education. They merely illustrate the kinds of options available to create new possibilities and lower barriers at every stage in the educational process. The cost of implementing these reforms would not be prohibitive if we were willing to take the large subsidies the government currently provides for upper-middle-class families who do not truly need them and direct them to poor students who deserve help much more. By moving in this direction, the government could not only enrich the lives of countless young people but enable them to engage their talents fully to the benefit of the entire society. Without such measures, opportunities for young people will continue to be less equal than they could be, and the moral basis of unequal earnings will remain suspect.

TOWARD A BETTER DISTRIBUTION OF TALENT

Overcoming the disadvantages of the public sector in competing for talented managers and professionals is a challenge of great importance to the society. In public education, no sensible person can suppose that our schools will improve without attracting abler people into teaching and giving them better working conditions. Teachers today typically rank somewhere near the bottom third of their college classes. They are further below the average in college grades and test scores then they were in 1970, when expectations for our schools were much more modest. Once hired, they often work under conditions that deaden motivation—isolated from their colleagues, performing demeaning nonacademic duties, meeting teaching schedules that leave too little time for preparation, lacking opportunities for adequate training, and serving under the direction of casually selected, poorly prepared principals.

Much the same is true of public officials. Americans have made it clear that they want the government to carry out a formidable set of responsibilities and feel that public officials should perform more effectively. Yet salaries for top career officials have fallen far behind earnings for comparable private-sector jobs over the past twenty years. Many more of the interesting, responsible government posts go to short-term political appointees than in any other advanced nation, depriving capable civil servants of challenging career opportunities. Politicians continue to scapegoat bureaucrats for problems that are often not of their making, while hampering their work with petty conflicts between Congress and the White House, constant investigations, inadequate training budgets, and other handicaps. So long as these conditions persist, it is idle to suppose that enough talented young people will wish to devote their lives to government service or that those who do will perform to the best of their ability.

The remedies for this state of affairs are quite straightforward. They have appeared in earlier chapters and in countless reports, books, and articles on the reform of the public schools and the civil service. We need but briefly summarize them here.

The first step is to maintain salary levels that will attract and retain better recruits for teaching and civil service positions. For the public schools, this implies keeping starting salaries at the level of average beginning pay for all college graduates. It also entails lifting pay scales thereafter to levels that will deter the ablest teachers from leaving within two or three years and enhance the prospect of retaining them over much longer periods of time. For the civil service, the critical steps are to keep compensation at average levels for comparable private-sector jobs and to eliminate the linkage to congressional salaries that penalizes civil servants for Congress' political problems in trying to raise its own pay.

Even these adjustments may not suffice to attract young people of unusual ability who can have their pick of many attractive jobs. Further steps are required, therefore, both to ensure enough candidates for hard-to-fill positions, such as math and science teachers, and to build a pool of exceptional talent for future leadership in the public schools and federal government. A modest step toward meeting those needs would be to provide attractive scholarships for students possessing the desired qualifications on the condition that they teach or enter the federal service for a certain number of years or else repay their grants as loans at market rates of interest.

Salaries, of course, will never rise far enough to rival those of major law firms and corporations, nor will money alone ever suffice to make the public sector attractive to capable people. Both the schools and the civil service must recruit more aggressively and streamline their hiring procedures. They must also offer more challenging opportunities for capable people who demonstrate proficiency on the job. For teachers, this implies the chance to assume greater responsibility either as principals and superintendents or in guiding younger colleagues and participating in deliberations about school policies and curriculum. For the civil service, it calls for substantial cutbacks in the number of political appointees so that government agencies can hold forth the prospect of enough positions of importance to attract the most talented young people.

Even successful efforts to recruit good people to the public sector will not suffice if they are not excited by their work and convinced that they can make a difference. The obstacles here are harder to surmount, because they are rooted in problems of bureaucracy and large organizations that are deeply imbedded in the traditions and structures of our schools and government institutions. At the heart of the matter, however, lies the issue of incentives, which poses a challenge for institutions in every sector of our society but seems particularly nettlesome in large public organizations.

ENHANCING MOTIVATION

As we have learned, efforts to motivate professionals by monetary rewards have run into serious difficulty in virtually every occupation and calling in which they have been tried. Inducing people to work hard but not too hard, to strive for appropriate goals in appropriate ways, to work in harmony and not succumb to petty rivalries and resentments, to respect assessments of one's performance and learn to benefit from them—all these aims turn out to be much harder to achieve than one might suppose. Still, it is not enough simply to abandon merit pay and substitute nothing in its place. Even absorbing tasks such as instructing college students often fail to inspire proper dedication when professors are not held accountable for how they teach and universities make no attempt to supply suitable incentives to improve the quality of instruction. Hence, building motivation remains a critical challenge, the more so because of the high social importance of the work professionals perform.

Fortunately, there are many ways of motivating professionals aside from paying them for performance. Giving recognition for good work, mobilizing peer pressure in a close-knit group, offering funds to carry out interesting tasks, holding forth the possibility of promotion, establishing clear goals, and supplying better feedback can all induce individuals to try harder. So can the threat of negative sanctions such as the fear of being fired, losing face, or letting down one's colleagues. In most cases, these possibilities are not mutually exclusive, and the choice of which incentives to stress varies from one work setting to another. Amid the many alternatives, several deliberate strategies for strengthening incentives deserve special comment.

An obvious way of building motivation, of course, is to introduce some form of competition. Competition, especially in our culture, produces a powerful urge to win, whether the prize is money, recognition, or simply the quiet satisfaction of prevailing over worthy adversaries. Indeed, as we have learned, the problem with competition is often that it is too powerful a stimulus, causing participants to blow the contest out of proportion by devoting too much time and effort to it or, worse yet, resorting to unethical means that require a proliferation of rules and safeguards to keep the rivalry within proper bounds.

Still, competition has advantages over the use of bonuses and similar monetary rewards. It can encourage methods of teamwork that bring participants together in a collaborative effort to succeed. It is usually free of the ambiguity that frequently surrounds merit pay, as the rules of the contest are typically clear enough that there is rarely much doubt over who has won and why. Moreover, the rules are normally established by authorities external to the organization so that success rarely depends on the fallible judgment of a superior. That is why one can accept the outcome of a sporting contest more easily than come to terms with the size of one's bonus. For this reason, competition tends to motivate with much less internal resentment and misunderstanding than merit pay often engenders.

Competition, of course, can usually work its magic only on those who share in the rewards. It is possible, notably in war, for an entire nation to be gripped by a passion to defeat the enemy. More often, at least in large organizations, only the leaders will be gripped by a sense of rivalry or feel that they have a stake in the eventual outcome. For the rest, some other device is needed to rouse them to devote their full energies to the common enterprise.

One method is to reward successful performance by giving money to groups rather than individuals. Many Japanese and some American companies pay bonuses to all the employees in the firm or in a particular division when the unit involved has earned a stipulated return.[15] Some states are experimenting with bonuses for the entire teaching staff of schools in which students make above-average academic progress. Law firms and health maintenance groups will typically pay larger amounts to their members when the organization enjoys an unusually profitable year.

Group rewards escape some of the problems that have dogged individual merit plans. The measure of success is usually prescribed in advance, is often determined by outside, impersonal events, and typically avoids the resentments that come from having supervisors make subjective judgments about the work of subordinates. In addition, because the reward depends on the work of the group, rather than the performance of each individual, professionals do not feel a sense of personal failure when bonuses do not materialize. By their very nature, group rewards have the further advantage of promoting teamwork and solidarity instead of provoking rivalry and tension.

In most other respects, however, group bonuses encounter the same difficulties as individual merit plans. If the measures of success are poorly defined, professionals may distort their efforts to gain a reward. In more than one school, for example, teachers have wasted valuable class time coaching their students on how to take short-answer tests to boost scores and obtain recognition. As with individual bonus plans, if the rewards for group performance are raised too high, participants may even resort to unethical means to achieve success. In one large city where officials promised bonuses to the staff in schools where SAT scores improved, teachers went so far as to persuade their dullest students to stay at home on days when the tests were given. Finally, as groups grow larger, opportunities for individual members to freeload may increase, especially in organizations in which the amount and quality of work performed by each participant are not immediately obvious to colleagues. In the 1960s, for example, when profits were distributed according to seniority, all partners gained when their law firms did well. Nevertheless, this prospect was not sufficient to induce all partners to work appropriately hard, especially as their firms grew larger and more impersonal. That is one reason why more and more firms felt impelled to abandon payment by seniority in favor of distributing profits according to individual performance.[16]

In contrast to merit pay and group rewards, the last major strategy for motivating executives and professionals does not use monetary incentives but seeks to create an organizational culture, a collective sense of mission, that elicits genuine commitment and enthusiasm from those who work within it. Much thought has been devoted to this subject in many kinds of institutions. The techniques that have emerged, as we have seen, are remarkably similar whether one looks at corporations, law offices, government agencies, or effective schools.

In all these organizations, a strong, successful culture requires a clearly defined and commonly shared set of goals and values, considerable participation from the professionals involved, frequent opportunities for discussion and collaborative problem solving, ample feedback and evaluation, carefully designed programs of training and renewal, and proper facilities and working conditions free of undue distraction or fear of penalty or job loss. Wherever such cultures arise, much of the credit is usually given to effective leaders, who articulate the goals and values, invite participation and collaboration, and build loyalty by protecting the professionals in their organization from interference or intimidation.

In trying to develop a strong culture, it helps to have a function that engenders enthusiasm naturally. Ray Kroc, founder of McDonald's, used to say that his secret of good management was making employees see the beauty in a perfectly made hamburger bun. "It can be done," he insisted. Fortunately, doctors, lawyers, managers, and teachers all work at tasks that are far more interesting than making hamburger buns. If Ray Kroc could succeed, therefore, it should be possible for heads of organizations to find ways to instill a strong sense of purpose and meaning in the work their executives and professionals perform.

Success in creating a strong culture and a committed work force brings great advantages. Because it rests on a genuine belief in the importance of the enterprise, it offers a surer guarantee that participants will work for the best interests of the organization than any reward that appeals to the selfish interests of employees. If the professionals involved sincerely want to perform well because the work matters, there is no reason to "game the system" by finding ways to achieve higher ratings by clever stratagems that serve no valid organizational interest. If participants are truly committed to the enterprise, they also stand a better chance of finding genuine satisfaction in their work without the rivalries and tensions that so often accompany performance-based rewards.

Although building a culture with a strong commitment to a common mission has great advantages in principle, it is difficult to achieve in practice. Even mustering the will to make a serious attempt can prove difficult. Some leaders will simply not understand how to go about creating such a culture. Others will be reluctant to share authority and invite genuine participation and collaboration, not only because they enjoy power but because they understandably fear being held accountable for an organization that they no longer completely control.

Profit-making organizations have the added problem of convincing subordinates that building a strong culture is not simply a manipulative scheme to increase profits for the owners. Leaders who merely talk about the corporation's mission and its values may quickly encounter cynicism on the part of employees. That is what happened to one well-meaning company that solemnly announced its eight-point "corporate credo" only to learn soon after that its cherished principles were commonly referred to in the trenches as "Profit and the Seven Dwarfs." After all, however one may try to disguise it, corporate efforts to build strong cultures *are* designed to increase profits. It takes considerable skill to acknowledge this fact and still persuade employees that profit making is compatible with other goals—such as serving people, working closely together, sharing authority, and creating better products—that can give genuine personal satisfaction to participants.

The task of putting this message across is not made any easier if those in charge earn huge salaries with the prospect of making even more through lavish stock options when corporate profits rise. The power of personal example is great, for better or for worse. If leaders have such an obvious private interest in the bottom line, all talk of other values is likely to seem hypocritical and false. Conversely, when leaders have made personal sacrifices for their beliefs, they speak more persuasively. That undoubtedly helps to explain why the editor of *American Lawyer* discovered that "at just about every [large law] firm where I found strong, credible leadership, I also found . . . a pervasive feeling that the leaders were taking out less than they were really worth by any commonsense standard."[17]

Public organizations have a different challenge in trying to instill a culture and a shared sense of mission. Because government agencies and schools exist to serve the public rather than to earn a profit, there is less difficulty in persuading members that appeals to mission and service are genuine. The public purposes of these organizations are their greatest asset in eliciting effort and enthusiasm from their members. Yet the way in which public-sector institutions are organized often dissipates this advantage. Fragmented authority pulls them in different directions and makes it difficult to maintain consistent values and objectives. Leaders are typically chosen too casually and serve too short a time to engage in the slow, patient task of transforming the aims, values, and work habits of those who work under them. For these reasons, alas, highly motivated public organizations continue to be the exception rather than the rule.

All things considered, building a culture of commitment is probably the best way of motivating managers and professionals. Unfortunately, it is also very difficult. In business, it requires executives to abandon authoritarian, hierarchical methods that are often hard for American managers to put aside. In the public sector, it calls for a kind of leadership that neither government agencies nor school districts have taken great pains to develop. Whatever the setting, it demands qualities of patience, credibility, and interpersonal skill that will always be in short supply.

RETHINKING OUR VALUES

Building an organizational culture that inspires commitment is a markedly different remedy from all those previously described. It does not involve manipulating rewards to align acquisitive instincts with organizational goals. Instead, it seeks to change the attitudes of executives and professionals and cause them to perceive a greater meaning in their jobs. Rather than alter the pay people receive for their work, it tries to change the value of work itself.

This approach has wider implications for the effort to cure the defects of our current compensation practices. All of the earlier remedies we have discussed are only partially effective, whether they involve raising tax rates for the well-to-do, increasing public-sector salaries, or shifting from individual bonuses to group rewards. To get at the roots of our compensation problems, we cannot simply make adjustments in rules and rewards. In the end, we must reexamine the values that have created the difficulties in the first place.

This is a disturbing message, difficult to implement and not particularly congenial to traditional practice in America. As a society, we much prefer to leave our values undisturbed while going to great lengths to create, in T. S. Eliot's words, "a system so perfect that no one needs to be good."[18] Thus, we are forever rearranging the legal and economic order in ways that will harness selfish desires to serve constructive ends, or at least contain them so that they can do no harm. Meanwhile, neither political party is inclined to do a great deal more. Republicans talked frequently about family values during the 1980s but did little to affect them except to oppose abortion. Democrats, on the other hand, found it awkward to speak of values for fear of offending gays, single parents, and other supportive groups involved in nontraditional life-styles.

One can appreciate the reasons for this reticence. There is little that public officials can do directly to affect people's beliefs. The formal powers of government are much better designed to alter institutions and legal frameworks than to shape how people think. Moreover, official efforts to mold people's values are suspect in America; they threaten individual autonomy and conjure up visions of Orwell's *1984*. The First Amendment itself is a bulwark against government actions to mold and manipulate what individual citizens believe.

One thing that governments *can* do, however, is to set examples of what is publicly honored and what is not. Limiting tax deductions for salaries above a certain size may not do much to deter boards of directors from overpaying executives, but it can still provide an expression of official disapproval for excessively generous compensation. Conversely, elected officials could undoubtedly have a positive effect on attitudes toward the civil service if they made a conscious effort to honor those who make a career of public service instead of ridiculing them as bureaucrats and blaming them, often unfairly, for the errors and shortcomings of government. Similarly, political leaders could doubtless help to restore the fallen image of public school teachers by finding ways to praise their dedication while taking care not to utter or condone false assertions, such as the oft-repeated statement that American students are performing less well academically than in earlier decades and that the fault lies chiefly with the schools. For aspiring teachers and civil servants alike, federal scholarship programs could signal the high importance that the nation attaches to attracting talented young people to careers in the public sector.

Important as such official actions are, the primary obligation for altering current compensatory practices in America lies elsewhere. It rests inescapably with those who shape the patterns of remuneration in our society—the boards of directors who set the pay of the corporate officials, the chief executives who often influence their own compensation, the senior law partners who establish the policies and financial goals for their firm, and the doctors who set their own fees, employ consultants to maximize their claims for reimbursement, and sometimes take a financial interest in medical facilities to bring in added revenue.

There are plenty of reasons and rationalizations to avoid thinking more deeply about these responsibilities. "Why me?" some will ask. "It is enough that I conform to the standards I see all around me." But this is hardly a sufficient reason for failing to seek a more thoughtful standard of personal behavior. Used-car dealers can hardly escape responsibility for telling the truth by pointing out how many of their fellow dealers lie.

"It won't do any good," others will insist, observing that the standards set by any one person can have but a tiny effect on the norms of conduct of society. Yet the principal object of developing personal values is not to change society but to change oneself for the better. Unless individuals are willing to accept this point and take their moral responsibilities seriously, there is little hope for improving ethical standards, either for themselves or for society.

"Look what other people are earning," still others will proclaim. More than a few CEOs have defended their paychecks by pointing to what some celebrated athlete earns shagging flies in Yankee Stadium or slam-dunking in Madison Square Garden. Yet this is the weakest rationalization of all for avoiding self-scrutiny. Most of these corporate officials would be the first to ridicule the doctrine of "comparable worth" and reject claims that their company should raise the salaries of secretaries because they are arguably performing as difficult a job as better-paid maintenance workers or security guards. It is grossly inconsistent for executives to turn around and use the same discarded rationale to justify their own pay. Besides, rather than point to entertainers and sports idols earning millions of dollars each year, executives could just as well compare themselves with cabinet secretaries, university presidents, and combat commanders who exercise as much or more responsibility for far lower salaries. With a myriad of examples to justify every conceivable result, little enlightenment can come from trying to compare the earnings of individuals holding very different kinds of jobs. For executives and professionals, there is no escape from the personal responsibility of having to do one's best, within the ample zone of discretion that the market allows, to decide what level of compensation is truly just and proper.

Even to speak of such responsibility will strike some readers as unrealistic. The power of money is very strong, and urging people to go against the grain and take more responsibility for their own remuneration may seem patently absurd. Still, the 1980s have a lesson to teach that may not be lost on everyone involved in fixing executive and professional compensation. The incomes of successful professionals did increase substantially in the past decade, even as the fortunes of most other members of society were declining. But the striking fact to emerge from this experience is not how much leading professionals earned but how little they seemed to enjoy the results. As we have seen, higher incomes have hardly been an unmixed blessing for the recipients. Rather, they have meant longer hours, more outside interference, greater controversy, and steadily growing levels of dissatisfaction. With enough reflection, more professionals may draw a lesson from this experience. When they do, it is not too much to hope that their attitudes toward compensation may change.

Now that we are free from the burdens of the cold war and about to enter a new era in our nation's development, we need to think again not only about our policies but about our values and ask whether the acquisitive, self-centered goals reflected in our compensation practices are truly what our society needs. Recent experience offers little reason to respond affirmatively. The principal failures of the past two decades—lagging productivity, shrinking savings, mounting deficits, growing poverty—all reflect an overweening desire to spend on ourselves and an inability either to care sufficiently for others or to keep from burdening future generations. After these excesses, our progress and prosperity in the coming decades will surely call for less emphasis on personal gain and greater stress on common sacrifice and sharing.

In the end, however, the main reason for thinking more deeply about our values is the effect they have us. As a wise saying goes, "It behooves us to be careful of what we are worshipping, for what we are worshipping we are becoming."[19] With this in mind, the ultimate question to emerge from our adventures with compensation is whether a preoccupation with material gain can produce either a deeply satisfying existence or a life that we look back upon with pride. All of us must ponder this question for ourselves. In doing so, we should remember that a long, almost unbroken tradition of secular and religious thought informs us that the answer is no. There is little in the experience of the past two decades to contradict this sobering judgment.

NOTES

Introduction

1. "From Murrow to Mediocrity," *New York Times* (March 10, 1987), Op. Ed. page.
2. This article is referred to, with the newspaper unspecified, in Kenneth Auletta, *Three Blind Mice: How the TV Networks Lost Their Way* (New York: Random House, 1991), p. 331.
3. This conversation is quoted in Auletta, *Three Blind Mice,* p. 334. My account of this entire episode is taken from Auletta's book.
4. Kevin Phillips, *The Politics of Rich and Poor: Wealth and the American Electorate in the Reagan Aftermath* (New York: Random House, 1990), p. 10.
5. "Party Tricks: Rehearsing for Campaign '92," *Harper's* (July 1991), p. 45.
6. Sidney Verba, *Elites and the Idea of Equality* (Cambridge, MA: Harvard University Press, 1987), p. 126.
7. See, e.g., *Public Opinion* (March–April 1989), which sets forth the results of a *New York Times* poll conducted on July 5–8, 1988, indicating that the public (63–27) favored raising taxes on those making more than $100,000 per year.

Chapter 1 The Role of Compensation

1. *An Inquiry Into the Nature and Causes of the Wealth of Nations* (New York: Modern Library, 1937), pp. 99–118.
2. Ibid., p. 99
3. Ibid., p. 102.
4. Ibid., p. 106.
5. Ibid., p. 103.
6. Christopher Jencks, Laurie Perman, and Lee Rainwater, "What is a Good Job? A New Measure of Labor Market Success," *American Journal of Sociology* 93 (1988): 1322–97.
7. See, e.g., Burkhard Strumpel (ed.), *Economic Means for Human*

Needs (Ann Arbor, MI: Institute for Social Research, University of Michigan, 1976), pp. 51–52. "Professionals appeared to be the best-adapted to our economic system. They were more satisfied with their jobs, their education and their living standard. Their job involvement was the highest and they were the most attached to its intrinsic rewards."

8. See, e.g., Congressional Budget Office, *Physician Reimbursement Under Medicare: Options for Change* (Washington, DC: Congress of the United States, 1986), p. 34, which puts the average rate of return for all physicians at 16 percent. Sherwin Rosen estimates the rate of return for lawyers at 16 percent in an unpublished paper, "The Market for Lawyers," October 10, 1991.
9. See, e.g., Knut Wicksell, *Value, Capital and Rent* (New York: Reinhart, 1954); John B. Clark, *The Distribution of Wealth: A Theory of Wages, Interest and Profits* (New York: Macmillan, 1902); Leon Walras, *Elements of Pure Economics: Or, the Theory of Social Wealth* (London: Allen & Unwin, 1954); Alfred Marshall, *Principles of Economics* (London: Macmillan for the Royal Economic Society, 1961).
10. Thomas Nagel, *Equality and Partiality* (New York: Oxford University Press, 1991), p. 128.
11. Quoted in Peter D. McClelland, *The American Search for Economic Justice* (Cambridge, MA: Basil Blackwell, 1990), p. 38.
12. *Looking Backward* (1886), chap. IX.
13. Thorstein Veblen, *The Theory of the Leisure Class* (New York: A. M. Kelley Mentor Edition, 1953).
14. Ibid., p. 39.
15. Ronald Inglehart, "Post-Materialism," *American Political Science Review* 75(1981):880.
16. *Survey of the Class of 1989* (Consortium for Higher Education, 1990).
17. *Bartlett's Familiar Quotations,* 16th ed. (Boston: Little Brown, 1992), p. 605.
18. Richard Freeman, *The Market for College-Trained Manpower* (Cambridge, MA: Harvard University Press, 1971).
19. See, e.g., Ronald Ehrenberg, "An Economic Analysis of the Market for Law School Students," *Journal of Legal Education* 39(1989): 627.
20. Eric Dey, Alexander Astin, and William S. Korn, *The American Freshman: Twenty-Five-Year Trends, 1966–1990* (Los Angeles: Higher Education Research Institute, UCLA, 1991).
21. Chester Barnard, *The Functions of the Executive* (Cambridge, MA: Harvard University Press, 1938), p. 143.

22. Edward Deci, *Intrinsic Motivation and Self-Determination in Human Behavior* (New York: Plenum, 1975); Mark Lepper and Greene, *The Hidden Costs of Reward: New Perspectives on the Psychology of Human Motivation* (Hillsdale, NJ: Halsted Press, 1978); Morton Deutsch, *Distributive Justice: A Social-Psychological Perspective* (New Haven: Yale University Press, 1985).
23. See *Forbes,* May 27, 1991, p. 212.
24. Abraham Maslow, *Toward a Psychology of Being,* rev. ed. (Princeton, NJ: Van Nostrand, 1968).
25. *Work and the Nature of Man* (Cleveland: World Publishing Co., 1986); "One More Time: How Do You Motivate Employees?," *Harvard Business Review* (Sept.– Oct. 1987), p. 109.
26. Lepper and Greene, *The Hidden Costs of Reward.* For a thoughtful appraisal of this line of work see J. T. Spence and R. L. Helmreich, "Achievement-Related Motives and Behavior," in Janet T. Spence (ed.), *Achievement and Achievement Motives: Psychological and Sociological Approaches* (San Francisco: W. H. Freeman, 1983), p. 10.
27. Beth A. Hennessey and Teresa M. Amabile, *Creativity and Learning* (Washington, DC: National Education Association, 1987).

Chapter 2 The Rise of the Professions

1. Quoted in Richard Harrison Shryock, "Benjamin Rush from the Perspective of the Twentieth Century," in *Medicine in America: Historical Essays* (Baltimore: Johns Hopkins Press, 1966), p. 237.
2. Quoted in Paul Starr, *The Social Transformation of American Medicine* (New York: Basic Books, 1982), p. 55.
3. "Currents and Counter Currents in Medical Science," in Oliver Wendell Holmes, *Medical Essays* (Boston: Houghton Mifflin & Co., 1899).
4. Editorial, "Does It Pay to Be a Doctor?," *Journal of the American Medical Association* 42(January 23, 1904):247.
5. Perry Miller, *The Life of the Mind in America* (New York: Harcourt, Brace & World, 1965), p. 102.
6. Charles Warren, *History of the American Bar* (Boston: Little, Brown & Co., 1911), p. 4; Roscoe Pound, *The Lawyer from Antiquity to Modern Times, With Particular Reference to the Development of Bar Associations in the United States* (St. Paul, MN: West Publishing, 1953), p. 163.
7. Pound, *The Lawyer from Antiquity to Modern Times,* pp. 139–40, 141.

8. Ibid., p. 137.
9. Quoted in Warren, *History of the American Bar,* p. 220.
10. Quoted in Gerald W. Gewalt (ed.), *The New High Priests: Lawyers in Post–Civil War America* (Westport, CT: Greenwood Press, 1984), p. 77.
11. Quoted in Laurence R. Veysey, *The Emergence of the American University* (Chicago: University of Chicago Press, 1965), pp. 6–7.
12. *Dent* v. *West Virginia,* 129 U.S. 114 (1888).
13. *Medical Education in the United States and Canada,* Bulletin No. 10, Carnegie Foundation for the Advancement of Teaching (1910).
14. Matzko, "The Best Men of the Bar: The Founding of the American Bar Association," in Gewalt (ed.), *The New High Priests,* pp. 75, 88.
15. David Tyack, *The Future of the Past,* in Donald Warren (ed.), *American Teachers* (New York: Macmillan, 1989), p. 408.
16. Howard R. Bowen, *Academic Compensation* (New York: TIAA: College Retirement Equities Fund, 1978), pp. 30, 32–33.
17. See Paul P. Van Riper, *History of the United States Civil Service* (Westport, CT: Greenwood Press, 1958), p. 542.
18. Quoted in ibid., p. 305.
19. F. W. Taussig and W. S. Barker, "American Corporations and Their Executives: A Statistical Inquiry," *Quarterly Journal of Economics* 40 (1925):1, 19.
20. John C. Baker, *Executive Salaries and Bonus Plans* (New York: McGraw-Hill, 1938). See also Detlev Vagts, "Challenges to Executive Compensation: For the Markets or the Courts?," *Journal of Corporate Law* 8(1985):232.
21. Bowen, *Academic Compensation,* pp. 30, 32, 33.
22. Baker, *Executive Salaries and Bonus Plans.*
23. Wilbur G. Lewellen, "Executives Lose Out, Even with Options," *Harvard Business Review* (Jan.–Feb., 1968), p. 127.
24. Burritt, "Professional Distribution of College and University Graduates," *U.S. Bureau of Education Bulletin* (1912), p. 19.
25. Margaret Gordon, "The Changing Labor Market for College Graduates," in Gordon (ed.), *Higher Education and the Labor Market* (New York: McGraw-Hill, 1974), pp. 27, 28, 31.
26. Ibid.
27. David A. Wise, "Academic Achievement and Job Performance," *American Economic Review* 65(1975):350.
28. Estelle Janes, Nabeel Alsalem, Joseph Conetz, and Duc-le To, "College Quality and Future Earnings: Where Should You Send Your Child to College," *American Economic Review* 79(1989):247.
29. Ronald F. Ferguson, "Paying for Public Education: New Evidence on How and Why Money Matters," *Harvard Journal on Legisla-*

tion 28(1991):464. Earlier studies have come to mixed conclusions about the link between teacher test scores and student achievement. Ferguson's work, however, is not only one of the most recent investigations; it is also based on an exceptionally large data base involving almost 900 school districts in Texas that enroll over 2.4 million students.

30. Robert E. Klitgaard, *Choosing Elites* (New York: Basic Books, 1985), p. 130.
31. Dael Wolfle, *America's Resources of Specialized Talent* (New York: Harper, 1954), pp. 321–22.
32. Sara L. Lightfoot, *Balm in Gilead* (Reading, MA: Addison-Wesley Publishing Co., 1988), p. 175.
33. Charles Manski and David A. Wise, *College Choice in America* (Cambridge, MA: Harvard University Press, 1983); Taubman and Wales, in F. Thomas Juster (ed.), *Education, Income and Human Behavior* (New York: McGraw-Hill, 1975), p. 47.
34. Taussig and Barker, "American Corporations and Their Executives: A Statistical Inquiry," *Quarterly Journal of Economics* 40(1925): 1.
35. Baker, *Executive Salaries and Bonus Plans.*
36. Wilbur G. Lewellen, "Executives Lose Out."

Chapter 3 What Happened After 1970

1. Jean-Jacques Servan-Schreiber, *The American Challenge* (New York: Atheneum, 1968), pp. 37, 89.
2. Robert H. Hayes and William J. Abernathy, "Managing Our Way to Economic Decline," *Harvard Business Review* (July–Aug. 1980): 67.
3. These figures are taken from the Executive Compensation Surveys published annually by *Forbes.*
4. Information supplied to me by Hay Management Consultants, 229 South 18th Street, Rittenhouse Square, Philadelphia, Pennsylvania, by letter dated June 26, 1992.
5. Michael L. Connell, *Starting Salary Offers: An Historical Perspective* (College Placement Council, 1991), p. 15. I have converted the figures to 1982 dollars.
6. These figures were supplied to me by the Harvard Business School placement office.
7. *Digest of Educational Statistics 1990,* Table 254, p. 275.
8. "Academe and the Boom in Business Studies," *Change* (Sept.–Oct. 1986), pp. 37, 40.
9. See annual editions of *An Admissions Office Profile of Candidates*

Taking the Graduate Admissions Test, Graduate Management Admissions Council.

10. *Digest of Educational Statistics 1990,* Table 254, p. 275.
11. Paul E. Barton and Richard J. Coley, *Performance at the Top: From Elementary Through Graduate School* (Princeton, NJ: Policy Information Center, Educational Testing Service, 1991), p. 62, Table 14. See also Rodney Hartnett, *Trends in Student Quality in Doctoral and Professional Education* (New Brunswick, NJ: Project on Trends in Academic Talent, Rutgers University, March 1985), p. 33.
12. Frank Goldberg and Roy Koenigsknecht, *Highest Achievers* (Evanston, IL: Graduate School of Northwestern University, 1985), p. 33. Figures for the 1980s were supplied to me by the Consortium on Higher Education from data collected from senior class surveys for the classes of 1982 and 1989.
13. Richard H. Sander and E. Douglas Williams, "Why Are There So Many Lawyers? Perspectives on a Turbulent Market," *Law and Social Inquiry,* 6(1989):431, 433.
14. Steven Brill, "The Law Business in the Year 2000," *American Lawyer* (Fall 1989, Supplement), p. 13.
15. *Bates and O'Steen* v. *Arizona State Bar,* 433 U.S., 350 (1977).
16. Sander and Williams, "Why Are There So Many Lawyers?", p. 435.
17. Compare "The American Law 75," *American Lawyer* (July–Aug. 1986), pp. 54-55, with "The American Law 100," *American Lawyer* (July–Aug. 1991), pp. 36, 38, 40.
18. Sander and Williams, "Why Are There So Many Lawyers?", p. 474.
19. Altman and Weil, *Survey of Law Firm Economics, 1972–1990* (Ardmore, PA: Altman & Weil Publications, 1991).
20. Sander and Williams, "Why Are There So Many Lawyers?", p. 450.
21. Altman and Weil, *Survey of Law Firm Economics.*
22. Ibid.
23. Clotfelter et al., *Economic Challenges in Higher Education,* p. 182.
24. See Richard Abel, *American Lawyers* (New York: Oxford University Press, 1989), p. 195; Zeldis, "Billables Up," *National Law Journal* (April 11, 1988):2; Derby, "Are You Keeping Up Financially?," *American Bar Association Journal* 71(1985):68; Marc Galanter and Paley, "The Transformation of the Big Law Firm," in Robert L. Nelson, David M. Trubek, and Rayman L. Solomon, *Lawyers' Ideals/Lawyers' Practices* (Ithaca, NY: Cornell University Press, 1992), pp. 56–61.

25. Sander and Williams, "Why Are There So Many Lawyers?", p. 456.
26. Ibid., pp. 459–61.
27. Ibid., p. 453. Figures for the last few years of the 1980s were supplied to me by the American Bar Association.
28. See American Bar Association, *A Review of Legal Education in the United States, Fall 1990, Law Schools and Bar Admission Requirements* (Chicago: American Bar Association, 1991), p. 66.
29. These figures were supplied by the American Bar Association.
30. Rodney Hartnett, *Trends in Student Quality in Doctoral and Professional Education,* p. 33; Sander and Williams, "Why Are There So Many Lawyers?," pp. 462–63.
31. Goldberg and Koenigsknecht, *Highest Achievers,* p. 33.
32. Sander and Williams, "Why Are There So Many Lawyers?", p. 477.
33. Howard R. Bowen, *Academic Compensation* (New York: TIAA: College Retirement Equities Fund, 1978), p. 33.
34. David Wilsford, *Doctors and the State* (Durham, NC: Duke University Press, 1991), p. 11.
35. *New York Times* (July 11, 1969), quoted in Paul Starr, *The Social Transformation of American Medicine* (New York: Basic Books, 1982), p. 381.
36. Cordtz, "Change Begins in the Doctor's Office," *Fortune* (January 1970), p. 84.
37. Richard L. Ernst and Donald E. Yett, *Physician Location and Specialty Choice* (Ann Arbor, MI: Health Administration Press, 1985), p. 9.
38. "Annual Report: Medical Education in the United States," *Journal of the American Medical Association,* 244 (Dec. 16, 1990): 2813.
39. These figures are taken from the annual spring surveys contained in American Medical Association Center for Health Policy Research, *Socioeconomic Characteristics of Medical Practice.*
40. Ibid. See especially AMA Center for Health Policy Research, "1990 Spring Survey," *Socioeconomic Characteristics of Medical Practice 1990/1991,* p. 154.
41. *Journal of the American Medical Association,* 266(Aug. 21, 1991):971.
42. Enrollment figures were obtained from Association of American Medical Colleges, Section for Student Services.
43. These results are obtained from my own survey of over 2,000 randomly selected Phi Beta Kappas graduating from college from 1970 to 1990.

44. Goldberg and Koenigsknecht, *Highest Achievers,* p. 33. Figures for the 1980s were supplied to me by the Consortium for the Financing of Higher Education based on data collected in surveys of the classes of 1982 and 1989 from member institutions.
45. Ibid.
46. *Digest of Educational Statistics,* Table 228 (1991).
47. *Research Universities and the National Interest: A Report from Fifteen University Presidents* (New York: Ford Foundation, 1977), p. 26.
48. National Research Council, *Survey Report 1982: Doctorate Recipients from United States Universities* (1983), p. 16.
49. *Digest of Educational Statistics,* Table 228 (1991).
50. U.S. Department of Education, National Center for Educational Statistics, *Faculty Salaries, Tenure, and Fringe Benefits of Full-Time Instructional Faculty in Institutions of Higher Education* (Washington, DC: U.S. Department of Education, February 1991).
51. *Digest of Educational Statistics* (Washington, DC: Department of Health, Education and Welfare, 1991), Table 228.
52. Ibid.
53. See generally William G. Bowen and Julie Ann Sosa, *Prospects for Faculty in the Arts and Sciences* (Princeton, NJ: Princeton University Press, 1989).
54. Barton and Coley, *Performance at the Top,* p. 63.
55. Eric Dey, Alexander Astin, and William S. Korn, *The American Freshman: Twenty-Five-Year Trends, 1966–1990* (Los Angeles: Higher Education Research Institute, UCLA, 1991), p. 55.
56. Barton and Coley, *Performance at the Top,* p. 63.
57. Bowen and Sosa, *Prospects for Faculty in the Arts and Sciences.*
58. Adelman, "The Standardized Test Scores of College Graduates, 1964–1982." Paper prepared for the Study Group on the Conditions of Excellence in American Higher Education, 1984.
59. Howard R. Bowen and Jack H. Schuster, *American Professors: A National Resource Imperiled* (New York: Oxford University Press, 1986), p. 227.
60. Goldberg and Koenigsknecht, *Highest Achievers,* p. 17.
61. Adelman, "Standardized Test Scores of College Graduates."
62. These figures come from a private survey conducted by the author of 2,000 randomly selected Phi Beta Kappas graduating from college from 1970 to 1990.
63. Goldberg and Koenigsknecht, *Highest Achievers,* p. 17.
64. Bowen and Schuster, *American Professors,* pp. 214, 220.
65. Morton Owen Schapiro, Michael P. O'Malley, and Larry H. Lit-

ten, "Progression to Graduate School from the 'Elite' Colleges and Universities," *Economics of Education Review* 10(1990), Table 3. Data from the 10 institutions with response rates of over 50 percent also show the proportion of top (A) students planning careers in higher education holding constant at 24 percent in 1982 and 1989.

66. James S. Coleman, *Equality of Educational Opportunity* (Washington, DC: American Federation of Teachers, 1966).
67. American Federation of Teachers, *1990 Teacher Salary Survey* (1991), p. 26.
68. Fiske, "Survey of Teachers Reveals Morale Problem," *New York Times* (September 19, 1982), pp. 1, 52; Duke, *Teaching—The Imperiled Profession* (Albany: State University of New York Press, 1984), p. 53.
69. Gary Sykes, "Public Policy and the Problem of Teacher Quality," in Lee Shulman, ed., *Handbook of Teaching and Policy* (New York: Longman, 1983), pp. 97, 111.
70. National Education Association, *Status of the American School Teacher, 1980–81* (1981), p. 18.
71. Ibid.
72. Carnegie Foundation for the Advancement of Teaching, *The Condition of Teaching* (Princeton, NJ: The Carnegie Foundation, 1990), p. 61.
73. *Digest of Educational Statistics* (Washington, DC: Department of Health, Education and Welfare, 1991), Table 235.
74. J. A. Shymansky and B. C. Aldridge, "The Teacher Crisis in Secondary School Science and Mathematics," *Educational Leadership* 40 (1982): 61–62.
75. See Richard J. Murnane, et al., *Who Will Teach?: Policies That Matter* (Cambridge, MA: Harvard University Press, 1991), pp. 21, 33.
76. W. Timothy Weaver, "Educators in Supply and Demand: Effects on Quality," *University of Chicago School Review* 86(1978):552, 577.
77. Dael Wolfle, *America's Resources of Specialized Talent* (New York: cit., *Harper,* 1954), pp. 321–22.
78. Murnane et al., *Who Will Teach?*, p. 35.
79. Data supplied to me from surveys conducted by the Consortium for Financing Higher Education for the senior classes of 1982 and 1989. These data show the percentage of A students electing a school teaching career dropping from 1.6 percent in 1982 to 0.7 percent in 1989.
80. Figures from the 1970s and 1980s are taken from a survey con-

ducted by the author in 1992 involving over 2,000 randomly selected Phi Beta Kappas graduating from college from 1970 to 1990. Figures from the 1950s and 1960s come from a similar survey reported in Bowen and Schuster, *American Professors,* p. 227.

81. W. Timothy Weaver, *America's Teacher Quality Problem: Alternatives for Reform* (New York: Praeger, 1983), p. 41.
82. Ibid., pp. 62–63.
83. Murnane et al., *Who Will Teach?,* pp. 69–70.
84. Vance and Schlechty, "The Distribution of Academic Ability in the Teaching Force," *Phi Delta Kappan* 64(1982):22.
85. *Digest of Educational Statistics* (1991), Tables 235, 236, pp. 255, 256.
86. Dey, Astin, and Korn, *The American Freshman,* p. 55.
87. Barton and Coley, *Performance at the Top,* p. 63.
88. Seymour Martin Lipset and William Schneider, *The Confidence Gap: Business, Labor, and Government in the Public Mind* (New York: Free Press, 1983).
89. Ibid., p. 17.
90. These calculations are derived from Office of Personnel Management, *Pay Structure of the Federal Civil Service for 1972–1990.*
91. *Leadership for America: Report of the National Commission on the Public Service* (Washington, DC: U.S. Government Printing Office, 1990), p. 3. (Hereafter cited as Volcker Commission.)
92. See note 90.
93. These figures were supplied to me by the Office of Personnel Management, Washington, D.C.
94. Volcker Commission, p. 65. See also Barry Z. Posner and Warren H. Schmidt, "Government Morale and Management: A Survey of Federal Executives," *Public Personnel Management* 17(1988):21.
95. U.S. Merit Systems Review Board, *Working for America: A Federal Employee Survey* (Washington, DC: The Board, June 1990).
96. Figures supplied to me by the Office of Personnel Management, Washington, D.C.
97. General Accounting Office, *Managing Human Resources: Greater OPM Leadership Needed to Address Critical Challenges* (1989).
98. U.S. Merit Systems Protection Board, *Federal Personnel Policies and Practices—Perspectives from the Workplace* (1987).
99. Martin Reck and Walter G. Mann, *Scientists and Engineers in Civilian Agencies* (Washington, DC: U.S. Office of Personnel Management, 1991); Patricia A. Harris, *Computer Specialists in Federal Agencies* (Washington, DC: U.S. Office of Personnel Management, 1991). Clark and Wachtel, "The Quiet Crisis Goes Public," *Government Executive* (June 1988), p. 14, report that 73

percent of government managers declared that their agency was experiencing a "brain drain."

100. All of the data relating to Phi Beta Kappas is taken from an unpublished survey conducted by the author involving 2,000 randomly selected Phi Beta Kappas graduating from college from 1970 to 1990.
101. Volcker Commission, p. 138.
102. Ibid., p. 252.
103. Daniel R. Levinson, *Attracting Quality Graduates to the Federal Government: A View of College Recruiting* (Washington, DC: U.S. Merit Systems Protection Board, 1988).
104. See James K. Conant, "Universities and the Future of the Public Service," *Public Administration Quarterly* 13(1989):342.
105. Ronald Sanders, "The Best and the Brightest: Can the Public Service Compete?," reprinted in Volcker Commission, p. 157.

Chapter 4 The 1970s and 1980s in Perspective

1. Tibor Scitovsky, "An International Comparison of the Trend of Professional Earnings," *American Economic Review* 66(1966):25.
2. Henry Phelps-Brown, *The Inequality of Pay* (New York: Oxford University Press, 1977), pp. 330–32; Adrian Wood, *A Theory of Pay* (New York: Cambridge University Press, 1978), pp. 201–202.
3. See Gosta Esping-Andersen, *The Three Worlds of Welfare Capitalism* (Cambridge, UK: Polity Press, 1990), p. 205.
4. See Stuart H. Altman, "The Mix of Physician Manpower and Its Effect on U.S. Health Care Expenditures: The U.S. vs. Other Industrialized Nations." Paper presented at the National Primary Care Conference, March 30, 1992, Washington, D.C., p. 7. See also *Health Care Systems in Transition: The Search for Efficiency,* OECD Social Policy Studies No. 7 (1990), p. 51; Sandier, "Health Services Utilization and Physician Income Trends," *Health Care Financing Review* 10(1989):33.
5. French figures are taken from David Wilsford, *Doctors and the State* (Durham, NC: Duke University Press, 1991), p. 136. Figures for the United States come from American Medical Association, *Socioeconomic Characteristics of Medical Practice* (1983).
6. *U.S. Health Care at the Crossroads,* OECD Health Policy Studies No. 1 (1992), p. 89.
7. Paul F. Milgrom and John Roberts, *Economics, Organization, and Management* (Englewood Cliffs, NJ: Prentice-Hall, 1992), p. 491; David Harrop, *World Paychecks: Who Makes What, Where, and Why* (London: Muller, 1982), p. 58.

8. See generally Richard Abel and Philip S. Lewis, *Lawyers in Society*, vol. 2 (Los Angeles: UCLA Press, 1988). See also Harrop, *World Paychecks.*
9. See, e.g., Graef S. Crystal, *In Search of Excess* (New York: W. W. Norton & Co., 1991), pp. 204 ff.
10. Ibid., 205–207.
11. Milgrom and Roberts, *Economics, Organization, and Management,* p. 491.
12. Compare "The Continental 20, *Legal Times of Washington* (April 12, 1990), with "The American Law 100," *American Lawyer* (July–Aug. 1991), p. 46.
13. "The Continental 20."
14. *American Lawyer,* pp. 24, 46 (giving numbers of partners for each firm and profits per partner).
15. U.S. Department of Education, National Center for Educational Statistics, *Faculty Salaries, Tenure and Fringe Benefits of Full-Time Instructional Faculty In Institutions of Higher Education* (Washington, DC: U.S. Department of Education, February 1991).
16. See *The Economist* (June 27–July 3, 1992), p. 65.
17. Ibid.
18. Geraldine Clifford and James Guthrie, *Ed School* (Chicago: University of Chicago Press, 1988), pp. 31, 33. See also Steven M. Barro and Larry Suter, *International Comparisons of Teachers' Salaries: An Exploratory Study* (Washington, DC: U.S. Department of Education, Survey Report, July 1988), pp. 15–17, 21.
19. Ronald Sanders, "The Best and the Brightest: Can the Public Service Compete?" Reprinted in Volcker Commission Report, *Leadership for America: Rebuilding the Public Service* (1989), p. 157.
20. Ezra Vogel, *Japan as Number One: Lessons for America* (Cambridge, MA: Harvard University Press, 1979), p. 55.
21. *The Economist* (June 27–July 3, 1992).
22. Mayntz, "German Federal Bureaucrats: A Functional Elite Between Politics and Administration," in Ezra Suleiman, ed., *Bureaucrats and Policy Making* (New York: Holmes & Meier, 1984), pp. 174, 181.
23. Cassesse, "The Higher Civil Service in Italy," in Suleiman, ed., p. 25.
24. *Los Angeles Times* (September 17, 1991), pp. H/B, H/C.
25. Singer, "The Effect of the Viet Nam War on Numbers of Medical School Applicants," *Academic Medicine* 64(1989):567.
26. David Mechanic, *Medical Sociology,* 2nd ed. (New York: Free Press, 1978).
27. See, e.g., Harvey and Shubat, *Physician Opinion on Health Care*

Issues, American Medical Association, 1989 (April 1989), p. 21.

28. See "AAMC Survey Lists Why People Turn Away from Medicine," *American Medical News* (June 5, 1987), p. 9; Charles E. Lewis et al., "How Satisfying Is the Practice of Internal Medicine?," *Annals of Internal Medicine* 114(1991):1. See also Steven A. Schroeder, "The Troubled Profession: Is Medicine's Glass Half Full or Half Empty?," *Annals of Internal Medicine* 116(1992):583.
29. Frank A. Sloan, "The Demand for Higher Education: The Case of Medical School Applicants," *Journal of Human Resources* 6 (1971):467.
30. Paul Jolly, Leanne Jolin, Jack Krakower, and Robert Beran, "Financing Medical Education, 1989–90," *Academic Medicine* 66 (1991):565.
31. See, e.g., Charles Manski, "Academic Ability, Earnings, and the Decision to Become a Teacher," in David Wise, ed., *Public Sector Payrolls* (Chicago: University of Chicago Press, 1987).
32. William G. Bowen and Neil Rudenstine, *In Pursuit of the Ph.D.* (Princeton, NJ: Princeton University Press, 1992), pp. 46–55.

Chapter 5 Corporate Executives

1. Graef S. Crystal, *In Search of Excess* (New York: W. W. Norton & Co., 1991), p. 28.
2. "E.g., The Flap Over Executive Pay," *Business Week* (May 6, 1991), p. 90.
3. The Gallup Poll, *Public Opinion* (1990), p. 178.
4. Kevin J. Murphy, "Top Executives Are Worth Every Nickel They Get," *Harvard Business Review* (March–April 1986):125.
5. *Time* (May 4, 1992), p. 48.
6. "Eclipse of the Public Corporation," *Harvard Business Review* (Sept.–Oct. 1989), pp. 61, 66.
7. Kurt Vonnegut, *God Bless You Mr. Rosewater* (New York: Dell, 1965), pp. 17–18.
8. Bryan Burrough and John Helyar, *Barbarians at the Gate: The Fall of RJR Nabisco* (New York: Harper & Row, 1990), p. 510.
9. Edward Lazear and Sherwin Rosen, "Rank Order Tournaments as Optimal Labor Contracts," *Journal of Political Economy* 89 (1981):841; Ronald Ehrenberg and Michael L. Bognanno, "Do Tournaments Have Incentive Effects?," *Journal of Political Economy* 98(1990):1307. It is possible, however, that big prizes may have adverse effects on players' motivation over the longer run. Thus, Michael Bamberger, in an Op. Ed. piece in the *New York Times* (April 10, 1992), suggests that European golfers have be-

come more competitive than American golfers because huge purses in United States tournaments have made it too easy to make a good living so that European competitors are "hungrier."

10. Charles A. O'Reilly, Brian G. Mein, and Graef S. Crystal, "CEO Compensation as Tournament and Social Comparison: A Tale of Two Theories," *Administrative Science Quarterly* 33(1988): 257.
11. Paul Milgrom and John Roberts, *Economics, Organization and Management* (Englewood Cliffs, NJ: Prentice-Hall, 1992), p. 426.
12. Michael Novak, *The Spirit of Democratic Capitalism* (New York: Simon & Schuster, 1982), p. 211.
13. Quoted in *Forbes* (May 28, 1990), p. 210.
14. Kevin J. Murphy, "Top Executives Are Worth Every Nickel They Get," *Harvard Business Review* (March–April 1986), p. 125.
15. David J. McLaughlin, "Does Compensation Motivate Executives?," in Fred Foulkes, ed., *Executive Compensation: A Strategic Guide for the 1990s* (Boston: Harvard Business School Press, 1991), p. 77.
16. Douglas M. Cowherd and David I. Levine, "Product Quality and Pay Equity Between Lower Level Employees and Top Management: An Investigation of Distributive Justice Theory," *Administrative Science Quarterly* 37(1992):302.
17. See James C. Abegglen and George Stalk, Jr., *Kaisha: The Japanese Corporation* (New York: Basic Books, 1985), pp. 195, 198.
18. See, e.g., Burkhard Strumpel, ed., *Economic Means for Human Needs* (Ann Arbor, MI: Institute for Social Research, University of Michigan, 1976), pp. 54–55.
19. Edward Lawler, *Pay and Organization Development* (Reading, MA: Addison-Wesley Pub. Co., 1981), p. 14.
20. See Herbert H. Meyer, "The Pay for Performance Dilemma," *Organizational Dynamics* 3(1975):39.
21. Clinton O. Longnecker and Dennis A. Gioia, "Neglected at the Top—Executives Talk about Executive Appraisal," *Sloan Management Review* (Winter, 1988):41.
22. Ibid., p. 43.
23. Ibid.
24. Ibid., p. 45.
25. D. L. De Vries et al., *Performance Appraisals on the Line* (New York: Wiley & Sons, 1981).
26. See the discussion of various studies to this effect in Herbert H. Meyer, "The Pay for Performance Dilemma," p. 39.
27. George T. Milkovich, *Pay for Performance: Evaluating Performance Appraisal and Merit Pay* (Washington, DC: National Academy Press, 1991), p. 106. See also James Medoff and Abraham,

"Are Those Paid More Really More Productive?," *Journal of Human Resources* 16(1981):186.

28. B. Holmstrom and Costa, "Managerial Incentives and Capital Management," in Milgrom and Roberts, *Economics, Organization and Management,* chap. 13, esp. p. 444.
29. See, e.g., G. Bennett Stewart, III, "Remaking the Public Corporation from Within," *Harvard Business Review* (July–Aug. 1990), p. 126.
30. See, e.g., Andrei Schleifer and Robert W. Vishny, "Management Entrenchment: The Case of Manager-Specific Investments," *Journal of Financial Economics* 25(1989):123, describing how managers try to protect their jobs by making themselves indispensable in ways that do not serve the shareholders or enhance value.
31. George T. Milkovich and Bonnie R. Rabin, "Executive Performance and Firm Performance: Research Questions and Answers," in Fred Foulkes, ed., *Executive Compensation,* p. 95. For further discussion of the link between corporate performance and executive pay, see Leonard, "Executive Pay and Firm Performance," *Industrial and Labor Relations Review* 43 (Special Issue, 1990):13S; John M. Abowd, "Does Performance-Based Managerial Compensation Affect Corporate Performance?," Ibid., p. 52S.
32. Quoted in James Boyd White, "How Should We Talk about Corporations? The Language of Economics and of Citizenship," *Yale Law Journal* 94(1985):1416.
33. E. g., Michael E. Porter, "Capital Disadvantage: America's Failing Capital Investment System," *Harvard Business Review* (Sept.–Oct., 1992), p. 65.
34. Milton Friedman, "The Social Responsibility of Business Is to Increase Its Profits," *New York Times* (September 13, 1970), Sunday Magazine, p. 32; Richard A. Rodewald, "The Corporate Social Responsibility Debate: Unanswered Questions About the Consequences of Moral Reform," *American Business Law Journal* 25 (1987): 443.
35. See Lester Thurow, *Head to Head: The Coming Economic Battle Among Japan, Europe and America* (New York: Morrow, 1992), p. 137.
36. See Philip Glouchevitch, *Juggernaut: The German Way of Business: Why It Is Transforming Europe—and the World* (New York: Simon & Schuster, 1992), pp. 106–107.
37. Seymour Martin Lipset and William Schneider, *The Confidence Gap: Business, Labor and Government in the Public Mind* (New York: Free Press, 1983), p. 175. In the poll cited by Lipset and Schneider, only 9 percent of the respondents felt that business should give primacy to stockholders' interests. Only 7 percent felt

that workers should receive primary consideration. Almost one-third, 32 percent, identified consumers and 35 percent mentioned the American people as the interests most deserving attention by corporations.

38. Michael C. Jensen and Kevin J. Murphy, "CEO Incentives—It's Not How Much You Pay, But How," *Harvard Business Review* (May–June 1990), p. 138.
39. Jensen and Murphy, "Performance Pay and Top-Management Incentives," *Journal of Political Economy* 98(1990):225, 250–51.
40. Kenneth Mason, "Four Ways to Overpay Yourself Enough," in Fred K. Foulkes, ed., *Executive Compensation,* p. 266.
41. Graef S. Crystal, *In Search of Excess* (New York: W. W. Norton & Co., 1991), p. 107.
42. Lester Korn, "Window of Danger in Executive Leadership," *Financier* (March 1982), p. 41. Note that scholars have not found empirical evidence of the problem referred to by Korn.
43. O'Reilly, Mein, and Crystal, "CEO Compensation as Tournament and Social Comparison: A Tale of Two Theories," *Administrative Science Quarterly* 33(1988):257.
44. *Washington Post* (February 14, 1992), pp. A1, A14.
45. Porter, "America's Capital Disadvantage," p. 65.

Chapter 6 Doctors

1. *New York Times* (February 16, 1981). Quoted in Paul Starr, *The Social Transformation of American Medicine* (New York: Basic Books, 1982), p. 419.
2. Simon Kuznets and Milton Friedman, *Income from Independent Professional Practice* (New York: National Bureau of Economic Research, 1945).
3. American Medical Association, Center for Health Policy Research, *Socioeconomic Characteristics of Medical Practice* (Chicago: Center for Health Policy Research, 1990/91).
4. Uwe E. Reinhardt, "A Framework for Deliberations on the Compensation of Physicians," *Journal of Medical Practice Management* 3(1987):85.
5. Kuznets and Friedman, *Income from Independent Professional Practice.*
6. Stuart Altman, "The Mix of Physician Manpower and Its Effect on U.S. Health Expenditures: The U.S. Versus Other Industrialized Nations." Paper presented at National Primary Care Conference, March 30, 1992, pp. 18–19.
7. Jerry Cromwell, Janet B. Mitchell, and William B. Stason, "Learning by Doing in CABG Surgery," *Medical Care* 28(1990):6.

8. Congressional Budget Office, *Physician Reimbursement Under Medicare: Options for Change* (Washington, DC: Congress of the United States, 1986), p. 32.
9. General Accounting Office, *Health Insurance: Vulnerable Payers Lose Billions to Fraud and Abuse* (Washington, DC: U.S. GAO, May 1992).
10. Jean M. Mitchell and Jonathan H. Sunshine, "Consequences of Physicians' Ownership of Health Care Facilities—Ventures in Radiation Therapy," *New England Journal of Medicine* 327(November 19, 1992):1497.
11. Jean M. Mitchell and Elton Scott, "Physician Ownership of Physical Therapy Services," *Journal of the American Medical Association* 268(October 21, 1992):2055.
12. Hillman, Olson, Griffith, et al., "Physicians' Utilization and Charges for Outpatient Diagnostic Imaging in a Medicare Population," *Journal of the American Medical Association* 268(October 21, 1992):2050.
13. Colwill, "Where Have All the Primary Care Applicants Gone?," *New England Journal of Medicine* 326(February 6, 1992):387. See also Paul B. Beeson, "Too Many Specialists, Too Few Generalists," *The Pharos* (Spring, 1991), p. 2.
14. Greenfield, Nelson, Zubkoff, Manning, et al., "Variations in Resource Utilization Among Medical Specialties and Systems of Care: Results from the Medical Outcome Study," *Journal of the American Medical Association* 269(1992):1624; Kravitz, Greenfield, Rogers, Manning, et al., "Differences in the Mix of Patients Among Medical Specialties and Systems of Care: Results from the Medical Outcomes Study," *Journal of the American Medical Association* 267(1991): 1617.
15. Altman, "The Mix of Physician Manpower," p. 18.
16. See generally, e.g., Richard L. Ernst and Donald E. Yett, *Physician Location and Specialty Choice* (Ann Arbor, MI: Health Administration Press, 1985), chap. 6; Daniel Funkenstein, "Factors Affecting Career Choices of Medical Students, 1958–1976," in Eileen C. Shapiro and Leah M. Lowenstein, eds., *Becoming a Physician: Development of Values and Attitudes in Medicine* (Cambridge, MA: Ballinger Publishing Co., 1979).
17. Quoted in Alain Enthoven, *Health Plan: The Only Practical Solution to the Soaring Cost of Medical Care* (Reading, MA: Addison-Wesley Pub. Co., 1980).
18. Steven A. Schroeder and Jonathan A. Showstack, "Financial Incentives to Perform Medical Procedures and Laboratory Tests: Illustrative Models of Office Practice," *Medical Care* 16(April 1978):289.

19. For a detailed study of these practices, see Marc A. Rodwin, *Medicine, Money and Morals* (New York: Oxford University Press, 1993).
20. See Altman, "The Mix of Physician Manpower," pp. 11, 12.
21. See notes 26, 27 below.
22. Joseph Newhouse, "Medical Care Costs: How Much Welfare Loss?" *Journal of Economic Perspectives* 6(1992):3.
23. William Hsiao et al., "Results and Policy Implications of the Resource-Based Relative Value Study," *New England Journal of Medicine* 319(Sept. 29, 1988):881.
24. *New York Times* (December 20, 1991), pp. A1, 16.
25. See, e.g., John Iglehart, "Germany's Health Care System," *New England Journal of Medicine* 324(February 14, 1991):503; (June 13, 1991):1750. See also Bradford L. Kirkman-Liff, "Physician Payment and Cost-Containment Strategies in West Germany: Suggestions for Medicare Reform," *Journal of Health Politics, Policy and Law* 15(1990):69; Kirkman-Liff, "Cost Containment and Physician Payment Methods in the Netherlands," *Inquiry* 26(1989): 468.
26. Luft, "HMO Performance: Current Knowledge and Questions for the 1980's, *Group Health Journal* 1(1980):34.
27. Manning, Leibowitz, Goldbert, et al., "A Controlled Trial of the Effect of a Pre-Paid Group Practice on the Use of Services," *New England Journal of Medicine* 310(1984):1505.
28. Luft, "HMO Performance."
29. Homer, "Methods of Hospital Use Control in Health Maintenance Organizations," *Health Care Management Review* 11(1986):15; Eisenberg and Williams, "Cost Containment and Changing Physicians' Practice Behavior: Can the Fox Learn to Guard the Chicken Coop?," *Journal of the American Medical Association* 246(1981): 2195.
30. Alan L. Hillman, Mark V. Pauly, and Joseph J. Kerstein, "How Do Financial Incentives Affect Physicians' Decisions and the Financial Performance of Health Maintenance Organizations?," *New England Journal of Medicine* 321(July 13, 1989):86.
31. Alain Enthoven, "Managed Competition: An Agenda for Action," *Health Affairs* 7(1988):25; Enthoven, *Health Plan.*

Chapter 7 Lawyers

1. See generally John P. Heinz and Edward O. Laumann, *Chicago Lawyers: The Social Structure of the Bar* (New York: Russell Sage Foundation, 1982).

2. Quoted in Jeffrey O'Connell, *The Law Suit Lottery* (New York: Free Press, 1979), p. 43.
3. "Ethical Perspectives on Legal Practice," *Stanford Law Review* 37 (1985):589, 628.
4. O'Connell, *The Law Suit Lottery,* p. 14.
5. Quoted in ibid., p. 17.
6. See, e.g., Terry Thomason, "Are Attorneys Paid What They're Worth?, Contingent Fees and the Settlement Process," *Journal of Legal Studies* 20(1991):187.
7. Chaney, Posner, Caplan, and Ward, "Standard of Care and Anesthesia Liability," *Journal of the American Medical Association* 261 (1989):1599.
8. Paul Weiler, *Medical Malpractice on Trial* (Cambridge, MA: Harvard University Press, 1991), p. 13. Weiler estimates that some 400,000 torts occur each year in American hospitals of which only 25,000 result in payments to the victim. Ibid., p. 175.
9. Deborah R. Hensler et al., *Compensation for Accidental Injuries in the United States* (Santa Monica, CA: Rand Corp., 1991).
10. For descriptions and analyses of no-fault plans, see Jeffrey O'Connell, *The Blame Game* (Lexington, MA: Lexington Books, 1987), pp. 107 ff.; Stephen J. Carroll et al., *No-Fault Approaches to Compensating People Injured in Automobile Accidents* (Santa Monica, CA: Rand Corp., 1991).
11. Dedicatory Address: "The Legal Profession Today," *Indiana Law Journal* 62(1987):151, 155.
12. For a general discussion of this problem, see William G. Ross, "The Ethics of Hourly Billing by Attorneys," *Rutgers Law Review* 44 (1991):1. See also Lerman, "Lying to Clients," *University of Pennsylvania Law Review* 138(1990):659.
13. Ross, "The Ethics of Hourly Billing," p. 93.
14. Quoted in Mark Stevens, *Power of Attorney: The Rise of the Giant Law Firms* (New York: McGraw-Hill, 1987), pp. 150–151.
15. For a detailed analysis of this trend, see Ronald J. Gilson and Robert H. Mnookin, "Sharing Among the Human Capitalists: An Economic Inquiry into the Corporate Law Firm and How Partners Split Profits," *Stanford Law Review* 37(1985):313.
16. The speech is quoted in part in Pollock, Turks, and Brahmins, *Upheaval at Milbank, Tweed* (1990), pp. 193–200; more extensive quotes appear in the materials prepared by Gary Singsen for his course at the Harvard Law School entitled "Legal Profession: The Megafirm" (1991).
17. Gilson and Mnookin, "Sharing Among the Human Capitalists," pp. 351–352.

18. See Steven Brill, "Toward a New Excellence: Strategies and Values for Tomorrow's Successful Firms," *American Lawyer* (November 1983):18.

Chapter 8 University Professors

1. U.S. Department of Education, National Center for Educational Statistics, *Faculty Salaries, Tenure, and Fringe Benefits of Full-Time Instructional Faculty in Institutions of Higher Education* (Washington, DC: U.S. Department of Education, February 1991).
2. National Science Foundation, *Activities of Science and Engineering Faculty in Universities and 4-Year Colleges 1978/79* (Washington, DC: National Science Foundation, 1981), pp. 1, 22, 35, 56.
3. Howard Bowen and Jack H. Schuster, *American Professors: A National Resource Imperiled* (New York: Oxford University Press, 1986), pp. 255–259.
4. William G. Bowen and Julie Ann Sosa, *Prospects for Faculty in the Arts and Sciences: A Study of Factors Affecting Demand and Supply* (Princeton, NJ: Princeton University Press, 1989), pp. 128–143.
5. Ibid., pp. 136–37.
6. Ibid., pp. 144–171.
7. Ibid., pp. 176–186.
8. See Ronald Ehrenberg, "Should Policies Be Pursued to Increase the Flow of New Doctorates?," in Charles T. Clotfelter et al., *Economic Challenges in Higher Education* (Chicago: University of Chicago Press, 1991), pp. 233 ff.
9. Alison M. Konrad and Jeffrey Pfeffer, "Do You Get What You Deserve? Factors Affecting the Relationship between Productivity and Pay," *Administrative Science Quarterly* 35(1990):258; McLaughlin, Montgomery, and Mahan, "Pay, Rank, and Growing Old with More of Each," *Research in Higher Education* II (1979):23; Marsh and Dillon, "Academic Productivity and Family Supplemental Income," *Journal of Higher Education* SI(1986):546.
10. See, e.g., Charles Sykes, *ProfScam: Professors and the Demise of Higher Education* (Washington, DC: Regnery Gateway, 1988).
11. Samuel E. Morison, *Three Centuries of Harvard* (Cambridge, MA: Harvard University Press, 1936), p. 260.
12. Quoted in Hugh Hawkins, *Between Harvard and America: The Educational Leadership of Charles W. Eliot* (New York: Oxford University Press, 1972), pp. 274–275.
13. *Report of Student Council Committee on Education,* June 12, 1939 (mimeo), p. 28.

14. The most authoritative survey of research on this topic is contained in Feldman, "Research Productivity and Scholarly Accomplishment of College Teachers as Related to Their Instructional Effectiveness: A Review and Exploration, *Research in Education* 26(1987):277.
15. See, e.g., Howard Bowen and Jack H. Schuster, *American Professors: A National Resource Imperiled,* pp. 255–259.
16. See Carol M. Boyer and Darrell R. Lewis, *And On the Seventh Day* (Washington, DC: Association for the Study of Higher Education, 1985), p. 43. "Faculty who consult, compared to their peers who do not, teach as many courses and devote as much of their professional work time to teaching and research, . . . publish more, subscribe to more professional journals, are more satisfied with their careers and their institutions and are at least as active in departmental and institutional governance." Ibid., p. V.
17. See Ronald Ehrenberg, "Decisions to Undertake and Complete Doctoral Study and Choices of Sector of Employment," in Clotfelter et al., *Economic Challenges in Higher Education,* pp. 174, 204.
18. See Clark Kerr, "Comments," *Minerva* 30(1992):149, 150; Henry Rosovsky, ibid., p. 187.
19. Carol M. Boyer and Darrell R. Lewis, pp. V, 55. More generally, see Barry M. Staw, "Motivation Research Versus the Art of Faculty Management," *Review of Higher Education* 6(1993):301.
20. For a more extended discussion of steps to improve the quality of teaching see Derek Bok, "The Improvement of Teaching," *Teachers College Record* 93(1991):236.
21. Lee Knefelkamp as quoted in Lynn Cheney, *Tyrannical Machines: A Report on Educational Practices Gone Wrong and Our Best Hopes of Setting Them Right* (Washington, DC: National Endowment for the Humanities, 1990).
22. Ernest Boyer, *Scholarship Reconsidered: Priorities of the Professoriate* (Princeton, NJ: The Carnegie Foundation, 1990), p. 33; John A. Centra, *Determining Faculty Effectiveness* (San Francisco: Jossey-Bass, 1979), p. 15; Darrell R. Lewis and Shirley M. Clark, *Faculty Vitality and Institutional Productivity* (New York: Teachers College Press, Columbia University, 1985), p. 155.
23. Most studies show that scholarly productivity either remains the same or increases after receipt of tenure. See, e.g., Lionel S. Lewis, "Academic Tenure: Its Recipients and Its Effects," *Annals of the American Academy* 448(1980):86. See also Theodore Walden, "Tenure and Academic Productivity," *Improving College and University Teaching* 27(1979):154.
24. Jack H. Schuster, quoted in *Chronicle of Higher Education* (March 29, 1989), p. A17.

25. Zwerling, "The Miami-Dade Story," *Change* (Jan.–Feb. 1988), p. 18.
26. On the general subject of faculty development and renewal, see Jack H. Schuster, Wheeler and Associates, *Enhancing Faculty Careers: Strategies for Development and Renewal* (San Francisco: Jossey-Bass, 1990); Lewis and Clark, eds., *Faculty Vitality and Institutional Productivity;* Roger G. Baldwin, "Faculty Vitality Beyond the Research University," *Journal of Higher Education* 61(March–April 1990):160.

Chapter 9 Teachers

1. For a more detailed description of these learning needs, see Lauren Resnick, *Education and Learning to Think* (Washington, DC: National Academy Press, 1987).
2. Larry Cuban, "Policy and Research Dilemmas in the Teaching of Reasoning: Unplanned Designs," *Review of Educational Research* 54(1984):661.
3. Statement by American Academy for the Advancement of Science, quoted in Marshall S. Smith and Jennifer O'Day, *Systemic School Reform: Politics of Education Association Yearbook, 1990* (1990), pp. 233, 240; see also Russell Rumberger, "The Shortage of Mathematics and Science Teachers: A Review of the Evidence," *Education Evaluation and Policy Analysis* 7(1989):355.
4. Charles Manski, "Academic Ability, Earnings and the Decision to Become a Teacher," in David Wise, ed., *Public Sector Payrolls* (Chicago: University of Chicago Press, 1987), p. 291. See also Vance and Schlechty, "The Distribution of Academic Ability in the Teaching Force: Policy Implications," *Phi Delta Kappan* (Sept. 1982), p. 22.
5. The importance of principals to effective schools has emerged from a number of different studies. For a review of the literature, see Susan J. Rosenholtz, "Effective Schools: Interpreting the Evidence," *American Journal of Education* 93(1985):352.
6. Quoted in Geraldine Clifford and James Guthrie, *Ed School* (Chicago: University of Chicago Press, 1988), p. 11.
7. Rumberger, "The Shortage of Mathematics and Science Teachers."
8. Richard J. Murnane et al., *Who Will Teach?* (Cambridge, MA: Harvard University Press, 1991), pp. 69–71; Richard J. Murnane and David K. Cohen, "Merit Pay," *Harvard Education Review* 56 (1986):1.
9. See Carnegie Foundation for the Advancement of Teaching, *The Condition of Teaching: A State-by-State Analysis* (Princeton, NJ: Carnegie Foundation, 1990), p. 63; Ernest Boyer, *High School: A*

Report on Secondary Education in America (New York: Harper & Row, 1983), p. 166.

10. See Clifford and Guthrie, *Ed School,* pp. 31, 33.
11. Charles Murray, *In Pursuit of Happiness and Good Government* (New York: Simon & Schuster, 1988), pp. 214–245. See also Lieberman, "Are Teachers Underpaid?," *The Public Interest* (Summer, 1986), p. 12.
12. Murnane et al., *Who Will Teach?,* pp. 36–37.
13. Manski, "Academic Ability," p. 291.
14. Ibid.
15. Murray, *In Pursuit of Happiness and Good Government,* p. 239.
16. Ronald F. Ferguson, "Paying for Public Performance: New Evidence on How and Why Money Matters," *Harvard Journal on Legislation* 28(1991):265.
17. Samuel B. Bacharach, Sharon Conley, and Joseph Shedd, "Beyond Career Ladders: Structuring Teacher Career Development Systems," *Teachers College Record* 87(1986):563.
18. E.g., Michael Kirst, in David Monk and Julie Underwood, eds., *MicroLevel School Finance: Issues and Implications for Policy* (Cambridge, MA: Ballinger Pub. Co., 1988); Gerald C. Hayward, "The Two Million Dollar School," Policy Paper No. PP. 88-5-5, *Policy Analysis for California Education* (May, 1988).
19. Eric A. Hanushek, "The Impact of Differential Expenditures on School Performance," *Educational Researcher* 18(1989):45, 47.
20. Daniel Lortie, *Schoolteacher: A Sociological Study* (Chicago: University of Chicago Press, 1975), p. 106; Susan Johnson, "Incentives for Teachers," *Educational Administration Quarterly* 22(1986): 54.
21. Boyer, *High School,* p. 158.
22. Carnegie Foundation for the Advancement of Teaching, *The Condition of Teaching* (1990), p. viii.
23. Ibid., p. xv.
24. Ibid., p. 40.
25. See Arthur Wise, Linda Darling-Hammond, and Berry, *Effective Teacher Selection: From Recruitment to Retention* (Santa Monica, CA: Rand Corp., 1987).
26. Perry, "New Teachers: Do the Best Get Hired?," *Phi Delta Kappan* 63(1981):113.
27. Ibid.
28. See Manski, "Academic Ability."
29. Murnane et al., *Who Will Teach?,* pp. 38–43.
30. The discussion in this section and the next owes much to Murnane et al., *Who Will Teach?,* chap. 7.

31. Ibid., p. 116. For a review of the research on this question, see Eric A. Hanushek, "The Economics of Schooling," *Journal of Economic Literature* 24(1986):1141, 1161.
32. See David M. Arfin, "The Use of Financial Aid to Attract Talented Students to Teaching: Lessons from Other Fields," *Elementary School Journal* 86(1986):405.
33. Quoted in Susan Johnson, "Merit Pay for Teachers: A Poor Prescription for Reform," *Harvard Education Review* 54(1984):175.
34. Wise et al., *Effective Teacher Selection.*
35. Alexander Kern and David H. Monk, eds., *Attracting and Compensating America's Teachers* (Cambridge, MA: Ballinger Pub. Co., 1988), p. 102.
36. See Lortie, *Schoolteacher;* Johnson, "Incentives for Teachers."
37. Richard M. Brandt, *Incentive Pay and Career Ladders for Today's Teachers* (Albany, NY: State University of New York Press, 1990).
38. See Richard J. Murnane and David Cohen, "Merit Pay and the Evaluation Problem: Why Most Merit Pay Plans Fail and a Few Survive," *Harvard Education Review* 56(1986):1.
39. Carnegie Foundation for the Advancement of Teaching, *The Condition of Teaching,* p. 40.
40. Ibid., p. 41.
41. Boyer, *High School,* p. 158.
42. For a useful elaboration of this theme, see Michael Smith and Jennifer O'Day, "Systemic School Reform," *Politics of Education Association Yearbook, 1990,* p. 233.
43. The Kentucky Education Reform Act specifies that a school in which the number of successful students declines by more than 5 percent will be designated a school in crisis. Such schools must develop an improvement plan and are eligible for state funds to implement it. They are also assigned a "distinguished educator" from another district who has power to transfer and dismiss personnel.
44. For a more extended discussion, see Samuel B. Bacharach, Sharon Conley, and Joseph Shedd, "Beyond Career Ladders: Structuring Teacher Career Development Systems," *Teachers College Record* 87(1986):563.
45. John Chubb and Terry Moe, *Politics, Markets, and America's Schools* (Washington, DC: Brookings Institution, 1990). This book presents the most influential of the proposals for a market-oriented, parental-choice school system.
46. For a careful critique of voucher systems and parental choice plans, see Liebman, "Voice Not Choice," *Yale Law Journal* 101 (1991): 259. See also William L. Boyd and Herbert J. Walberg, eds., *Choice in Education: Potential and Problems* (Berkeley, CA: McCutchan,

1990); "Politics, Markets, and America's Schools: A Symposium," *Teachers College Record,* 93(1991):37.

47. Chester Finn, *We Must Take Charge* (New York: Free Press, 1991), p. 153.
48. National Center for Education Statistics, *The State of Mathematics Achievement: NAEP's 1990 Assessment of the Nation and the Trial Assessment of the States* (Washington, DC: The Center, 1991). See also Richard J. Murnane, "A Review Essay: Comparisons of Public and Private Schools: Lessons from the Uproar," *Journal of Human Resources* (1984), p. 263.

Chapter 10 Federal Officials

1. *Report of the President's Commission on Compensation of Career Federal Executives* (Feb. 1988).
2. Quoted in Fred Malek, *Washington's Hidden Tragedy: The Failure to Make Government Work* (New York: Free Press, 1978).
3. *Leadership for America: Rebuilding the Public Service* (hereafter cited as Volcker Report) (Washington, DC: U.S. Government Printing Office, 1989).
4. "Most Federal Workers Need Only Be Competent," *Wall Street Journal* (May 21, 1986), p. 32.
5. Gallup, *Public Opinion* (1990), p. 178. According to this poll, 41 percent of the public feel that appointed officials are paid "a lot too much"; 18 percent feel they are paid "a little too much"; while only 10 percent feel they are paid "a little too little" or "a lot too little."
6. *USA Today* (March 30, 1989), p. 10A.
7. Statement before Commission on Executive, Legislative and Judicial Salaries, Washington, D.C., November 21, 1988.
8. Cited in Volcker Report, p. 83.
9. Ibid., p. 267.
10. Seymour Martin Lipset and William Schneider, *The Confidence Gap: Business, Labor and Government in the Public Mind* (New York: Free Press, 1983), p. 304.
11. Quoted in Steven Kelman, *Making Public Policy: A Hopeful View of American Government* (New York: Basic Books, 1987), p. 272.
12. See Volcker Commission, pp. 62–63; and Daniel Katz et al., *Bureaucratic Encounters* (1975) for an extended discussion of the much better public perceptions of efficiency held by those who have had direct personal experience with government agencies.
13. Quoted in Leonard Silk and David Vogel, *Ethics and Profits: The Crisis of Confidence in American Business* (New York: Simon & Schuster, 1976), p. 46.

14. National Academy of Public Administration, *Leadership in Jeopardy: The Fraying of the Presidential Appointments System* (Washington, DC: National Academy of Public Administration, 1985), p. 29.
15. James Q. Wilson, *Bureaucracy: What Government Agencies Do and Why They Do It* (New York: Basic Books, 1989), p. 275.
16. Ronald Sanders, "The Best and the Brightest: Can the Public Service Compete?" Reprinted in Volcker Commission, p. 157.
17. Quoted in Larry Lane and James Wolf, *The Human Resource Crisis in the Public Sector: Rebuilding the Capacity to Govern* (New York: Quorum Books, 1990), p. 157.
18. Sanders, "The Best and the Brightest."
19. U.S. Merit Systems Review Board, *Attracting and Selecting Quality Graduates to the Federal Government: A View of College Recruiting* (Washington, DC: The Board, 1988).
20. A bill to this effect has been introduced in Congress. See *Congressional Record,* July 16, 1991, pp. E2547–48.
21. U.S. Merit Systems Review Board, *Why Are Employees Leaving the Federal Government? Results of an Exit Survey* (Washington, DC: The Board, 1990).
22. See Volcker Report, pp. 192–198.
23. Ibid., p. 193.
24. See, generally, Hugh Heclo, *A Government of Strangers: Executive Politics in Washington* (Washington, DC: Brookings Institution, 1977).
25. See National Research Council: Alan K. Campbell and Linda S. Dix, eds., *Recruitment, Retention and Utilization of Federal Scientists and Engineers* (Washington, DC: National Academy Press, 1990), pp. 15–16.
26. Ibid., pp. 12–13.
27. U.S. Merit Systems Review Board, *Attracting and Selecting Quality Applicants for Federal Employment,* p. 17.
28. Buddy Robert S. Silverman, "Why the Merit Pay System Failed in the Federal Government," *Personnel Journal* 62(1983):284.
29. James L. Perry, Beth Ann Petrakis, and Theodore K. Miller, "Federal Merit Pay, Round II: An Analysis of the Performance Management and Recognition System," *Public Administration Review* 49 (1989):29.
30. U.S. Merit Systems Protection Board, *Federal Personnel Policies and Practices—Perspective from the Workplace* (1987), cited in Volcker Report, p. 143.
31. Volcker Report, p. 279.
32. National Research Council, *Pay for Performance: Evaluating Per-*

formance Appraisal and Merit Pay (Washington, DC: National Academy Press, 1991), p. 30.

33. Mark W. Huddleston, *The Government's Managers: Report of the Twentieth Century Fund Task Force on the Senior Executive Service* (New York: Priority Press, 1987). See also U.S. Merit Systems Protection Board, *The Senior Executive Service: Views of Former Federal Executives* (Washington, D.C., 1989), p. 18.
34. National Research Council, *Pay for Performance,* p. 135.
35. Silverman, "Why the Merit Pay System Failed," p. 294. See also Gerald T. Gabris, ed., "Why Merit Plans Are Not Working: A Search for Alternative Pay Plans in the Public Sector—A Symposium," *Review of Public Personnel Administration* 7(1987):28.
36. These developments are discussed at length in David E. Osborne and Ted Gaebler, *Reinventing Government: How the Entrepreneurial Spirit Is Transforming the Public Sector* (Reading, MA: Addison-Wesley Pub. Co., 1992).
37. Jameson Doig and Erwin Hargrove, eds., *Leadership and Innovation: A Biographical Perspective on Entrepreneurs in Government* (Baltimore: Johns Hopkins University Press, 1987). See also Herbert Kaufman, *The Administrative Behavior of Federal Bureau Chiefs* (Washington, DC: Brookings Institution, 1981).
38. Martha Derthick, *Agency Under Stress: The Social Security Administration in American Government* (Washington, DC: Brookings Institution, 1990), p. 184.
39. John Kotter and James Heskett, *Corporate Culture and Performance* (New York: Free Press, 1992), pp. 104–105.
40. "Candid Reflections of a Businessman in Washington," *Fortune* (January 29, 1979), p. 39.
41. For an extended discussion of these problems, see William T. Gormley, Jr., *Taming the Bureaucracy: Muscles, Prayers, and Other Strategies* (Princeton, NJ: Princeton University Press, 1989).

Chapter 11 Summing Up

1. Quoted in Graef Crystal, *In Search of Excess* (New York: W. W. Norton & Co., 1991), p. 26.
2. See Melvin Kohn, *Work and Personality: An Inquiry into the Impact of Social Stratification* (Norwood, NJ: Ablex Pub. Co., 1983); Burkhard Strumpel, *Economic Means for Human Needs: Social Indicators of Well-Being and Discontent* (Ann Arbor, MI: Survey Research Center, University of Michigan, 1970).
3. Slemrod's study is reported in Paul Krugman, "The Rich, the Right and the Facts," *The American Prospect* (Fall, 1992), p. 19. Krug-

man's article contains a careful rebuttal of the argument that turnover among the rich is very high.

4. Michael Novak, *The Spirit of Democratic Capitalism* (New York: Simon & Schuster, 1987), pp. 211–212.
5. *Fortune* reports that the top 1% of all taxpayers in 1990 (a group totaling just over 1 million people) had an average after-tax income of slightly more than $400,000 and that all taxpayers in this group had pretax incomes in 1991 in excess of $350,000. *Fortune* (June 29, 1992), pp. 42–43.
6. Figures supplied to me by Independent Sector in Washington, D.C., based on Internal Revenue Service data.
7. *Wealth and Poverty* (New York: Basic Books, 1981), p. 62.
8. Milton Friedman and Rose Friedman, *Free to Choose* (Tel Aviv: Devir, 1990 pbk), p. 139.
9. This figure was supplied to me by Independent Sector, Washington, D.C., based on Internal Revenue figures and compiled for Independent Sector by Price, Waterhouse.
10. See Charles T. Clotfelter, "The Impact of Tax Reform on Charitable Giving: A 1989 Perspective," in Joel Slemrod, ed., *Do Taxes Matter? The Impact of the Tax Reform Act of 1986* (Cambridge, MA: MIT Press, 1990), p. 203.
11. *Theory of Moral Sentiments* (London: Printed for A. Millar, A. Kincaid, and J. Bell in Edinburgh, 1759), part IV, chap. i.
12. These figures were supplied to me by the Opinion Research Corporation based on its annual *General Social Survey*.
13. Frank M. Andrews and Stephen B. Withey, *Social Indicators of Well-Being: Americans' Perceptions of Life-Quality* (New York: Plenum Press, 1976), pp. 286–287.
14. Richard Easterlin, "Does Economic Growth Improve the Human Lot?," in Paul A. David and Melvin W. Reder, *Nations and Households in Economic Growth: Essays in Honor of Moses Abramovitz* (New York: Academic Press, 1974).
15. See Nigel Tomes, "Income Distribution, Happiness, and Satisfaction: A Direct Test of the Interdependent Preferences Model," *Journal of Economic Psychology* 7(1986):425, finding that in communities where the poor are relatively better off, residents are less satisfied than in communities where the poor are relatively worse off.
16. Irving Kristol, *Two Cheers for Capitalism* (New York: Basic Books, 1978), p. 267.
17. Gosta Esping-Andersen, *The Three Worlds of Welfare Capitalism* (Cambridge, UK: Polity Press, 1990), p. 205.
18. Department of Health and Human Services, *Seventh Report to the*

President and Congress on the Status of Health Personnel in the United States (March 1990), p. VI–22.

19. For a discussion of the problems involved in international comparisons, see Friedman, "Lawyers in Cross-Cultural Perspective," in Richard L. Abel and Philip S. C. Lewis, *Lawyers in Society: Comparative Theories,* vol. 3 (Los Angeles: UCLA Press, 1988), pp. 1, 5.
20. See Dean Robert C. Clark, "Why So Many Lawyers? Are They Good or Bad?," *Fordham Law Review* 61(1992):275.
21. Rodney T. Hartnett, *Trends in Student Quality in Doctoral and Professional Education* (New Brunswick, NJ: Project on Trends in Academic Talent, Rutgers University, March 1985), pp. 33, 36.
22. W. Timothy Weaver, "Education in Supply and Demand: Effects on Quality," *School Review* 86(1978):552.
23. Vance and Schlechty, "The Structure of Teaching Occupation and the Characteristics of Teachers: A Sociological Interpretation" (unpublished manuscript, 1982).
24. Data on Phi Beta Kappas in this paragraph are taken from a private survey of 2,000 Phi Beta Kappas graduating from 1970 to 1990 conducted by the author in the spring of 1992.
25. The figures cited in this paragraph were supplied to me by the Consortium on the Financing of Higher Education and were derived from surveys of the senior classes of 1982 and 1989.
26. Ronald Sanders, "The Best and the Brightest: Can the Public Service Compete?," in *Leadership for America: Report of the National Commission on the Public Service* (Washington, DC: U.S. Government Printing Office, 1990), p. 157.
27. Culler, "Most Federal Workers Need Only Be Competent," *Wall Street Journal* (May 21, 1986), p. 32.
28. Altman, "The Mix of Physician Manpower and Its Effect on U.S. Health Expenditures: The U.S. Versus Other Industrialized Nations." Paper presented at National Primary Care Conference, March 30, 1992.
29. Thomas W. Harrell and Bernard Alpert, "Attributes of Successful MBAs: A 20-Year Longitudinal Study," *Human Performance* 2 (1989):301.
30. Walter Kiechel, "New Debate About Harvard Business School," *Fortune* (November 9, 1987), pp. 34, 35.
31. Ibid.
32. James Tobin, "On the Efficiency of the Financial System," *Lloyds Bank Review* (July 1984), p. 14.
33. See, e. g., Kevin M. Murphy, Andrei Schleifer, and Robert Vishny, "The Allocation of Talent: Implications for Growth," *Quarterly Journal of Economics* 106(1991):503; I, too, am guilty of consid-

erable oversimplification on this point. See Derek C. Bok, "A Flawed System of Law Practice and Training," *Journal of Legal Education* 33(1983):570.

34. Ronald J. Gilson, "The Devolution of the Legal Profession," *University of Maryland Law Review* 49(1990):869.
35. See Ronald J. Gilson, "How Many Lawyers Does It Take to Change an Economy?," *Law and Social Inquiry* 17(1993):635.
36. For a more extended discussion, see Marc Galanter, "Why the 'Haves' Come Out Ahead: Speculations on the Limits of Legal Change," *Law and Society Review* 9(1974):95.
37. *Thinking for a Living: Education and Wealth of Nations* (New York: Basic Books, 1992).

Chapter 12 The Impact of Values

1. Albert G. Keller, ed., *The Challenge of Facts and Other Essays* (New Haven: Yale University Press, 1914), p. 90.
2. McCready, "On the Influence of Trades, Professions and Occupations in the United States in the Production of Disease," *Transactions of the Medical Society of the State of New York (1836–37)* III, pp. 146–47. See also Alexis de Tocqueville, *Democracy in America,* Vintage ed. (New York: New American Library, 1956), pp. 53, 403.
3. Robert G. McCloskey, *American Conservatism in the Age of Enterprise: A Study of William Graham Sumner, Stephen J. Field, and Andrew Carnegie, 1865–1910* (Cambridge, MA: Harvard University Press, 1951), p. 12.
4. James B. Bryce, *The American Commonwealth* (New York: The Commonwealth Pub. Co., 1907), p. 745.
5. Edward Everett, *Orations and Speeches,* vol. II (Boston: Little, Brown, 1878), p. 294.
6. Robert S. Lynd and Helen M. Lynd, *Middletown in Transition: A Study in Cultural Conflicts* (New York: Harcourt, Brace & Co., 1937), pp. 63, 409.
7. de Tocqueville, *Democracy in America,* p. 198.
8. Bryce, *The American Commonwealth,* p. 537.
9. See, generally, E. J. Dionne, *Why Americans Hate Politics* (New York: Simon & Schuster, 1991); Samuel H. Beer, "In Search of a New Public Philosophy," in Anthony King, ed., *The New American Political System* (Washington, DC: American Enterprise Institute for Public Policy Research, 1978).
10. Jeffrey G. Williamson and Peter H. Lindert, *American Inequality: A Macroeconomic History* (New York: Academic Press, 1980).

11. Eric Dey, Alexander Astin, and William S. Korn, *The American Freshman: Twenty-Five-Year Trends, 1966–90* (Los Angeles: Higher Education Research Institute, UCLA, 1987).
12. Quoted in Beer, "In Search of a New Public Philosophy," p. 43.
13. "Party Tricks: Rehearsing for Campaign '92," *Harper's* (July 1991), pp. 45–46.
14. Kevin Phillips, *The Politics of Rich and Poor: Wealth and the American Electorate in the Reagan Aftermath* (New York: Random House, 1991), p. 43.
15. Quoted in Volcker Report, p. 63.
16. Quoted in John Chancellor, *Peril and Promise: A Commentary on America* (New York: Harper & Row, 1991), p. 115.
17. George Gallup, Jr., *The Gallup Poll: Public Opinion 1992* (Wilmington, DE: Scholarly Resources, Inc., 1992), p. 109.
18. Ibid.
19. See, generally, Michael H. Best, *The New Competition: Institutions of Industrial Restructuring* (Cambridge, UK: Polity Press, 1990). Best begins his book with the following observation from Konosuki Matsushita: "We (the Japanese) will win and you will lose. You cannot do anything about it because your failure is an internal disease. . . . You firmly believe that sound management means executives on one side and workers on the other, on the one side men who think and on the other side men who can only work.

    "We are aware that business has become terribly complex. Survival is very uncertain in an environment filled with risk, the unexpected and competition. . . . We know that the intelligence of a few technocrats—even very bright ones—has become totally inadequate to face these challenges. Only the intellects of all employees can permit a company to live with the ups and downs and the requirements of the new environment."
20. Gerald R. Salancik and James R. Meindl, "Corporate Attributions as Strategic Illusions of Management Control," *Administrative Science Quarterly* 29(1984):238; see also James R. Meindle, Sanford B. Erlich, and Janet M. Dukerich, "The Romance of Leadership," *Administrative Science Quarterly* 30(1985):78.
21. E.g., Allen, Panian, and Lotz, "Management Succession and Organizational Performance—A Recalcitrant Problem Revisited," *Administrative Science Quarterly* 24 (1979):167.
22. Stanley Lieberson and James F. O'Connor, "Leadership and Organizational Performance," *American Sociological Review* 37 (1972): 117.
23. Bill Saparito, "The Tough Cookie at RJR-Nabisco," *Fortune* (July 18, 1988), p. 32.

24. ABC-Harris Poll, Sept. 1979, quoted in Seymour Martin Lipset and William Schneider, *The Confidence Gap: Business, Labor, and Government in the Public Mind* (New York: Free Press, 1983), p. 390.
25. George F. Will, *Statecraft as Soulcraft: What Government Does* (New York: Simon & Schuster, 1983), pp., 130–131.
26. See Lawrence E. Gladieux and Gwendolyn L. Lewis, *The Federal Government and Higher Education: Traditions, Trends, Stakes and Issues* (New York: College Entrance Examination Board, 1987), p. 7.
27. Marian W. Edelman, *Families in Peril: Agenda for Social Change* (Cambridge, MA: Harvard University Press, 1987), pp. 40–41.
28. Isabel V. Sawhill, "Young Children and Families," in Henry J. Aaron and Charles L. Schultze, eds., *Setting Domestic Priorities: What Can Government Do?* (Washington, DC: The Brookings Institution, 1992), p. 168.
29. Ibid.
30. Speech at Education Summit, University of Virginia, September 28, 1989 (White House Transcript), quoted in M. Edith Rasell and Lawrence Mishel, "Shortchanging Education: How U.S. Spending on Grades K–12 Lags Behind Other Industrial Nations," Briefing Paper (Washington, DC: Economic Policy Institute), p. 1.
31. Ibid.
32. "There's No Such Thing as a Free Lunch" (1975), p. 31, quoted in Peter D. McClelland, *The American Search for Economic Justice* (Cambridge, MA: Basil Blackwell, 1990), pp 261–262.
33. Angus Campbell, Philip Converse, and Willard Rodgers, *The Quality of American Life* (Ann Arbor, MI: Inter-university Consortium for Policy and Social Research, 1976), p. 287.
34. Quoted in Chancellor, *Peril and Promise,* p. 124.
35. American Bar Association, *In the Spirit of Public Service: A Blueprint for the Rekindling of Lawyer Professionalism* (Chicago: The Commission, 1986).
36. Schneyer, "Professionalism as Politics: The Making of a Modern Legal Ethics Code," in Robert L. Nelson, David M. Trubek, and Rayman L. Solomon, eds., *Lawyers' Ideals/Lawyers' Practices: Transformations in the American Legal Profession* (Ithaca, NY: Cornell University Press, 1992), p. 95.
37. See Michael Millemann, "Mandatory Pro Bono in Civil Cases: A Partial Answer to the Right Question," *University of Maryland Law Review* 49(1990):18; Esther F. Lardent, "Mandatory Pro Bono in Civil Cases: The Wrong Answer to the Right Question," *University of Maryland Law Review* 49(1990):78.
38. Barr, "Doers and Talkers," *American Lawyer* (July–Aug. 1990), p. 51.

39. E.g., Carlton Young, Mayden, and Molod, "Greed Is Good?," *Barrister* 15(1988):13.
40. David Luban, "The Noblesse Oblige Tradition in the Practice of Law," *Vanderbilt Law Review* 41(1988):717.
41. General Accounting Office, *Health Insurance: Vulnerable Payers Lose Billions to Fraud and Abuse* (Washington, DC: GAO, May 1992).
42. See, e.g., "Lawyer Fraud Put at All-Time High," *Boston Globe* (January 27, 1993), p. 13.
43. See, e.g., Johnson and Coyle, "On the Transformation of the Legal Profession: The Advent of Temporary Lawyering," *Notre Dame Law Review* 66(1990):359, 363, reporting a rise in the number of billable hours for associates of New York City firms from 1,780 in 1982 to 2,290 in 1989. See also Zeldis, "Billables Up," *National Law Journal* (April 11, 1988), p. 2.
44. *The State of the Legal Profession: 1990* (Chicago, IL: American Bar Association: Young Lawyers Division, 1991), p. 54.
45. Juliet Schor, *The Overworked American: The Unexpected Decline of Leisure* (New York: Basic Books, 1991), p. 130.
46. David E. Osborne and Ted Gaebler, *Reinventing Government: How the Entrepreneurial Spirit Is Transforming the Public Sector* (Reading, MA: Addison-Wesley, 1992), p. 87.
47. Quoted in Theodore Marmor and Jerry Mashaw, "Checking the Nation's Pulse: America's Health Insurance Fever," *Washington Post* (November 17, 1991).
48. Robert Putnam, *Making Democracy Work: Civic Traditions in Modern Italy* (Princeton, NJ: Princeton University Press, 1993).
49. Osborne and Gaebler, *Reinventing Government,* pp. 326–327.
50. See, generally, Lipset and Schneider, *The Confidence Gap,* pp. 48–49.
51. Ibid., p. 17.
52. Josephson Institute for the Advancement of Ethics, *The Ethics of American Youth: A Warning and a Call to Action* (Los Angeles: Josephson Institute, 1990), p. 56; See also *Time* (July 9, 1990), p. 64.

Chapter 13 Searching for Remedies

1. The most careful, comprehensive (and sympathetic) review of these arguments appears in Walter J. Blum and Harry Kalven, *The Uneasy Case for Progressive Taxation* (Chicago: University of Chicago Press, 1953).
2. The literature on the effect of higher taxes and savings on the incen-

tive to work is discussed in some detail by Peter D. McClelland, *The American Search for Economic Justice* (Cambridge, MA: Basil Blackwell, 1990), pp. 196–197. For a more extended treatment, see Barry Bosworth, *Tax Incentives and Economic Growth* (Washington, DC: Brookings Institution, 1984).

3. Patient care hours per week rose slightly in the latter half of the 1980s but the increase began before the reduction in rates from the 1986 tax form. The number of weeks practiced per year, conversely, fell slightly in the last half of the 1980s. See AMA, *Socioeconomic Characteristics of Medical Practice 1990/1991* (Chicago: Center for Health Policy Research, 1991), p. 30. Data relevant to the tax cut of 1981 are somewhat harder to assess. Figures from the AMA show a large jump in hours of patient care per week from 1980 to 1982, but the authors state that these figures should be discounted as the method of obtaining data changed during this period. If hours of patient care had in fact increased dramatically, doctors' incomes would likewise have risen by an unusual amount. AMA data do not reveal this to be the case.
4. Milton Friedman, *Capitalism and Freedom* (Chicago: University of Chicago Press, 1962), p. 174.
5. See e.g., Glenn Jenkins, "Tax Reform: Lessons Learned," in Dwight Perkins and Michael Roemer, eds., *Reforming Economic Systems in Developing Countries* (Cambridge, MA: Harvard Institute for International Development, Harvard University Press, 1991), pp. 294, 299.
6. See, e.g., Lawrence Lindsey, *The Growth Experiment: How the New Tax Policy Is Transforming the U.S. Economy* (New York: Basic Books, 1990).
7. Ernest Boyer, *Ready to Learn* (Princeton, NJ: Princeton University Press, 1991), p. 7.
8. Jonathan Kozol, *Savage Inequalities: Children in America's Schools* (New York: Crown Publishers, 1991).
9. Ibid., pp. 4–5.
10. Report of the Commission on Responsibilities for Financing Postsecondary Education, *Making College Affordable Again* (1993), pp. 3–4.
11. Since college enrollment rates are lower for poor students than those of well-to-do students, even among young people of comparable ability, and since dropout rates for poorer students are much higher, it seems likely that inadequate aid is in fact closing off opportunities for low-income students. See Michael S. McPherson and Morton O. Schapiro, *Keeping College Affordable: Government and*

Educational Opportunity (Washington, DC: Brookings Institution, 1991).

12. E.g., Chester Finn, *We Must Take Charge* (New York: Free Press, 1991).
13. For an alternative plan that also raises tuition at public colleges and universities, see McPherson and Schapiro, *Keeping College Affordable*, p. 187.
14. For a more extended discussion of such a plan, see Barry Bluestone, Alan Clayton-Mathews, John Havens, and Howard Young, "Generational Alliance: Social Security as a Bank for Education and Training," *The American Prospect* (Summer, 1990), p. 15.
15. See, generally, Alan S. Blinder, ed., *Paying for Productivity: A Look at the Evidence* (Washington, DC: Brookings Institution, 1990).
16. See Ronald J. Gilson and Robert H. Mnookin, "Sharing Among Human Capitalists," *Stanford Law Review* 37(1985):313.
17. See Steven Brill, "Toward a New Excellence: Strategies and Values for Tomorrow's Successful Firms," *American Lawyer* (November 1983), p. 18.
18. Quoted in Barry Schwartz, *The Battle for Human Nature: Science, Morality, and Modern Life* (New York: W. W. Norton & Co., 1987), p. 247.
19. Quoted in Schuman, "Beyond the Waste Land: Law Practice in the 1990's," *Hastings Law Journal* 42(1990):1, 5.

INDEX

9 780743 236324